THE LEASING HANDBOOK

THE LEASING HANDBOOK

EVERYTHING PURCHASING
MANAGERS NEED TO KNOW
COMPLETE WITH FACTS,
FIGURES, FORMS &
CHECKLISTS

KALMAN I. PERLMAN

PROBUS PUBLISHING COMPANY
CHICAGO, ILLINOIS
CAMBRIDGE, ENGLAND

ISBN 1-55738-242-5

Printed in the United States of America

BB

2 3 4 5 6 7 8 9 0

Dedicated to
Ida, Esther and Martin

Table of Contents

Preface

This handbook was written to serve as a guide and ready reference for the purchasing manager and others involved in the quest of capital assets. The professional will discover that leasing is an attractive financial alternative to outright purchasing in the acquisition of that capital asset.

This book leads the professional through the many methods of analysis of the economic soundness of an acquisition and includes the various types of leases available to meet a particular need along with the effects of the tax laws as well as the warranties and remedies that available to either party under a lease contract.

The purchasing manager is a key player in the acquisition process, before and after a financial decision. He (or she) must have knowledge of the different methods of analyzing capital investments to ascertain their potential value to the company. He (or she) should have knowledge of what constitutes a lease contract, the rights and liabilities of either party, the effects of the ever changing tax laws, etc.

Leasing is now annually a 130 billion dollar industry and is the fastest growing and largest single source of capital for plant and equipment in the United States. More than 80 percent of American and foreign companies utilize leasing as a source for the acquisition of needed equipment.

It is my hope that this book will serve as a guide and reference to those professionals involved in the acquisition of capital assets.

Chapter 1 introduces the reader to the field of leasing from both the lessor's and lessee's viewpoints, and a brief overview of the various means of capital acquisition. Chapter 2 enumerates the various types of leases from a tax and from an accounting viewpoint. Chapter 3 discusses the tax effects of the cash flow problems that arise in any acquisition.

Chapter 4 reviews the economic analysis of capital asset acquisition and the cost of money. Chapter 5 discusses the time value of money and expands on the various methods of calculating the discounted cash flow which is essential in any financial decision.

Chapters 6 through 12 review and discuss the Uniform Commercial Code provisions and their legal effect on the lease contracts. Chapter 13 discusses the various parties and documents involved in a lease agreement. Chapter 14 presents an overview of the various fields in the lease industry.

There is a glossary of the common terms encountered in the leasing industry and precalculated factor tables used in the economic analysis of projected acquisitions of capital assets. The index also is very detailed to help the book serve as a handy reference.

I wish to acknowledge with thanks to the following for suggestions and/or information supplied in the writing of this book: Norman L. Chapman of Security Pacific Leasing Company; J.R. English of Caterpillar Financial Services; Steve Grundon of Ellco Leasing Corporation; Carol K. Suddath of Eaton Financial Corporation; and Dr. Martin A. Tanner, division of Biostatics, of the University of Rochester, and to the American Association of Equipment Lessors.

Kalman I. Perlman

CHAPTER 1

Introduction to Leasing

BACKGROUND

Leasing, as we know it today, evolved from "land tenure" or land leasing. Even primitive communities had some system of land tenure with the chief having titular control although the land itself was in possession of others of his tribe. Primitive people held the land as a sacred trust from their dead ancestors who rewarded them with the productivity of the land.

Around 1500 B.C., the Phoenician culture flourished and was a controlling factor in the sea commerce of the Mediterranean Sea by chartering (leasing) ships to merchants who were more concerned in moving their wares than in owning the vessels outright.

In this country, land tenure was introduced by the British colonists. The king held titular right to the land by right of discovery and granted land charters to trading companies and to prominent persons. These persons granted "leases" to the settlers who worked the land and paid their "lessors" compensation, usually a percentage of the productivity.

During the great depression of the 1930s, when a great many stores and manufacturing outlets became vacant or occupants were on the verge of vacating the premises, the landlords, to gain or retain occupancy of their premises, gladly offered leases with compensation based on a percentage of the business operation. This percentage leasing spread to mineral and other mining leases with a reduced risk of speculation of mineral, oil, and other resources.

Equipment leasing on a large scale was started by AT&T and IBM, which manufactured sophisticated equipment (telecommunication equipment and computers), and their service and maintenance created a monopolistic leasing market. The leasing industry, which began its modern growth in the late 1950s, exploded by the 1960s, and now almost any product can be leased from aircraft, oceangoing vessels, railroad cars, and trucks to office furniture, computers, and even televisions, lamps, etc.

Tax laws, the Federal Comptroller of Currency rulings, and the update of the Bank Holding Company Act, and other regulatory changes have contributed to the explosive growth of modern equipment leasing. Over $310 billion in lease receivables are outstanding in the industry.[1]

In today's rapidly changing technology with the need to remain competitive yet solvent (maintain adequate cash flow), many firms have become more concerned with product affordability among other acquisition considerations. These firms focus on the relationship among equipment productivity, operating costs and acquisition cost of the right piece of equipment for the required job.

The key factor to success in business operation is to maintain a healthy cash flow. That is, the total cash receipts from sales minus the cash expenditure to realize those sales. Cash flow statements provide management with an insight as to its liquidity and operating success.

WHY LEASE (Lessor's viewpoint)

Equipment manufacturers utilize leasing as a means of increasing the "sales" of their products. The manufacturer or dealer can offer vendor leasing or arrange financing through financial institutions

1 U.S. Dept. of Commerce, 1987 Industrial Outlook 53-1.

or leasing companies. In any case, the manufacturer has moved his wares by providing an attractive alternative to his customer.

WHY LEASE (Lessee's viewpoint)

The lessee has many and varied reasons for leasing instead of purchasing such equipment.

1. The lessee may need the equipment for a short period of time. For example, in construction, the contractor needs that "digging" equipment for a few days on the present job and may not need its use again for months or even a year or longer.

2. The lessee may wish to experiment with a new process, or a new product, which requires equipment which the lessee does not own and is too expensive to purchase for this purpose.

3. The lessee may have insufficient capital, or credit, to make an outright purchase and will use leasing as a source for intermediate or long-term financing, depending on the useful life of the equipment.

4. The lessee may view leasing as a tax advantage for its company, or as a means to defer taxes.

5. There are many times when a piece of equipment is in short supply and the manufacturer, or owner, may only be willing to lease and not to sell.

FINANCIAL ALTERNATIVES FOR ACQUISITION OF CAPITAL ASSETS[2]

There are many considerations that come into play when an asset has to be replaced or new one acquired. The big question for top

2 Financial Merchandising, Model I, Cat Financial (1989).

management is "How do we pay for this capital asset?" Management has several options available, each with its own advantages, to obtain the needed asset.

Purchase

A cash purchase with available funds is normally the lowest cost method for acquiring needed equipment when those funds are not needed for other expenditures. The purchaser gets immediate ownership (legal title) and all the benefits that come with ownership. The cost is entered on the balance sheet together with the depreciation value, subject to the method used.

An outright purchase converts liquid assets (cash) into a fixed asset (equipment) thus weakening the current ratio (ratio of current assets to current liabilities) which is an important ratio for credit lines.

If a cash resource is depleted in order to acquire the asset, then flexibility to cover cash flow shortages becomes a serious problem. In 1977, the State of Illinois froze the level of reimbursements for Medicaid to hospitals, and many hospitals felt the impact of this slowdown in payments, and had to draw upon their reserves of cash to pay vendors to maintain operation.

Financial Loan

Cash may be limited, even for the biggest corporations, which means that these firms will avoid using their cash resources to pay for anything. Conservation of capital is the major reason for equipment users to look to loan financing, or leasing, as an alternative means for acquiring the needed equipment.

The bank extends a company a loan to make the purchase. Although this method preserves capital, that loan may have an impact on future available credit. Some capital will have to be used as a down payment, for most banks do not offer 100 percent loan financing. As with a cash purchase, this transaction appears on the balance sheet.

Lease

A properly structured lease can provide many financial advantages to the lessee not available with ownership.

1. Leasing can free working capital for other investments that are more productive. A lease is not a loan and does not appear on the balance sheet, thus, does not affect the borrowing power of credit line of the user. Lease payments may provide a tax deductible business expense and thereby reducing tax liability, particularly the recent Alternative Minimum Tax (AMT).

2. Some companies have limited funds or have reached their limit of borrowing power for capital investments and turn to leasing as a viable means of increasing their capitalization. Leasing can provide up to 100 percent financing of equipment, thus, providing a new source for obtaining needed equipment which otherwise could not be obtained on a fixed operating budget. It is much easier to obtain top management's approval for needed equipment under a lease plan than as a capital expenditure.

3. Leasing has the advantage, particularly for the fleet user, of being able to reduce operating expenses by replacing overaged equipment without a large capital outlay, by establishing realistic replacement schedules. This must be done before maintenance costs become excessive. Leasing also eliminates the problems of technological changes, obsolescence and disposal of the old equipment.

4. Leasing provides a hedge against inflation for although the acquisition of the new equipment is at today's dollar value, you pay for its use over the term of the lease with "cheaper" dollars.

5. One may need some piece of equipment for a very short period of time, after which, if purchased, would remain

unused; that would be expensive. Leasing permits the "rental" of such equipment for a short period of time "to try it out" in evaluating the value of the equipment.

6. Leasing simplifies bookkeeping and accounting functions because it reduces the paperwork and administrative requirements. There is no need to establish depreciation schedules and interest payments in the journal and on statements. Leasing is considered an "off-balance-sheet" transaction preserving borrowing power or credit line.

Rent

Rental programs offer many of the benefits of leasing with three major distinguishing characteristics:

1. The contract period for rental provides complete flexibility, with contract periods as brief as an hour, day, week, or month up to one year. Remember, as the rental term is extended, the economic benefits diminish.

2. Rental equipment includes provisions for complete maintenance by the lessor unless special provisions are stated to the contrary.

3. Rental provides an inexpensive means "to try" a new piece of equipment without long-term commitment. It can be considered a paid demonstration.

LEASING VS. RENTING

The leasing and rental industries are considered two separate entities although both perform the same service, which is to permit others to possess and use goods, not owned by users, for a period of time for compensation. The distinguishing factor between leasing and renting is the duration of time. The American Rental Association indicates that there are at least 10,000 rental outlets in this country.

The profitability from rentals is a great value both to the lessor and renter. For example, many stores rent carpet cleaners for those do-it-yourself persons for an average of $18 for a 24-hour period. These machines cost about $365 and have an economic life of five years. From the renter's point of view who may need the use of the machine for one day, $18 represents a great savings over the unwarranted purchase of a $360 machine. From the lender's point of view, renting the machine is very profitable. If rented one day per week for one year, the lender would gross $936 ($19 x 52), and if two days per week, the gross profit would be better. With a 5-year economic life for the machine, the lender would gross $4,680 for only a one-day-per-week rental, which is not a bad gross on a $365 investment.

There are outlets which both rent and lease their goods. For example, an automobile dealer can both rent the car for a day, week, or month, and can lease that car for one or more years.

Figure 1.1, in simplified form, gives some of the major reasons for acquiring equipment under each of the above basic three methods; purchase, lease and rent. The three methods can be further divided into a variety of finance and lease alternatives.

Figure 1.1

Cash	Finance	Lease	Rental	Customer Criteria
X	X			Wants Ownership
		X		Optional Ownership
		X	X	Use and Return Only
		X	X	Off-Balance-Sheet Financing
	X	X		100% Financing (No Down Payment)
X	X			Cash Surplus - Trade-In
		X	X	Expense 100% of Payments
X	X			Needs Depreciation/Interest Write-Offs
		X	X	Affected by AMT (Alternative Minimum Tax)
X				Lowest Total Cost (For Ownership)
		X		Lowest Monthly Payment (For Use)
			X	Future Business Uncertain
			X	Temporarily Avoid Debt
			X	Try Out Machine
		X		Improve Cash Flow
	X	X	X	Planned Equipment Replacement
		X	X	Eliminate Equipment Disposal Concerns

Reprinted with permission from "Financial Merchandising" Module 1, page 3. Caterpillar Financial Services Corporation.

CHAPTER 2

Types of Leases[1]

WHAT IS A LEASE?

"A lease means the transfer of the right to possession and use of goods for a term in return for consideration, but a sale, including a sale on approval or a sale or return, or retention or creation of a security interest, is not a lease. Unless the context clearly indicates otherwise, the term includes a sublease." [UCC 2A-103(j)]

"A lease is defined as an agreement conveying the right to use property, plant, or equipment (land or depreciable assets or both) usually for a stated period of time." [L-10 ¶.101]

WHAT IS A LEASE AGREEMENT?

"A lease agreement means the bargain, with respect to the lease, of the lessor and the lessee in fact as found in their language or by implication from other circumstances including course of dealing or usage of trade or course of performance as provided by this Article. Unless the context clearly indicates otherwise, the term includes a sublease agreement." [UCC 2A-103(k)]

---

1 Uniform Commercial Code, 1987 Edition (UCC) Article 2A. "Accounting for Leases," 1990 Edition. Internal Revenue Service, 1990 Publications.

WHAT IS A LEASE CONTRACT?

"A lease contract means the total legal obligation that results from the lease agreement as affected by this Article and any other applicable rules of law. Unless the context clearly indicates otherwise, the term includes a sublease contract." [UCC 2A-103(1)]

TYPES OF LEASES

There are two classifications of leases: the capital or finance lease and the operating or true lease with variations of each. Those variations are expressed by different names based on the marketing, or financing, conditions.

The type of lease transaction ultimately chosen is based on the intent of both, the lessor and the lessee, in a particular situation.

The Internal Revenue Service (IRS) sets forth guidelines to be used in determining the treatment, for Federal tax purposes, of leases of equipment used in the trade or business of the lessee (Rev. Rul. 55-540).

The Capital Lease (for tax purposes)[2]

The IRS considers that agreements of the type described below will generally be held as sales of personal property contracts.

1. Agreements which provide for a "rental" over a comparatively short period of time in relation to the expected life of the equipment. Such payments fully cover the normal purchase price plus interest. Title usually passes to the lessee upon payment of a stated amount of "rental," or on the termination of the agreement upon payment of an amount, which when added to the "rental" paid, approximates the normal purchase price of the equipment plus interest.

---

2 IRS Ruling 55-540, Section 2.02(c), (d) and (e).

2. Agreements which provide for the payment of "rental" for a short original term in relation to the expected life of the equipment, approximates the purchase price of the equipment, plus interest, while the "rentals" during the remaining useful life of the equipment are insignificant when compared to the initial rental. These agreements may or may not provide for an option to acquire legal title to the equipment upon termination of the initial period or at any stated time thereafter.

3. Agreements similar to #2 above, but with the added factor that the manufacturer of the equipment purports to sell the equipment to a credit or finance company, which will either take an assignment of an existing agreement with the user, or itself later enter into such agreement with the user (lessee).

Capital Lease other than leverage leases (for accounting purposes)[3]

If at its inception a lease meets one or more of the following criteria, the lease shall be classified by the lessee as a capital lease. Otherwise, it shall be classified as an operating lease (FAS13 ¶7).

1. The lease transfers ownership of the property to the lessee by the end of the *lease term*.

2. The lease contains a *bargain purchase option* (FAS13 ¶7b).

3. The lease term is equal to 75 percent or more of the *estimated economic life of the leased property*. However, if the beginning of the lease term falls within the last 25 percent of the total estimated economize life of the leased property, including the earlier years of use, this criteria shall

3 "Accounting for Leases," 1990 Edition.

not be used for purposes of classifying the lease (FAS13 ¶7c).

4. The present value at the beginning of the lease term of the *minimum lease payments*, excluding executory costs . . . equals or exceeds 90 percent of the excess of the *fair value of the leased property* to the lessor at the inception of the lease . . . . However, if the beginning of the lease term falls within the last 25 percent of the total estimated economic life of the leased property, including earlier years of use, this criteria shall not be used for purposes of classifying the lease (FAS13 ¶7d).

Explanation of the terms used above:

"*Lease term* is the fixed noncancellable term of the lease plus all periods . . . of renewal options" (FAS13 ¶5f).

"*Bargain purchase option* is a provision allowing the lessee, at this option, to purchase the leased property for a price which is sufficiently lower than the expected fair value of the property at the date the option becomes exercisable, that exercise of the option appears . . . to be reasonably assured" (FAS13 ¶5d).

"*Estimated economic life of leased property* is the estimated remaining period during which the property is expected to be economically usable by one or more users, with normal repairs and maintenance, for the purpose for which it was intended at the inception of the lease, without limitation by the lease term" (FAS13 ¶5g).

"*Minimum lease payments,* from a lessee's viewpoint, is the minimum rental payments called for by the lease term plus any guarantee of the residual value at the expiration of the lease" (FAS13 ¶5j).

"*Fair value of the leased property* is the price for which the property could be sold in an arm's length transaction between unrelated parties" (FAS13 ¶5c).

The 90-percent test is stated as a lower limit rather than as a guideline (FIN 19 ¶4).

Operating Lease (for tax purposes)[4]

1. "Short-term agreements which usually concern mobile equipment or relatively small articles of equipment whose 'composition for use' provisions are usually expressed in terms of hourly, daily, or weekly rental and the rental rates are relatively high in relation to the value of the article. There may be an option to purchase the equipment at a price fixed in advance which will approximate the fair market value of the equipment at the time of the election to exercise the option. In this type of agreement, all costs of repairs, maintenance, taxes, insurance, etc., are the obligations of the lessor."

2. "Agreements whose amounts payable, called rental rates, are ordinarily based on the normal operations, or use, plus a surcharge for operation in excess of normal stated usage. In some instances the rental is based on units produced or mileage operated. Termination of the agreement at stated periods is provided upon due notice by either party. If the agreement includes an option to purchase, the option price has no relation to the amounts paid as rentals."

3. "Agreements which are indicative of an intent to rent the equipment and are not directly related to the normal purchase price, provided, if there is an option to purchase, that price approximates the anticipated fair market value on the option date. Agreements of the type described above will be considered by the IRS as true leases (operating leases), in absence of other facts or circumstances which denote a passing of title or an equity interest to the lessee."

"The Internal Revenue Code (IRC) of 1954 provides that there shall be allowed a deduction of all ordinary and

4 IRS Ruling 55-540, Section 2.02(a) and (b).

necessary expenses paid . . . including rentals . . . for use or possession . . . of property to which the user has not taken nor is taking title or in which he has no equity."

Operating Lease (for accounting purposes)[5]

There is no formal classification of operating leases. However, there are two basic types that have gained wide usage.

The first type can be described as service oriented operating leases, known as rentals. Examples are daily or weekly rental of an automobile, the monthly use of a telephone, or the short-term rental use of a copier or a computer. In these arrangements, the lessor provides the services connected with these leases, such as maintenance, insurance and the taxes which are associated with ownership.

The second type of operating lease is one which has the characteristics of the capital lease, but is treated as an operating lease for accounting purposes; that is, it is an "off-balance-sheet" treatment. This means that the balance sheet does not indicate ownership of the asset. The corporation uses the asset, but does not own it. This type of lease is commonly called "FASB 13 Operating Lease" and is often written for one, two, or more years.

The criteria for an operating lease would be the opposite of a capital lease, and could be listed as:

1. Title to the asset must not automatically pass to the lessee as one of the conditions of the lease term.

2. The lease must not contain an option to purchase the asset at a bargain price.

3. The lease term must be for less than 75 percent of the economic life of that asset.

4. The present value of rental, or lease, payments, excluding executory costs (insurance, maintenance, taxes, etc.), must

5 "Accounting for Leases," 1990 Edition.

be less than 90 percent (not equal to) of the fair market value of the asset.

The rationale of the criteria is to determine the intent of the parties to a lease transaction. A lease that does not transfer all the benefits and liabilities associated with ownership is said to be an operating lease.

Ownership Intent—Capital Leases

When a corporation has the intent of ownership of the property, there are several lease alternatives to consider: (1) sales-type lease; (2) direct finance lease; or, (3) leverage lease.

From the lessor's viewpoint, if at inception a lease meets one of the four criteria listed above [under "Capital lease (for accounting purposes)], and in addition, meets both of the following criteria, it shall be classified as a sales-type lease, or a direct financing lease. Otherwise, it shall be classified as an operating lease (FAS13 ¶8). The criteria are:

1. Collectibility of the minimum lease payments is reasonably predictable (FAS13 ¶8a).

2. No important uncertainties surround the amount of unreimbursable costs yet to be incurred by the lessor under the lease (FAS13 ¶8b).

SALES-TYPE LEASES

These are classified as leases that give rise to manufacturer's, or dealer's, profit (or loss) to the lessor (i.e., the fair value of the leased property at the inception of the lease is higher, or lower, than its cost or carrying amount, if different) and that meet the four criteria for capital leases and both of the above criteria (FAS13 ¶6bi).

DIRECT FINANCING LEASES

These are classified as leases other than leveraged leases that do not give rise to manufacturer's, or dealer's, profit (or loss) to the lessor but meet one or more of the criteria for capital leases and both of the above criteria under ¶8 (FAS13 ¶6bii).

LEVERAGED LEASES

A leveraged lease is direct financing lease that additionally has all of the following characteristics:

1. It involves at least three parties: a lessee, a long-term creditor, and a lessor, commonly called the equity participant (FAS13 ¶42b).

2. The financing provided by the long-term creditor is nonrecourse as to the general credit of the lessor (although the creditor may have recourse to the specific property leased and the unremitted rentals relating to it). The amount of the financing is sufficient to provide the lessor with substantial "leverage" in the transaction (FAS13 ¶42c).

3. The lessor's net investment declines during the early years once the investment has been completed and rises during the later years of the lease before its final elimination (FAS13 ¶42d).

OWNERSHIP INTENT—OPERATING LEASES

There is no company intent of ownership when they wish to use an asset for a short period of time.

There is no company intent of ownership when using rapidly changing highly technical equipment, as the computer, which permits an upgrading without capital investment and no worry about obsolescence or disposal.

There are times when a company wants to evaluate an asset and then determine its desire to purchase the asset if satisfactory and utilizes the operating lease with the option to purchase the asset.

Most lease-with-option-to-purchase disputes have been judicated in tax courts. The criteria applied by the courts has been the *intent to purchase test*. This test declares that if the option can be exercised within a time period that is less than the property's useful life, and the lease payments cover what would be the purchasing price, then a sale was intended.

"HELL OR HIGH WATER" CLAUSE

A "hell or high water" clause in a lease may prejudice its status as a true lease. Such clauses stipulate that the lessee pays the full value of the asset to the lessor regardless of what happens to the equipment. This clause is used to protect the lessor against any financial loss in the lease agreement.

OPERATING LEASE VERSUS CONDITIONAL SALE CONTRACT[6]

Whether an agreement, which in form is a lease, is in substance a conditional sales contract depends on the *intent* of the parties as evidenced by the provisions of the agreement, read in light of the facts and circumstances existing at the time the agreement was executed.

In absence of compelling persuasive factors of contrary, implication an intent warranting treatment of a transaction, for tax purposes, as a purchase and sale rather than as a lease, or rental, agreement may in general be said to exist if one or more of the following conditions are present:

---

6 IRS Ruling 55-540, Section 4.01.

1. Portions of the periodic payments are made specifically applicable to an equity to be acquired by the lessee (Truman Bowen vs. Commissioner, 12 T.C. 446, acquiescence, C.B. 1951-2-1).

2. The lessee will acquire title upon payment of a stated amount of "rentals" which under the contract the lessee is required to make (Harvey vs. Rhode Island Locomotive Works, 93 U.S. 664; Robert A. Taft vs. Commissioner, 27 B.T.A. 808; Truman Bowen vs. Commissioner, supra.).

3. The total amount which the lessee is required to pay for a relatively short period of use constitutes an inordinately large portion of the total sum required to be paid to secure the transfer of title (Truman Bowen vs. Commissioner, supra.).

4. The agreed "rental" payments materially exceed the current fair rental value. This may be indicative that the payments include an element other than compensation for the use of the property (William A. McWaters et al. vs. Commissioner, Tax Court Memorandum Opinion, entered June 1950; Truman Bowen vs. Commissioner, supra.).

5. The asset may be acquired under a purchase option at a price which is nominal in relation to the value of the asset at the time of entering into the original agreement, or which is a relatively small amount when compared with the total payments which are required to be made (Burroughs Adding Machine Company vs. Bogdon, 9 Fed. 2d 54; Holeproof Hosiery Company vs. Commissioner, 11 B.T.A. 547. Compare H.T. Benton et al., vs. Commissioner, 197 Fed. 2d 745).

6. Some portion of the periodic payment is specifically designated as interest, or otherwise, recognizable as equiva-

lent of interest (Judson Mills vs. Commissioner, 11 T.C. 25, acquiescence, C.B. 1949-1, 2).

SALES AND LEASEBACK

This type of transaction occurs when one company converts its fixed assets (buildings, equipment, etc.) into liquid assets (cash) thereby improving its balance sheet. The transaction involves the sale of the property by one company to another (usually a financial institution) which in turn leases the same property back to the original seller. In this type of transaction, the original owner receives needed cash from the sales transaction, and yet retains the use of the property through a lease.

For example:

1. Xerox Credit Corporation recently purchased the operations center of a West Coast bank and leased it back to the bank for 25 years;

2. the Oakland, California, government arranged for the sale and leaseback of two dozen city-owned buildings, including City Hall, generating some $250 million in cash; and,

3. Security Pacific Leasing Corporation recently purchased and leased back the General Reinsurance Building in downtown Stanford, Connecticut.[7]

VENDOR LEASES

This is a lease directly from the manufacturer, or dealer or through its financial subsidiary (captive leasing) company, which provides the financing to the manufacturer's, or dealer's, customers. The manufacturer and dealer use this method as a tool in the marketing of their products.

---

7 Harvey Shapiro, "Equipment Leasing," *Forbes*, March 24, 1986.

For example, The Caterpillar Financial Service Corporation (Cat Corporation) is a captive financing company which provides a variety of financial arrangements to customers for Caterpillar equipment. This role strengthens Caterpillar and its dealers' position in the marketplace by providing consistent, competitive and supportive financing.[8]

MASTER LEASES

A master lease is an open-ended contract for equipment needed now and in the future. It is similar to an open-ended purchase order which contains the price, terms and conditions, but does not contain the kind and quantity of merchandise for the future. This is the same in a master lease where the lease rate and terms are indicated with the kind and quantity of equipment to be provided by the lessor as the lessee requests them.

This type of leasing arrangement is usually used when leasing trucks or cars or when leasing office equipment, such as computers, during cyclical business times.

SAFE HARBOR LEASE

The Economic Recovery Tax Act of 1981 (ERTA) made dramatic changes in equipment leasing and financing by creating a new type of tax-oriented equipment lease—the *safe harbor lease*—by permitting the transfer of tax benefits.

ERTA broadened the definition of a true lease as set forth under Revenue Procedure 75-21, Section 4, by permitting a fixed-price purchase option, the lease of limited-use property, extended the authorized length of the lease term, and for lessees to loan the lessor up to 90 percent of the purchase price.

Safe harbor leases made it easy for a profitable company to act as a "nominal lessor" and use the unused tax benefits of a marginal profit lessee. This was accomplished through a *tax benefit*

8 Financial Merchandising, Module 3, Cat Financial.

transfer lease (TBT lease) in which the lease payments offset the debt payments. The only money changing hands was the payment for tax benefits. Thus, the marginal lessee transferred the "tax title" to the more profitable lessor who could use the tax benefits to shelter income.

The safe harbor and TBT leasing was repealed in 1982 and phased out on December 31, 1983, through the Tax Equity and Fiscal Responsibility Act of 1982 (TEFRA).

FINANCE LEASE

This tax-oriented type lease was established by the Tax Equity and Fiscal Responsibility Act of 1982 (TEFRA) called the finance lease. This was to replace the repealed safe harbor lease and become effective January 1, 1984, but was postponed to January 1, 1988, by the Deficit Reduction Act of 1984 (DRA) and repealed in 1986 by the Tax Reform Act (TRA).

Internal Revenue Code (IRC) Section 68(f)(8) states the following rules for finance leases:

(A) In case of any agreement with respect to any finance lease property,

(i) a lessee has the right to purchase the property at a fixed price which is not less than 10% of the original cost of the property to the lessor, or

(ii) the property is of type not readily usable by any other person other than the lessee, shall not be taken into account in determining whether such agreement is a lease.

(B) (i) "Finance lease property" means recovery property which is new section 38 property of the lessor, which is leased within 3 months after such property was placed into service, and which if acquired by the lessee, would have been new section 38 property of the lessee.

(ii) The cost basis of all finance lease property which is placed into service, before January 1, 1990, and with respect to which the taxpayer is a lessee, shall not exceed an amount equal to 40% of the taxpayer's qualified property during such calendar year.

(C) The parties to a finance agreement characterize such agreement as a lease, and the lessor under such agreement would be treated as the owner of the property.

The lessor could reduce its federal income tax by only 50 percent as a result of tax benefits from safe harbor or finance leases entered into before September 30, 1985.

True lease structures were changed by neither the ERTA nor the TEFRA, and the guidelines, as set forth in Revenue Procedure 75-21, remain valid.

TRAC LEASES

In case of any qualified motor vehicle agreement, the fact that such agreement contains a *"terminal rental adjustment clause"* (TRAC) shall not be taken into account in determining whether such agreement is a true lease.[9]

The term "terminal rental adjustment clause" means a provision of an agreement which permits or requires the rental price to be adjusted upward or downward by reference to the amount realized by the lessor under the agreement upon the sale or other disposition of such property. In other words, the residual risk is shifted to the lessee.

TRAC leases have been around for 30 or so years in the motor vehicle leasing industry. Basically, the lease provides for a schedule of lease payments, together with an *estimated* residual value at

9 Public Law 97-248, Section 210, 96 Stat. 447.

the end of the lease term. The agreement provides that the *actual* value will be determined by a sale or otherwise, and thus either a payment will be made by the lessee or credit given by the lessor to reflect the difference between the estimated and actual residual value.

The lessee who takes good care of the vehicle would be "rewarded" while the careless lessee would be penalized for poor care.

LEASE SYNDICATION AND BROKERAGE

This occurs when a leasing entity acts as an intermediary, or broker, by matching the investor with the lessee. These activities usually involve millions of dollars, such as in the aircraft industry financing. Sometimes the leasing entity invests with other investors, or arranges with other investors to finance the entire financial agreement. There is a brokerage fee paid for this service. For example, South Pacific Leasing made arrangements with investors to finance Air Canada with $260 million to acquire four 767-200 ER aircraft; South Pacific received a fee for its service.

TAX-EXEMPT POLITICAL SUBDIVISION LEASES

This is a cost effective alternative for the acquisition of assets (land, buildings and equipment, etc.) by state, county and city governments. The income to the lessor is tax-exempt, but no deductible depreciation is applicable.

According to the Government Finance Officers Association, estimates of municipal leases being signed, are at the rate of five billion dollars a year, and the leases include everything from fire trucks to buildings. For example:

1. Oklahoma City leases two helicopters for its police department;
2. Oakland, California, leases some of its fire trucks, and;

3. Reeves County, Texas, leased an entire facility, a correctional center (jail), which was arranged by the First Continental Finance Group of Dallas.[10]

WET AND DRY LEASES

These types of leases refer to the aircraft industry. A *dry* lease refers to the aircraft lease financing as the primary object. A *wet* lease refers to a lease where, in addition to aircraft financing, there is fuel and maintenance during the lease term.

NET LEASES

This is a financial lease whereby the lessee in addition to making lease payments agrees to assume the obligation of maintenance, insurance, property taxes, etc., and assumes risks of ownership.

NET-NET LEASES

These are similar to the net lease with the additional lessee's obligation to guarantee the residual value to the lessor at a pre-determined value. The lessee is responsible for any difference between the actual sale and the pre-determined value.

INTERNATIONAL LEASES

These types of leases are offered in most industrial countries and are generally in the form of dollar-dominated cross-border tax leasing arrangements for large multinational corporations establishing facilities in the United States.

Cross-border leasing, where the lessor and the lessee are in different countries, is a substantial part of the international market for aircraft, ships, and other big-ticket items. For example, Security

10 Shapiro, "Equipment Leasing."

Pacific Leasing Corporation arranged for Japanese lease financing of four McDonnell Douglas MD82 aircraft for American Airlines in the amount of $104 million.

Leasing has become a global industry, and the disappearing trade barriers and freer flow of capital and goods should provide increase involvement in world-wide equipment finance leasing during the next decade for United States lessors.

FUTURE FOR LEASING[11]

Domestic demand for leasing equipment should grow about seven percent per year for the early 1990s. Globalization will have an impact on the large lessors, but all lessors should see increased business dynamics in world economy.

Efficient management and remarketing of equipment (residual resale) will be the core for growth in the leasing industry.

Five factors that equipment lessors must consider for their future:

1. Domestic and global economy;

2. Rapid advance in high technological equipment;

3. Trends in the leasing industry;

4. Merger and acquisition of companies; and,

5. The regulatory climate (now leasing is a "self-regulatory business" with no legal obstacles).

---

11 American Association of Equipment Lessor, 1990 Industry Future Council Report.

CHAPTER 3

Tax Effect on Cash Flow

INTRODUCTION

Every business has a definite goal for every financial decision it makes: mainly to achieve a target market share, maximize profits and survive in the competitive arena. Usually an increase of one percent in the market share can result in a 0.5 percent increase in profits thus assuring that company's survival.

When making a purchase-or-lease decision it is necessary to understand the basics of taxation and depreciation, especially as they relate to the acquisition and disposal of assets. From these one can have an indication of the after-tax cash flow.

WHAT IS DEPRECIATION?

Depreciation is the annual deduction one takes to recover the cost of a business or income-producing property that is used for more than one year. Depreciation is the cost of the continuing waste (wearing out) of an asset as it is being used. This depreciation is spread out over the useful life or recovery period of an asset.

Depreciation is an important consideration whenever an asset is to be acquired. If an asset is purchased, depreciation is recognized as a tax-deductible expense and has an effect on the cash inflow (for these is no cash outflow); the greater the depreciation, the lower the taxes which result in higher after-tax cash flow.

WHAT CAN BE DEPRECIATED?

Property is depreciable if it meets the following requirements:

- It must be used in a business or held for the production of income.
- It must have a determinable life usage and that life must be more than one year.
- It must be something that wears out, decays, gets used up, becomes obsolete, or loses value from natural causes.

Land itself can never be depreciated.

Depreciation property may be either *tangible* or *intangible*. Tangible property is any property which can be seen or touched. Tangible property can be depreciated only if it can wear out, decay, or lose value from natural causes, be used up, or become obsolete. If the property is leased or rented, it cannot be depreciated; only the owner of the property may depreciate it.

Intangible property may be depreciated if you can determine its useful life; this includes patents, copyrights, agreements not to compete, franchises, designs, drawings and patterns. Customer and subscription lists may sometimes be depreciable. Goodwill is not depreciable because its useful life cannot be determined. Trademark and trade names may not be depreciated; they must be capitalized.

MODIFIED ACCELERATED COST RECOVERY SYSTEM (MACRS)[1]

The modified accelerated cost recovery system applies to new and used tangible property (recovery property) placed in service after 1986, and must be depreciated under the MACRS.

1 IRS Publication 534, 1990 issue.

Several factors enter the determination as to how much depreciation to deduct. They include:

- The depreciable basis for the property;
- When the property was placed in service;
- The property class of the asset;
- Which convention applies; and,
- Which MACRS recovery method you choose to use.

COST BASIS

The basis is a measure of total investment cost in that asset owned, and includes the purchase price plus sales tax, plus freight charges, installation and testing costs. This is the basis for depreciation.

When an asset is depreciated, a certain percentage of the basis is deducted each year.

WHEN PLACED IN SERVICE[2]

For depreciation purposes, an asset is considered placed in service when such asset is in a condition or state of readiness and available for a specific assigned task, whether in trade or business, for the production of profit.

For example, a machine was ordered November 10, 1989, and delivered on December 20, 1989, but was not installed and operational until January 10, 1990. In this case, depreciation of the machine started January 10, 1990, when it was ready to perform its desired function, not on the date of purchase.

---

2 IRS Publication No. 534 (1990).

MACRS PROPERTY CLASS LIVES AND RECOVERY PERIODS[3]

The annual depreciation amount depends upon the depreciation method used as well as the asset's useful life or recovery period. The useful life may be estimated, based on experience or based on one of the various class lives established by the Internal Revenue Service (IRS). The Tax Reform Act of 1986 (TRA) provides that tangible, personal property will be depreciated over a 3-, 5-, 7-, 10-, 15-, or 20-year period. IRS Publication number 534 contains a listing for most assets under the "Table of Class Lives and Recovery Periods." The table has a description of assets included in each asset class. At the end of each asset description of assets included in each asset class. At the end of each asset description are listed the class life, the MACRS recovery period and the alternate MACRS recovery period for each asset described.

3-year property—includes property with a class file of four years or less. Examples: over-the-road tractor units, any race horse that is over two years old when placed in service, and breeding hogs.

5-year property—includes property with a class life more than four years but less than ten years. Examples: taxis, buses, heavy-duty general purpose trucks (actual unloaded weight of 13,000 pounds or more), computers and peripheral equipment, office machinery (typewriters, calculators, copiers, etc., and any property used in connection with research and experimentation.

7-year property—includes property with a class life of ten years or more but less than 16 years. Examples: office furniture and fixtures (desks, files, etc.) and property that does not have a class life and that has not been designed by law in any other class.

10-year property—includes property with a class life of 16 years or more but less than 20 years. Examples: vessels, barges, tugs, and similar water transportation equipment, and any tree or vine-bearing fruit or nuts.

---

3 IRC Section 168(e).

15-year property—includes property with a class life of 20 years or more but less than 25 years. Examples: roads, shrubbery, wharves (if depreciable), and as designated, any municipal waste-water treatment plant.

20-year property—includes property with a class of 25 years or more such as any municipal sewers.

Non-residential real property—includes any real property that is not residential rent property and Section 1250 property with a class life of 27.5 years or more. This property is depreciated over 31.5 years.

Residential rental property—includes any real property that is a rental building or structure (including mobile homes) for which 80% or more of the rental income for the tax year is rental income from the dwelling units. This property is depreciable over 27.5 years.

SALVAGE VALUE

Salvage value is the estimated value of an asset at the end of its useful life. It represents the value expected for that asset after it can no longer be used productively and profitably. It is important to accurately determine the correct salvage value for the asset so that one may correctly depreciate the depreciable portion of the asset. Assets may not be depreciated below their reasonable salvage value.

Net Salvage

Net salvage value is the salvage value of an asset after deducting what it costs to dispose of such asset. If the cost to dispose of the asset is more than the estimated salvage value, the net salvage value is zero. The salvage value can never be less than zero.

With personal property that has a useful life of three years or more, if the salvage value is less than 10% of the basis, the salvage value may be ignored when figuring the depreciation.

DEPRECIATION METHODS

Use the MACRS for all tangible property placed into service after 1986. Intangible property must be depreciated by the straight-line method.

For property in the 3-, 5-, 7-, 10-year class, use the 200% declining balance method over the 3, 5, 7, and 10 years. For property in the 15- or 20-year class, use the 150% declining balance method. For all these classes of property, one can change to the straight-line (S/L) method for the first tax year for which that method, when applied to the adjusted basis at the beginning of such year, will yield a larger depreciation deduction.

Instead of using the declining balance method, you may elect to use the straight-line method. Once made, you cannot change the method.

Declining Balance Method

Declining balance methods use the total cost of an asset rather than the depreciable value. To compute the MACRS deduction, first determine the declining rate of depreciation. This rate is determined by dividing the specific declining percentage (200% or 150%) by the useful life or recovery period.

A 5 year rate for 200% calculated:

$$\frac{200\ \%}{5\ \text{yr.}} = \frac{2.00}{5} = 0.40 \text{ or } 40\%$$

and this rate is multiplied by that year's basis (total cost - cumulative depreciation) to attain that year's depreciation deduction.

A 15 year rate for 150% is calculated:

$$\frac{150\ \%}{15\ \text{yr.}} = \frac{150}{15} = 0.10 \text{ or } 10\%$$

and this rate multiplied by that year's adjusted basis (total cost - cumulative depreciation) which gives that year's depreciation deduction.

The following table shows the applicable declining balance rate for each class of property and the first year for which it is changed to the straight-line method which gives the greater deduction allowed.

Class	*Declining Balance Rate*	*Year*
3	66.67%	3rd
5	40.00%	4th
7	28.57%	5th
10	20.00%	7th
15	10.00%	7th
20	7.50%	9th

Straight-line Method

The 200% declining balance method may be used for new residential real estate, and for new property having a useful life of 3 years or more.

The 150% declining balance method is used for new real estate, other than residential, and used for property having a useful life of 3 years or more.

The straight-line depreciation method may be used for all new and used property. Its rate determination is calculated by dividing the number 1 by the years remaining in the recovery period multiplied by the depreciable value of the property.

Example 3-1: A firm purchases two assets, Asset A and Asset B, for $100,000 each with a useful life of ten years each. Asset A will have a salvage value of $20,000 at the end of its useful life while Asset B has no expected salvage value. What is the depreciation of each?

Table 3.1 summarizes the depreciation for Asset A and Asset B:

Table 3.1

Year	*Rate x Basis - Cumulation Depreciation*		*Depreciation*	*Cumulative Depreciation*
1	0.20 x $100,000	=	$20,000.00	20,000.00
2	0.20 x (100,000 - 20,000)	=	16,000.00	36,000.00
3	0.20 x (100,000 - 36,000)	=	12,800.00	48,800.00
4	0.20 x (100,000 - 48,800)	=	10,240.00	59,040.00
5	0.20 x (100,000 - 59,040)	=	8,192.00	67,232.00
6	0.20 x (100,000 - 67,232)	=	6,553.00	73,785.60
7*	0.25 x (100,000 - 73,785.60)	=	6,553.00	80,339.20
8	"	=	6,553.00	86,892.80
9	"	=	6,553.00	93,446.40
10	"	=	6,553.00	100,000.00

*After six years, the continued depreciation will not provided for the full depreciation; thus, the IRS permits the straight-line depreciation method for the final four years in order to yield a larger annual depreciation deduction for each of the remaining years of useful life. The calculations are determined by dividing the remaining depreciable value ($100,000 less $73,785.60, the accumulative depreciation) of $26,214.40 by the remaining four years resulting in $6,553.60 per year.

Asset A calculations: $100,000 – $20,000 = $80,000 depreciable amount.

$$\text{Annual Depreciation} = \frac{\$100{,}000}{10} - \frac{\$20{,}000}{10} = \$8{,}000$$

The amount is $8,000 for each year that depreciation is applicable, which in this case is 10 years until the basis (depreciable value) in the asset is recovered.

Asset B calculations: No salvage value is expected in this case, thus the depreciable value is the total cost of $100,000 to be recovered over 10 years.

$$\text{Annual Depreciation} = \frac{\$100{,}000}{10} = \$10{,}000$$

The amount is $10,000 per year for 10 years.

The Internal Revenue Service directs that the first year for Asset A is calculated as 1/10th of the depreciable value ($100,000 - $20,000) resulting in $8,000 for that first year. For the second year, take 1/9th of the depreciable value, ($80,000 - $8,000 = $72,000), to result in $8,000, the same as the first year. The third year, take 1/8th of the depreciable value, ($72,000 - $8,000 = $64,000), again resulting in $8,000 as the third-year depreciation deduction, etc.

Double-declining-balance Method (DDB)

When using the double-declining-balance depreciation methods, the salvage value is not deducted from the total cost of the asset.

In reference to the above examples, Asset A and Asset B, and using the DDB method, we find that 200% ÷ 10 years = 2.00/10 = 0.20 or 20%. This rate is multiplied by the total cost (the basis) to arrive at the depreciation deduction for the first year. That sum, deducted from the total cost, gives the depreciable sum for the second-year basis which is again multiplied by the same rate of 20%, etc.

The depreciation deductions end when the remaining book value equals the salvage value. Asset A has a salvage value of $20,000 thus permitting the total depreciation equal to $80,000. The 6th year accumulated depreciation deduction was $73,785.60, and that leaves $6,214.40 to be deducted in the 7th year for a total of $80,000.

Asset B has no salvage value and thus can be depreciated to the full $100,000 as depicted in the above tabulation.

Sum-of-the-year's-digits Method (SYD)

This method applies to a changing rate to the constant depreciable value to arrive at the annual depreciation deduction. The denominator is the sum of the digits representing the total years of useful life for the asset. In the above example which has a 10-year useful life, the sum of the years 1+ 2+ 3+ 4+ 5+ 6+ 7+ 8+ 9+ 10 = 55 which remains the constant denominator. The numerator changes each year since it represents the remaining years of useful life of the asset. In the above example, the first year's fraction would be 10/55 of the depreciable value to arrive at the first year's depreciation deduction. The second year's fraction would be 9/55 of the original depreciable value. The third year's fraction would be 8/55, etc. Table 3.2 summarizes the 10 years of depreciation.

Table 3.2 Ten Years of Depreciation

	Asset A - $80,000 Basis Depreciable Value			*Asset B - $100,000 Basis Depreciable Value*		
Year	*Fraction of Basis*	*Yearly Depreciation*	Cumulative Depreciation	*Fraction of Basis*	*Yearly Depreciation*	*Cumulative Depreciation*
1	10/55	$14,545.45	$14,545.45	10/55	$18,181.82	$18,181.82
2	9/55	13,090.91	27,636.36	9/55	16,363.64	34,545.46
3	8/55	11,636.36	39,272.72	8/55	14,545.45	49,090.91
4	7/55	10,181.82	49,454.54	7/55	12,727.27	61,818.18
5	6/55	8,727.27	58,181.81	6/55	10,909.09	71,717.17
6	5/55	7,272.73	65,454.54	5/55	9,090.91	81,818.18
7	4/55	5,818.18	71,272.72	4/55	7,272.73	89,090.91
8	3/55	4,363.64	75,636.36	3/55	5,454.55	94,545.46
9	2/55	2,909.09	77,818.82	2/55	3,636.36	98,181.82
10	1/55	1,454.55	80,000.00	1/55	1,818.18	100,000.00

WHAT IS TAXATION?

Taxation is the system of levying a tax upon persons or property by a governmental body to raise revenue for the support of that taxing body.

Federal taxation is concerned with taxes on operating (ordinary) income, taxes on capital gains and losses, recapture of depreciation, etc. There is also state and city taxes to consider. Taxes are real cash outflow and must be taken into account when evaluating any capital expenditure.

FEDERAL TAXATION OF OPERATING INCOME[4]

The Tax Reform Act of 1986 reduced and simplified the number of tax brackets from five to three. The new brackets and tax rates are:

Tax Year	*Taxable Income*	*Tax Rate*
After July 1, 1987	0 to $50,000	15%
	$50,000 to 75,000	25%
	75,000 to ——	34%
	over $335,000 *	flat 34%

* Under previous law, an additional 5% surtax was levied on corporate income between $1,000,000 and $1,405,000 in an attempt to recapture the benefit of the lower tax rates. The Tax Reform Act of 1986 retains the 5% surtax, but is levied on corporate income between $100,000 and $335,000 which puts the tax of 39% for this phasing out group. For corporations with taxable income above $335,000, the tax rate is a flat 34%.

4 IRS Publication 334 (1990).

NET OPERATING LOSS (NOL)

If your deductions for the year are more than your income for the year, you may have a net operating loss. Generally, you carry back any NOL to three tax years before the NOL year, and then forward for up to 15 years till the loss is equalized. For example, if you had a net operating loss for the year 1990, you can carry that loss back to year 1987, and if you still have more loss, you would be able to carry that amount forward until the year 2005. If you still had any NOL left over after 2005, you would not be allowed to recoup that sum.

CAPITAL GAINS AND LOSSES

When a corporation acquires and disposes of an asset then capital gains or losses can occur. The treatment of capital gains and losses depends on how long you own the asset before you sell or exchange it.

If you hold a capital asset one year or less, the gain or loss from its disposition is short term. If you hold a capital asset longer than one year, the gain or loss on its disposition is long term.

Capital losses are allowed in full against capital gains plus up to $3,000 of ordinary income.

Short-term capital gains are taxed at part of ordinary income. Long-term capital gains are taxed at 28%, or at the rate applied to ordinary income, whichever is lower.

DEPRECIATION RECAPTURE

All gains on the disposition of capital assets depreciated under the MACRS method is recaptured as ordinary income to the extent of the previously allowed depreciation deductions.

Example 3-2: In example 3-1, Asset A had the original cost of $100,000 with a useful life of 10 years and a salvage value of

---

$20,000. At the end of six years, the corporation disposes of the asset for $100,000.

The tax effect would be that difference between the sales price of $100,000 and the book value (original cost of $100,000 less the cumulative depreciation of $73,785.60 using the DDB method) of $26,214.40 and represents the recaptured depreciation which is taxed at ordinary (operating) income.

Example 3-3: In the above example, the sales price was $110,000 which is $10,000 above the original cost thus representing a long-term capital gain of $10,000 which is taxed as such. The recaptured depreciation value is taxed as ordinary income.

DEPRECIATION AS A PREPAID EXPENSE

Accounting for depreciation charges for tangible assets (buildings, furniture, equipment, etc., used in the production of goods and/or services) is carried as if the cost was prepaid expense and spread over the useful life of that asset. Accounting Research Bulletin No. 22, issued by the American Institute of Accountants, describes the accounting concept of depreciation as:

"Depreciation accounting is a system of accounting which aims to distribute the cost of other basic value of tangible capital assets, less salvage, if any, over the estimated useful life of the unit (which may be a group of assets) in a systemic and rational manner. It is a process of allocation, not of valuation. Depreciation for the year is the portion of the total charge under such a system that is allocated to the year. Although the allocation may properly take into account occurrences during the year, it is not intended to be a measurement of the effect on all such occurrences."

DEPRECIATION AND THE BALANCE SHEET

Depreciation, in either a direct purchase or a capital lease, is generally shown on the asset side of the balance sheet as a deduction from the appropriate fixed asset account, as indicated below:

Current Assets		
Cash	$ 18,000.00	
Accounts receivable	14,000.00	
Inventory	15,000.00	
Total		$47,000.00
Fixed Assets		
Buildings	$100,000.00	
Less accumulative depreciation (2 years)	20,000.00	
Total		$80,000.00
Equipment	$ 50,000.00	
Less accumulative depreciation	18,000.00	
Total		$32,000.00

Reviewing the above, we see that the book value of the building and the equipment are $80,000.00 and $32,000.00, respectively, after two years of usage and deduction of the depreciation accounts. The remaining amount (book value) is the amount to be charged (depreciated) against future accounting periods.

The capital lease is a financial lease where there is a transfer of all benefits and risks inherent in ownership of the asset to the lessee who records all such transactions on the balance sheet.

The operating lease provides the lessee with an off-balance sheet financing transaction. That is, there is no reflection of the asset acquired and used on the balance sheet. This type of transaction provides for the lease (rental) payments to be expenses on the lessee's income statement as they occur.

ALTERNATIVE MINIMUM TAX (AMT)

In addition to the regular income tax, the Internal Revenue Code (IRC) imposes an alternative minimum tax (AMT) on both corporate and non-corporate taxpayers. The AMT applies to the extent that it exceeds the taxpayer's regular tax and is imposed at the rate of 20% for corporations (increases to 24% for 1991) on the excess of the taxpayer's alternative minimum taxable income (AMTI) above the exemption amount. AMTI is computed by reference to the taxpayer's taxable income plus tax preference terms and certain other adjustments. The AMT is imposed on corporation's AMTI less a $40,000 exemption.

The AMT was enacted by the Tax Reform Act of 1986 (TRA), effective January 1, 1987, to insure that all taxpaying entities with economic income pay some amount of tax, despite their allowable deductions. Tax preference items include deductions created by the accelerated cost recovery system.

LEASING AND THE AMT

The Tax Reform Act of 1986 added the AMT as a new factor in the purchase-or-lease decision making process. The more equipment a corporation owns, the more depreciation deductions are generated under the accelerated cost recovery system which is considered a preference item, and may be subject to AMT liability.

Leasing might prove attractive to such corporations (subject to AMT liability) for payments under a true (operating) lease do not create a preference item.

In fact, leasing provides corporations with possession and use of equipment for as long as needed at a predictable cost (rental payments), which permits the corporations to be more flexible in its management of its cash flow. The benefits of higher productivity and profit comes from the use of the equipment, not the ownership of them.

CHAPTER 4

Economic Analysis of Equipment Acquisitions

Businesses are continuously having requests for capital expenditure. If the business is the keep abreast in the market of competition, equipment must be upgraded periodically or new equipment acquired to keep pace with the rapid changes in technology. In particular, data processing and programming encourage capital outlays with the promise of more efficient operation.

Persons involved in the analysis of financial decisions should have an understanding of the time value of money. They should be able to perform the calculations associated with the analysis of capital expenditures. They should understand the concept, mathematics and uses for computing interest rates, cash discounts, etc.

No matter what technique of analysis is used, management cannot make a decision unless the information is reliable. The most important component in any capital expenditure decision is the amount and the timing of the cash flows expected over the next span of accounting periods.

WHAT IS INTEREST?

Interest is the fee, rent, or charge paid for the use of money. Investors or savers "loan" their money to financial institutions or projects for which they receive interest or rent for the use of their money. Other people and businesses "borrow" money from these financial institutions for a fee (interest) depending on the amount and time this money is used. Many people and businesses acquire goods and services on "credit." That is, they get to utilize the goods and services now and pay for them in the future. The financial institutions pay for these goods and services now and are repaid for the credit extended (use of the money) in the form of interest by those people and businesses over the agreed period of time.

Interest is a key cost in today's business because most, if not all, at one time or another, have to borrow money. Whether you lease or purchase, interest cost is involved when you have to use another's money. Interest cost is a real cash outflow and can effect the profitability of a proposed capital investment.

TERMINOLOGY IN INTEREST CALCULATIONS

There is *simple interest, add-on interest,* and *compound interest* used in the calculation of "fee" payment for the use of money.

The amount of money invested, borrowed, or unpaid is known as the *principal.*

The *interest rate* is the rate of the fee expressed as a percentage of the principal per period of time.

Time is a factor in every calculation of interest. In modern business, the Julian calendar (exact time), based on the solar year of 365 days, is used. Every fourth year, one day is added and that year is computed on a 366-day basis. A period of time can be expressed as the number of days, months, or years.

WHAT AFFECTS INTEREST RATES?

The rate of interest charged varies with the situation existing at the time of borrowing. Two of the most important factors are: (1) the money supply and (2) the risk involved. If the money supply is scarce, or "tight," then the rates will tend to be higher. When the risk factors increase, the rates tend to to be higher.

The risk factors a financial institution will investigate before approving a loan include:

- The stability of the business (business history);
- Whether this is a short-term loan or a long-term loan;
- Will there be a down payment and to what extent; and,
- Past credit history and loan security.

SIMPLE INTEREST

Simple interest is commonly stated as the *annual percentage rate (APR)*. Simple interest is calculated solely on the unpaid principal from one period to the next. The formula for such calculation is:

$$I = P \times i \times t$$

I = Simple interest earned or charged
P = Principal amount of money invested or borrowed
i = Annual interest rate, expressed as a percentage per $100 of principal
t = Time expressed in years, or parts thereof

In order to compute for any of the above variables, the other three items have to be known. When an investment, or loan, is made, the amount invested or borrowed, the rate of the interest and the length of the time involved are known, the interest paid or earned can be calculated.

Example 4-1: Municipal bonds are issued at a specified simple interest rate with interest earned and paid semi-annually. When \$5,000 is invested for five years at 6% simple interest, the interest payments every half-year are calculated as follows:

$$\begin{aligned} I &= P \times i \times t \\ &= 5{,}000 \times 6\% \times \tfrac{1}{2} \text{ year} \\ &= 5{,}000 \times 0.06 \times 0.5 = 150 \end{aligned}$$

In this case, the semi-annual payment will be \$150, and will remain the same throughout the five-year term of the investment, since the principal and the interest rate remain the same.

Example 4-2: A firm borrows \$5,000 for one year at 10% simple interest, payable at the year's end. What is the interest cost?

$$\begin{aligned} I &= P \times i \times t \\ &= \$5{,}000 \times 10\% \times 1 \text{ year} \\ &= \$5{,}000 \times 0.10 \times 1 \\ &= \$500 \text{ (the total interest cost)} \end{aligned}$$

ACCUMULATED SUM OF SIMPLE INTEREST

The accumulated sum to be paid or received at the term's end is the interest added to the principal, and has the formula:

$$S = P + I$$

S, (accumulated sum), is also known as the *maturity value* or *future value*.

In example 4-1, we have \$150 paid every 1/2 year for 10 payments (2 yearly payments for 5 years) for a total of \$1,500 and the accumulated sum is:

$$\begin{aligned} S &= \$5{,}000 \text{ principal} + \$1{,}500 \text{ total interest} \\ &= \$6{,}500 \end{aligned}$$

In example 4-2, the entire amount is repaid at the year's end, and the accumulated sum is:

S = \$5,000 principal + \$500 total interest
= \$5,500

It is essential that the interest rate and the time period involved be consistent with each other. When a 12% annual rate is indicated, the time period must be expressed in years, or parts thereof. If the interest is quoted as 1 1/2% per month, then the time period must be expressed in months.

Ordinary simple interest, based on a 360-day year, is used primarily for commercial loans and mortgage payments. When calculating, we use our formula (I = P × i × t), but we replace the "t" with n/360 where "n" represents the number of days, and our formula reads:

$$I = P \times i \times n/360$$

Example 4-3: Ordinary simple interest of 8% on a \$5,000 investment for 270 days is calculated:

I = \$5,000 × 8% × 270/360
= \$5,000 × 0.08 × 0.75
= \$300

Exact simple interest is based on a 365-day year and is used when the exact time is required. In this case, the "t" is replaced with n/365 and the formula becomes:

$$I = P \times i \times n/365$$

Example 4-4: With the same conditions as above except a 365-day year is used. The calculations are:

I = \$5,000 × 8% × 270/365
= \$5,000 × 0.08 × 0.73973
= \$295.89

ADD-ON INTEREST

As the name implies, add-on interest is that interest charge which is added to the principal at the beginning of the loan term. This method is not used in most regions as many jurisdictions require that all interest charges be expressed as an annual percentage rate.

Example 4-5: When $5,000 is borrowed at a 12% add-on interest rate for one year, what will the monthly payments be?

$$\begin{aligned} I &= P \times i \times t \\ &= \$5{,}000 \times 12\% \times 1 \\ &= \$5{,}000 \times 0.12 \times 1 \\ &= \$600 \text{ total add-on interest} \end{aligned}$$

The $600 is added to the principal of $5,000 resulting in $5,600, which is divided by 12 months to arrive at a monthly payment of $446.67.

COMPOUND INTEREST

Whereas *simple interest* is defined as the interest earned on a principal amount for a specific time and at an expressed interest per year, *compound interest* is the procedure whereby the interest earned by a principal for a specified period is reinvested, and that amount (P + I) is again earning interest. This second earned interest is again reinvested and added to the first interest-added-amount to give *us* a new third principle, which continues to earn interest for the designated period, etc. This is sometimes referred to as "interest-on-interest" calculations. The formula for such transactions is:

$$S = P(1 = i)^n$$

S = Compound sum (P + I) due after "n" periods (at maturity)
P = Initial principal (amount of money invested or borrowed)
i = Nominal interest rate (stated annual rate) converted to an effective interest rate (rate per compounding period)

n = Number of compounding periods

Example 4-6: When one invests \$5,000 at 12% APR, what would be the sum total of the earnings when compounded annually, semi-annually, quarterly, or monthly for one year?

By using the formula for simple interest, we can calculate the interest earnings for each period of time. The formula is:

$$I = P \times i \times t$$

For an annual interest rate, the calculation is:

I = \$5,000 × 12% × 1 year	
= \$5,000 × 0.12 × 1 =	\$600.00

For semi-annual (2 interest periods), the calculation is:

I = \$5,000 × 12% × 1/2 year	
= \$5,000 × 0.12 × 0.5 =	\$300.00
= (5,000 + 300) × 0.12 × 0.5 =	318.00
	618.00

For quarterly (4 interest periods/year), the calculation is:

I = \$5,000 × 12% × 1/4 year	
= \$5,000 × 0.12 × 0.25 =	\$150.00
= (5,000 + 150) × 0.12 × 0.25 =	154.50
= (5,000 + 150 + 154.50) × 0.12 × 0.25 =	159.14
= (5,000 + 150 + 154.50 + 159.14) × 0.12 × 0.25 =	163.91
	627.55

To obtain the total sum of interest earnings for a one-year period of time, we simply add the individual earnings. We see that the more frequently the interest period is compounded, the larger is the sum of the interest earned. Thus, a principal whose interest is compounded daily earns more interest than one compounded monthly which earns more interest than one compounded quarterly, etc.

In the above examples, the calculations are the long, time consuming mathematical method for determining the total interest earned. The monthly calculations would be more time consuming. To facilitate computations, all financial institutions have the use of precalculated *compound-amount factor table* (Table I, Appendix), also known as the *compound-interest factor table* (see below for full explanation), which permits a quick determination of the maturity value of any fund. From the final sum, we deduct the principal to arrive at the total interest earned.

The compound interest formula, $S = P(1 + i)^n$, is where the exponent (represented by "n") indicates the number of times the base number is used as a factor in the calculations. For example:

$$(1 + i) \times (1 + i) = (1 + i)^2$$
$$(1 + i)^3 \times (1 + i) = (1 + i)^4$$
$$(1 + i)^{10} \times (1 + i)^{20} = (1 + i)^{30}$$

The expression $(1 + i)^{10}$, when multiplied by $(1 + i)^{20}$, will result in the expression $(1 + i)^{30}$, telling us that when the base numbers are multiplied by themselves, the multiplication is accomplished by simply *adding* their exponents.

INTEREST RATES PER COMPOUNDING PERIOD

In most cases, the interest rate is expressed as the annual interest rate, and the corresponding rate per compounding period can be calculated using the formula:

$$i = \frac{r}{n}$$

i = Interest per compounding period
r = Annual interest rate
n = Number of compounding periods per year

In our example 4-6, for the semi-annual compounding calculations, we have 2 compounding periods in 1 year. Thus, the 12% annual interest rate is divided by 2 to arrive at a 6% rate for each semi-annual interest rate. With 2 interest compounding periods, we look at the compound-amount factor table under the "n" column to number 2, then across to the 6% column to find the factor number (1.123600), which when multiplied by $5,000 results in $5,618.00 as the total sum received after one year. Deducting the principal of $5,000, we have the earned interest, $618.00, the same as above.

For quarterly compounding calculations, we divide the 12% annual rate by 4 (4 quarters per year) to arrive at 3% per quarter. Again, looking at the compound-amount factor table under the "n" column to number 4 and across to the 3% column to read the factor number (1.125509), which when multiplied by $5,000 gives the result of $5,627.55. This amount, reduced by the principal, tells us the interest earned is $627.55, the same as above.

For the monthly compounding calculations, we divide the 12% by 12 (12 months per year) to arrive at 1% per month. Looking at the compound-amount factor table under the "n" column to number 12, across to the 1% column, we read the factor number of 1.126825, which when multiplied by $5,000 results in the sum of $5,634.13. This, reduced by the $5,000 principal, tells us the interest that was earned amounts to $634.13.

The use of the compound-amount factor tables offers a quicker and easier method for the calculation of compound interest earned by indicating the maturity value of the principal at the term's end.

Example 4-7: Your firm makes a $500,000 investment for five years at an annual rate of 6%, compounded quarterly. What sum will the firm receive at maturity?

Here we have a five-year investment earning interest quarterly (4 times a year) or 20 compounding periods. The 6% annual interest rate equates to 1.5% (6 ÷ 4) per compounding period (per quarter). Using our compound interest formula and our compound-amount factor table under the "n" column to number 20 and across to 1.5% column, we calculate:

$S = P(1 + i)^n$
$S = \$500{,}000 (1 + 0.015)^{20}$
$S = \$500{,}000 (1.1346855)$
$S = \$673{,}427.50$ (the amount to receive at maturity)

The interest earned on this investment is $173,427.50.

EFFECTIVE INTEREST RATES

Interest rates are usually expressed as annual interest rates, and are referred to as the nominal rate. When compounding is computed more frequently than annually (semi-annually, quarterly, monthly, or even daily), an effective annual interest rate can be determined by using the formula:

$$r = (1 + \frac{i}{m})^{m} - 1$$

r = effective annual interest rate
i = nominal interest rate
m = number of compounding periods per year

Example 4-8: Determine the effective rate for 8% compounded quarterly.

1. 8% ÷ 4 (4 quarters/year) to arrive at 2%

2. the bracket $1 + (\frac{0.08}{4})^{4} = (1+0.02)^{4}$

and we look at our compound-amount factor table (Table I) under the "n" column to 4 and across to the 2% column to read a factor of 1.082432, and our formula reads:

$r = (1 + 0.02)^4 - 1$
$r = 1.082432 - 1 = 0.082432 = 8.24\%$

Example 4-9: Determine the effective rate for 12% compounded semi-annually.

$$r = 1 + (\frac{0.12}{2})^{2} - 1$$
$$r = (1 + 0.06)^{2} - 1$$
$$r = 1.1236 - 1 = 0.1236 = 12.36\%$$

Example 4-10: Determine the effective rate for 12% compounded quarterly.

$$r = 1 + (\frac{0.12}{4})^{4} - 1$$
$$r = (1 + 0.03)^{4} - 1$$
$$r = 1.125509 - 1 = 0.125509 = 12.55\%$$

Example 4-11: Determine the effective annual rate for 12% compounded monthly.

$$r = 1 = (\frac{0.12}{12})^{12} - 1$$
$$r = (1 + 0.01)^{12} - 1$$
$$r = 1.126825 - 1 = 0.126825 = 12.68\%$$

From the above, one can see that the more frequently the interest is compounded, the greater the effective rate will be.

Financial institutions may all offer the same nominal interest rate, but the effective interest rate depends on the frequency their institution compounds interest.

TOTAL INTEREST COST

When looking at the interest rate, consider the frequency of compounding and the length of time involved to ascertain the *total interest cost*. You have to select that which will meet the company's needs and match the projected cash flows with the needed cash outflow to make the investment attractive.

INTEREST AT WORK

You are evaluating three comparable machines with a five-year useful life.

You receive from:	*Dealer A*	*Dealer B*	*Dealer C*
Selling Price	$102,000	$100,000	$98,000

The best buy would be from Dealer C, but how many companies have this amount of cash available to make outright purchase without causing anxiety over the cash flow to meet daily business operations. Thus, we request each of the dealers to present a financial package for the acquisition of their machine.

All dealers requested a 20% down payment and the balance paid over a three-year period at their specified interest rates. You make a summary like this:

	Dealer A	*Dealer B*	*Dealer C*
Selling Price	$102,000	$100,000	$98,000
20% Down Payment	20,400	20,000	19,600
Amount to Finance	81,600	80,000	78,400
Interest Rate	9%	12%	15%
Interest Cost*	7,344	9,600	11,760
Total Cost	$109,344	$109,600	$109,760

* approximate for illustration only

Although Dealer C had the lowest selling price, it became the highest *total cost*. One way to reduce the total cost is by increasing the down payment, thus, reducing the amount to be financed. Had Dealer C offered financial arrangements with a 25% down payment, and with the same 15% interest charge, the result would have been $109,025, making it an attractive alternative.

Another method to reduce total cost is to pay off the financial obligation in a shorter period of time. This reduces the interest charges. The longer it takes to pay off a debt, the greater will be the interest costs. You have to pay for the use of someone's money.

CALCULATIONS FOR PERIODS EXCEEDING LISTINGS OF COMPOUND-AMOUNT FACTOR TABLE

From the compound-amount factor — $[(1 = i)^n]$ — all other factors can be computed, for the above expression appears in all other factor formulas.

When the compound periods exceed the table listings, we utilize the law of exponents from algebra. When a like expression is multiplied by itself, the exponents are simply added:

$$(1 + i)^2 + (1 + i)^3 = (1 + i)^5$$

The factor-compound factor table lists up to 120 compounding periods, and we can determine any number of periods beyond by combining any two or more factors to equal the desired factor.

Example 4-12: With monthly compounding periods for 20 years at a 0.5% interest rate per month, what would the factor be?

To calculate, we need any combination of exponents which will equal 240 (12 compound periods per year × 20 years) factor.

To accomplish this, we can multiply $(1 + 0.005)^{120}$ by $(1 + 0.005)^{120}$ which results in $(1 + 0.005)^{240}$. We look at the compound-amount factor table to 120 under the "n" column and across to the 0.5% column to read factor 1.819396734. This factor number multiplied by itself results in 3.310204476 as the factor for 240 compounding periods at 0.005 (0.5%).

To prove this, we can use any combination of exponents equal to 240.

1. The factor for 60 compounding periods at 0.5% is 1.348850153, and when multiplied by itself four (4) times, we get 3.310204479 for 240 periods.

2. The factor for 80 compounding periods at 0.5% is 1.490338568, and when multiplied by itself three (3) times, we get 3.310204476 for 240 periods.

3. We can multiply the factors for 60, 80, and 100 compounding periods, 1.348850153 × 1.490338568 x 1.646668942, to arrive at 3.31020538, for 240 compounding periods.

Further proof can be seen by multiplying the factor for 40 compounding periods at 0.5% by itself three (3) times and comparing the result with the factor listed for 120 compounding periods.

FACTOR TABLES EXPLAINED

All the factor tables have numbers which are multipliers that when applied to a dollar amount will provide a short-cut calculation to attain the desired result instead of the long, time consuming mathematical process.

It should be remembered that factor tables from different financial institutions use different decimal places. A few financial institutions use only three (3) decimal places, most use five (5), or six (6) decimal places and a few use seven (7), or eight (8) places.

As the compound-amount factor expression — $[(1 + i)^n]$ — forms part of all other factor tables, the author has computed the compound-amount factors to the ninth (9th) decimal place for those individuals who may wish for a more exacting figure. All other tables are to the sixth (6th) decimal place, which is used most often.

The general rule for reducing the number of decimal places is:

1. When the digit, to the right of the last desired decimal place, is five (5) or larger, the last desired decimal digit is raised to the next higher numeral.

2. When that digit, to the right of the last desired decimal digit, is *less* than five (5), those remaining digits are dropped.

Example 4-13: For four (4) compounding periods at 8%, we look at the compound-amount factor table under the "n" column to number four (4) and across to the 8% column, and we read a factor of 1.360 488 960. When using five (5) decimal places, the factor becomes 1.360 49, increasing the last digit to the next higher numeral. When six (6) decimal places are desired, the factor becomes 1.360 489, again increasing the last desired decimal place.

Example 4-14: For five (5) compounding periods at 8%, we find the factor to be 1.469 328 077. When five (5) decimal places are desired, the factor reads 1.469 33, increasing the last digit. If six (6) decimal places be desired, the factor will read 1.469 328, and the last 3 digits are dropped.

READING THE FACTOR TABLES

The left-hand column on all factor tables, *the "n" column*, represents the total number of compounding interest periods involved. For a five-year (5) investment, compounded annually, we look under the "n" column to number 5 and then across to the desired percentage column.

If we had semi-annual compounding periods, we would look under the "n" column to number 10 (2 times a year for 5 years).

If we had quarterly compounding periods, we would look under the "n" column to number 20 (4 compounding periods per year for 5 years).

If we had monthly compounding periods, we would look under the "n" column to number 60 (12 monthly compounding periods per year for 5 years).

CHAPTER 5

Time Value of Money

INTRODUCTION TO CASH FLOW

Out of all the variable methods considered in the making of a capital expenditure decision, the cash flow evaluation is the most important. A capital expenditure is regarded as a long-term investment, and the return on that investment should be measured in terms of the cash flow it generates and the cash flow required to support the investment.

What Is Cash Flow?

Cash flow is the movement of cash into and out of any business. A restricted viewpoint can represent the cash flow in regard to a specific investment or operation. The generally accepted viewpoint refers to the cash receipts from sales and the cash expenditures to obtain these sales. An all encompassing viewpoint, cash flow indicates all sources and uses of cash during a specific period of time.

Cash flow is a measure of corporate strength that consists of net income after expenditures and taxes that have been paid. All businesses have two such movements: the cash inflow and the cash outflow.

Cash inflow is the cash receipts received from sales derived as a result of the use of assets (equipment and inventory), from revenue derived from investments, from the reduction of operating costs and from depreciation.

Cash inflow can be the result of cost savings as a reduction in direct labor costs. The net result of these savings is a reduction in the cash outflow for wages and for labor thus increasing cash inflow.

Cash inflow may result from a reduction of working capital requirements. Many companies no longer maintain a large inventory stock, which requires large cash outlays, but now operate on a Just-in-Time delivery system for inventory supplies requiring smaller cash outflows.

Although depreciation is considered an expense, there is no cash outflow thus increasing cash inflow.

Cash outflow is the disbursement of cash needed to acquire assets and supplies used in the creation of sales, for the purchase of investments, and for the maintenance, operating and repair costs.

Cash outflow for any acquisition can be made as a single payment or over an extended period of time.

Cash outflow is needed for the operation of equipment, supplies, and direct labor to create the finished product or service needed for sales.

Incremental Cash Flows

The principle of incremental cash flows states that every proposed project should be evaluated by considering all the cash inflows and outflows caused by the investment decision. Consideration must be given to the amount and timing of cash flows, rather than to the accounting concept of expense and income.

Importance of Cash Flows

In every financial decision making process, there exists a definite goal or goals management strives to achieve. These include, among others: (1) survival of the business enterprise; (2) maximizing profits; and, (3) achieving a target market share.

When an asset is to be acquired, the accuracy in estimating the expected costs and projected revenues are of great importance for future profits. But, no matter how great the profit is forecast in the long run, business operation cash availability is more important today than in the future. Therefore, one of the main considerations in the acquisition decision, be it purchase or lease, is the timing of the cash flows. This may be difficult in actual business situations due to economic or unstable market conditions.

The cash flows in any business need to be managed so as to maintain sufficient available cash with which to operate the ongoing business as needed. The accounting department, under established rules and regulations, acts as the recorder for all cash inflows and outflows. These cash flows must be coordinated to avoid insolvency or excess cash reserve.

Insolvency occurs when the corporation is unable to pay its debts when they become due because of insufficient available cash as a result of poor cash flow management.

Excess cash results from management allowing cash to build up and not to earn its potential by investment in operational activities or through other investments which can earn more.

Lease payments are flexible, they can be tailored to the user's (lessee's) cash flow movements, be they seasonal, cyclical, or periodic. This flexibility makes leasing an attractive alternative in the acquisition of assets.

The Cash Flow Statement

Management utilizes all financial statements to ascertain the positive performance of its business operation. Management is concerned with the various ratios to measure the firm's ability to meet its obligations and thus to measure the effectiveness with which the firm's assets are utilized.

The cash flow statement reveals the sources and uses of funds, and thus, indicates the availability of working capital (cash) to

Figure 5.1 Cash Flow Statement

XYZ Corporation
Cash Flow Statement —Dec. 31, 19xx

Sources of Cash

Operations income (Sales)	$150,000	
Plus depreciation expense*	10,000	
Investment income (Bonds, etc.)	20,000	
Disposal of assets	5,000	
Total		$185,000

Uses of Cash

Accounts payable (Supplies)	$ 80,000	
Assets acquisition	50,000	
Dividends (On stock)	10,000	
Total		140,000
Increase in cash balance		$ 45,000

* Depreciation expense does not require any outflow of cash; thus, the cash inflow balance is increased by that amount.

meet current obligations. By comparison with previous periods, any and all changes in the "cash" standing can be determined.

A cash flow statement (Figure 5.1), to be of value to management, must present all the information which is: (1) correct; (2) complete; (3) relevant; and, (4) up-to-date. Because of the continuous changes in cash balances, a cash flow statement is usually prepared weekly, or monthly, to permit constant project progress.

TIME VALUE OF MONEY

That the movement of money has a time value is a basic concept in financial management. Money has a time value because everyone has the opportunity to invest today's money at a designated interest rate to earn a larger amount of money in the future.

The procedure of determining the equivalent present value of future funds is known as *discounting*.

DISCOUNTED CASH FLOW (DCF)

The investment planning for the acquisition of assets is known as *capital budgeting*, and this includes everything from plant facilities to equipment. Capital budgeting involves the preparation of costs and estimated future revenues and/or savings, and the choosing of the method for evaluating the proposed capital expenditure.

In order to evaluate the acceptance or rejection of any investment, the evaluation must arrive at an expected rate of return on that investment, considering taxes and cash flows (when they occur and in what amounts).

The acquisition of these assets requires crucial managerial decisions based upon estimates of future cash flows, which are at best, uncertain.

CONCEPT OF DISCOUNTED CASH FLOW

The d*iscounted cash flow technique* is used by many firms when evaluating a capital budget proposal, where it is necessary to know the net present value of future projected revenues or savings.

The concept is based upon the summation of the discounted future cash inflows and cash outflows to their present values. The time value of money is an essential consideration in the evaluation, that is, to convert all future cash flows to their equivalent dollar value today in order to compare equal dollars coming in with the same value dollars going out.

COMPUTATION OF DISCOUNTED CASH FLOW

Example 5-1: Your firm, in evaluating a proposed investment of $250,000 in a new machine with a 10-year useful life, expects to have an annual cash inflow of $55,000 per year for the next 10 years. The expected revenue will be $30,000 and the straight-line depreciation will be $25,000 per year. The firm expects the rate of return to be 15%. With this projection, will this meet the firm's expected rate of return of 15%?

Solution #1

The cash inflows are spread over a 10-year period. Management knows that the $55,000 today is not equivalent to the $55,000 received after one or more years. The future cash inflows must be converted to their present value equivalent. Calculations may be computed as follows using the present value factors of 15% for each $55,000 for each of the 10 years (see Table 5.1).

Table 5.1

Years	*Net Cash Flow*	*15% Present Value Factor*	*Present Value of Net Cash Flows*
1	$55,000	0.869565	$47,826.08
2	55,000	0.756144	41,587.92
3	55,000	0.657516	36,163.38
4	55,000	0.571753	31,446.42
5	55,000	0.497177	27,344.74
6	55,000	0.432328	23,778.04
7	55,000	0.375937	20,676.54
8	55,000	0.326902	17,979.61
9	55,000	0.284262	15,634.46
10	55,000	0.247185	13,595.18
		Total Present Value	$276,032.32
		Investment	250,000.00
		Net Present	$26,032.32

Solution #2

A quicker and easier method of calculation is to look at the *uniform series/present value factor table* (Table IV) under the "n" column to number 10 and then across to the 15% column to find a factor of 5.018769, and when multiplied by $55,000 results in $276,032.30 as the present value of all the receipts over the ten-year period.

When a firm invests in anything, it expects to derive a stream of future cash inflows sufficient to recover the investment plus a satisfactory return on that investment.

DISCOUNTED CASH FLOW SUMMARY

The background of mathematical methods is essential for the different discounted cash flow evaluations of capital expenditures.

The three discounted cash flow techniques that are used most to evaluate the economic value of a capital expenditure proposal are:

- The net present value;
- The internal rate of return; and,
- The index of profitability.

The net present value technique is considered the most reliable by most financial analysts. Other evaluation methods are also described.

THE CONCEPT OF PRESENT VALUE (PV)

The present value, of an amount expected to be received in the future, is the amount which, if invested today at a rate of return, would accumulate to that future amount.

Would you rather receive $1.00 today or $1.00 next year? Most people would rather take $1.00 now than wait one year to receive that $1.00. That $1.00 today could be "working" earning interest, so that by next year you would receive $1.00 plus earned interest. The analysis is that when the risk and uncertainty are reviewed, there is the realization that:

1. A dollar now—*the present value* —is worth more than that dollar in the future;

2. The longer you have to wait to receive that dollar, the greater the uncertainty of its *future value*; and,

3. The difference between the present value and the future value is the *interest* for that period of waiting.

Therefore, no business will invest $1.00 today unless there is the expectation to receive more than that $1.00 at a future date. By the same reasoning, if one expects to receive $1.00 a year from now, one should know what the present value of that $1.00 is today.

PRESENT VALUE CALCULATIONS

Present value calculations determine what the value of money of the future would be worth today, and use the compound-interest formula for such calculations. The compound interest formula is $S = P\,(1 + i)^n$ and P can be considered the *present value of S*. Solving for the present value, we rearrange the formula to read $PV = [\frac{1}{(1+i)^n}]$. Since multiplication of decimals is easier than division of decimals, the formula is further rearranged to become the *single payment/present value formula* or simply the *present value formula:*

$$PV = S\,[\frac{1}{(1+i)^n}]$$

PV = Present value
S = Compound sum (Future value or Maturity sum)
i = Interest or discount rate
n = Number of compounding periods

The bracket expression $[\frac{1}{(1+i)^n}]$ is known as the single *payment/present value factor* or simply as the *present value factor,* and is the reciprocal of the compound-amount factor.

Example 5-2: A firm holds a 10-year promissory note for \$250,000 from one of its customers and needs money now, and so approached the bank to sell the note. If discounted at 12%, how much would the firm expect to receive for the 10-year note?

In our example, we have:

S = \$250,000 as the face value of the note in the future;
i = 12% annual interest rate (discount rate); and,
n = 10-year waiting period for the note to mature.

Hand calculations would be time consuming, so we utilize the *single payment/present value factor table* (Table II). These tables provide a factor (multiplier) which, when applied to the dollar amount of a future value, will reveal the present value of that amount. You will note that all present value factor numbers are less than 1.0, for the present value will always be less than the future value.

To solve our example, we look at the present value factor table under the "n" column to number 10 and then across to the 12% column to find factor number 0.321973, and our formula reads:

$$PV = 250{,}000 \times [\frac{1}{(1+0.12)^{10}}]$$
$$PV = \$250{,}000\ (0.321973)$$
$$PV = \$80{,}493.25$$

Thus, \$80,493.25 would be the sum the firm would receive now—*the present value*—for that \$250,000 note due in 10 years.

When either the time period, or the discount rate, is decreased, the present value amount increases, and vice versa.

Example 5-3: All conditions are the same as in Example 5-2 above, except that the time the note becomes due is reduced to 5 years. What is the present value?

Again, looking at the present value factor table under the "n" column to number 5 and then across to the 12% column, read factor 0.567427; and our present formula becomes:

PV = \$250,000 (0.567427)
PV = \$141,856.75

Thus, under these conditions the present value of \$141,865.75 would be receiving by the firm for that 5-year note.

Example 5-4: All conditions are the same as in Example 5-2 above, except the discount rate is reduced to 8%. What is the present value?

We still have a 10-year note but the discount rate is 8%. We look at the present value factor table under the "n" column to number 10 and across to the 8% column to find factor number 0.425890, and our formula reads:

PV = \$250,000 (0.425890)
PV = \$106,472.50

In this case, the firm would receive today the sum of \$106,472.50 for that 10-year note.

Example 5-5: The firm needs \$500,000 in 5 years, and its bank offers 12% compounded quarterly. What amount has to be invested today to accumulate the needed \$500,000?

S = \$500,000 as the future value
i = 12% ÷ 4 = 3% interest paid per quarter
n = 20 (4 quarters/year × 5 years) compounding periods

Our PV formula reads:

$$PV = 500{,}000 \times \left[\frac{1}{(1+0.03)^{20}} \right]$$

Looking at the present value factor table for the intersection of number 20 under the "n" column and the 3% column to find a factor of 0.553676 and our formula becomes

PV = $500,000 (0.553676)
PV = $276,838.00

The firm would have to invest $276,838.00 today, compounded at 12% quarterly, to accumulate $500,000 in 5 years.

This can be proven by looking at the compound-amount factor table under the "n" column to number 20 and then across to the 3% column to read a factor of 1.806111, which when multiplied by $276,838.00 equals $500,000.16.

FACTS ABOUT THE PRESENT VALUE FACTOR TABLE

In Example 5-2, we looked to number 5 under the "n" column and moved across to the 12% column to find the factor number. Did you notice that as you moved across to 12% column, the factor numbers decreased? The higher the interest rate earned, the less money has to be invested today to reach that future amount.

Now, go down the 12% column, or any percentage column (as the compounding periods increase), and the present value factor numbers will decrease. The greater the number of compounding periods, the smaller the amount is required to earn that future amount.

THE NET PRESENT VALUE TECHNIQUE (NPV)

The net present value method of evaluation is based on the concept of the present value.

The net present value is the algebraic sum of the present values of all cash inflows and cash outflows associated with the proposed capital expenditure. All cash inflows are treated as *positive* cash flows and all cash outflows are treated as *negative* cash flows.

To compute the net present value, you need to know:

1. The appropriate after-tax (realistic) rate of return desired[1];

---

1 The firm will take into account all risk factors when arriving at a rate of return which is realistic.

2. Computation of the present value for the future cash flows[2];
3. The present value of the cash outflow needed for the investment. This includes the price, delivery, installation costs, etc.; and,
4. The summation of these present value determinations (net present value).

Once the net present value is calculated, the following criteria are a reliable method of evaluation for a capital expenditure decision:

1. If the NPV is greater than zero, the proposal is economically attractive and will produce financial rewards;

2. If the NPV is zero, the proposal is neither economically attractive nor unattractive; and,

3. If the NPV is negative, the proposal is economically unattractive.

A solid rule to follow in the selection of economically attractive bids is to select the bid with the *highest* NPV. In a lease versus a purchase (cash outlay or borrow-or-buy) decision, the NPV should be done for each of the alternative proposals.

PROFITABILITY INDEX

The profitability index measures the return per dollar of investment and is used to rank the various projects. Each project must be evaluated using the present value of the cash inflows and outflows.

Example 5-6: A firm has three projects with the following statistics:

---

2 Discounted at the expected rate of return.

Project Name	*A*	*B*	*C*
PV of cash inflows	$10,500	$18,000	$28,000
PV of cash outflows (investment)	10,000	19,750	30,000
Net Present Value	500	1,750	2,000

To determine the profitability index, the present value of cash inflows is divided by the investment (cash outflows). The calculations are:

For Project A $\dfrac{10{,}500}{10{,}000} = 1.05000$

For Project B $\dfrac{19{,}750}{18{,}000} = 1.0972$

For Project C $\dfrac{30{,}000}{28{,}000} = 1.0714$

The projects would be ranked B, C, and then A.

COMPOUND SUM OF AN ANNUITY (FUTURE VALUE OF AN ANNUITY)

It may be necessary for a firm to deposit a certain sum of money each interest compounding period (annually, semi-annually, quarterly, etc.) in order to accumulate a desired sum at a specific future time. Annuities, pension and retirement plans are the main users of this compound interest application.

WHAT IS AN ANNUITY?

An annuity is a series of periodic payments, usually of equal amounts, made at regular intervals of time. The word "annuity" refers to payments made yearly. A broader view includes payments made in parts of the year.

We will assume that equal payments are made at the end of a compounding period for a specified period of time.

CALCULATIONS FOR THE FUTURE VALUE OF AN ANNUITY

To determine the amount that will accumulate, after a period of time, we use the formula:

$$F = A\left[\frac{(1+i)^n - 1}{i}\right]$$

F = The future value (compound sum) of a series of deposits made at the end of a compounding period for n periods
A = The amount of periodic deposit
i = The interest rate per period
n = The number of periodic deposits (number of compounding periods)

The expression in the brackets is commonly referred to as a *uniform series/compound-amount factor,* found in Table III, and is constructed for deposits made at the end of an interest compounding period.

Example 5-7: A firm deposits $5,000 at the end of each year for 5 years earning 8%. What will the investment be worth after 5 years?

Calculations can be made by computing the compounding earning for each deposit and totaling the sums.

At the end of year 1:	$5,000 x $(1+0.08)^4$ or 1.360489	=	$6,802.45
2:	$5,000 x $(1+0.08)^3$ or 1.259712	=	6,298.56
3:	$5,000 x $(1+0.08)^2$ or 1.166400	=	5,832.00
4:	$5,000 x $(1+0.08)^1$ or 1.080000	=	5,400.00
5:	$5,000 x no interest	=	5,000.00
	Future value (sum accumulated)		$29,333.01

The calculations can be simplified and done more quickly by referring to the uniform series/compound-amount factor table under the "n" column to number 5 and then across to the 8% column to read factor number 5.866600. We now have:

FV = \$5,000 × (5.866600)
= \$29,333.00 (the same as above)

Example 5-8: The same circumstances, as in Example 5-7 above, except that the payments were made at the start of each year. What will the accumulated sum be?

The calculations will contain those above but modified by the interest earned on the first deposit at the start of year 1 for 5 years, and deducting the last deposit for it had been made at the start of year five (5). The computation is:

\$5,000 at start of year 1 × (1+0.08)5 or (1.469328)	\$ 7,346.64
Plus Future Value calculations from above	29,333.00
Less last deposit at end of year 5	- 5,000.00
Accumulated Sum	\$ 31,679.64

It should be noted that when the deposits are made at the *start* of each year, more interest is earned and the accumulated sum is larger.

Example 5-9: A firm deposits \$1,250 at the *end* of each quarter into an account for 5 years earning 8% annual interest rate compounded quarterly. What will be the accumulated sum (future value) in 5 years?

Here we have:

A = \$1,250 deposited each quarter
i = 8% ÷ 4 (4 quarters/year) = 2% per compounding period
n = 20 (4 quarters/year × 5 years) compounding periods

The formula becomes:

$$FV = \$1,250 \left[\frac{(1+2\%)^{20}-1}{2\%} \right]$$

$$FV = \$1{,}250 \left[\frac{(1+0.02)^{20}-1}{0.02} \right]$$

Looking at the uniform series/compound-amount factor table, we find the factor 24.297370 at the intersection of numbers 20 and 2%. Our formula reads:

$$FV = \$1{,}250 \times (24.297370)$$
$$FV = \$30{,}371.71 \text{ (at the end of 5 years)}$$

Example 5-10: Same conditions as above, except the annual interest rate is 12%. What will the accumulated sum be?

Again, we look at the uniform series/compound-amount factor table to read factor 26.870374 at the intersection of number 20 and 3%. Our formula reads:

$$FV = \$1{,}250 \left[\frac{(1+3\%)^{20}-1}{3\%} \right]$$
$$FV = \$1{,}250 \left[\frac{(1+0.03)^{20}-1}{0.03} \right]$$

$$FV = \$1{,}250 \times (26.870374)$$
$$FV = \$33{,}587.97 \text{ (at the end of 5 years)}$$

PRESENT VALUE OF AN ANNUITY

When one acquires an asset, either by installment purchase or by lease, there are payments to be made regularly in a constant amount over a definite period of time. An *annuity* is a series of periodic payments. The present value of an annuity is the worth today of the annual sum or series of payments made during the year for a period of years.

Each future value of these payments must be discounted to obtain its present value. Then the present values are added for the series of payments.

Example 5-11: A firm leases a piece of equipment for 5 years, with a down payment of $60,000 and annual payments of $60,000 at each year's end during the lease term. Using a 6% discount rate, what is the present value of the lease?

We can calculate the present value of each payment, thus:

Down Payment					$60,000.00
$60,000 end of year	1	x factor	0.943396	resulting in	56,603.76
"	2	"	0.889996	"	53,399.76
"	3	"	0.839619	"	50.377.14
"	4	"	0.792094	"	47.525.64
"			Present Value		267,906.30

The present value of this stream of payments can be calculated with greater ease and speed using the formula:

$$PV = A\left[\frac{(1+i)^n - 1}{i(1+i)^n}\right]$$

PV = Present Value of annuity
A = Annual year-end payments

The bracket expression in the above formula is known as the *uniform series/present value factor* (Table IV), and is the reciprocal of the capital recovery factor.

Looking at the uniform series/present value factor table under the "n" column to number 4 (although this a 5-year lease, there was a down payment, so we have only four (4) payments to make) and across to 6% to read factor number 3.465106, our formula becomes:

$$PV = \$60,000 + \$60,000 \times (3.465106)$$
$$PV = \$60,000 + \$207,906.36$$
$$PV = \$267,906.36$$

Example 5-12: A firm purchased a machine for $20,000 with a 10-year useful life, and expects to receive an annual cash inflow of

$3,200 for 10 years. Determine the present value if discounted at 8%.

Looking at the uniform series/present value factor table under the "n" column to the number 10 and across to the 8% column to find factor 6.710081, our formula reads:

$$PV = \$3,200 \times (6.710081)$$
$$PV = \$21,472.26$$

CAPITAL RECOVERY

In financial situations, it is necessary to determine the annual payments needed to repay a debt. *Amortization* is the procedure for extinguishing a debt or recapturing a capital expenditure. Amortizing a loan or debt is the process of repaying that debt by installment payments. The *capital recovery* is quickly calculated by using the formula:

$$A = PV \left[\frac{i(1+i)^n}{(1+i)^n - 1} \right]$$

A = Annual year payment (or period)
PV = Present value
i = Interest rate per period
n = Number of compounding periods

The bracketed expression is the reciprocal of the uniform series/present value factor and is known as the capital recovery factor, also known as the amortization factor (Table V).

Example 5-13: You get a bank loan for $10,000 for 5 years at the annual rate of 10%, compounded quarterly. What is the amount of quarterly payments to be made to retire the loan in five years? Here we have:

PV = $10,000
i = 10% ÷ 4 (4 quarters/year) = 2.5% (0.025)

n = 20 (4 quarters/year × 5 years) compounding periods

Utilizing our formula and capital recovery table, we have:

A = $10,000 × (0.064147)
A = $641.47

You will make 20 quarterly payments totaling $12,829.40, thus telling us the interest cost for the loan is $2,829.40.

ANNUAL-CAPITAL-CHARGE METHOD

This method is valuable in the fact that the time value of money, as well as the cash flows over the useful life of the asset, is considered.

Example 5-14: A firm builds a new plant costing $10,000,000 with a life expectancy of 30 years. The operating cost of this facility is projected at $750,000 per year. If the firm operates at an 8% rate of return, what is the equivalent annual charge?

This annual charge is composed of two parts: the amortized $10,000,000 over 30 years at 8% and the annual operating charge of $750,000. We look at the capital recovery factor table to the number 30 under the "n" column and across to the 8% column to find a factor of 0.088827; our calculations are:

A = $10,000,000 × (0.088827)
A = $88,827

This equivalent charge for the loan is $88,827 added to the annual operating cost of $750,000 to give a total annual equivalent charge of $838,827.

INTERNAL RATE OF RETURN (IRR)

The internal rate of return is similar to the net present value. Where the net present value uses a predetermined discount rate, the IRR looks for a discount rate which will equalize the after cash inflows and outflows, that is, when the net present value equals zero. This discount rate is known as the *internal rate of return* for any proposed investment.

There is no magic formula to resolve the internal rate of return. We select the discount rates that will produce NPVs close to zero, and then interpolate between these to determine the actual NPV of zero.

Example 5-15: In Example 5-1 we used management's expected rate of return of 15% to arrive at a NPV of $26,032.40. To obtain the discount rate and the NPV of zero, we can try a 17% rate, and look at the uniform series/present value factor table for 10 compounding periods at 17% to find the factor 4.658604, which when multiplied by $55,000 results in $256,223.22 indicating the NPV to be a *positive* $6,223.32.

We can repeat trying 18% and we find a factor of 4.494086 that when multiplied by $55,000 results in $247,174.73 compared to our investment of $250,000 which results in a *negative* $2,825.27.

From the above, we can see that the IRR lies between 17% and 18%, and by linear interpolation, we can solve for the NPV of zero, illustrated in Figure 5.2.

Figure 5.2

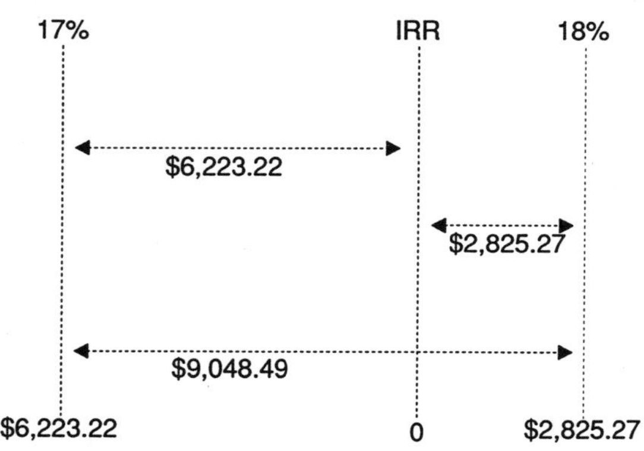

The zero point (internal rate of return) is $6,223.32/$9,048.49 or 0.68776 of the distance above the 17% to 17.69%.

From the other side, we divide $2,825.27 by $9,048.49 to give 0.3122 indicating the distance under 18% to arrive at 17.69%.

Once the internal rate of return is computed, it is compared with the expected rate of return to determine whether or not a project is acceptable. If the IRR equals or exceeds the required rate, the project will be considered acceptable.

The IRR considers the time value of money and the estimated revenues over the entire economic life of the investment. The IRR can be used to compare investments having different degrees of risk; the greater the risk, the greater the IRR. It is an excellent device for comparing alternative investment projects.

WHAT IS A SINKING FUND?

A sinking fund exists when the firm's goal is to accumulate a particular sum of money by a future date with regular deposits, usually at the end of an interest compounding period, to pay off its debt or other obligation.

CALCULATIONS FOR A SINKING FUND

What a firm has to know is the amount of each regular deposit required. The known facts are the future sum (S), the interest rate per period (i), and the compound time periods (n). With these known, it is simple to calculate the periodic payment (A) required.

Utilizing the uniform series/compound-amount formula:

$$S = A \frac{[(1 + i)^n - 1]}{[1]}$$

By rearranging the formula to solve for A, we have

$$A = S \frac{[1]}{[(1 + i)^n - 1)]}$$

where the bracketed expression is the reciprocal of the factor of the first formula above, and is known as the sinking fund factor (Table VI).

Example 5-16: A firm issues $10,000,000 in bonds at an 8% annual interest maturing in 20 years. What amount must be deposited at the end of each year to accumulate this $10,000,000 due in 20 years?

Looking at the sinking fund factor table under the "n" column to the number 20, then across to the 8% column to find the factor of 0.021852, our formula reads:

A = $10,000,000 × (0.021852)
A = $218,520

This is the amount to be deposited at the end of each year for 20 years to accumulate the needed $10,000,000.

To verify this, we need to look at the uniform series/compound-amount factor table under the "n" column to the number 20 and then across to the 8% column to find a factor of 45.761964. Thus the first formula reads:

S = $218,520 (45.761964)
S = $9,999,904.37 (rounded to $10,000,000)

The slight difference in the amounts is due to the decimal places used in the factor table. If we repeated both calculations using 8 decimals in the factors.

In the first solution, we would have:

A = $10,000,000 × (0.2185221)
A = $218,522.10

In the proving example, we would have:

S = $218,522.10 × (45.76196430)
S = $10,000,000.53

As mentioned before, the factor tables of the different financial institution used in their calculations. In our example, when using 8 decimal places, you will note a more exacting result.

PAYBACK ANALYSIS

In making economic analyses of alternate capital investments, many purchasing agents and others use the payback analysis technique among other methods.

Payback analysis computes the length of time that is required to repay the cost of the asset through the savings it generates. This is accomplished by the following formula:

$$\text{Payback period (in years)} = \frac{\text{net investment}}{\text{annual operating savings}}$$

Example 5-17: A firm invests $100,000 in a machine with a useful life of 10 years. The annual savings generated from the new machine is $20,000. What is the payback period?

$$\text{Payback period} = \frac{\$100{,}000}{\$20{,}000} = 5 \text{ years}$$

This does not take into account the fact that the machine will continue to generate $20,000 for each of the remaining 5 years of useful life.

This method of economic analysis is popular among some executives because it is simple to calculate, but it has its drawbacks. It does not consider the profits that are still generating after the net investment has been paid back.

This payback analysis does not take into consideration the time value of money. True, it saves $20,000 per year; however, that $20,000 received at the end of years 1, 2, 3, 4, or 5 does not have the equivalent value. That $20,000 today would be worth more at the end of year 1, and still more at the end of year 2, and so on.

LEASING APPRAISAL

Equipment users have a wide selection of alternative methods available to them for the acquisition of that equipment. Availability of funds may be scarce, even for large companies, which translates that every means of avoidance of cash outlay will be used, whenever possible.

The acquisition alternatives are:

1. Cash purchase or loan financing when the firm wants to own the equipment and all the benefits that go with ownership;

2. Lease with purchase option is for a firm that needs the equipment and reserves the right to own equipment at the end of the lease term; and,

3. True leasing, where the firm has no desire to own the equipment, only to use the equipment for a definite period of time and to pay for such use while producing income.

Leasing can be the answer to top management's, "There is no money in the budget for that item." Another advantage of leasing is the opportunity to replace over-aged equipment without the worry of disposal costs. Also, the replacement with more efficient up-to-date models, increasing the efficiency of production or the savings on operating costs, can be accomplished with ease and without a large outlay of capital, if any.

Every lessee must read the potential lease contract, for every lease lists an "insured value" provision providing a liability schedule of the lessee to the lessor if the equipment is lost or damaged, or that it becomes unusable during the lease term due to a casualty. The casualty values must also include the residual value to the lessor.

SELECTION OF THE LESSOR

The company has made the decision to finance the acquisition of an asset through leasing. Now comes the most important step—the selection of the lessor. Just as in the procedure for the purchase of goods, the selection of the vendor is not based solely on any one consideration, but on a combination of price, quality, service, etc.

It is known that the interest rate in a lease financial transaction is an important consideration in the selection of a lessor, but it is not the only consideration. According to a 1989 Gallup survey for the American Association of Equipment Lessors, 91 percent of the business executives polled said that the interest rate is not the most important consideration in the lessor selection process. The lessor sought after is one that is creative, provides a lease structure to match the lessee's needs, and is ready to give that "value-added service" when requested by the lessee.

Of vital importance to the lessee is that the lessor be one who makes a firm commitment to complete the lease transaction from its own resources (is adequately capitalized). There are some leasing companies and individuals who are in reality uncapitalized and work as brokers for a fee by seeking a third party to enter into a lease transaction with the lessee; then they walk away. Most are reliable brokers, such as established leasing companies and financial institutions (banks) which act in the interest of the lessee, and not merely for a fee but for repeat business.

Other points for evaluation include:

1. Is the lessor established in the equipment industry and does the lessor have a good reputation among his or her colleagues?

2. Is the lessor familiar with the legal and tax considerations relating to the particular lease (be it a tax-oriented or non-tax-oriented lease)?

3. Will the lessor be available to the lessee for any consultation throughout the term of the lease?

To summarize: (1) integrity; (2) continuity; and, (3) access of the lessor are very important factors in the selection of a lessor.

The lessee should have some knowledge of the lease rates for that particular equipment so that when bids are received, they should not vary too much.

Always have legal counsel review the lease agreement before committing your company.

In the case of a leveraged lease transaction, the lessee should chose the lessor who can offer you a combination of seasoned experience and expertise in the leasing needs of a corporation like yours. When the leasing company invests its own funds (usually 20% to 40% of the cost) and seeks other investors for the remainder, the lessee knows that the lessor is doing the best for the lessee.

There are reliable established leasing corporations, acting as a packager or broker, which initiate and arrange for the funding of a leveraged lease transaction. These leasing corporations are not just interested in earning a fee, but have a continuity of interest in the transaction, have seasoned leasing professionals available for consultation throughout the lease term and are concerned with continuing relationship with the lessee and the investor.

Reliability and responsiveness are two important characteristics of an established creditable leasing corporations, and should be investigated before a selection is made.

Remember, the two key factors that determine business success are:

1. How much money is taken in, and
2. How little money is spent.

CHAPTER 6

The Uniform Commercial Code and the Lease[1]

(General Provisions)

INTRODUCTION

Under present law, the leasing of personal property transactions are governed partly by common law principles relating to personal property, partly by the principles relating to real estate leases, and partly by reference to Article 2 (Sales) and Article 9 (Secured transactions) of the Uniform Commercial Code (UCC).

The lease is closer in spirit and form to the sale of goods than to the creation of a security interest. The obligations of the parties are bilateral and the common law of leasing is dominated by the need to preserve the freedom of contract. The UCC, as a result of case law analysis as it applies to the leasing of personal property, finds it necessary to codify leasing transactions both for business

1 All Article 2A – Leases – provisions listed are copyright ©1987 by The American Law Institute and the National Conference of Commissioners on Uniform State Laws. Reprinted with permission of the Permanent Editorial Board for the Uniform Commercial Code.

2 Source § 2A-101.

and consumer leasing. This Article 2A (Leases) attempts to resolve several issues in leasing transactions (2A-101).

1. It is necessary to determine whether the transaction is a true lease or a security interest disguised as a lease. If the latter, the lessor will be required to file a financing statement or other action to perfect its interest in goods against a third party. True leases have no such requirement (2A-301).

2. The lease of personal property is sufficiently similar to the sale of goods that many courts have reached the decision of applying the warranties of Article 2 (Sales) to lease transactions (2A-210 through 2A-216).

3. Many leasing transactions involve goods subject to a certificate of title statutes, and this Article 2A is subject to them [2A-104(1) (b)].

4. Consumer leasing transactions are subject to consumer protection statutes and they supersede those in this Article [2A-104(1)(a) and (d)].

5. Certain lease contracts, known as "Finance Leases," substitute the seller of the goods for the lessor as the party responsible to the lessee with respect to warranties and the like (2A-209 and 2A-407).

6. Sale and leaseback transactions are on the rise. Many state statutes look at these transactions closely to avoid fraudulent actions, where possession is retained by the seller as fraudulent *per se* or *prima facia* fraudulent. Section 2A-308(3) changes this position, "if the buyer bought for value and in good faith."

7. This Article provided remedies for the lessor in case of lessee default (2A-523 through 2A-531). It also provided

remedies for the lessee in case of lessor's default (2A-508 through 2A-522). Damages are available to either party in case of default by the other under 2A-504.

The codification of this Article 2A was greatly influenced by the fundamental tenet of common law: the freedom of the parties to contract. This permitted the parties to vary the effect of the provisions of this Article, subject to certain limitations including those that relate to the obligation of good faith, diligence, reasonableness and care [1-102(3)].

This Article 2A applies to leases of personal property, not to sales or security interests disguised as leases. It leaves the consumer protection to Federal and state statutes and so-called products liability case law.

LEASES SUBJECT TO OTHER STATUTES

This Article creates the theme of regulations for lease transactions and this Article supersedes all prior legislation dealing with leases, except as indicated in this section. Section 2A-104 states:

(1) A lease, although subject to this Article, is also subject to and applicable:

(a) statute of the United States;

(b) certificate of title statute of this State; (list any certificate of title statutes covering automobiles, trailers, mobile homes, boats, farm tractors, and the like);

(c) certificate of title statute of another jurisdiction (Section 2A-105); or

(d) consumer protection statute of this State.

(2) In case of conflict between the provisions of this Article, other than Sections 2A-105, 2A-304(3) and 2A-305(3), and

any statute referred to in subsection (1), the provision of that statute control.

(3) Failure to comply with any applicable statute has only the effect therein.

Consumer protection in lease transaction is primarily left to other laws. For example, in (1)(a), a statute of the United States that governs consumer leasing in the Consumer Leasing Act, 15 U.S.C. (1982) and its implementing Regulation M, 12 C.F.R. (1986); mandates disclosure of certain leasing terms, . . . and regulates the advertising of lease terms.

In (1)(d) there is the state Uniform Consumer Credit Code, 7A U.L.A. (1974) which governs consumer lease transaction within and without the definition of consumer lease under this Article.

Several provisions of this Article do contain special rules that may not be varied by agreement in the case of consumer lease; Sections 2A-106, 2A-108, and 2A-109(2). These prevent any one-sided agreement in favor of the lessor.

TERRITORIAL APPLICATION OF ARTICLE OF GOODS COVERED BY CERTIFICATE OF TITLE

This provision reflects a policy that it is reasonable to require holders of interests in goods covered by a certificate of title to police the goods or risk losing their interests when a new certificate of title is issued by another jurisdiction. Section 2A-105 states:

> Subject to provisions of Sections 2A-304(3) and 2A-305(3), with respect to goods covered by a certificate of title issued under a statute of this State or of another jurisdiction, compliance and the effect of compliance or noncompliance with a certificate of title statute are governed by the law (including the conflict of law rules) of the jurisdiction issuing the certificate until the earlier of (a) surrender of the certificate, or (b) four months after

the goods are removed from that jurisdiction and thereafter until a new certificate of title is issued by another jurisdiction.

Generally, the lessor or creditor whose interest is indicated on the most recently issued certificate of title will prevail over other interests indicated on other certificates of title issued previously by other jurisdiction.

LIMITATION ON POWER OF PARTIES TO CONSUMER LEASE TO CHOOSE APPLICABLE LAW AND JUDICIAL FORUM

This provision protects the consumer from certain lessors who attempt to induce a consumer lessee to agree that the applicable law will be a jurisdiction that has little effective consumer protection, or to agree that the applicable forum will be a forum that is inconvenient for the lessee in case of litigation. Section 2A-106 states:

(1) If the law chosen by the parties to a consumer lease is that of a jurisdiction other than a jurisdiction in which the lessee resides at the time of the lease agreement becomes enforceable or 30 days thereafter or in which the goods are to be used, the choice is not enforceable.

(2) If the judicial forum chosen by the parties to a consumer lease is a forum that would not otherwise have jurisdiction over the lessee, the choice is not enforceable.

Section (2) prevents enforcement of potentially abusive jurisdictional consent clauses in consumer leases.

This section has no effect on forum clauses used in leases that are not consumer leases; such clauses are, as a matter of current law, "prima facie valid." (See The Bremen v. Zapata Offshore Co., 407 U.S. 1, 10 (1972)).

WAIVER OR RENUNCIATION OF CLAIM OR RIGHT AFTER DEFAULT

Consideration is not necessary to the effective renunciation or waiver of rights or claims arising out of an alleged breach of a lease contract, and as in all commercial dealings, there must be "good faith." (1-201). Section 2A-107 states:

> Any claim or right arising out of an alleged default or breach of warranty may be discharged in whole or in part without consideration by a written waiver or renunciation signed and delivered by the aggrieved party.

UNCONSCIONABILITY

The term "unconscionability" is not defined by the UCC, and it is up to the courts to prevent oppression and unfair surprises in lease contracts. It is up to the purchasing agent to read and understand all clauses of every contract and raise objections to unconscionable clauses. Written objections are the best evidence in case of litigation.

This section makes it possible for courts to police explicitly against the lease contracts or clauses which they find to be unconscionable, and provides that the courts may refuse to enforce a particular clause or the entire leasing contract if the court finds that clause or entire contract unconscionable. Section 2A-108 declares:

> (1) If the court as a matter of law finds a lease contract or any clause of a lease contract to have been unconscionable at the time it was made the court may refuse to enforce the lease contract, or it may enforce the remainder of the lease contract without the unconscionable clause, or it may limit the application of any unconscionable clause as to avoid the unconscionable result.

(2) With respect to a consumer lease, if the court as a matter of law finds that a lease contract or any clause of a lease contract has been induced by unconscionable conduct or that unconscionable has occurred in the collection of a claim arising from a lease contract, the court may grant appropriate relief.

(3) Before making a finding of unconscionability under subsection (1) or (2), the court . . . shall afford the parties a reasonable opportunity to present evidence as to the setting, purpose, and effect of the lease contract or clause thereof, or of the conduct.

(4) In an action in which the lessee claims unconscionability with respect to a consumer lease:

(a) If the court finds unconscionability under subsection (1) or (2), the court shall award reasonable attorney's fees to the lessee.

(b) If the court does not find unconscionability and the lessee claiming unconscionability has brought or maintained an action he [or she] knew to be groundless, the court shall award reasonable attorney's fees to the party against whom the claim was made.

(c) In determining the attorney's fees, the amount of the recovery on behalf of the claimant under sub-section (1) and (2) is not controlling.

The test of unconscionability is to determine whether a particular clause involved was so one-sided as to be unconscionable under the circumstances existing at the time of the making of the lease contract. This is to prevent unfair surprises and oppression (see Campbell Soup Co. v. Wentz, 172 F. 2d 80, 3d Cir. 1948; and Dillman & Assoc. v. Capitol Leasing Co., 110 Ill. App. 3d 335, 342, 442 N.E. 2d 311, 316 App. Ct. 1982).

Subsection (4)(b) is independent of, and thus will not override, a term in the lease agreement that provides for the payment of attorney's fees.

OPTION TO ACCELERATE AT WILL

This lease provision permitting acceleration at will of the lessor or when the lessor feels insecure is of critical importance to the lessee. Section 2A-109 states:

(1) A term providing that one party or his [or her] successor in interest may accelerate payment or performance or require collateral or additional collateral "at will" or when he [or she] deems himself [or herself] insecure or in words of similar import must be construed to mean the he [or she] has the power to do so only if he [or she] in good faith believes that the prospect of payment or performance is insecure.

(2) With respect to a consumer lease, the burden of establishing good faith under subsection (1) is on the party who exercises the power; otherwise the burden of establishing lack of good faith is on the party against whom the power has been exercised.

The action to accelerate does not depend on any specific criteria, but on the discretion of the lessor. This section places the burden on the lessor to justify his or her acceleration of rentals in a consumer lease.

CHAPTER 7

Formation and Construction of Lease Contracts

STATUTE OF FRAUDS

The purchasing agent must always be on guard to protect his [or her] company from all legal entanglements, and must be on the lookout against fraudulent conduct on part of the lessor or supplier in lease contracts.

Fraud has been defined as the intentional deceit of the truth in order to induce another party to contract to that party's injury. Section 2A-201 states:

> (1) A lease contract is not enforceable by way of action or defense unless:
>
> (a) the total payments to be made under a lease contract, excluding payments for options to renew or buy, are less than $1,000; or
>
> (b) there is a writing, signed by the party against whom enforcement is sought or by that party's authorized agent, sufficient to indicate that a lease contract has

been made between the parties and to describe the goods leased and the lease terms.

(2) Any description of leased goods or of lease terms is sufficient and satisfies subsection (1)(b), whether or not it is specific, if it reasonably identifies what is described.

(3) A writing is not insufficient because it omits or incorrectly states a term agreed upon, but the lease contract is not enforceable under subsection (1)(b) beyond the lease term and the quantity of goods shown in the writing.

(4) A lease contract that does not satisfy the requirements of subsection (1), but which is valid in other respects, is enforceable:

(a) if the goods to be specifically manufactured or obtained for the lessee and are not suitable for lease or sale to others in the ordinary course of the lessor's business, and the lessor, before notice of repudiation is received and under circumstances that reasonably indicate that the goods are for the lessee, has made either a substantial beginning of their manufacture or commitments for their procurement;

(b) if the party against whom enforcement is sought admits in that party's pleading, testimony or otherwise in court that a lease contract was made, but the lease is not enforceable under this provision beyond the quantity of goods admitted; or

(c) with respect to goods that have been received and accepted by the lessee.

(5) The lease term under a lease contract referred to in subsection (4) is:

(a) if there is a writing signed by the party against whom enforcement is sought or by that party's authorized agent specifying the lease term, the term so specified:

(b) if the party against whom enforcement is sought admits in that party's pleading, testimony or other wise in court a lease term, the term is specified;

(c) a reasonable lease term.

This section is modeled after Section 2-201 (Sales) revised to conform to the custom and usage in lease transactions, and reflects on the differences between a lease contract and a sale of goods contract. In particular, subsection (1)(b) adds a requirement that the writing "describe the goods leased and the lease term." Subsection (2) sets forth the minimum criterion for satisfying the requirement.

Subsection (4) creates no exception for transactions where payment has been made and accepted. Unlike a buyer in a sales transaction, the lessee does not tender payment in full for goods delivered, but only payment of rent for one or more months.

Subsection (5) establishes the criteria for supplying the lease term if it is omitted, as the lease contract may still be enforceable under subsection (4).

FINAL WRITTEN EXPRESSION: PAROL OR EXTRINSIC EVIDENCE

Care must be exercised when reviewing that lease contract you negotiated. Be sure that it contains all the terms and conditions you agreed to, and does not contain unwanted terms and conditions. Section 2A-202 states:

> Terms with respect to which the confirmatory memoranda of the parties agree or which are otherwise set

forth in a writing intended by the parties as a final expression of their agreement with respect to such terms as are included therein may not be contradicted by evidence of any prior agreement or of a contemporaneous oral agreement but may be explained or supplemented:

(a) by course of dealing or usage of trade or by course of performance; and

(b) by evidence of consistent additional terms unless the court finds the writings to have been intended also as a complete and exclusive statement of the terms of the agreement.

Subsection (a) makes admissible evidence that the course of prior dealings between the parties and the usages of trade are taken for granted when the agreement was phrased. Unless carefully negated, they become an element of the meaning of the words used. Similarly, the course of actual performance by the parties is considered the best indication of what the parties intended the writing to mean.

Evidence can be introduced which explains an ambiguity or omission of terms, and does not contradict the written agreement terms, but rather clarifies them.

FORMATION OF LEASE CONTRACT IN GENERAL

Leasing contracts, just as any commercial contract, recognize the basic policy of having a contract by any manner of expression be it oral or in writing. To be enforceable, they must meet the qualifications of the provisions of this Article. Section 2A-204 states:

(1) A lease contract may be made in any manner sufficient to show agreement, including conduct by both parties which recognizes the existence of a lease contract.

(2) An agreement sufficient to constitute a lease contract may be found although the moment of its making is undermined.

(3) Although one or more terms are left open, a lease contract does not fail for indefiniteness if the parties have intended to make a lease contract and there is a reasonably certain basis for giving an appropriate remedy.

Subsection (1) states that appropriate conduct by the parties may be sufficient to establish a lease contract. Subsection (2) depicts a situation where the interchange of correspondence does not disclose the exact point at which the deal was closed, but the conduct of the parties indicates that a binding agreement has been undertaken.

Subsection (3) recognizes that if the parties *intended* to enter into a binding lease contract, the contract is valid in law despite the missing terms, if there is a reasonably certain basis for giving appropriate remedy.

The more terms the parties leave open, the less likely it is that they have intended to conclude a binding contract, but their actions are conclusive despite the omissions.

FIRM OFFERS

This section gives the effect to the deliberate intention of a merchant to make a current offer. Section 2A-205 states:

> An offer by a merchant to lease goods to or from another person in a signed writing that by its terms gives assurance it will be held open is not revocable, for lack of consideration, during the time stated or, if no time is stated, for a reasonable time, but in no event may the period of irrevocability exceed 3 months. Any such term of assurance on a form supplied by the offeree must be separately signed by the offeror.

This section is intended to apply to current "firm" offers, not to long term options, and an outside time limit of three months during which time such offers remain irrevocable has been set.

There is also the protection against inadvertent signing of a firm offer when contained in a form prepared by the offeree by requiring that such clause be separately authenticated by the offeror. This is to prevent an unconscionable result which otherwise would flow from other terms appearing in the form.

Whereby oral firm offers are made and relied upon without more evidence, such offers are revocable under this section since authentication by a writing is the essence of this section.

If supported by consideration, the offer may continue for as long as the parties specify. This section deals with firm offers not supported by consideration.

OFFER AND ACCEPTANCE IN FORMATION OF LEASE CONTRACTS

This section also liberalizes the stringent requirement for contracts under common law of meeting the exact terms and conditions of an offer. Section 2A-206 declares:

(1) Unless otherwise unambiguously indicated by language or circumstances, an offer to make a lease contract must be construed as inviting acceptance in any manner and by any medium reasonable in the circumstances.

(2) If the beginning of a requested performance is a reasonable mode of acceptance, an offeror who is not notified of acceptance within a reasonable time may treat the offer as having lapsed before acceptance.

Subsection (1) intends to make acceptance flexible and its applicability to be enlarged as new media of communication are developed; as today, communication can be "faxed" to the offeror, except when offeror specifies a definite manner of acceptance.

Subsection (2) states that the beginning of performance by the lessee can be effective in binding the lessor if followed within a reasonable time by a notice of acceptance.

Things a purchasing agent should understand in any contract dealing:

1. The offer must be communicated to the offeree, for only the offeree has the legal power to accept or reject an offer. In United States v. Thayer (209 U.S. 39, 28 S.Ct. 426), the court held, "An offer is nothing until it is communicated to the party to whom it is made."

2. "Everyone has the right to select and determine with whom he will contract. Another cannot be thrust upon him without consent." (Arkansas Valley Smelting Co. v. Belden Min. Co., 127 U.S. 379, S.Ct. 1308).

3. Any offer can be revoked by the offeror before acceptance, provided no time is stated in the offer. Exception per Section 2A-205.

COURSE OF PERFORMANCE OR PRACTICAL CONSTRUCTION

This section should be read in conjunction with Section 2A-208. The parties themselves know what they meant by the words of their agreement, and their actions under that agreement is the best indication of what they meant. Section 2A-207 states:

(1) If a lease contract involves repeated occasions for performance by either party with the knowledge of the nature of the performance and opportunity for objection to it by the other, any course of performance accepted or acquiesced in without objection is relevant to determine the meaning of the lease agreement.

(2) The express terms of a lease agreement and any course of performance, as well as any course of dealing and usage of trade, must be construed whenever reasonable as consistent with each other, but if that construction is unreasonable, express terms control course of performance, course of performance controls both course of dealings and usage of trade, and course of dealing controls usage of trade.

(3) Subject to the provisions of Section 2A-208 on modification and waiver, course of performance is relevant to show a waiver or modification of any term inconsistent with the course of performance.

Although a specific term may control the course of performance under subsection (2), subsection (3) allows same course of dealing to show waiver or modification, if Section 2A-208 is satisfied.

MODIFICATION, RESCISSION AND WAIVER

Very often parties to a lease contract may subsequently want to modify their existing contract and to do so without modification. This Section 2Al-208 does this as stated:

(1) An agreement modifying a lease contract needs no consideration to be binding.

(2) A signed lease agreement that excludes modification or rescission except by a signed writing may not be otherwise modified or rescinded, but, except as between merchants, such a requirement on a form supplied by a merchant must be separately signed by the other party.

(3) Although an attempt at modification or rescission does not satisfy the requirements of subsection (2), it may operate as a waiver.

(4) A party who has made a waiver effecting an executory portion of a lease contract may retract the waiver by reasonable notification received by the other party that strict performance will be required of any term waived, unless that retraction would be unjust in view of a material change of position in reliance on the waiver.

The requirement that any modification must meet the statute of fraud was omitted in this section [it is a requirement in sales contracts, 2-209(3)], as it is unfair to allow an oral modification which takes it a few dollars over the dollar limit.

Modification must meet the "good faith" test. That is, good faith between merchants means "honesty in fact and observance or reasonable commercial standards of fair dealing in the trade" [2-103(1)(b)].

Resolution of the issue is left to the courts based on the facts of each case.

LESSEE UNDER FINANCE LEASE AS BENEFICIARY OF SUPPLY CONTRACT

The lessee should not only carefully read the entire lease contract, but should also read the purchase contract between lessor and manufacturer or supplier in a supply contract to ascertain that all understandings and representations, warranties, and the like, between the lessee and manufacturer or supplier, be made part of that written purchase contract. This should be done before signing anything. Section 2A-209 states:

(1) The benefit of the supplier's promise to lessor under the supply contract and all of the warranties, whether express or implied, under the supply contract, extends to the lessee to the extent of the lessee's leasehold interest under a finance lease related to the supply contract, but subject to the terms of the supply contract, but subject to the terms of the supply contract, but subject to the terms of the sup-

ply contract and all of the supplier's defenses or claims arising therefrom.

(2) The extension of the benefit of the supplier's promises and warranties to the lessee [Section 2A-209(1)] does not:

(a) modify the rights and obligations of the parties to the supply contract, whether arising therefrom or otherwise, or

(b) impose any duty or liability under the supply contract on the lessee.

(3) Any modification or rescission of the supply contract by the supplier and the lessor is effective against the lessee unless, prior to the modification or rescission, the supplier has received notice that the lessee has entered into a finance lease related to the supply contract. If the supply contract is modified or rescinded after the lessee enters the finance lease, the lessee has a cause of action against the lessor, and against the supplier if the supplier has notice of the lessee's entering the finance lease when the supply contract was modified or rescinded. The lessee's recovery from such action shall put the lessee in as good a position as if the modification or rescission had not occurred.

In a finance lease, the lessor's function is extremely limited. The lessee looks to the supplier of the goods for warranties and the like. This expectation is reflected in subsection (1). As a matter of policy, this provision may not be excluded. However, the supplier is not precluded, under a supply contract, from disclaiming or modifying warranties [see Sections 2-312(2) and 2-316], nor from limiting rights and remedies of the lessor, as the buyer, and from liquidating damages (see Sections 2-718 and 2-719). These provisions are enforceable against the lessee as beneficiary.[1]

1 See, Triangle Underwriters v. Honeywell, 604 F. 2d 737 (2d Cir 1979).

Subsection (2) states a rule that extends the benefits of subsection (1) to the lessee. This statutory extension is not a modification of the supply contract.

Subsection (3) declares the rules that apply to the modification or rescission of supply contracts, and recognizes the potential cause of action by the lessee against the lessor and the supplier.[2]

The purchasing agent should watch for such merger clauses which read something like, "This agreement constitutes the entire agreement and supersedes all prior communications between the parties, including oral and written proposals."

The existence and extent of a cause of action by a supplier against the lessee is left to the courts to resolve based on the facts of each case.

2 See Earman Oil Co. v. Burroughs Corp. 625 F. 2d 1291 (5th Cir 1990).

CHAPTER 8

Warranties

EXPRESS WARRANTIES

All express and implied warranties of Article 2 (Sales) are revised to reflect the difference between a sale of goods and a lease of goods, and are stated in Articles 2A-210 through 2A-216.

Express warranties go to the essence of any bargaining agreement, and the buyer must be cautious for any disclaimers in the final written agreement form. Section 2A-210 states:

(1) Express warranties by the lessor are created as follows:

(a) Any affirmation of fact or promise made by the lessor to the lessee which relates to the goods and becomes part of the basis of the bargain creates an express warranty that the goods will conform to the affirmation or promise.

(b) Any description of the goods which is made part of the basis of the bargain creates an express warranty that the goods will conform to the description.

(c) Any sample or model that is part of the basis of the bargain creates an express warranty that the whole of the goods will conform to the sample or model.

(2) It is not necessary to the creation of an express warranty that the lessor use the formal words, such as "warrant" or "guarantee," or that the lessor have specific intention to make a warranty, but an affirmation merely of the value of the goods or a statement purporting to be merely the lessor's opinion or commendation of the goods does not create a warranty.

Buyers should be able to distinguish between statement of fact and statement of opinion. Any statement that you rely upon and is the basis for the contract, be sure that statement of fact is included in the final agreement form to avoid misunderstanding and litigation.

Many federal and state courts have adjudicated lease disputes on the basis that the lease of goods is sufficiently similar to the sale of goods.

Leases intended as security leases are governed by the provision in Article 9 (Secured Transactions) and by Article 2 (Sales) for they are considered to be sales of equipment with a reservation of title to provide a security interest in the goods.[1]

WARRANTIES AGAINST INTERFERENCE AND AGAINST INFRINGEMENT; LESSEE'S OBLIGATION AGAINST INFRINGEMENT

The warranty of quiet possession was abolished in regard to the sale of goods, but reinstated in lease contracts for the need by the lessee for protection greater than that afforded to the buyer, as stated in 2A-211:

(1) There is in a lease contract a warranty that for the lease term no person holds a claim to or interest in the goods that arose from an act or omission of the lessor, other

---

1 Hawkins, William D., *The Impact of the Uniform Commerical Code on Equipment Leasing,* 1972 Ill. F.L. 446.

than a claim by way of infringement or the like, which will interfere with the lessee's enjoyment of its leasehold interest.

(2) Except in a finance lease there is in a lease contract by a lessor who is a merchant regularly dealing in goods of the kind a warranty that the goods are delivered free of the rightful claim of any person by way of infringement or the like.

(3) A lessee who furnishes specifications to a lessor or supplier shall hold the lessor and supplier harmless against any claims by way of infringement or the like that arises our of compliance with the specifications.

Subsection (1) states the essence of the lessee's expectation, with the exception of infringement or the like, is the warranty of quiet possession, that is, the use and enjoyment of the goods for the term of the lease.

Subsection (2) excludes the finance lease from extending this warranty of quiet possession. The lessee, under a finance lease, looks to the supplier for warranties and the like.

IMPLIED WARRANTY OF MERCHANTABILITY

Goods delivered under a lease agreement, except a finance lease, by a lessor in a given line of trade must of the quality that is generally acceptable in that line of trade under the description of the goods used in the lease agreement. A specific designation of goods by the lessee does not exclude the lessor's obligation that the goods be fit for the general purposes of such goods. Section 2A-212 states:

(1) Except in a finance lease, a warranty that the goods will be merchantable is implied in a lease contract if the lessor is a merchant with respect to the goods of that kind.

(2) Goods to be merchantable must be at least such as:

(a) pass without objection in the trade under the description in the lease agreement;

(b) in the case of fungible goods, are of average fair quality within the description;

(c) are fit for the ordinary purposes for which the goods of that type are used;

(d) run, within the variation permitted by the lease agreement, of even kind, quality, and quantity within each unit and among all units involved;

(e) are adequately contained, packaged, and labeled as the lease agreement may require; and

(f) conform to any promise or affirmation of fact made on the container or label.

(3) Other implied warranties that may arise from course of dealing or usage of trade.

Common law assumes warranties as implementing the parties' presumed intention, thus recognizing two implied warranties: that of merchantability and that of fitness for a particular purpose. These are incorporated in Article 2 (Sales) as well as in Article 2A (Leases). These warranties impose strict liability, without regard to negligence or fault, and are applicable to lessors who are merchants of the trade under true leases.

In Glen Dick Equipment Co. v. Galey Construction Co. [97 Idaho 216, 225, 541 P.2d 1184, 1193 (1975)], the court held that where the lessee of the three motor scraper units was aware of the defects when it entered into oral modification of the lease agreement, it waived its right to seek damages flowing from alleged fraudulent misrepresentation made at the time the written lease agreement was entered into and waived any rights arising from any express warranties covering the defects.

IMPLIED WARRANTY OF FITNESS FOR A PARTICULAR PURPOSE

Section 2A-213 states the requirements for implied warranty of fitness for a particular purpose.

> Except in a finance lease, if the lessor at the time the lease contract is made has reason to know of any particular purpose for which the goods are required and that the lessee is relying on the lessor's skill or judgement to select or furnish suitable goods, there is in the lease contract an implied warranty that the goods will fit for that purpose.

It should be noted that in order for an implied warranty of fitness for a particular purpose to arise in a lease transaction, it must be shown that the lessor was made aware of the lessee's need, that the lessor recommended the product, and that the lessee leased the product as recommended.[2]

Where, though lessor of car-washing equipment might have been aware of lessee's need, it made no suggestion or recommendation as to the choice . . . and there was no indication that the lessee made his selection on any basis other than his own inspection of the manufacturer's literature . . . no implied warranty of fitness for a particular purpose existed.[3]

EXCLUSION OR MODIFICATION OF WARRANTIES

Express warranty can be excluded when there is no statement of fact or promise relating to the characteristics of the goods leased, as provided in Section 2A-214(1):

---

2 Source: All-States Leasing Company v. Noah BASS, 96 Idaho 873, 879, 538 P2d, 1177, 1178 (Aug. 6, 1975).

3 Ibid.

> Words or conduct relevant to the creation of an express warranty and words conduct tending to negate or limit a warranty must be construed wherever reasonable as consistent with each other; but subject to the provisions of Section 2A-202 on parol or extrinsic evidence, negation or limitation is inoperative to the extent that the construction is unreasonable.

Implied warranties, that of merchantability and that fit for a particular purpose, can be disclaimed by the provisions in Section 2A-214(2):

> Subject to subsection (3), to exclude or modify the implied warranty of merchantability, or any part of it the language must mention "merchantability," be by a writing and be conspicuous. Subject to subsection (3), to exclude or modify any implied warranty of fitness the exclusion must be in writing and be conspicuous. Language to exclude all implied warranties of fitness is sufficient if it is in writing, is conspicuous and states, for example, "There is no warranty that the goods will fit for a particular purpose."

A *warranty against interference and against infringement* can be disclaimed by the provisions of Section 2A-214(4) which states:

> To exclude or modify a warranty against interference or against infringement (Section 2A-211) or any part of it, the language must be specific, be by a writing, and be conspicuous, unless the circumstances, including course of performance, course of dealing, or usage of trade, give the lessee reason to know that the goods are being leased subject to a claim or interest of any person.

Other methods to disclaim warranties are stated under Section 2A-214(3):

Notwithstanding subsection (2), but subject to subsection (4),

(a) unless the circumstances indicate otherwise, all implied warranties are excluded by expressions like "as is," or "with all faults," or by other language that in common understanding calls the lessee's attention to the exclusion of warranties and makes plain that there is no implied warranty, if in writing and conspicuous;

(b) if the lessee before entering into the lease contract has examined the goods or the sample or model as fully as desired or has refused to examine the goods, there is no implied warranty with regard to defects that an examination ought in the circumstances to have revealed: and

(c) an implied warranty may also be excluded or modified by course of dealing, course of performance, or usage of trade.

This section provides, that to exclude or modify the implied warranty of merchantability or fitness for a particular purpose or against interference or infringement, the language must be in writing and conspicuous.

"Conspicuous" as defined by Section 1-201(10) is intended to indicate some method of making a term attention-calling. But the test is whether attention can reasonably be expected to be called to it.

A writing is not conspicuous if it is only in slight contrast with the rest of the instrument. Since the concept of conspicuousness is one of reasonableness and notice, the circumstances play a crucial role if the language is conspicuous. The concept of conspicuousness is what a reasonable person ought to have noticed.[4]

Just as the lessee wants to obtain the best deal and all the protective measures that can be obtained, the lessor wants protec-

---

4 FMC Finance Corp. v. Murphee, 632 F.2d 413 (1980). See also Overland Bond Investment Corp. v. Howard, 9 Ill. App. 3d 348, 292 N.E.2d 168 (1972).

tion from all possible liabilities and utilizes the disclaimer clause to reduce the potential liabilities.

Therefore, it becomes the absolute duty of the purchasing agent to read the entire lease agreement to ascertain that what he negotiated for is included in the final written lease agreement.

CUMULATION AND CONFLICT OF WARRANTIES EXPRESS OR IMPLIED

Section 2A-215 provides guidance when there are two or more warranties appearing in a lease transaction:

> Warranties, whether express or implied, must be construed as consistent with each other and as cumulative, but if that construction is unreasonable, the intention of the parties determines which warranty is dominant. In ascertaining the intention the following rules apply:
>
> (a) Exact or technical specifications displace an inconsistent sample or general language of description.
>
> (b) A sample from an existing bulk displaces inconsistent general language of description.
>
> (c) Express warranties displace inconsistent implied warranties other than an implied warranty of fitness for a particular purpose.

IDENTIFICATION

Section 2A-217 deals with the manner of identifying goods to the lease contract so that an insurable interest in the lessee and rights set forth in the next section will accrue. The guidelines are:

> Identification of goods as goods to which a lease contract refers may be made at any time and in any manner ex-

plicitly agreed to by the parties. In absence of explicit agreement, identification occurs:

(a) when the lease contract is made if the lease contract is for a lease of goods that are existing and identified;

(b) when the goods are shipped, marked, or otherwise designated by the lessor as goods to which the lease contract refers, if the lease contract is for a lease of goods that are not existing and identified; or

(c) when the young are conceived, if the lease contract is for a lease of unborn young of animals.

This section provides that "explicit agreement" by the parties clarifies any confusion of identification. Only in the absence of "explicit agreement" are the rules of subsections (a), (b) and (c) applicable.

Subsection (b) contains a certain amount of ambiguity in reference to when the goods are designated. This issue has been left to the courts to decide, case by case.

INSURANCE AND PROCEEDS

This Section 2A-218 should be read together with Section 2A-217, since the identification of the goods creates an insurable interest in the lessee. Section 2A-218 states:

(1) A lessee obtains an insurable interest when existing goods are identified to the lease contract even though the goods identified are nonconforming and the lessee has the option to reject them.

(2) If a lessee has an insurable interest only by reason of the lessor's identification of the goods, the lessor, until default or insolvency or notification to the lessee that identi-

fication is final, may substitute other goods for those identified.

(3) Notwithstanding a lessee's insurable interest under subsections (1) and (2), the lessor retains an insurable interest until an option to buy has been exercised by the lessee and the risk of loss has passed to the lessee.

(4) Nothing in this section impairs any insurable interest recognized under any other statute or rule of law,

(5) The parties by agreement may determine that one or more parties have an obligation to obtain and pay for insurance covering the goods and by agreement may determine the beneficiary of the proceeds of the insurance.

Subsection (2) provides a rule allowing substitution of goods by the lessor under certain circumstances.

Subsection (3) states the rule, regarding the lessor's insurable interest, shall be deemed to be exercised at the lease term's end, when the lessee has the option to buy the goods.

Subsection (5) reflects the trend in today's lease transaction by shifting the responsibility and cost between the parties.

RISK OF LOSS

Section 2A-219 states the rules related to the retention of passage of risk of loss in today's lease transactions. The rules are:

(1) Except in the case of a finance lease, risk of loss is retained by the lessor and does not pass to the lessee. In the case of a finance lease, risk of loss passes to the lessee.

(2) Subject to the provisions of this Article on the effect of default on risk of loss (Section 2A-220), if risk of loss is to pass to the lessee and the time of passage is not stated, the following rules apply:

(a) If the lease contract requires or authorizes the goods to be shipped by carrier

(i) and it does not require delivery at a particular destination, the risk of loss passes to the lessee when the goods are duly delivered to the carrier, but

(ii) if it does require delivery at a particular destination and the goods are there duly tendered while in the possession of the carrier, the risk of loss passes to the lessee when the goods are there duly so tendered as to enable the lessee to take delivery.

(b) If the goods are held by a bailee to be delivered without being moved, the risk of loss passes to the lessee on acknowledgement by the bailee of the lessee's right to possession of the goods.

(c) In any case not within subsection (a) or (b), the risk of loss passes to the lessee on the lessee's receipt of the goods if the lessor, or, in the case of a finance lease, the supplier, is a merchant; otherwise the risk passes to the lessee on tender of delivery.

This section does not concern with the responsibility for loss caused by a wrongful act of either the lessor or lessee.

EFFECT OF DEFAULT ON RISK OF LOSS

Section 2A-220 reflects the effects of default on the risk of loss by stating:

(1) Where the risk of loss is to pass to the lessee and the time of passage is not stated:

(a) If a tender or delivery of goods so fails to conform to the lease contract as the give a right of rejection, the risk of their loss remains with the lessor, or, in the case of a finance lease, the supplier, until cure or acceptance.

(b) If the lessee rightfully revokes acceptance, he [or she], to the extent of any deficiency in his [or her] effective insurance coverage, may treat the risk of loss as having remained with the lessor from the beginning.

(2) Whether or not risk of loss is to pass to the lessee, if the lessee as to conforming goods already identified to the lease contract repudiates or is otherwise in default under the lease contract, the lessor, or, in the case of a finance lease, the supplier, to the extent of any deficiency in his [or her] effective insurance coverage may treat the risk of loss as resting on the lessee for a commercially reasonable time.

Section 2A-220(1)(b) does not allow a lessee under a finance lease to consider the risk of loss as having remained with the supplier from the beginning. This is appropriate given the limited circumstances under which the leasee under a finance lease is allowed to revoke acceptance (see Section 2A-516 and 2A-517).

CASUALTY TO IDENTIFIED GOODS

This section deals with goods that are totally or partially destroyed without fault of either lessor or lessee before risk of loss passes to the lessee. If the risk of loss has passed to the lessee, this section has no application. Section 2A-221 states:

If a lease contract requires goods identified when the lease contract is made, and the goods suffer casualty without fault of the lessee, or lessor or the supplier before delivery, or the goods suffer casualty before risk of loss passes to the lessee pursuant to the lease agreement, or Section 2A-219, then:

(a) if the loss is total, the lease contract is avoided; and

(b) if the loss is partial or the goods have so deteriorated as to no longer conform to the lease contract, the lessee may nevertheless demand inspection and at his [or her] option either treat the lease contract as avoided, or, except in a finance lease that is not consumer lease, accept the goods with due allowance from the rent payable for the balance of the lease term for the deterioration or the deficiency in quantity but without further right against the lessor.

Subsection (b) gives the lessee the express right to inspect the goods in order to determine whether he [or she] wishes to avoid the lease contract entirely or to take the goods with a rental adjustment.

CHAPTER 9

Performance of Lease Contract (Repudiated, Substituted and Excused)

INSECURITY: ADEQUATE ASSURANCE OF PERFORMANCE

Actual performance is the essential purpose of a lease contract. The lessor needs protection against the credit of the lessee, and also against the supplier or manufacturer for delivery of those goods. Section 2A-401 states:

(1) A lease contract imposes an obligation on each party that the other's expectation of receiving due performance will not be impaired.

(2) If reasonable grounds for insecurity arise with respect to the performance of either party, the insecure party may demand in writing adequate assurance of due performance. Until the insecure party receives that assurance, if commercially reasonable the insecure party may suspend any performance for which he [or she] has not already received the agreed return.

(3) A repudiation of the lease contract occurs if assurance of due performance adequate under the circumstances of the particular case is not provided to the insecure party within a reasonable time, not to exceed 30 days after receipt of a demand by the other party.

(4) Between merchants, the reasonableness of grounds for insecurity and the adequacy of any assurance offered must be determined according to commercial standards.

(5) Acceptance of any nonconforming delivery or payment does not prejudice the aggrieved party's right to demand adequate assurance of future performance.

This section provides the method by which the aggrieved party may treat a lease contract as breached if his [or her] reasonable grounds for insecurity are not cleared up within a reasonable time.

A lessee who falls behind in his [or her] "lease rental payment" impairs the lessor's expectation of due performance. By the same reasoning, a lessee who utilizes goods upon delivery, or learns that the lessor is also supplying others with the same goods, may have reasonable grounds for insecurity.

In subsection (5), "adequate assurance" of future performance can occur when the lessee accepts and uses nonconforming goods, and has the promise of the lessor (who has a good reputation) that future deliveries would be conforming.

When either party has reasonable grounds for insecurity, that party may demand, in writing, adequate assurance of performance from the other.

ANTICIPATORY REPUDIATION

Anticipatory repudiation centers upon an overt communication of intention or any action which renders the performance impossible, or indicates that further performance will not be forthcoming. Section 2A-402 states:

If either party repudiates a lease contract with respect to a performance not yet due under lease contract, the loss of which performance will substantially impair the value of the lease contract to the other, the aggrieved party may:

(a) for a commercially reasonable time, await retraction of repudiation and performance by the repudiating party;

(b) make demand pursuant to Section 2A-401 and await assurance of future performance adequate under the circumstances of the particular case; or

(c) resort to any right or remedy upon default under the lease contract or this Article, even though the aggrieved party has notified the repudiating party that the aggrieved party await the repudiating party's performance and assurance and has urged retraction. In addition, whether or not the aggrieved party is pursuing one of the foregoing remedies, the aggrieved party may suspend performance or, if the aggrieved party is the lessor, proceed in accordance with the provisions of this Article on lessor's right to identify goods to the lease contract notwithstanding default or to salvage unfinished goods (Section 2A-524).

After repudiation, the aggrieved party may immediately resort to any remedy available as long as he [or she] acts in good faith (Section 1-203). But, before taking any remedy action, the lessee must notify the lessor that the lessee considers the repudiation final, or else the lessee may discover that he [or she] has two shipments of goods since the lessor has the right to retract repudiation. As Section 2A-403 states:

(1) Until the repudiating party's next performance is due, the repudiating party can retract the repudiation unless, since the repudiation, the aggrieved party has canceled the

lease contract or materially changed the aggrieved party's position or otherwise indicated that the aggrieved party considers the repudiation final.

(2) Retraction may be by any method that clearly indicates to the aggrieved party that the repudiating party intends to perform under the lease contract and includes any assurance demanded under Section 2A-401.

(3) Retraction reinstates a repudiating party's rights under a lease contract with due excuse and allowance to the aggrieved party for any delay occasioned by the repudiation.

SUBSTITUTED PERFORMANCE

There must be a true commercial impracticality to excuse the agreed to performance and thereby justify a substituted performance. Section 2A-404 provides:

(1) If without fault of the lessee, the lessor and the supplier, the agreed berthing, loading, or unloading facilities fail or the agreed type of carrier becomes unavailable or the agreed manner of delivery otherwise becomes commercially impracticable, but a commercially reasonable substitute is available, the substitute performance must be tendered and accepted.

(2) If the agreed means or manner of payment fails because of domestic or foreign governmental regulation:

(a) the lessor may withhold or stop delivery or cause the supplier to withhold or stop delivery unless the lessee provides a means or manner of payment that is commercially a substantial equivalent; and

(b) if delivery has already been taken, payment by the means or in the manner provided by the regulation discharges the lessee's obligation unless the regulation is discriminatory, oppressive, or predatory.

EXCUSED PERFORMANCE

The test for excused performance includes the "test of commercially impracticability" as contrasted with "impossibility" or "frustration of performance." Increase in price alone does not excuse performance unless the rise in cost was due to some unforeseen contingency, such as a war, an embargo, or an unforeseen shutdown of major sources of the supply. Section 2A-405 states:

Subject to Section 2A-404 on substituted performance, the following rules apply:

(a) Delay in delivery or nondelivery in whole or in part by a lessor or a supplier who complies with paragraphs (b) and (c) is not a default under the lease contract if performance as agreed has been made impracticable by the occurrence of a contingency the nonoccurrence of which was a basic assumption on which the lease contract was made or by compliance in good faith with any applicable foreign or domestic governmental regulation or order, whether or not the regulation or order later proves to be invalid.

(b) If the causes mentioned in paragraph (a) affect only part of the lessor's or the supplier's capacity to perform, he [or she] shall allocate production and deliveries among his [or her] customers but at his [or her] option may include regular customers not then under contract for sale or lease as well as his [or her] own requirements for further manufacture. He [or she] may so allocate in any manner that is fair and reasonable.

(c) The lessor seasonably shall notify the lessee and in case of a finance lease the supplier seasonably shall notify the lessor and the lessee, if known, that there will be delay or nondelivery and, if allocation is required under paragraph (b), of the estimated quota thus made available for the lessee.

PROCEDURE ON EXCUSED PERFORMANCE

This section establishes the mechanics for providing certainty to when a supervening and excusing contingency "excuses" the delay and "discharges" the contract, as stated in Section 2A-406 as follows:

(1) If the lessee receives notification of a material or indefinite delay or an allocation justified under Section 2A-405, the lessee may by written notification to the lessor as to any goods involved, and with respect to all of the goods if under an installment lease contract the value of the whole lease contract is substantially impaired (Section 2A-510):

(a) terminate the lease contract [Section 2A-505(2)]; or

(b) except in a finance lease that is not a consumer lease, modify the lease contract by accepting available quota in substitution, with due allowance from the rent payable for the balance of the lease term for the deficiency but without further right against the lessor.

(2) If, after receipt of a notification from the lessor under Section 2A-405, the lessee fails so to modify the lease agreement within a reasonable time not exceeding 30 days, the lease contract lapses with respect to any deliveries affected.

The provision in (1)(a) allows the lessee under a lease, including a finance lease, the right to terminate the lease for excused performance. However, subsection (1)(b) excludes a finance lease, which is not a consumer lease, from the right to modify a lease. This exclusion is the reason for the codification of the next section on irrevocable promises.

IRREVOCABLE PROMISES: FINANCE LEASES

This section extends the benefits of the well-known "hell or high water" clause in a finance lease, which is not a consumer lease. Section 2A-407 states:

> (1) In case of a finance lease which is not a consumer lease the lessee's promises under the lease contract becomes irrevocable and independent upon the lessee's acceptance of the goods.
>
> (2) A promise that has become irrevocable and independent under subsection (1):
>
> (a) is effective and enforceable between the parties, and by or against the third parties including assignees of the parties, and
>
> (b) is not subject to cancellation, termination, modification, repudiation, excuse, or substitution without the consent of the party to whom the promise runs.

From the above, we can see that covenants in a finance lease are irrevocable and independent due to the function of the finance lessor in any three-party relationship. The lessee looks to the supplier to perform the essential covenants and warranties.

In reference to finance leases that are not consumer leases, the courts have enforced "hell or high water" clauses [in re O.P.M. Leasing Servs., 21 Bankr. 993, 1006 (Bankr. S.D.N.Y. 1982)].

Consumer obligation to pay for defective goods or the like are not tenable under case law [Unico v. Owen, 50 N.J. 101, 232 A.2d 405 (1967)]. The Uniform Consumer Credit Code §§ 3.403-405, 7A U.L.A. 126-31 (1974) and federal statute [15 U.S.C. § 1666i (1982)] also afford protection to the ultimate consumer.

CHAPTER 10

Default in General

DEFAULT PROCEDURES

Section 2A-501 declares the procedures in default, as stated:

(1) Whether the lessor or the lessee is in default under a lease contract is determined by the lease agreement and this Article.

(2) If the lessor or the lessee is in default under the lease contract, the party seeking enforcement has rights and remedies as provided in this Article and, except as limited by this Article, as provided in the lease agreement.

(3) If the lessor or the lessee is in default under the lease contract, the party seeking enforcement may reduce the party's claim to judgment, or otherwise enforce the lease contract by self-help or any available judicial procedure or nonjudicial procedure, including administrative proceeding, arbitration, or the like, in accordance with this Article.

(4) Except as otherwise provided in this Article or the lease agreement, the rights and remedies referred to in subsection (2) and (3) are cumulative.[1]

(5) If the lease agreement covers both real property and goods, the party seeking enforcement may proceed under this Part as to the goods, or under other applicable law as to both the real property and the goods in accordance with his [or her] rights and remedies in respect of the real property, in which case this Part does not apply.

Section 2A-502 regarding *notice after default*, it states:

Except as otherwise provided in this Article or the lease agreement, the lessor or lessee in default under the lease contract is not entitled to notice of default or notice of enforcement from the other party to the lease agreement.

This section makes it clear that absent agreement to the contrary or provision in this Article to the contrary, as in Section 2A-516(3), the party in default is not entitled to notice of default or enforcement. Revocation of an acceptance requires notification [Section 2A-517(2)].

Except to restrictions of Sections 2A-105, 106 and 108(1) and (2), parties to a lease agreement have freedom to provide for the rights and remedies in addition to or in substitution for those provided in this Article, and Section 2A-503 states the rules for *modification or impairment of rights and remedies* as follows:

(1) Except as otherwise provided in this Article, the lease agreement may include rights and remedies for default in addition to or in substitution for those provided in this Article and may limit or alter the measure of damages recoverable under this Article.

---

1 Dekove, Leases of Equipment: Puritan Leasing Company v. August; A Dangerous Decision, 12 U.S. F.L. Rev. 257, 276-280 (1978).

(2) Resort to a remedy provided under this Article or in the lease agreement is optional unless the remedy is expressly agreed to be exclusive. If circumstances cause an exclusive or limited remedy to fail of its essential purpose, or provision for an exclusive remedy is unconscionable, remedy may be had as provided in this Article.

(3) Consequential damages may be liquidated under Section 2A-504, or may otherwise be limited, altered, or excluded unless the limitation, alteration, or exclusion is unconscionable. Limitation of consequential damages for injury to the person in case of a consumer goods is prima facie unconscionable but limitation of damages where the loss is commercial is not.

LIQUIDATION OF DAMAGES

Consistent with the common law for freedom to contract with respect to bailments for hire, this section reflects greater flexibility with respect to leases of goods. Section 2A-504 declares:

(1) Damages payable by either party for default, or any other act or omission, including indemnity for loss or diminution of anticipated tax benefits or loss or damage to lessor's residual interest, may be liquidated in the lease agreement but only at an amount or by a formula that is reasonable in light of the then anticipated harm caused by the default or other act or omission.

(2) If the lease agreement provides for liquidation of damages, and such provision does not comply with subsection (1), or such provision is an exclusive or limited remedy that circumstances cause to fail of its essential purpose, remedy may be had as provided in this Article.

(3) If the lessor justifiably withholds or stops delivery of goods because of lessee's default or insolvency (Section

2A-525 or 2A-526), the lessee is entitled to restitution of any amount by which the sum of his [or her] payments exceeds:

(a) the amount to which the lessor is entitled by virtue of terms liquidating the lessor's damages in accordance with subsection (1); or

(b) in absence of those terms, 20 percent of the then present value of the total rent the lessee was obliged to pay for the balance of the lease term, or, in the case of a consumer lease, the lesser of such amount or $500.

(4) A lessee's right to restitution under subsection (3) is subject to offset to the extent the lessor establishes:

(a) a right to recover damages under the provisions of this Article other than subsection (1); and

(b) the amount or value of any benefits received by the lessee directly or indirectly by reason of the lease contract.

One of the liquidating damages formula used by the leasing industry provides that the sum of the lease payments past due, accelerated future lease payments, and the lessor's estimated residual interest, less the net proceeds of disposition of the leased goods, is the lessor's damages.

Another common liquidated damages formula utilizes a periodic depreciation allocation as a credit to the amount due in mitigation of a lessor's damages.

A third formula provides for a fixed number periodic payments to liquidate damages. Many leases contain a "stipulated loss schedule" whereby the lessee provides for liquidating damages.

The enforcement of these formulas, or others, in a lease is determined by the facts of each case. [In re Noack, 44 Bank. 172,

174-75 (Bankr.E.D. Wis. 1984)]. Subsection (1) emphasizes that fixing of unreasonably large amounts of liquidated damages is voided. The parties are free to negotiated any formula, restrained by the rule of unreasonableness.

CANCELLATION AND TERMINATION AND EFFECT OF CANCELLATION, TERMINATION, RESCISSION, OR FRAUD ON RIGHTS AND REMEDIES

This Section 2A-505 provides a safeguard to a person holding a right of action from any unintentional loss of rights by the use of terms as "cancellation," "rescission," or the like. Section 2A-505 states:

> (1) On cancellation of the lease contract, all obligations that are still executory on both sides are discharged, but any right based on prior default or performance survives, and the canceling party also retains any remedy for default of the whole lease contract or any unperformed balance.
>
> (2) On termination of the lease contract, all obligations that are still executory on both sides are discharged but any right based on prior default or performance survives.
>
> (3) Unless the contrary intention clearly appears, expressions of "cancellation," "rescission" or the like of the lease contract may not be construed as a renunciation or discharge of any claim in damages for an antecedent default.
>
> (4) Rights and remedies for material misrepresentation or fraud include all rights and remedies available under this Article for default.
>
> (5) Neither rescission nor a claim for rescission of the lease contract nor rejection or return of the goods may bar or

be deemed inconsistent with a claim for damages or other right or remedy.

Unless the cancellation of a lease contract expressly states that it is "without reservation of rights," or the like, it cannot be considered a repudiation under this section.

STATUTE OF LIMITATIONS IN LEASE CONTRACTS

"An action for default under a lease contract, including breach of warranty or indemnity, must be commenced with 4 years after the cause of action occurred. The lease contract can by agreement reduce the period of limitation to not less than one year" [Section 2A-506(1)].

"A cause of action for default accrues when the act or omission on which the default or breach of warranty is based is or should have been discovered by the aggrieved party, or when the default occurs, whichever is later. A cause of action for indemnity accrues when the act or omission on which the claim for indemnity is based is or should have been discovered by the indemnified party, whichever is later" [Section 2A-506(2)].

CHAPTER 11

Default by Lessor

LESSEE'S REMEDIES IN GENERAL

Every purchasing agent should know what remedies are available to the firm when the lessor is in default or in breach of the lease contract. The purchasing agent must not only read the entire lease contract but must permit the firm's legal counsel to review the document before signing. In case of any legal action, the purchasing agent must consult with the firm's lawyer to ascertain the legal position of such action.

Section 2A-508 declares:

(1) If a lessor fails to deliver the goods in conformity to the lease contract (Section 2A-509) or repudiates the lease contract (Section 2A-402), or a lessee rightfully rejects the goods (Section 2A-509) or justifiably revokes acceptance of the goods (Section 2A-517), then with respect to any goods involved, and with respect to all of the goods if under an installment lease contract the value of the whole lease contract is substantially impaired (Section 2A-510), the lessor is in default under the lease contract and the lessee may:

(a) cancel the lease contract [Section 2A-505(1)];

(b) recover so much of the rent and security as has been paid, but in the case of an installment lease contract the recovery is that which is just under the circumstances;

(c) cover and recover damages as to all goods affected whether or not they have been identified to the lease contract (Sections 2A-518 and 2A-520), or recover damages for nondelivery (Sections 2A-519 and 2A-520).

(2) If the lessor fails to deliver the goods in conformity to the lease contract or repudiates the lease contract, the lessee may also:

(a) if the goods have been identified, recover them (Section 2A-522); or

(b) in a proper case, obtain specific performance or replevy the goods (Section 2A-521);

(3) If a lessor is otherwise in default under a lease contract, the lessee may exercise rights and remedies provided in the lease contract and this Article.

(4) If a lessor has breached a warranty, whether express or implied, the lessee may recover damages [Section 2A-519(4)].

(5) On the rightful rejection or justifiable revocation of acceptance, a lessee has a security interest in goods in the lessee's possession or control for any rent and security that has been paid and any expenses reasonably incurred in their inspection, receipt, transportation, and care and custody and may hold those goods and dispose of them in good faith and in a commercially reasonable manner, subject to the provisions of Section 2A-527(5).

(6) Subject to the provisions of Section 2A-407, a lessee, on notifying the lessor of the lessee's intention to do so, may deduct all or any part of the damages resulting from any default under the lease contract from any part of the rent still due under the same lease contract.

This section lists the rights and remedies available to the lessee upon the lessor's default, unless otherwise agreed to by the parties in the lease contract. "Freedom to contract" permits the parties to create a new scheme of rights and remedies when default occurs.

Regarding the finance lease, absent supplementary principles of law and equity to the contrary, the lessee's acceptance of the goods has no rights or remedies against the lessor, because of the lessor's limited obligations in a finance lease. The lessee will look to the supplier for performance.

LESSEE'S RIGHTS ON IMPROPER DELIVERY; RIGHTFUL REJECTION

Under an installment lease contract, if the goods or the tender or delivery does not conform to the lease contract, the lessee may:

- reject or accept the whole; or,
- accept any commercial unit or units and reject the rest.

Lessee's notification of rejection to the lessor must be made within a reasonable time, for without such seasonable notification, the rejection is ineffective (Section 2A-509).

INSTALLMENT LEASE CONTRACTS; REJECTION AND DEFAULT

An "installment lease contract" is one which requires or authorizes the delivery of goods in separate lots to be separately accepted.

Under Section 2A-510, provisions provide:

(1) Under an installment lease contract a lessee may reject any delivery that is nonconforming if the nonconformity substantially impairs the value of that delivery and cannot be cured or the nonconformity is a defect in the required documents; but if the nonconformity does not fall within subsection (2) and the lessor or the supplier gives adequate assurance of its cure, the lessee must accept that delivery.

(2) Whenever nonconformity or default with respect to one or more deliveries substantially impairs the value of the installment lease contract as a whole there is a default with respect to the whole. But, the aggrieved party reinstates the installment lease contract as a whole if the aggrieved party accepts a nonconforming delivery without seasonably notifying of cancellation or brings an action with respect only to past deliveries or demands performance as to future deliveries.

Substantial impairment of the value of an installment refers not only to the quality of the goods, but also on such factors as time, quantity, assortment, and the like.

Subsection (2) is designed to continue the installment lease contract further when there is no overt cancellation.

MERCHANT LESSEE'S DUTIES TO RIGHTFULLY REJECTED GOODS

This section recognizes that there are duties imposed upon the merchant lessee by good faith and commercial practice to follow any reasonable instructions of the lessor as to reshipping, storing, delivery to a third party, or the like in case of rightfully rejected goods. As per Section 2A-511:

(1) Subject to any security interest of a lessee [Section 2A-508(5)], if a lessor or a supplier has no agent or place of business at the market of rejection, a merchant lessee, after rejection of goods in his [or her] possession or control, shall follow any reasonable instructions received from the lessor or the supplier with respect to the goods. In the absence of those instructions, a merchant lessee shall make reasonable efforts to sell, lease, or otherwise dispose of the goods for the lessor's account if they threaten to decline in value speedily. Instructions are not reasonable if on demand indemnity for expenses is not forthcoming.

(2) If a merchant lessee [subsection (1)] or any other lessee (Section 2A-512) disposes of the goods, he [or she] is entitled to reimbursement either from the lessor or the supplier or out of the proceeds for reasonable expenses of caring for and disposing of the goods and, if the expenses no disposition commission, to such commission as is usual in the trade, or if there is none, a reasonable sum not exceeding 10% of the gross proceeds.

(3) In complying with this section or Section 2A-512, the lessee is held only to good faith. Good faith conduct hereunder is neither acceptance or conversion nor the basis of an action for damages.

(4) A purchaser who purchases in good faith from a lessee pursuant to this section or Section 2A-512 takes the goods free of any rights of the lessor and the supplier even though the lessee fails to comply with one or more of the requirements of this Article.

It is important to note that "good faith" is defined differently from for others [Section 1-201(19)]. Also, in subsection (5), provision is made for a good faith buyer to take a good title from the lessee against the lessor and the supplier.

LESSEE'S DUTIES AS TO RIGHTFULLY REJECTED GOODS

Lessees have a statutory obligation in reference to rightfully rejected goods that threaten to decline in value speedily and are not perishable. Section 2A-512 states the rules with respect to the lessee's treatment of such goods in his possession. They are:

(1) Except as otherwise provided with respect to goods that threaten to decline in value speedily (Section 2A-511) and subject to any security interest of the lessee [Section 2A-508(5)]:

   (a) the lessee, after rejection of goods in the lessee's possession shall hold them with reasonable care at the lessor's or supplier's disposition for a reasonable time after the lessee's seasonable notification of rejection;

   (b) if the lessor or the supplier gives no instructions within a reasonable time after notification of rejection, the lessee may store the rejected goods for the lessor's or the supplier's account or ship them to the lessor or the supplier or dispose of them for the lessor's or the supplier's account with reimbursement in the manner provided in Section 2A-511; but

   (c) the lessee has no further obligations with regard to goods rightfully rejected.

(2) Action by the lessee pursuant to subsection (1) is not acceptance or conversion.

This section is designed to accord all reasonable leeway to a rightfully rejecting lessee acting in good faith.

CURE BY LESSOR OF IMPROPER TENDER OR DELIVERY; REPLACEMENT

This section permits a lessor or supplier who has made a nonconforming delivery to make a conforming delivery within the lease contract time upon seasonable notification to the lessee. Section 2A-513 declares:

> (1) If any tender or delivery by the lessor or the supplier is rejected because nonconforming and the time for performance has not yet expired, the lessor or the supplier may seasonably notify the lessee of the lessor's or the supplier's intention to cure and may then make a conforming delivery within the time provided in the lease contract.
>
> (2) If the lessee rejects a nonconforming tender that the lessor or the supplier had reasonable grounds to believe would be acceptable with or without money allowance, the lessor or the supplier may have a further reasonable time to substitute a conforming tender if he [or she] seasonably notifies the lessee.

Subsection (2) seeks to avoid injustice to the lessor or supplier by reason of surprise rejection by the lessee. The lessor or supplier is not protected unless he [or she] had "reasonable grounds to believe" that the tender would be acceptable. Such reasonable grounds can be in prior course of dealing, in course of performance or during usage of trade as well as in particular circumstances surrounding the making of the lease contract.

WAIVER OF LESSEE'S OBJECTIONS

This section presents a policy of permitting the lessee to give a quick and informal notice of defects in a tender without penalty for omissions in the statement, and at the same time, protecting the lessor or the supplier who is reasonably misled by the lessee's failure to state curable defects. Section 2A-514 states:

(1) In rejecting goods, a lessee's failure to state a particular defect that is ascertainable by reasonable inspection precludes the lessee from relying on the defect to justify rejection or to establish default:

(a) if, stated seasonably, the lessor or the supplier could have cured it (Section 2A-513); or

(b) between merchants if the lessor or the supplier after rejection has made a request in writing for a full and final written statement of all defects on which the lessee proposes to rely.

(2) A lessee's failure to reserve rights when paying rent or other consideration against documents precludes recovery of the payment for defects apparent on the face of the documents.

In subsection (2), when payment is required against the documents, they must be inspected before payment, and payment constitutes acceptance of the documents. They do not constitute an acceptance of the goods or impair any options or remedies of the lessee for their improper delivery. The lessee "waives" only what is apparent on the face of the documents.

ACCEPTANCE OF GOODS

Section 2A-515 states:

(1) Acceptance of goods occurs after the lessee has had a reasonable opportunity to inspect the goods and

(a) the lessee signifies or acts with respect to the goods in a manner that signifies to the lessor or the supplier that the goods are conforming or that the lessee will take or retain them in spite of their nonconformity; or

(b) the lessee fails to make an effective rejection of the goods [Section 2A- 509(2)].

(2) Acceptance of a part of any commercial unit is acceptance of that entire unit.

Under this section, "acceptance" as applied to goods means that the lessee, pursuant to the lease contract, takes those particular goods which have been appropriated to the lease contract.

Acceptance amounts only to the performance by the lessee of one part of his [or her] legal obligation.

Subsection (2) supplements the policy of the section on lessee's rights on improper delivery, recognizing the validity of a partial acceptance but insisting that the lessee exercise this right only as to whole commercial units.

EFFECT OF ACCEPTANCE OF GOODS; NOTICE OF DEFAULT; BURDEN OF ESTABLISHING DEFAULT AFTER ACCEPTANCE; NOTICE OF CLAIM OR LITIGATION TO PERSON ANSWERABLE

Section 2A-516 continues the prior basic policies with respect to acceptance of goods while making a number of minor though material changes in the interest of simplicity and commercial convenience declares:

(1) A lessee must pay rent for any goods accepted in accordance with the lease contract, with due allowance for goods rightfully rejected or not delivered.

(2) A lessee's acceptance of goods precludes rejection of the goods accepted. In case of a finance lease, if made with the knowledge of a nonconformity, acceptance cannot be revoked because of it. In any other case, if made with knowledge of nonconformity, acceptance cannot be revoked because of it unless the acceptance was on the reasonable assumption that the nonconformity would be seasonably cured. Acceptance does not of itself impair any other remedy provided by this Article or the lease agreement for nonconformity.

(3) If a tender has been accepted:

(a) within a reasonable time after the lessee discovers or should have discovered any default, the lessee shall notify the lessor and the supplier, or be barred from any remedy;

(b) except in case of a consumer lease, within a reasonable time after the lessee receives notice of litigation for infringement or the like (Section 2A -211) the lessee shall notify the lessor or be barred from any remedy over for liability established by the litigation; and

(c) the burden is on the lessee to establish any default.

(4) If a lessee is sued for breach of a warranty or other obligation for which the lessor or supplier is answerable over:

(a) The lessee may give the lessor or the supplier written notice of the litigation. If the notice states that the lessor or the supplier may come in and defend and that if the lessor or the supplier does not do so he [or she] will be bound in any action against him [or her] by the lessee by any determination of fact common to the two litigations, then unless the lessor or the supplier after seasonable receipt of the notice does come in and defend he [or she] is so bound.

(b) The lessor or the supplier may demand in writing that the lessee turn over control of the litigation including settlement if the claim is one for infringement or the like (Section 2A-211) or else be barred from any remedy over. If the demand states that lessor or the supplier agrees to bear all expense and to satisfy any adverse judgement, then unless the lessee after seasonable receipt of the demand does turn over control the lessee is so barred.

(5) The provisions of subsections (3) and (4) apply to any obligation of a lessee to hold the lessor or the supplier harmless against infringement or the like (Section 2A-211).

Subsection (2) creates a special rule for finance leases, precluding revocation of acceptance of known nonconforming goods.

Subsection (3)(a) requires the lessee to give notice of default to the lessor. In case of a finance lease, notice of default must be given to both, the lessor and the supplier. When the finance lease creates a security interest, the rule may be contrary. [General Electric Credit Corporation of Tennessee v. Ger-Bek Machine Company, 806 F.2d 1207 (3rd Cir. 1986)].

REVOCATION OF ACCEPTANCE OF GOODS

Section 2A-517 states the rules, rights and duties involved in the revocation of nonconforming goods, as is stated:

(1) A lessee may revoke acceptance of a lot or commercial unit whose nonconformity substantially impairs its value to the lessee if he [or she] accepts it:

(a) except in case of a finance lease, on the reasonable assumption that its nonconformity would be cured and it has not been seasonably cured; or

(b) without discovery of the nonconformity if the lessee's acceptance was reasonably induced either by the lessor's assurances or, except in the case of finance lease, by the difficulty of discovery before acceptance.

(2) Revocation of acceptance must occur within a reasonable time after the lessee discovers or should have discovered the ground for it and before any substantial change in condition of the goods which is not caused by nonconformity. Revocation is not effective until the lessee notifies the lessor.

(3) A lessee who revokes has the same rights and duties with regard to the goods involved as if the lessee had rejected them.

COVER; SUBSTITUTE GOODS

Section 2A-518 provides the lessee with a remedy enabling him/her to obtain the goods essential for his/her needs, and are:

(1) After default by a lessor under the lease contract [Section 2A-508(1)], the lessee may cover by making any purchase or lease of or contract to purchase or lease goods in substitution for those due from the lessor.

(2) Except as otherwise provided with respect to damages liquidated in the lease agreement (Section 2A-504) or determined by agreement of the parties [Section 1 -102(3)], if a lessee's cover is by lease agreement substantially similar to the original lease agreement and the lease agreement is made in good faith and in a commercially reasonable

manner, the lessee may recover from the lessor as damages

(a) the present value, as of date of default, of the difference between the total rent for the lease term of the new lease agreement and the total rent for the remaining lease term of the original lease agreement and

(b) any incidental or consequential damages less expenses saved in consequence of lessor's default.

(3) If a lessee's cover is by lease agreement that for any reason does not qualify for treatment under subsection (2), or is by purchase or otherwise, the lessee may recover from the lessor as if the lessee had elected not to cover and Section 2A-519 governs.

Subsection (1) provides the lessee with the means of actions to remedy the default by the lessor. The decision to cover is a commercial judgement, not a statutory mandate.

Subsection (2) puts forth the rule for determining the amount of lessee's damages providing the original lease agreement was silent or had no agreement to the contrary. The damages are established using the new lease agreement if the following three criteria are met:

- The lessee's cover is by lease agreement;
- The new lease agreement is substantially similar to the original lease agreement; and,
- Such cover was done in good faith and in a commercially reasonable manner.

If the lessee's cover does not satisfy the above criteria, then Section 2A-519 governs.

LESSEE'S DAMAGES FOR NON-DELIVERY, REPUDIATION, DEFAULT AND BREACH OF WARRANTY IN REGARD TO ACCEPTED GOODS

Section 2A-519 provides the basic rule governing the measure of lessee's damages for non-delivery or repudiation by the lessor, or for rightful rejection or revocation of acceptance by the lessee, in absence of agreement to the contrary, if the lessee does not cover or if cover does not qualify under Section 2A-518. Section 2A-519 states:

> (1) Except as otherwise provided with respect to damages liquidated in lease agreement (Section 2A-504) or determined by agreement of the parties [Section 1 -102(3)], if a lessee elects not to cover or a lessee elects to cover and the cover is by lease agreement that for any reason does not qualify for treatment under Section 2A-518(2), or is by purchase or otherwise, the measure of damages for non-delivery or repudiation by the lessor or for rejection or revocation of acceptance by the lessee is the present value as of the date of the default of the difference between the then market rent and the original rent, computed for the remaining lease term of the original lease agreement together with incidental and consequential damages, less expenses saved in consequence of lessor's default.
>
> (2) Market rent is to be determined as of the place for tender or, in cases of rejection after arrival irrevocation of acceptance, as of the place of arrival.
>
> (3) If the lessee has accepted the goods and given notification [Section 2A-516(3)], the measure of damages for non-conforming tender or delivery by a lessor is the loss resulting in the ordinary course of events from the lessor's default as determined in any manner that is reasonable together with incidental and consequential damages, less expenses saved in consequence of the lessor's default.

(4) The measure of damages for breach of warranty is the present value at the time and place of acceptance of the difference between the value of the use of the goods accepted and the value if they had been as warranted for the lease term, unless special circumstances show proximate damages of a different amount, together with incidental and consequential damages, less expenses saved in consequence of the lessor's default or breach of warranty.

This section emphasizes the standard rule that the lessee must deduct, from his/her damages, any expenses saved as a result of the default or breach.

LESSEE'S INCIDENTAL AND CONSEQUENTIAL DAMAGES

Subsection (1) of Section 2A-520 lists some examples of incidental damages resulting from a lessor's default, and subsection (2) lists examples of consequential damages resulting from a lessor's default; the lists are not exhaustive.

(1) Incidental damages resulting from a lessor's default include expenses reasonably incurred in inspection, receipt, transportation, and care and custody of goods rightfully rejected or goods the acceptance which is justifiably revoked, any commercially reasonable charges, expenses or commissions in connection with effecting cover, and any other reasonable expenses incident to the default.

(2) Consequential damages resulting from a lessor's default include;

(a) any loss resulting from general or particular requirements and needs of which the lessor at the time of contracting had reason to know and which could not reasonably be prevented by cover or otherwise; and

(b) injury to person or property proximately resulting from any breach of warranty.

Subsection (1) is intended to provide the lessee reimbursement for reasonable expenses in connection with the handling of goods due to a lessor's default.

Subsection (2) allows the lessee to recover consequential damages resulting from a lessor's breach. Loss may be determined in any manner which is reasonable under the circumstances.

Any lessor who does wish to be responsible for consequential damages has available the section on contractual limitation of remedy (Sections 1-106, 2-7718 and 2-719).

LESSEE'S RIGHT TO SPECIFIC PERFORMANCE OR REPLEVIN

Section 2A-521 provides the policy as to specific performance and injunction against breach, and reads:

(1) Specific performance may be decreed if the goods are unique or in other proper circumstances.

(2) A decree for specific performance may include any terms and conditions as to payment of the rent, damages, or other relief that the court deems just.

(3) A lessee has a right of replevin, detinue, sequestration, claim and delivery, or the like for goods identified to the lease contract if after reasonable effort the lessee is unable to effect cover for those goods or the circumstances reasonably indicate that the effort will be unavailing.

This section seeks to further a more liberal attitude than some courts have shown in connection with the specific performance of lease contracts.

In subsection (1) there is a new concept of "unique" goods. The test of uniqueness must be made in terms of the total situation which characterizes the lease contract. Inability to cover is strong evidence of "other proper circumstances."

LESSEE'S RIGHT TO GOODS ON LESSOR'S INSOLVENCY

The lessee is given a right to the goods on lessor's insolvency occurring within 10 days after he or she receives the first rent of their lease contract, as stated in Section 2A-522:

> (1) subject to subsection (2) and even though the goods have not been shipped, a lessee who has paid a part or all of the rent and security for goods identified to a lease contract (Section 2A-217) on making and keeping good a tender of any unpaid portion of the rent and security due under the lease contract may recover the goods identified from the lessor if the lessor becomes insolvent within 10 days after receipt of the first installment of rent and security.
>
> (2) A lessee acquires the right to recover goods identified to a lease contract only if they conform to the lease contract.

Subsection (2) is stated to prevent the unjust enrichment of the lessee is the lessee were permitted to recover goods that were greatly superior in quality or quantity to that called for in the lease contract.

CHAPTER 12

Default by Lessee

LESSOR'S REMEDIES IN GENERAL

The purchasing agent must not do anything to create a default in the lease contract before he/she consults with the legal department to ascertain if he/she is on solid legal grounds for such action. In case of lessee's default, the lessor's rights are stated in Section 2A-523:

(1) If a lessee wrongfully rejects or revokes acceptance of goods or fails to make a payment when due or repudiates with respect to a part or the whole, then, with respect to any goods involved, and with respect to all of the goods if under an installment lease contract the value of the whole lease contract is substantially impaired (Section 2A-510), the lessee is in default under the lease contract and the lessor may:

(a) cancel the lease contract [Section 2A-505(1)];

(b) proceed respecting goods not identified to the lease contract (Section 2A-524);

(c) withhold delivery of the goods and take possession of goods previously delivered (Section 2A-525);

(d) stop delivery of the goods by any bailee (Section 2A-526);

(e) dispose of the goods and recover damages (Section 2A-527), or retain the goods and recover damages (Section 2A-528), or in a proper case recover rent (Section 2A-529).

(2) If a lessee is otherwise in default under a lease contract, the lessor may exercise the rights and remedies provided in the lease contract and this Article.

LESSOR'S RIGHT TO IDENTIFY GOODS TO LEASE CONTRACT

Section 2A-524 gives an aggrieved lessor the right at time of lessee's default to identify to the lease contract any conforming finished goods, and also the right to complete manufacture exercising reasonable commercial judgement, as stated:

(1) A lessor aggrieved under Section 2A-523(1) may:

(a) identify to the lease contract conforming goods not already identified if at the time the lessor learned of the default they were in the lessor's or the supplier's possession or control; and

(b) dispose of goods [Section 2A-527(1)] that demonstrably have been intended for a particular lease contract even though those goods are unfinished.

(2) If the goods are unfinished, in the exercise of reasonable commercial judgement for the purpose of avoiding loss

> and of effective realization, an aggrieved lessor or the supplier may either complete manufacture and wholly identify the goods to the lease contract or cease manufacture and lease, sell, or otherwise dispose of the goods for scrap or salvage value or proceed in any other reasonable manner.

The lessor's reasonable commercial judgement to complete manufacture will reduce the damages. In case of damage disagreement, the burden is upon the lessee to show the commercial unreasonable nature of the lessor's action in completing manufacture.

LESSOR'S RIGHT TO POSSESSION OF GOODS

This section, among others, are to codify the lessor's common law right to protect the lessor's reversionary interest in the goods. Section 2A-525 states:

> (1) If a lessor discovers the lessee to be insolvent, the lessor may refuse to deliver the goods.
>
> (2) The lessor has on default by the lessee under the lease contract the right to take possession of the goods. If the lease contract so provides, the lessor may require the lessee to assemble the goods and make them available to the lessor at a place to be designated by the lessor which is reasonably convenient to both parties. Without removal, the lessor may render unusable any goods employed in trade or business, and may dispose of goods on the lessee's premises (Section 2A-527).
>
> (3) The lessor may proceed under subsection (2) without judicial process if that can be done without breach of peace or the lessor may proceed by action.

The concept of stoppage has been extended to include goods in possession of any bailee who has not yet delivered to the lessee.

In subsection (3), appropriate case action includes injunctive relief [see Clark Equipment Co. v. Armstrong Equipment Co., 431 F.2d 54 (5th Cir. 1970), cert. denied, 402 U.S. 909 (1971)].

This section is intended to supplement and not displace principles of law and equity in respect to the protection of reversionary interest.

LESSOR'S STOPPAGE OF DELIVERY IN TRANSIT OR OTHERWISE

This section expands the remedy to cover situations other than insolvency. As stated in Section 2A-526:

1. A lessor may stop delivery of goods in the possession of a carrier or other bailee if the lessor discovers the lessee to be insolvent and may stop delivery of carload, truckload, planeload, or large shipments of express or freight if the lessee repudiates or fails to make a payment due before delivery, whether for rent, security or otherwise under the lease contract, or for any other reason the lessor has a right to withhold or to take possession of the goods.

2. In pursuing its remedies under subsection (1), the lessor may stop delivery until

   (a) receipt of the goods by lessee;

   (b) acknowledgement to the lessee by any bailee of the goods, except a carrier, that the bailee holds the goods for the lessee; or

   (c) such an acknowledgement to the lessee by a carrier via reshipment or as warehouseman.

3. (a) To stop delivery, a lessor shall so notify as to enable the bailee by reasonable diligence to prevent delivery of the goods.

(b) After notification, the bailee shall hold and deliver the goods according to the directions of the lessor, but the lessor is liable to the bailee for any ensuing charges or damages.

(c) A carrier who has issued a non-negotiable bill of lading is not obliged to obey a notification to stop received from a person other than the consignor.

In subsection (1), the right to stop shipments in all situations except insolvency is limited to carload, truckload, planeload or larger shipments. Stoppage of shipments is a burden to carriers, especially small shipments, thus this limitation on size of loads to be stopped.

Improper stoppage is a breach by the lessor if it effectively interferes with the lessee's right to due tender. If the bailee obeys an unjustified order to stop delivery, he/she may also be liable to the lessee. Therefore, subsection (3)(b) gives him/her the right of indemnity against the lessor in such a case.

After effective stoppage under this section, the lessor's rights in the goods are the same as he/she had never made a delivery.

LESSOR'S RIGHT TO DISPOSE OF GOODS

Meticulous conditions and restrictions of the prior statutory provisions are disapproved by this Article and replaced by the standards of "commercial reasonableness." Section 2A-527 states:

(1) After a default by a lessee under the lease contract [Section 2A-523(1)], or after the lessor refuses to deliver or takes possession of goods (Section 2A-525 or 2A-526), the lessor may dispose of the goods concerned or the undelivered balance thereof by lease, sale or otherwise.

(2) Except as otherwise provided with respect to damages liquidated in the lease agreement (Section 2A-504) or determined by agreement of the parties [Section 1 -102(3)], if

the disposition is by lease agreement substantially similar to the original lease agreement and the lease agreement is made in good faith and in a commercially reasonable manner, the lessor may recover from the lessee as damages

(a) accrued and unpaid rent as of the date of default,

(b) the present value of the date of default of the difference between the total rent for the remaining lease term of the original lease agreement and the total rent for the lease term of the new lease agreement, and

(c) any incidental damages allowed under Section 2A-530, less expenses saved in consequence of the lessee's default.

(3) If the lessor's disposition is by lease agreement that for any reason does not qualify for treatment under subsection (2), or is by sale or otherwise, the lessor may recover from the lessee as if the lessor had elected not to dispose of the goods and Section 2A-528 governs.

(4) A subsequent buyer or lessee who buys or leases from the lessor in good faith for value as a result of a disposition under this section takes the goods free of the original lease contract and rights of the original lessee even though the lessor fails to comply with one or more of the requirements of this Article.

(5) The lessor is not accountable to the lessee for any profit made on any disposition. A lessee who has rightfully rejected or justifiably revoked acceptance shall account to the lessor for any excess over the amount of the lessee's security interest [Section 2A -508(5)].

In subsection (1), the lessor's right to disposition of the goods must be made as a commercial judgement, not a statutory mandate.

Subsection (2) sets forth the criteria for establishing the damages, and if the lessor's disposition does not qualify under subsection, then Section 2A-528 will govern.

Subsection (4) protects the subsequent buyer or lessee who buys or leases in good faith for value. Subsection 5 provides that a lessor is not accountable to the lessee for any profit realized from a disposition. The fundamental premise of "bailment for hire" holds that a lessee under a lease of goods has no equity of redemption to protect.

LESSOR'S DAMAGES FOR NON-ACCEPTANCE OR REPUDIATION

This section provides the basic rule governing the measure of the lessor's damages for non-acceptance or repudiation, and in case of inadequate measure of damages, puts forth additional measures for damages so as to put the lessor in as good a position as the lessee's performance would have. Section 2A-528 declares:

(1) Except as otherwise provided with respect to damages liquidated in the lease agreement (Section 2A-504) or determined by agreement of the parties [Section 1 -102(3)], if a lessor elects to retain the goods or a lessor elects to dispose of the goods and disposition is by lease agreement that for any reason does not qualify for treatment under Section 2A-527(2), or is by sale or otherwise, the lessor may recover from the lessee as damages for non-acceptance or repudiation by the lessee (a) accrued and unpaid rent as of date of default, (b) the present value as of the date of default of the difference between the total rent for the remaining lease term of the original lease agreement and the market rent at the time and place for tender computed for the same term, and (c) any incidental damages

allowed under Section 2A-530, less expenses saved in consequence of the lessee's default.

(2) If the measure of damages provided in subsection (1) is inadequate to put a lessor in as good a position as performance would have, the measure of damages is the profit, including reasonable overhead, the lessor would have made from full performance by the lessee, together with any incidental damages allowed under Section 2A-530, due allowance for costs reasonably incurred and due credit for payments or proceeds of disposition.

Subsection (2) is intended to give the lessor the benefit of the bargain, and a court should consider any reasonable benefit of profit expected by the lessor from the performance of the lease agreement [see Honeywell, Inc. v. Lithonia Lighting, Inc., 317 F.Supp. 406, 413 (N.D. Ga. 1970)].

In calculating profit, the concept of present value should be given effect [Taylor v. Commercial Credit Equipment Corporation, 170 Ga. App. 322, 316 S.E. 2d 788 (Ct. App. 1984)].

LESSOR'S ACTION FOR RENT

This Section 2A-529, and the two previous sections, provides the lessor with three alternative methods of computing damages recoverable from the defaulting lessee, as stated:

(1) After default by the lessee under the lease contract [Section 2A-523(1)], if the lessor complies with subsection (2), the lessor may recover from the lessee as damages:

(a) for goods accepted by the lessee and for conforming goods lost or damaged within a commercially reasonable time after risk of loss passes to the lessee (Section 2A-219), (i) accrued and unpaid rent as of date of default, (ii) the present value as of the date of default of the rent for the remaining lease term of the lease agreement, and

(iii) any incidental damages allowed under Section 2A-530, less expenses saved in consequence of lessee's default; and

(b) for goods identified to the lease contract if the lessor is unable after reasonable effort to dispose of them at a reasonable price or the circumstances reasonably indicate that effort will be unavailing, (i) accrued and unpaid rent as of the date of default, (ii) the present value as of the date of default of the rent for the remaining lease term of the lease agreement, and (iii) any incidental damages allowed under Section 2A-530, less expenses saved in consequence of lessee's default.

(2) Except as provided in subsection (3), the lessor shall hold for the lessee for the remaining lease term of the lease agreement any goods that have been identified to the lease contract and are in the lessor's control.

(3) The lessor may dispose of the goods at any time before collection of the judgement for damages obtained pursuant to subsection (1). If the disposition is before the end of the remaining lease term of the lease agreement, the lessor's recovery against the lessee for damages will be governed by Section 2A-527 or Section 2A-528.

(4) Payment of the judgment for damages obtained pursuant to subsection (1) entitles the lessee to use and possession of the goods not then disposed of for the remaining lease term of the lease agreement.

(5) After a lessee has wrongfully rejected or revoked acceptance of goods, has failed to pay rent then due, or has repudiated (Section 2A-402), a lessor who is held not entitled to rent under this section must nevertheless be awarded

> damages for non-acceptance under Sections 2A-527 and 2A-528.

Subsections (2), (3) and (4) should be viewed together. An illustration would best explain these. Mr. A leases computers for two years and defaults on his rental payments. Mr. B, his lessor, recovers the computers and obtains a judgement against Mr. A, the lessee, for damages pursuant to subsection (1).

The lessor must hold these computers for the lessee for the balance of the lease term. This eliminates possibility of double recovery by the lessor. It also preserves the value of the leasehold estate of the lessee [Subsection (2)].

If the lessor determines that the lessee is "judgement proof" then the lessor may elect to dispose of the computers before collection of the damage judgement. Damage recovery is then governed by Section 2A-527 or 2A-528 [Subsection (3)].

Subsection (4) declares that if the damage judgement is satisfied, the lessee regains the right to use and possession of the computers for the balance of the original lease. A partial satisfaction of the judgement does not establish a right for the lessee to the use and possession of the computers.

Sections 2A-501(2) and (4) declare that rights and remedies provided in this Article are cumulative.

LESSOR'S INCIDENTAL DAMAGES

Section 2A-530 authorizes reimbursement of the lessor for expenses reasonably incurred by him/her as a result of the lessee's default, as stated:

> Incidental damages to an aggrieved lessor include any commercially reasonable charges, expenses, or commission incurred in stopping delivery, in the transportation, care and custody of goods after lessee's default, in connection with return or disposition of the goods, or otherwise resulting from the default.

STANDING TO SUE THIRD PARTIES FOR INJURY TO GOODS

Section 2A-531 has provisions that apply only after the identification of goods. Prior to that time only the lessor has the right of action, as stated:

(1) If a third party so deals with goods that have been identified to a lease contract as to cause actionable injury to a party to the lease contract (a) the lessor has a right of action against the third party, and (b) the lessee also has a right of action against the third party if the lessee;

(i) has a security interest in the goods;

(ii) has an insurable interest in the goods; or

(iii) bears the risk of loss under the lease contract or has since the injury assumed the risk as against the lessor and the goods have been converted or destroyed.

(2) If at the time of the injury the party plaintiff did not bear the risk of loss as against the other party to the lease contract and there is no arrangement between them for disposition of the recovery, his [or her] suit or settlement, subject to his [or her] own interest, is as a fiduciary for the other party to the lease contract.

(3) Either party with the consent of the other may sue for the benefit of whom it may concern.

CHAPTER 13

The Lease Agreement

In any lease transaction the key document is the lease agreement. It provides for all the rights and obligations of the parties involved. A lease agreement spells out the physical description of the equipment and where such equipment will be located and enumerates the terms and conditions of the agreement.

As with any bilateral contract, the lease agreement is discharged by the agreed performance by both parties in almost every lease transaction. The few times, usually 5% or less, that a dispute arises, is the primary reason that all parties have a clear understanding of the terminology used in the lease agreement.

Repudiated, substituted and excused performance of a lease contract are governed by Article 2A, Part 4, of the Uniform Commercial Code. When either party is in default under a lease contract, the UCC provides the rights and remedies for such action.

NON-LEVERAGED LEASES

Non-leveraged leases are sometimes called direct or single-investor leases, and are two-party transactions involving a *lessee* and a *lessor*. A non-leveraged lease can be considered a bilateral contract, where one party promises to perform certain conditions for the promise of the other party. Here, in a non-leveraged lease transaction, we have the promise of the lessor to purchase specific equipment and lease such equipment to the lessee for the lessee's promise to lease the equipment and make certain lease payments (rent) for the use of the equipment.

The *lessee* selects the type and quantity of the equipment from the manufacturer or dealer, negotiates the price, warranties, delivery and other terms and conditions pertaining to the equipment.

The *lessor* supplies the necessary funds necessary for the acquisition of the specified equipment. This may be accomplished by the lessor using his/her own funds or by borrowing some or all of the funds from others (banks or financial institutions) on a full recourse basis to the investors. Many times a manufacturer or dealer will sell its equipment through its subsidiary captive financial company, which develops a rental schedule of payments for the equipment. It is an attractive method the manufacturer uses to move his/her equipment.

The lessor is not responsible for any conditions, such as to warranties agreed to by the lessee and manufacturer, or dealer, and writes a disclaimer clause into the lease agreement which is acknowledged by the lessee signing the lease contract. The lessor is responsible for the purchase price of the equipment upon delivery and acceptance of the equipment by the lessee, who is legally the agent of the lessor, to receive the equipment.

The lessee can assign the purchase order to the lessor when placing the order himself/herself, but the supplier has to consent to such assignment which is the norm for such transactions, and in which case the lessor is billed directly for the equipment.

LEVERAGED LEASES

Leveraged leases are three-party transactions involving a *lessee,* a *lessor* and a *non-recourse investor*. A leveraged lease is always a true lease. It is more complex than a non-leveraged lease in the required documentation and the number of participants involved.

There can be several owner participants and several loan participants.

The *lessee,* just as in a non-leveraged lease, selects the type and quantity of the desired equipment, and negotiates with the manufacturer or dealer the price, warranties, delivery schedule and other terms and conditions pertaining to the equipment. The lessee also negotiates with a lessor as to the rental payments and other rights and obligations of both parties.

The *lessor* becomes the owner of the leased equipment by providing a minimum of 20% of the purchase price. The lessor is the owner or equity participant.

There can be several *owner participants,* also referred to as *equity participants,* that provide the 20% or more of the purchase price of the leased equipment. The lessor, as owner of the leased property, can claim all the tax benefits associated with ownership. The tax benefits are based on the entire cost of the equipment although they provide only a portion of that cost, and this risk is known as the "leverage" of the lessor.

Then there are the *loan participants,* or *investors,* such as banks or the financial institutions, which provide the balance of the funds needed to make the purchase of the leased equipment. Such loans are secured by (1) a lien or mortgage on the leased equipment, or (2) assignment of the lease and all rents payable by the lessee. The Security Notes are on a non-recourse to the lessor.

An *owner trustee* is usually selected when there are several owner participants, and holds title to the leased goods. The owner trustee represents the owner participants (equity participants) acting as lessor for all in executing all documents including the lease agreement. The owner trustee has only those powers granted under the trust agreement.

This arrangement makes it convenient for the lessee and the loan participants to deal with one another.

The *indenture trustee* is selected by the several loan participants to represent their interests. The indenture trustee is sometimes referred to as the *security trustee* for he/she represents the secured interest of the loan participants, also known as the *debt participants.*

The *trust indenture* is an agreement whereby the owner trustee assigns to the indenture trustee all of the owner trustee's interest as granted to him/her by the equity participants.

The indenture trustee collects the lease payments from the lessee, pays the debt payments (principal plus interest) to the loan participants, and forwards the remainder to the owner trustee, who distributes that sum among the equity participants.

The use of a single trustee to perform as an owner trustee and an indenture trustee is becoming increasingly common in usage, for many claim such an arrangement is simpler and reduces costs. The only disadvantage arises when the lessee is in default; there is a conflict of interest between the interests of the equity participants and the loan participants as to what actions should be taken.

A *lessee guarantor* is a party which guarantees the obligations of the lessee under the lease contract. The party may be related to the lessee group or may be a third party such as a bank or other financial institution.

The *manufacturer or dealer* supplies the asset to be leased. The terms and conditions, contained in the purchase contract regarding the warranty of merchantability or warranty for a particular purpose, are very important not only to the lessee but to show to the equity participants and the loan participants that the asset will perform as required by the lessee.

A *packager or broker* is used in the arrangement for a leveraged lease transaction. From a lessee's viewpoint, the packager should be a leasing company which will become one of the equity participants in the lease transaction.

The *key documents* to a leveraged lease transaction are: (1) the participation agreement; (2) the lease agreement; (3) the owner trust agreement; and, (4) the indenture trust agreement.

The *participation agreement* is the document which identifies all the participants to the lease transaction and their respective obligations for the acquisition of the leased equipment.

The *lease agreement* is executed between the lessee and the owner trustee, acting as lessor, which spells out the rights and obligations of all parties involved.

The *owner trust agreement* names an owner trustee to represent all of the equity participants, and enumerates the duties and responsibilities of the owner trustee.

The *indenture trust agreement* appoints an indenture trustee to act for the loan participants, and spells out the obligations involved.

The owner trustee assigns the lease agreement to the indenture trustee along with a lien or security interest in the leased equipment.

MASTER LEASES

The master lease operates in the same manner as the open-ended purchase contract or blanket purchase order. That is, the master lease facilitates the delivery of the equipment needed now and guarantees delivery of subsequent other needed equipment when required. The master lease establishes the line of credit intended to the lessee by the lessor (the leasing company).

The master lease can be written for any length of time, but usually states the dollar limit for the equipment to be leased under the agreement. The rates, terms and conditions for all equipment to be leased can be negotiated at the time of entering into a master lease agreement. Some master leases contain the provision that the lessor will supply requested additional equipment with the rates and terms negotiated at the time of delivery.

The master lease agreement (Figure 13.1), eliminates the need to negotiate all conditions each time another piece of equipment is needed. Master leasing is used in the trucking transportation industry where the lessee has seasonal or cyclical requirements for additional trucks, and a phone call to the lessor will provide that need. The same is true in the office technology equipment field, such as in computers, copiers, etc., when additional units are needed during the holiday seasons, and this saves time and cost of negotiating a new lease.

Figure 13.1

MASTER LEASE AGREEMENT NO. __________
PAGE One of _______

MASTER LEASE AGREEMENT

This Master Lease Agreement (the "Lease") entered into this __________ day of ______________________, 19_____, by and between hereinafter referred to as "Lessor", and ____, hereinafter referred to as "Lessee".

WITNESSETH:

1. LEASE, TERM, RENTAL. For and in consideration of the covenants and agreements to be kept and performed by the Lessee pursuant to this Lease, Lessor hereby leases to Lessee the property (said property, together with any replacements, additions, repairs and accessories incorporated therein and/or affixed thereto, is hereinafter collectively referred to as "Equipment") described in the Equipment Lease Schedule or Schedules (hereinafter sometimes referred to as the "Schedule or Schedules (hereinafter sometimes referred to as the "Schedule" or collectively "Schedules"), now or hereafter attached hereto and by reference made a part hereof.

The term of the Lease, aggregate rental and rental payments for any particular item or items of Equipment shall be as specified in the Schedule(s) which describes such item(s). All rent shall be paid at the office of the Lessor, or as other wise directed by Lessor in writing.

2. SELECTION OF EQUIPMENT. The Lessee has selected both the Equipment of the type and quantity which is the subject of this Lease, the applicable Schedule and the supplier from whom the Lessor purchased the Equipment. Lessor warrants that at the time of delivery of Equipment under this Lease and the applicable Schedule, Lessor had such title to the Equipment as Lessor derived from the manufacturer, vendor or other transferor to the Lessor, and that Lessor has the right to enter into this Lease. EXCEPT AS PROVIDED IN THE IMMEDIATELY PRECEDING SENTENCE, LESSOR MAKES NO REPRESENTATION AND DISCLAIMS ANY AND ALL WARRANTIES, EXPRESS OR IMPLIED, AS TO THE DESIGN, COMPLIANCE WITH SPECIFICATIONS, CONDITION, QUALITY, WORKMANSHIP, OR THE SUITABILITY, ADEQUACY, OPERATION, USE OR PERFORMANCE OF THE EQUIPMENT, INCLUDING, BUT NOT LIMITED TO, MERCHANTABILITY OR FITNESS FOR A PARTICULAR PURPOSE. ANY DELAY IN DELIVERY SHALL NOT AFFECT THE VALIDITY OF THIS LEASE OR ANY SCHEDULE. The Lessee understands and aggrees that neither the supplier nor any salesman or any agent of the supplier is an agent of the Lessor. No salesman or agent of the supplier is authorized to waive or alter any term or condition of the Lease, and no representation as to the Equipment or any other matter by the supplier shall in any way affect the Lessee's duty to pay the rent and perform its other obligations as set forth in the Lease. Lessee shall inspect the Equipment within three (3) business days after delivery thereof to the Lessee. Unless within said period the Lessee gives notice to Lessor as provided in Paragraph 14 of this Lease, specifying any defects in or any other proper objections to the Equipment, it shall be conclusively presumed that Lessee has fully inspected and accepted the Equipment, that the Equipment is in proper working order, that the Equipment is in full compliance with the terms of the Lease and applicable Schedule and in good condition and repair.

Notwithstanding any provision of this Lease to the contrary, after acceptance of each such item of Equipment by Lessee and receipt of the manufacturer's warranty by Lessee, if any, Lessee agrees to settle any and all claims directly with the manufacturer and will not assert any such claims against Lessor or Lessor's assignee, if any. In no event shall Lessee have any right of set-off, withhold any rent or any other payment due hereunder or be relieved of any obligations, such payments and obligations being absolute and unconditional. Notwithstanding any provision herein to the contrary, in no event shall Lessor be liable for any consequential or special damages with respect to any aspect of the Equipment or the use or operation thereof.

3. INSTALLMENT, MAINTENANCE AND REPAIR. Neither the Lessor nor any assignee shall have any obligation to install, erect, test, adjust or service the Equipment. The Lessee, at its sole cost and expense, shall:

A. At Lessor's option, pay all charges in connection with the installation and operation of the Equipment;
B. Comply with all laws, ordinances, regulations, requirements and rules with respect to the use, maintenance and operation of the Equipment;
C. Take good and proper care of the Equipment and make all repairs and replacements necessary to maintain, preserve and keep the Equipment in good condition and working order as of the date of installation and placement into service, ordinary wear and tear excepted. The Lessee shall not make any alterations, additions or improvements to the Equipment without the prior written consent of the Lessor. All repairs, replacements, parts, accessories and improvements of whatsoever kind or nature furnished or affixed to the Equipment shall belong to and become part of the Equipment;
D. At Lessor's option, pay all taxes, assessments, licenses, registration fees and other governmental charges levied on the Equipment, or relating to this Lease, exclusive of franchise taxes and taxes measured by the income of the Lessor. At Lessor's option, the Lessee shall file all returns required in connection herewith, including, but not limited to, personal property tax, and furnish copies thereof to the Lessor. The assumption of liability in this Paragraph will continue in full force and effect notwithstanding the expiration or other termination of this Lease or the applicable Schedule;
E. Any or all advances made by Lessor to preserve the Equipment or to pay any premiums for insurance thereon or to discharge and pay all taxes, liens or encumbrances thereon shall be added to the unpaid balance of rentals due hereunder, and shall be repayable by the Lessee to Lessor immediately, together with interest thereon at the rate of Eighteen Percent (18%) per annum, or the maximum rate allowed by law, whichever is less.

4. INSURANCE AND INDEMNITY. Lessee assumes the entire risk of loss or damage to the Equipment from any cause whatsoever, and the obligation of Lessee to pay the rentals herein provided shall not in any manner be affected and shall remain in full force and effect irrespective of any damage, loss or destruction of the Equipment. In the event of any damage, loss or destruction of the Equipment, Lessee shall repair or replace the Equipment involved to return the Equipment to the condition it was as of the date of installation and placement into service, ordinary wear and tear excepted, and any such repaired or replaced Equipment shall belong to Lessor and shall be subject to the terms of this Lease.

Figure 13.1 (continued)

Lessee agrees, at its sole cost and expense, to procure and maintain insurance for the Equipment for the full replacement value thereof, with companies approved by Lessor, against such risks, including the liability of Lessor from public liability and property damage. Such insurance shall expressly cover both Lessor and Lessee, as their interests may appear, and any proceeds, whether resulting from loss, damage or return premium, shall be paid by the insurance carriers to Lessor to be held in trust by Lessor for the purpose of defraying the cost and expense of repairing or replacing the Equipment involved, or at the option of Lessor, to be applied toward the payment of the obligations of Lessee hereunder. Lessee agrees to provide Lessor with a certificate of insurance. Such insurance coverage shall also provide that it shall not be materially changed or cancelled without at least thirty (30) days prior written notice to Lessor.

Lessee agrees to and does hereby indemnify, protect and hold harmless Lessor, its successors and assigns, from and against any suit, charge, claim, expense, loss or liability (including, but not limited to, reasonable attorney's fees and expenses, penalties and interest) imposed upon or asserted against Lessor or which are incurred by Lessor in any manner relating to or arising from this Lease or the ownership of or the leasing, use, suitability or adequacy for any purpose, operation, condition, delivery, return or other disposition of any Equipment (including without limitation, latent, and other defects, whether or not discoverable by Lessor or Lessee) subject to this Lease. Lessee shall indemnify Lessor against any alleged, claimed or actual negligence arising from or concerning the delivery, condition, maintenance, inspection, operation, specifications of or quality of any Equipment. The assumption of liability and indemnities in this Paragraph shall continue in full force and effect notwithstanding the expiration or other termination of this Lease or the applicable Schedule.

5. USE, LOCATION, REMOVAL AND INSPECTION. Equipment shall be used only in the lawful business of the Lessee and located as shown on the applicable Schedule. The Lessee, without the prior written consent of the Lessor, shall not remove the Equipment from such location nor part with possession or control thereof. The Lessor, upon prior reasonable notice to the Lessee, shall have the right to inspect the Equipment during the Lessee's normal business hours.

6. TIME IS OF THE ESSENCE. Time is of the essence of this Lease, and no waiver by Lessor or any breach or default shall constitute a waiver of any other breach or default by Lessee or waiver of any of Lessor's rights.

7. DEFAULT. If Lessee fails to pay any rent or other amount herein required within five (5) days after the same is due and payable, or if Lessee fails to observe, keep or perform any other provision of this Lease required to be observed, kept or performed by Lessee, or if Lessee ceases doing business as a going concern, or if a petition is filed by or against Lessee under the Bankruptcy Act or any amendment thereto (including a petition for reorganization or an arrangement), or if a receiver is appointed for Lessee or its property, or if Lessee commits an act of bankruptcy, becomes insolvent, makes an assignment for the benefit of creditors, offers a composition or extension of any of its indebtedness, or if Lessee, without Lessor's prior consent, attempts to remove, sell, transfer, encumber, sublet or part with the possession of the Equipment, or if the Equipment is subject to execution or other process of law, or if Lessor deems itself reasonably insecure, Lessor shall have the right to exercise any one or more of the following remedies: (a) To declare the entire amout of rent hereunder immediately due and payable without notice or demand to Lessee; (b) To sue for and recover from the Lessee an amount equal to the unpaid balance of the rent due and to become due during the term of this Lease and/or the loss of the Lessor's residual value of the Equipment; (c) To enter upon Lessee's premises, with or without notice, and without any right or cause of action for trespass, to take possession of any or all items of Equipment without demand or notice wherever same may be located without any court order or other process of law; or (d) To secure a writ of replevin for the Equipment without notice or demand from a court of competent jurisdiction (which notice the Lessee hereby knowingly, voluntarily and intelligently waives). Upon retaking possession of any or all items of Equipment, the Lessor, at its option, may (i) Lease repossessed Equipment or any part thereof to any third party on such terms and conditions as the Lessor may reasonably determine or (ii) sell the Equipment or any part thereof to the highest bidder at a public auction or at private sale and credit the amount so realized, less expenses incurred in connection with such disposition, to the unpaid balance of rent and other financial obligations due and to become due hereunder. Lessee hereby waives any and all damages occasioned by such taking of possession. Any said taking of possession shall not constitute a termination of this Lease, and shall not relieve Lessee of its obligations hereunder unless Lessor expressly so notifies Lessee in writing.

Should any legal proceedings be instituted by Lessor to recover any monies due and to become due hereunder and/or for the possession of the Equipment, Lessee shall be liable and pay for all reasonable attorney's fees and costs incurred.

To further secure the payment of all obligations under this Lease, except in states in which it may not be permitted by law, the Lessee and all guarantors, if any, hereby jointly and severally irrevocably authorize(s) any attorney of any court of record to appear for them, or any one or more of them, in such court, during term time or vacation, at any time after the stated or accelerated maturity hereof, and confess a judgment without process against them, or any one or more of them, in favor of the legal holder of this Lease for such sum as may appear to be due and unpaid thereon, together with interest, costs and reasonable attorney's fees, with minimum attorney's fees of $50.00, and to waive and release all errors which may intervene in such proceeding and consent to immediate execution upon such judgment, hereby ratifying and confirming all that said attorney may do by virtue hereof. The Lessee and all guarantors, if any, hereby consent to the Lessor granting, at its option, one or more extensions for the time of payment or performance of any of the obligations of this Lease or any Schedule in connection herewith, hereby waiving all notice thereof. If Lessee fails to pay when due any rent or other amount required herein to be paid Lessor, Lessee shall pay to Lessor a service charge of Five Percent (5%) of the amount of payment which is delinquent plus interest at the rate of Eighteen Percent (18%) per annum or the maximum rate allowed by law, whichever is less.

8. RETURN OF EQUIPMENT. Upon expiration or termination of the Lease of Equipment as set forth in the applicable Schedule, the Equipment covered under said Schedule shall be immediately returned by the Lessee to the Lessor (at Lessee's expense) in as good condition as received, less normal wear and tear, to such place as is then specified by Lessor, carefully crated, shipped freight prepaid and properly insured. In the event Lessee fails to return Equipment at the end of the lease rental period covered by the applicable Schedule(s), and without written notice of such Schedule(s) expiration by Lessor to Lessee, the Lessee shall pay to the Lessor rent at the rate of double the monthly rate as designated in the applicable Schedule(s) for such Equipment.

9. SIGNATURE, AUTHORIZATION. The Lessee's duly authorized and empowered signator authorizes any Department Head, Manager or other designated Personnel to execute the Schedule(s) pursuant and subject to this Lease on its behalf. The subject Schedule(s) now or hereafter executed and attached shall be deemed part and parcel of this Lease.

10. ASSIGNMENT BY LESSOR. This Lease, the Schedule(s), the Equipment and all rights of Lessor hereunder may be assigned, pledged, mortgaged, transferred or otherwise disposed of, either in whole or in part, without notice to Lessee. In the event Lessor assigns this Lease or the payments due or to become due hereunder or any other payment or interest herein, whether as security for any of its indebtedness or otherwise, no breach or default by Lessor hereunder or pursuant to any other agreement between Lessor and Lessee, should there be one, shall excuse performance by Lessee of any provision hereof, including, but not limited to, the Lessee's obligation to pay rent, it being understood that in the event of such default or breach by Lessor that Lessee shall pursue any right on account thereof solely against Lessor and not against such assignee. No such assignee shall be obligated to perform any duty, covenant or condition required to be performed by Lessor under the terms of this Lease.

Subject to the foregoing, this Lease inures to the benefit of, and is binding upon, the successors and assigns of the parties hereto.

Figure 13.1 (continued)

11. ASSIGNMENT BY LESSEE. Without the prior written consent of Lessor, Lessee agrees not to transfer or assign this Lease or any interest hereunder or to sublease, assign, transfer or create a security interest in any or all of the Equipment or in any manner, except as herein provided, surrender or part with the possession, custody or control thereof. Replacements, additions, repairs or alterations made to or placed in or upon the Equipment shall become a component part thereof, and title therein shall immediately vest in Lessor and shall be included under the terms and provisions of this Lease.

12. OWNERSHIP, PERSONAL PROPERTY. The Equipment shall at all times remain the property of the Lessor, and the Lessee shall have no right or property interest therein but only the right to use the same under this Lease. The parties hereto agree that there is no sale of the Equipment to the Lessee, and further, that no right, title or interest, legal or equitable, in the Equipment so leased, or in any part thereof, shall vest in the Lessee. The Lessor may require Lessee, at Lessee's expense, to display notice of Lessor's ownership by affixing to the Equipment its identifying plate, stencil or other indicia of ownership. The Equipment shall always remain and be deemed personal property even though the Equipment may hereafter become attached or affixed to realty.

13. CREDIT AND FINANCIAL INFORMATION, ADVANCE LEASE PAYMENTS. Lessor may require from time to time, and Lessee agrees to furnish, statements setting forth the financial condition and operations of Lessee and any guarantor of this Lease. The Lessee and any guarantor represent and warrant that all credit and financial information submitted to the Lessor herewith or at any other time during the term of this Lease is true and correct. Lessee's advance lease payments are a security deposit which may be applied to the final lease payments, at the option of the Lessor.

14. NOTICES. Service of all demands under this Lease shall be sufficient if given personally or mailed by certified mail to the party involved at its respective address hereinafter set forth, or at any such other address as such party may provide in writing from time to time. Any such notices mailed to such address shall be effective when deposited in the United States Mails, duly addressed and with postage prepaid.

15. ADDITIONAL DOCUMENTS. At the request of the Lessor, the Lessee shall execute and deliver to the Lessor such documents as the Lessor shall deem necessary or desirable for the purpose of recording or perfecting Lessor's interest under this Lease and/or the Equipment.

16. ADDITIONAL SCHEDULE(S) AMENDMENTS. This Lease and all Schedules added hereto as designated by the Lease Number above shall be construed as one Lease (the term "Lease" as used herein shall mean this instrument and all Schedules attached hereto and incorporated herein from time to time) and a default on this Lease or on any other lease between the parties hereto shall be deemed a default on all leases between the parties. Except as provided herein, this Lease and all Schedules contain the entire agreement between the parties, and may not be altered, modified, terminated or discharged except in writing.

17. WAIVER. No delay or omission to exercise any right, power or remedy accruing to Lessor upon any breach or default by Lessee under this Lease shall impair any such right, power or remedy of Lessor, nor shall be construed as a waiver of any such breach or default, or of any similar breach or default thereafter occurring, nor shall any waiver of a single breach or default be deemed a waiver of any subsequent breach or default. All waivers under this Lease must be in writing. All remedies either under this Lease or by law afforded to Lessor shall be cumulative and not alternative.

18. LIABILITY. Whenever the context of this Lease requires, the singular number includes the plural, and whenever the word "Lessor" is used herein, it shall include all assignees of Lessor. If there shall be more than one Lessee named in this Lease and/or guarantor, the liability of each shall be joint and several.

19. ENTIRE AGREEMENT. This Lease constitutes the entire understanding of the parties and shall not be altered or amended except by an agreement in writing signed by the parties hereto or their successors or assigns.

20. NET LEASE. This Lease is a net lease and the Lessee hereby acknowledges that it shall be solely responsible for the maintenance and/or repairs of the Equipment.

21. MISCELLANEOUS. Any provision of this instrument prohibited by law in any state, as to such state, shall be effective to the extent of such prohibition without invalidating the remaining provisions of this instrument. This instrument shall be governed and construed in accordance with the laws of the State of Illinois. This Lease and all Schedules hereto shall be deemed to have been accepted and entered into by Lessor in DuPage County, Illinois, and in the event that any litigation or other legal proceedings shall arise under and/or in connection with the Lease, such litigation or other legal proceeding shall be conducted in a local, federal or state court located within DuPage County, Illinois. Furthermore, the Lessee hereby accepts and consents to personal jurisdiction and venue in any local, federal or state court located within DuPage County, Illinois, and the Lessee waives any and all defenses and/or rights in opposition thereto. The Lessee represents that the Equipment is being leased for business purposes and agrees that under no circumstances shall this Lease be deemed or construed as a consumer contract. By execution hereof, the undersigned hereby certifies that he has read this Lease and that he is duly authorized to execute this Lease on behalf of the Lessee.

Accepted this ______ day of ______________, 19 ________.

By: ______________________________

As its: ______________________________

Executed this ______ day of ______________, 19 ________.

LESSEE:

____

____
Authorization Signature

____
Title

____
Typed or Printed Signature

____
Address

____
City State Zip

Figure 13.1 (continued)

GUARANTY

In consideration of the financial interest of the undersigned in the Lessee, and other good and valuable consideration, the undersigned, jointly and severally, guaranty performance to the Lessor of all of the terms and conditions contained in the above Lease by Lessee to be performed, and the prompt payment when due of all sums due thereunder, hereby waiving any modifications, amendments or extensions of payment and notices thereof. The undersigned further agrees that in the event of default by Lessee of any of the terms or conditions of this Lease, the Lessor shall have the right to pursue all legal remedies directly against the undersigned which Lessor is entitled to pursue against the Lessee under the Lease, without having first exhausted any and all such legal remedies against the Lessee. In the event that any litigation or other legal proceeding shall arise under and/or in connection with the Lease and/or this Guaranty, such litigation or other legal proceeding shall be conducted in a local, federal or state court located within DuPage County, Illinois. Furthermore, the undersigned hereby accepts and consents to personal jurisdiction and venue in any local, federal or state court located within DuPage County, Illinois, and the undersigned waives any and all defenses and/or rights in opposition thereto.

INDIVIDUAL GUARANTOR(S)

Signature ______________________________

Typed Signature ______________________________

Address: ______________________________
Street City State Zip Code

DATED: ______________________________

Signature ______________________________

Typed Signature ______________________________

Address: ______________________________
Street City State Zip Code

DATED: ______________________________

CORPORATE GUARANTOR

____
Full Legal Name of Corporation

(AFFIX CORPORATE SEAL)

BY: ______________________________

Typed Signature ______________________________

As its: ______________________________

Address: ______________________________

Attest: ______________________________

____
City State Zip

DATED: ______________________________

CHAPTER 14

Various Fields of Leasing

INTRODUCTION

Equipment leasing continues to grow in the 1990s, reflecting an increase in capital equipment expenditures. During the 1980s, equipment leasing grew more than twice as fast as business investment in capital equipment. In 1989, the volume of leasing is estimated at $123 billion in original equipment cost. The demand in the 1990s should grow at the rate of 7% annually.

The strongest demand for leasing was for computer, transportation and telecommunications equipment, followed by office and medical equipment.

The loss of certain tax benefits under The Tax Reform Act of 1986 has increased the volume of operating and direct finance leasing markets and decreased the leveraged leasing activity.

New technology can make some equipment, such as computers and specialized production equipment, obsolete long before it wears out. A short-term operating lease offers the lessee protection against obsolescence and the cost of disposal, shifting such risks to the lessor.

Leases for equipment requiring frequent maintenance and service, such as the automobile, truck, medical, etc., are constructed to include or be accompanied by maintenance and service contracts. With the reduction of tax benefits for equipment ownership, full-service leasing has been made more attractive for equipment users. Lessees have found that such service contracts are less costly than undertaking these services themselves, both in money and trouble.

AUTOMOBILE LEASING

These days the public is bombarded through newsprint, radio and television with "fantastic" offers of leasing those high priced automobiles. Twenty-five years ago, there were about 5% of the automobiles under lease. Today, in the 1990s, there is the expectation that 40 percent of the vehicles will be leased.

With today's soaring automobile prices and the IRS's phased out tax benefit for buying an automobile on time, leasing has become an attractive alternative for that person who likes to drive a new car every two, three, or even four years. This attractiveness for leasing doesn't make it acceptable for everyone with the fine print penalties and disclaimers that the lessee should carefully read before signing. Anyone who expects to keep an automobile for five years or more should definitely purchase, borrow to purchase, but not lease that car.

Types of Automobile Leases

Two types of automobile leases are offered: the *closed-end* and *open-end* lease types. Usually, the consumer is offered the closed-end lease, whereby the lessee leases the automobile for a definite monthly "rental" payment, and at the end of the lease term returns the automobile to the lessor without any further obligation, provided the vehicle was properly cared for and the maximum allowed mileage was not exceeded. There is usually a 10- to 20-cent per mile charge for the overage mileage. The greater the mileage, the less the lessor will obtain for that vehicle.

In an open-end lease, the risk of the resale of the automobile is shifted to the lessee. The returned automobile must yield the estimated predetermined price; if not, the lessee is charged with the difference. The lessor is assured to get that estimated value. (For more on vehicle leasing, see TRAC leases, page 22.)

The Lease "Rental" Payments

Those monthly "rental" payments should be considered in the same manner as the payment of rent for an apartment, something you utilize but do not own.

In estimating those lease payments, the lessor knows that the automobile you lease today will be worth only a fraction of its initial sales price when you return that automobile at lease's end.

The leasing companies look at two primary costs: the cost of the money they had to borrow in order to purchase you car, and the amount of the car's value you, the lessee, are expected to use up during the lease term (depreciation). The less a car is expected to depreciate, the lower your monthly payments and the greater the residual value anticipated at lease's end.

The leasing company calculates the amount of each monthly payment so that at the end of the lease term, those payments will cover: (1) the cost of the vehicle; (2) the cost of financing; (3) general overhead costs; and, (4) a fair profit. One key factor in this determination is the estimated value the lessor expects to receive when that leased automobile is returned and disposed.

In closed-end lease, the actual value the lessor receives for that leased automobile represents the lessor's profit or loss. In this type of lease, the lessee has no obligation other than returning the automobile less normal wear and within the maximum agreed mileage. In this case, lessor bears the risk of profit or loss.

In an open-ended lease, the lessee has all the risk since the lessor is guaranteed a definite value for the leased automobile at lease end.

Key factors for the lessee to consider is: (1) how much depreciation are you paying, and (2) what is the interest rate the leasing company is assuming.

Other Costs

Some leases have *insurance costs* built into the lease agreement. Others do not. If that automobile is totaled or stolen, especially during the early portion of the lease, standard insurance policies fall far short of covering the balance owed on the lease. Most leasing companies are insisting that the lessee purchase "gap" insurance, which is a one-time cost of approximately $200 to $500.

There is also that *early termination charge* for that person who leases an automobile for three to four years, and then decides after six months or one year to terminate the lease. Those charges could be a nightmare and should be negotiated before signing the three- to four-year lease.

There is the *excessive mileage charge* which could be from ten to twenty-five cents per mile for that extra driving.

Then there is that *excessive wear and tear charge,* which if not properly taken care of will cost more than you bargained for.

Fleet Leasing

About 40% of the higher priced automobiles are "dumped" into the fleet sales, usually to rental companies like Hertz, etc. The Detroit automobile manufacturers are hush-hush about the fleet sales. American automobile manufacturers have too many plants with too much capacity for their shrinking market share of automobile sales. Many are consolidating their plants and even shutting others to reduce operating costs and remain competitive. Each car maker follows this pattern to keep its respective factories going.

This is the main reason the "Big Three" have been buying up rental companies. Chrysler has purchased Thrifty, Dollar and Snappy. Ford has purchased 49% of Hertz and has a quota arrangement with Budget. General Motors owns shares of Avis and National. Even Mitsubishi has purchased Value Rent A Car.

When those "company cars" you lease are five or more, you are eligible for fleet prices and should negotiate the payments, maintenance, etc. Shop for a lessor who can provide fleet-management services which include maintenance, records, individual vehicle records, etc. Shopping around brings the best deal.

The fleet deals are being made for short-lease terms so that car makers can look forward to "selling" new ones at the end of the lease term. And when the individual dealer lessor complains about competing with Hertz's and Avis's used car sales, the car manufacturer (factories) is buying back the old rentals.

LEASING VERSUS BUYING

Auto manufacturers have the answer to those who cannot afford to purchase that new car. Borrow it. They are promoting leasing as never before. The question: does it make sense to borrow that car instead of buying it?

Many companies have found that automobile (or truck) leasing is a favorite method of reducing costs, and at the same time eliminating the hassle in purchasing, owning, maintaining and eventually disposing of the vehicle. The 1986 changes in the tax laws have repealed the investment tax credits and phased out the credit for interest on borrowing funds for a car purchase which has given leasing a favorable margin over purchasing.

With purchasing, the automobiles depreciate in value, so that cash or a down payment would be better invested elsewhere. When you lease, you are not putting a rapidly depreciating asset on your balance sheet. This helps keep the debt down, especially in growing or struggling companies. Leasing does not require a down payment. Usually lessors request the first and last month's payment, and sometimes, a security deposit.

If your credit is good and you do not expect to drive more than 15,000 miles per year, then you should consider leasing.

A key factor is the residual value of that automobile at lease end, for that amount is deducted from the selling price and the resultant is the amount upon which monthly payments are calculated.

Another aspect of leasing is the finance costs. By adding the total monthly payments plus the residual value and deducting the selling price, this reveals what the potential lessee will be paying in interest and other fees.

Extra charges for excessive damage to the automobile induces the lessee to "treat" that car with care. After all, the automobile is only loaned to you.

Points to Negotiate

1. The *purchase price* is used by leasing companies to calculate those monthly payments. Lessees can bargain that purchase price down through negotiations.

2. The predicted *residual value* of that automobile can also be negotiated. The higher the value you agree upon, the lower those monthly payments.

3. *Cost reduction* by finding a lease that does not require a down payment. Shop around; you don't "give away" money for something you do not own.

4. Carefully review that *end-of-lease fine print* which adds charges for "extras" like extra mileage, or excessive wear and tear. Arrive at a definite charge for these and others before you sign that lease.

Beware of Headaches

1. Get a closed-end lease. The lessor takes the risk in obtaining that full residual value at lease end. In an open-end lease, you, the lessee, assume that risk. Look carefully for the "terminal rental clause" in the lease.

2. Don't fall for that down payment gimmick. Very seldom is this required due to expensive cars and "tottering" credit.

3. Beware of the penalties for early termination of the lease. This can be negotiated and included in the terms of the lease.

4. Negotiate the mileage limitations and the penalty for exceeding this.

5. You may be liable for excess wear and tear. Reliable lessors provide guidelines for acceptable damage.

6. Check the lease to determine if you have an option to purchase the car at lease end, and the method of determining the purchase price.

7. The usual lease acquisition or administrative fee of approximately $250 is standard. Don't pay too much. Shop around.

8. Whether you purchase or lease, be sure you know the sales price upon which your payments are based. Do your homework and compare it with other dealer's sales price.

LEASE SHOPPING "PAYS"

The lessee should shop around and do it with the same zeal as to purchase, to bring lease payments down. In May 1990, I was quoted $469 for a Cadillac Sedan de Ville for 36 months, whereas a year ago, the lease payments were $650 per month. This car had a selling price of $33,000. A Dodge Grand Caravan LE, with a purchase price of $20,078, could be leased for 36 months at a monthly payment of $379.

In 1941, Chrysler and Ford, followed by General Motors in 1952, signed consent decrees permitting outside lenders such as banks and other financial institutions to participate in their subsidized interest rate programs. These consent decrees expired in 1982 when the Big Three renewed their subsidized financing programs. With cut-throat competition, due to the bargain lease payments (some financed at 2.9% for a 48-month lease), General Motors Acceptance Corporation (GMAC) did $794 million of business the first quarter of 1990, double the previous quarter. Banks cannot compete with those subsidized interest rates because a bank's cost of funds are higher than the rates offered by the captive finance companies.

The primary incentive for many corporations to lease is the conversion of fixed assets into working capital. Corporate fleets account for approximately 15% of all automobiles on the road.

AVIATION LEASING

Aviation is a field in itself. Leasing corporations must have global expertise in aircraft financing for leveraged leasing is the mainstay of aircraft leasing. This can be accomplished domestically or internationally.

No airline has the funds available to purchase an aircraft when one aircraft has a price tag of approximately $20,000,000. The leasing company can be one of the investors or can act as a broker and arrange for the financial mechanics to permit the airline to acquire the needed aircraft.

These leasing companies sometime look to other countries for investors to back such acquisition. This is known as "cross border" leveraged lease financing, whereby the leasing company, for a fee, acts as the broker.

The lease arrangement can be for a *dry lease* where the lessor's primary function is to arrange for the financing. The airline will provide the fuel and maintenance of the aircraft. In a *wet lease,* the lessor has to provide funds for the aircraft itself plus funds for the fueling and maintenance of the aircraft.

With tax reform, the demand for leveraged leasing is down, but the need for the supply of money to finance deals is still there. Lessors are demanding and getting longer lease terms which translate into lower monthly payments. Airlines are demanding (and getting) lease terms of 22 to 25 years instead of the previous 14 to 15 years.

TRUCK LEASING

Truck leasing is similar to automobile leasing, and is mostly for fleet arrangements since trucks are used for delivery of goods. The fleet leases should have arrangements for lessors to provide fleet-management services and maintenance, and the lease should include provisions for replacement of trucks. The leases should also include a provision that enables lessees to request additional trucks for increased delivery requirements during the holiday or seasonal period. Sears Roebuck, of Chicago, a retail and catalogue outlet, leases its trucks and drivers from Ryder for its delivery services.

Many manufacturers and distributors of products lease a whole truck for the movement of their wares. Others lease "space" on a truck. When "less than truckload" delivery is wanted, phone a truck carrier who makes the pickup and delivery service. You may not realize the fact that you actually "leased" space on the truck along with others for the delivery service.

RAILROAD CAR LEASING

Railroad cars are leased by manufacturers, mining companies, grain shippers, and automobile manufacturers among others, for the transportation of their products. Railroad cars can be flatbeds carrying trucks, automobiles and containers loaded with merchandise. Then there are tank cars to carry fluid products like oil, gasoline, etc. Railroad cars are built to accommodate every commodity that can be shipped by rail.

Manufacturers or bulk delivery companies of wheat or oat granaries who utilize the railroad for transportation of their products, usually have a railroad track siding running from the main tracks to the loading platforms of their plants. Then, whenever there is a need for railroad cars, they are delivered empty to these plant loading and transport.

The lessee can lease any number of railroad cars to meet any need, be it occasionally or on a time period basis (or for a month or so), or the lessee can lease those railroad cars on a cyclical basis as required.

In mining, as in coal mining, the loaded railroad cars move from the mine shaft to the mine's siding to the main railroad line for transportation.

When the purchasing agent places an order for goods overseas, the railroad "bridges" the transportation route by carrying the goods from the ship to its destination near the plant.

The same precautions must be used when leasing of railroad cars as with any other from of transportation.

WATER CARRYING VESSEL LEASING

Leasing or chartering vessels or space on them has been going on since ancient times, as in the Middle East when merchants wanted to ship their wares from Phoenicia (now known as Lebanon) to other ports in the Mediterranean. The merchants were interested in using the ships, not in owning them. The same is true today where manufacturers and other merchants are interested in moving their wares to market. They lease the entire vessel with or without the crew, or lease the space available on a particular vessel.

The growth in ocean and inland waterway commerce and the revolutionary changes in marine technology has resulted in the upgrading and building of high tankers, larger drybulk carriers, refrigerated ships, etc., to meet specialized needs. In general, vessels have become larger and more sophisticated.

The inland waterways, such as the Mississippi River, have the leasing of barges and roll-on/roll-off vessels to transport all sorts of goods and of vehicles carrying goods plus passengers. The trip can be a short one across the river or either down stream or up stream to any landing available along the river.

For the purchasing agent interested in obtaining the best rates for his/her inbound bulk cargo, without the limitations of regularly scheduled vessels, ship chartering (leasing) may be lucrative answer. Potential charterers have a variety of options in the present overtonnage market.

Agreements, between charterer and vessel owner to make a vessel available, fall into three categories:

1. *Voyage charter*—This kind of agreement covers a particular cargo's movement from one designated port to another at a negotiated rate for the goods loaded. The shipowner is responsible for all vessel operations.

2. *Time charter*—In this kind of agreement, the charterer obtains the vessel for a period of time to carry any cargo that the charter contract does not specifically prohibit anywhere within the charter provision's broad limitations.

3. *Bareboat charter*—In this agreement, the shipowner transfers full control of the vessel to the charterer. The charterer must operate the ship, purchase the fuel and food, pay for maintenance and drydock expenses and generally manage the ship.

The most commonly used contract is the voyage charter. This imposes the lease operation responsibility upon the shipowner and is the most convenient method for moving bulk commodities.

OFFICE EQUIPMENT LEASING

The leasing company, upon the selection of the potential lessee, purchases the equipment from reliable, usually major, manufacturers with established services and support capabilities. Remember, the lessor has no knowledge of the equipment you lease and looks to those manufacturers that will "come to the rescue" when needed. The lessee should provided for such services and support when negotiating the purchase prior to the lease arrangement. See Figure 14.1 of an example for an equipment lease.

High technology equipment such as computers, copiers, fax machines, etc., are constantly being upgraded; therefore, you, the lessee, should make provisions in the lease that after a time you should have the newer model replace the one you are presently using.

There are many companies, usually smaller ones, that rent office space and then lease their needed office furniture. Look out for the fine print which penalizes you for excessive wear and tear on that furniture. If you think of expansion for the near future, you may want to consider a master lease arrangement.

LAND FACILITY LEASING

If you lease business property from a third party or you enter into a lease agreement via a sale and leaseback, you can deduct as additional rent any real estate taxes you pay for the lessor.

All costs (commissions, fees, etc.) that you pay to acquire a lease on business property are considered capital costs and are amortized over the term of the lease.

Should you add a building or other permanent improvements to the leased property, you are only allowed to depreciate the cost of the improvements using the modified accelerated recovery system. If you do not keep the improvements when the lease ends, you can claim a gain or loss based on the adjusted basis at that time.

In all such transactions, it is strongly advised to have legal counsel.

COMMERCIAL EMPLOYEE LEASING

Unlike the temporary help agencies where you hire (lease) one or two persons to replace a temporary vacancy in your business, commercial employee leasing of permanent, full-time employees, is for that small- or medium-sized company which does not have the time to handle the administrative responsibilities and other regulations regarding employer-employee matters. These companies save time and spend more energy on beefing up their profits.

Figure 14.1 Sample Equipment Lease

INSTRUCTIONS FOR COMPLETING AN EQUIPMENT LEASE APPLICATION

PLEASE PRINT

STEP 1. Please fill in all of the blank spaces on THE APPLICATION for leasing/renting. THE APPLICATION is on the reverse side of this form.

STEP 2. Please have the lessee sign and date the shaded areas authorizing the release of credit information to the lessor. This will help expedite your lease request.

INSTRUCTIONS FOR ENTERING INTO THE LEASE AGREEMENT

STEP 3. Please type or print the lessee's correct and full legal name and address in the shaded box. Just below the shaded area please include the name of the person to contact and the phone number.

STEP 4. Please type or print the name and address of the supplier of the equipment. Just below the supplier information please list the name of the sales representative and the phone number.

STEP 5. Enter complete description of equipment, including model number and serial number if known.

STEP 6. Please complete the shaded areas identifying the correct term, number of payments, payment amount, total initial payment, and description of initial payment. In the box marked "tax" please insert the word "use" for use tax or "included" for sales tax included in the lease payment. (See note below.)

STEP 7. Please read the EQUIPMENT LEASE AGREEMENT (both sides). Please sign and date in the shaded areas.

STEP 8. Please read THE LEASE GUARANTY and sign in the shaded area. Your signature should be witnessed. Please have your witness sign and date this section just below your signature.

STEP 9. Please read the DELIVERY AND ACCEPTANCE RECEIPT, and sign in the shaded areas.

NOTE: For equipment to be located in one of the following Sales Tax States, you must add the applicable sales tax for that state to the equipment cost before calculating the monthly payment. (Subject to change.)

California • Hawaii • Illinois • Louisiana •
Maine • Michigan • South Dakota

Figure 14.1 Sample Equipment Lease (continued)

DATE

STEP 1
Supplier________________ Salesperson________________
STREET ADDRESS CITY STATE ZIP ( ) PHONE

PLEASE PRINT
Name of Customer________________ Phone ( )________
Address________________ How Long at Present Address________
City________ County________ State________ Zip________
To the Attention of________________ Title________
(authorized person to sign lease, and to whom any correspondence may be directed)
Description of Business________________ Please check: Corp. ☐ Partnership ☐ Individual ☐ How long in business________years

STEP 2 To Whom This May Concern:
Please accept this as my authorization and my request to release to the leasing company any credit information they may request. This request includes payment history and credit balances for trade references as well as balances on deposit and bank/loan references. I hereby authorize any photostatic copies of this authorization.

By:________________ Title________________ Date________________

Banks:	Name and Address	Telephone	Acct. Number(s)	Acct. Officer
1.		( )		
2.		( )		

Credit & Trade References

Name	City, State	Telephone
		( )
		( )
		( )
		( )

DESCRIPTION OF EQUIPMENT TO BE LEASED/RENTED

No. Machines	Make and Model (and Serial No.'s if available)	Cost per Unit	Total Cost

Lease Term Desired________ Total________
Advance Payment(s)________ Less Trade-in________
Lease Factor________ Sub-Total________
State, County & City Taxes (when applicable)________
Lease Payment________ Balance________

Special Instructions or Information________________

PLEASE INCLUDE AND COMPLETE THE FOLLOWING

	CO-LESSEE OR PREVIOUS ADDRESS
Name________	Name________
Home Address________	Home Address________
City, State & Zip________	City, State & Zip________
Home Phone ( )________	Home Phone ( )________
Social Security Number____/____/____	Social Security Number____/____/____

Figure 14.1 Sample Equipment Lease (continued)

EQUIPMENT LEASE AGREEMENT

LEASE NUMBER
CUSTOMER NUMBER

NAME AND ADDRESS OF LESSEE
(Complete Legal Name)

STEP 3

SUPPLIER OF EQUIPMENT
(Complete Address)

STEP 4

PERSON TO CONTACT | TELEPHONE NO ( ) | SALESPERSON | TELEPHONE NO ( )

TERMS AND CONDITIONS OF EQUIPMENT LEASE AGREEMENT ("LEASE")

1. LESSOR hereby leases to LESSEE, and LESSEE hereby leases from LESSOR, the personal property set forth hereinbelow, upon the terms and conditions hereinafter set forth (hereinafter sometimes referred to as the "Agreement" or "Lease").

2. The property leased hereunder (hereinafter sometimes referred to as the "Leased Property" or "Equipment") is as follows:

STEP 5 DESCRIPTION OF EQUIPMENT LEASED (Include make, year, model, identification and model numbers or marks)

EQUIPMENT TO BE DELIVERED AND LOCATED AT

STEP 6 3. SCHEDULE OF LEASE PAYMENTS DURING INITIAL TERM OF LEASE.

TERM OF LEASE NUMBER OF MONTHS	NUMBER OF PAYMENTS	AMOUNT OF EACH LEASE PAYMENT			TOTAL INITIAL PAYMENT	INITIAL PAYMENT REPRESENTING
		PAYMENT	TAX	OTHER		First_____ & Last_____ (OTHER)_____MOS (OTHER)_____MOS

ADDITIONAL PROVISIONS

LESSEE'S first monthly payment shall be due upon delivery of the Equipment to LESSEE and all subsequent payments shall be due on or before the first day of each calendar month thereafter

4. LESSOR HEREBY DOES NOT MAKE AND DISCLAIMS ANY AND ALL WARRANTIES, EXPRESS OR IMPLIED, WITH RESPECT TO THE LEASED PROPERTY, INCLUDING, BUT NOT LIMITED TO WARRANTIES OF MERCHANTABILITY OR FITNESS FOR A PARTICULAR PURPOSE. LESSEE HAS MADE THE SELECTION OF THE LEASED PROPERTY BASED UPON ITS OWN JUDGMENT, AND EXPRESSLY DISCLAIMS ANY RELIANCE UPON ANY STATEMENTS OR REPRESENTATIONS MADE BY LESSOR. LESSOR IS NOT RESPONSIBLE FOR ANY REPAIRS, SERVICE OR DEFECTS IN THE LEASED PROPERTY OR THE OPERATION THEREOF.

LESSEE SHALL INSPECT THE EQUIPMENT WITHIN THREE (3) BUSINESS DAYS AFTER DELIVERY THEREOF TO THE LESSEE. UNLESS WITHIN SAID PERIOD THE LESSEE GIVES NOTICE TO LESSOR AS PROVIDED IN PARAGRAPH 17 OF THIS LEASE, SPECIFYING ANY DEFECTS IN OR OTHER PROPER OBJECTIONS TO THE EQUIPMENT, IT SHALL BE CONCLUSIVELY PRESUMED THAT LESSEE HAS FULLY INSPECTED AND ACCEPTED THE EQUIPMENT, THAT THE EQUIPMENT IS IN PROPER WORKING ORDER, THAT THE EQUIPMENT IS IN FULL COMPLIANCE WITH THE TERMS OF THIS LEASE AND IN GOOD CONDITION AND REPAIR. NOTWITHSTANDING ANY PROVISION OF THIS LEASE TO THE CONTRARY, AFTER ACCEPTANCE OF EACH SUCH ITEM OF EQUIPMENT BY LESSEE AND RECEIPT OF THE MANUFACTURER'S WARRANTY BY LESSEE, IF ANY, LESSEE AGREES TO SETTLE ANY AND ALL CLAIMS DIRECTLY WITH THE MANUFACTURER AND WILL NOT ASSERT ANY SUCH CLAIMS AGAINST LESSOR OR LESSOR'S ASSIGNEE, IF ANY. IN NO EVENT SHALL LESSEE HAVE ANY RIGHT OF SET-OFF, WITHHOLD ANY RENT OR ANY OTHER PAYMENT DUE HEREUNDER OR BE RELIEVED OF ANY OBLIGATIONS, SUCH PAYMENTS AND OBLIGATIONS BEING ABSOLUTE AND UNCONDITIONAL. NOTWITHSTANDING ANY PROVISION HEREIN TO THE CONTRARY, IN NO EVENT SHALL LESSOR BE LIABLE FOR ANY CONSEQUENTIAL OR SPECIAL DAMAGES WITH RESPECT TO ANY ASPECT OF THE EQUIPMENT OR THE USE OR OPERATION THEREOF.

This Lease, consisting of the foregoing AND THE REVERSE SIDE HEREOF, sets forth the entire agreement between LESSOR and LESSEE. No agreements or understandings shall be binding on either of the parties hereto unless specifically set forth in this Agreement. The term "LESSEE" as used herein shall mean and include any and all LESSEES who sign hereunder, each of whom shall be jointly and severally bound hereby. LESSEE agrees that the depositing or endorsing of any check or other negotiable instrument shall not be deemed as acceptance hereof until such time as LESSOR accepts a copy hereof and so notifies LESSEE.

By execution hereof, the undersigned hereby certifies that he has read this Agreement, INCLUDING THE REVERSE SIDE HEREOF, and that he is duly authorized to execute this Lease on behalf of the LESSEE.

THIS AGREEMENT CANNOT BE CANCELLED. THIS AGREEMENT IS FOR BUSINESS PURPOSES ONLY.

ACCEPTED this_____day of_____, 19_____

BY:_____

Executed this _____ day of _____, 19 _____

LESSEE:_____

BY **STEP 7**

Authorized Signature and Title

(Continued on reverse side hereof)

Type Signature

LEASE GUARANTY

In consideration of the financial interest of the undersigned in the LESSEE, and other good and valuable consideration, the undersigned, jointly and severally, guaranty performance to the LESSOR of all of the terms and conditions contained in the above Lease by LESSEE to be kept and performed, and the prompt payment when due of all sums due thereunder, hereby waiving any modifications, amendments or extensions of payment and notices thereof. The undersigned further agree(s) that in the event of default by LESSEE of any of the terms or conditions of this Lease, the LESSOR shall have the right to pursue all legal remedies directly against the undersigned which LESSOR is entitled to pursue against the LESSEE under the Lease without having first exhausted any and all such legal remedies against the LESSEE. THE UNDERSIGNED, IN ORDER TO INDUCE LESSOR TO ENTER INTO THIS LEASE AND FOR OTHER GOOD AND VALUABLE CONSIDERATION, THE RECEIPT AND SUFFICIENCY OF WHICH IS HEREBY ACKNOWLEDGED, AGREES THAT ALL ACTIONS OR PROCEEDINGS ARISING DIRECTLY, INDIRECTLY OR OTHERWISE IN CONNECTION WITH, OUT OF, RELATED TO, OR FROM THIS LEASE SHALL BE LITIGATED AT LESSOR'S DISCRETION AND ELECTION, ONLY IN COURTS HAVING SITUS WITHIN THE STATE OF ILLINOIS. THE UNDERSIGNED HEREBY CONSENTS AND SUBMITS TO THE JURISDICTION OF ANY LOCAL, STATE OR FEDERAL COURT LOCATED WITHIN THE STATE OF ILLINOIS. THE UNDERSIGNED HEREBY WAIVES (1) ANY RIGHT THE UNDERSIGNED MAY HAVE TO TRANSFER OR CHANGE THE VENUE OF ANY LITIGATION BROUGHT AGAINST THE UNDERSIGNED BY LESSOR HEREUNDER; AND (2) ANY RIGHT TO TRIAL BY JURY.
IN ADDITION, THE UNDERSIGNED HEREBY CONSENTS TO THE LESSOR GRANTING, AT ITS SOLE OPTION, ONE OR MORE EXTENSIONS OF THE TIME OF PAYMENT OR PERFORMANCE OF ANY OF THE OBLIGATIONS OF LESSEE UNDER THIS LEASE, HEREBY WAIVING ANY AND ALL NOTICE THEREOF AND ANY RIGHT TO OBJECT THERETO WITHOUT WAIVING ANY OF LESSOR'S RIGHTS HEREUNDER.

_____ Individually (Guarantor)

_____ Witness

Date

STEP 8 _____ Individually

_____ Witness

Date

DELIVERY AND ACCEPTANCE RECEIPT

The undersigned hereby certifies that all the equipment above is in accordance with the terms of the said Equipment Lease Agreement ("Lease"), has been delivered, inspected, installed is in good working condition, and accepted by the undersigned as satisfactory. The decals, labels, etc., if required and supplied, have been applied to the equipment as listed in said Lease. The undersigned hereby approves payment by the LESSOR or you to the Supplier.

LESSEE _____

by **STEP 9**

Authorized Signature and Title

Date _____

Figure 14.1 Sample Equipment Lease (continued)

EQUIPMENT LEASE SCHEDULE NO.____________
SIDE One of Two Sides

EQUIPMENT LEASE SCHEDULE

Attached to and made a part of Master Lease Agreement Number________________, by and between , as Lessor, and__________

____,
as Lessee

A. EQUIPMENT LEASED

Item No.	Quantity	Description

DATED: ____________________________

Lessee:

____

BY: ______________________________

____
Title

Figure 14.1 Sample Equipment Lease (continued)

EQUIPMENT ACCEPTANCE NOTICE

As evidenced by this Equipment Acceptance Notice, we acknowledge receipt, in good condition and satisfactory installation and proper working order, of all of the items described in Equipment Lease Schedule Number ____________________, (the "Schedule"), and certify that the Lessor has fully and satisfactorily performed each, every and all covenants and conditions to be performed by it under the Master Lease Agreement referred to in the Schedule. We also approve payment by you to the supplier or vendor.

We accept the above-mentioned Equipment, programmed or not programmed (if applicable), and waive, insofar as and its assignees are concerned, any reservations as to condition, correctness, capability or capacity of the Equipment or associated software, and understand that any defects or shortcomings of the Equipment, its operation or programming, without reservation, will not be grounds for withholding any installment of rental due or to become due under the aforementioned Master Lease Agreement. We further agree that this Acceptance shall be a bar to any claim in any legal proceeding of the Equipment leased being defective or inoperative.

____
Name of Lessee

BY: ______________________________

As Its: ______________________________
(Title)

Date: ______________________________

Figure 14.1 Sample Equipment Lease (continued)

EQUIPMENT LEASE SCHEDULE NO.____________
SIDE Two of Two Sides

B. TERM: The term of this Lease Schedule, with respect to each item of Equipment listed herein, receipt whereof is hereby acknowledged and accepted, is for a term of ____________________ months, commencing on ________________________, 19 ______.

C. LEASE PAYMENTS: Lessee shall pay Lessor at the office of Lessor, or at such other place as Lessor may hereafter designate, the sum of $ _________________ per month, commencing ____________________, 19 ____ and on the first day of each and every consecutive month thereafter, for a period of __________________ months, the lease term hereunder. The first and last ____________________ payment(s) in the total amount of $ __________________ being payable at time of signing this Schedule.

(a) SPECIAL PAYMENT PROVISIONS: ____

____

____

____

D. LOCATION: The Equipment shall be located at ______________________________________
__________________________, City of ____
County of ______________________, State of ____

This Lease Schedule is attached to and made a part of that certain Master Lease Agreement Number____________________ dated __________________________________, 19______, between the parties hereto, and all terms and conditions of said Master Lease Agreement are incorporated herein by this reference and made a part hereof.

LESSEE:

Dated: ____________________________________ ______________________________________

BY: ____________________________________

____
Title

Accepted:

BY: ____________________________________

____
Title

Date of Acceptance: ____________________________

The leasing company provides all the personnel services needed to control costs and reduce personnel burdens. Among the services they provide are:

1. Employee recruitment services—they advertise, screen and test potential employees.

2. Financial accounting—the client (lessee) informs lessor of the hours and wage changes. The leasing company computes the salary, tax deductions, 401(k) contributions and insurance costs.

3. Tax accounting and IRS considerations—they handle all tax deposits and fillings to governmental agencies. The leasing company is responsible for all employment related taxes provided in Subtitle C of the IRC.

4. Compliance with human resources law—the leasing company is the legal employer of those people working for you, and are legally liable for compliance with all human resource laws, such as wrongful termination, administrative confirmation and document preparation required under the Immigration Reform and Control Act of 1986 and under Occupational Safety and Health Administration (OSHA).

The leasing company can provide health benefits at a lower rate than the individual small- or medium-sized companies which have a small number of employees in their plants. They also arrange for pension plans for their employees, for the employee is not an employee of the company he/she works in.

EMPLOYEE LEASING BENEFITS

1. Relieves the small company owner of many administrative duties.

2. Provides employees with more comprehensive benefits.

3. Although the leasing company is the legal employer, the lessee company retains control over who works for the company.

EMPLOYEE LEASING DISADVANTAGES

1. More expensive for companies with low overhead and/or efficient operations, and

2. Most leasing companies won't handle unions. The commercial employees companies the author knows of are:

    - Consolidated Employment Benefits Corporation (CEB COR) headquartered in Chicago, Illinois;

    - National Staff Network, headquartered in Van Nuys, California; and

    - Employee Staff Leasing, Inc., headquartered in Dearborn, Michigan.

Glossary

Accelerated payments—A schedule of payments which decreases over the term (in year one, 50%; in year two, 40%; in year three, 30%, etc.). This type of payment schedule: (1) eliminates down payments; and (2) reduces the interest cost because the debt is repaid at a faster rate.

Accelerated Cost Recovery System (ACRS)—A depreciation schedule enacted by the Economic Recovery Tax Act of 1981 and listed under Section 168 of the Internal Revenue Code.

Accounting for book and tax—In the financial world there are two types of accounting. One is to satisfy the tax requirements by using "tax books," and the other is to satisfy accounting purposes as defined by the Financial Accounting Standards Board (FASB). FASB Statement 13 sets for the rules for financing and leasing which are followed when an auditor certifies financial statements. There are similarities between the two rules, but their terminology is different and serves different particular purposes.

ACRS—Accelerated Cost Recovery System

ACRS (Modified)—Modified Acceleration Cost Recovery System

Accrued interest—(1) Interest that has been earned but not collected. (2) Interest earned but not paid since last payment.

Advance rent—(1) Payment required of lessee when they sign the lease contract and before they obtain the use of the equipment. (2) The advance payments reduce the total amount of the lease amount either by lowering the monthly amount or reducing the number of payments.

Alternative Minimum Tax (AMT)—This tax was enacted by the Tax Reform Act of 1986 to ensure that a minimum tax is paid by profitable companies which extensively have use of tax preference items, such as double deduction depreciation. Leasing may be a method whereby a company limits its exposure to AMT.

Application survey—Valuation by manufacturer's or lessor's representative on the lessee's operation and how the equipment will be used. It includes equipment application, usage, maintenance and the environment, and the equipment's residual value.

Amortization—The procedure whereby a debt is reduced over a set period of time. It is that portion of the monthly payment that is the principal, not the interest.

Assets—This is the sum of tangible and intangible properties owned by an entity.

Assets (current)—Liquid assets. Cash, inventories, and accounts receivable, all of which are subject to constant change.

Assets (fixed)—Assets intended for continued use and operation of an entity. Includes land, buildings, equipment, furniture and intangibles such as patents.

Asset-based financing—Similar to a finance lease except the lessor has a lien on the equipment and is not the legal owner.

Assignment—The written transfer of a security interest in equipment in a finance contract to a third party. (The manufacturer or dealer assigning his rights and interests in a conditional sale to a financial institution.)

Audited financial statement—A document disclosing an entity's economic condition at the end of a particular fiscal year as verified by an independent auditor.

Balloon payment—The final payment of a finance contract which is larger than the regular payments.

Balance sheet—A document which is a summary of a company's assets, liabilities and proprietorship of its business to portray its financial condition at a given period of time.

Bank line of credit—See lease credit.

Bargain purchase option—A lease provision whereby the lessee has the option to purchase the leased asset for a price predetermined at lease inception which is substantially lower than the expected market value.

Bargain renewal option—A provision in the lease agreement allowing the lessee, at his option, to renew the lease for a rental much lower than the expected fair market rental. This is usually done so as to be reasonably assured of renewal.

Base rate—(1) The periodic cost (payment) for rent of leased equipment. Taxes may or may not be included. (2) The floating interest rate quoted on the basis of the prime rate.

Base term—The minimum period of time that a lessee will have possession and use of equipment.

Basis points—The fraction division of a percentage of interest. There are 100 basis points in one percent.

Big-ticket item—That market segment which deals with leases with property valued over $2 million dollars, and are usually leveraged leases.

Book value—That portion of the original cost of an asset remaining on the books. It represents that amount which has not yet been depreciated.

Broker—A person or company who, for a fee, arranges the financing between lessors and lessees of an asset.

Capital lease—FAS 13 §7 sets forth the following criteria for classifying a capital lease:

(1) The lease transfers ownership of the property to the lessee at the end of the lease term.

(2) The lease contains a bargain purchase option.
(3) The lease term is equal to 75% or more of the estimated economic life of the leased property. (Economic life in the hands of one or more lessees, with normal maintenance).
(4) The present value of the minimum lease payments, excluding executory costs, equals or exceeds 90% of the excess value of the leased property. A lessee shall compute the present value of the minimum lease payments using its incremental borrowing rate.

Captive finance company—A finance institution owned by the manufacturer or dealer of the product it finances. It may or may not finance products of other companies.

Cash flow—Refers to the amount of cash flowing into a firm and the amount of cash flowing out of that firm.

Casualty value—See insured value.

Certificate of acceptance—A document whereby the lessee acknowledges that the equipment to be leased has been delivered and is acceptable having been manufactured or constructed in accordance with the specifications of the lease contract.

Collateral—Real or personal property pledged as security for a loan or for the equipment financed or leased.

Comptroller's ruling—The interpretation rendered by the U.S. Comptroller of Currency defining the leasing activities in which the national banks may engage (12 CFR 7.3400).

Conditional sale—Per IRS Ruling 55-540 Section 4, a lease agreement where the intent of the parties to transfer ownership as evidenced by the facts of the transaction. For tax purposes, the lessee is considered the owner of the property from the outset of the transaction.

Consumer lease—Per Title USC §1667, a consumer lease means a lease contract for the use of personal property for a period of time exceeding 4 months and an obligation not exceeding $25,000, primarily for personal, family, or household purposes.

Cost of capital—(1) Refers to the discount rate that equates the present value of estimated future cash flows. (2) Refers to the cost of funds invested in some project.

Credit—(1) The term associated with the ability of an entity to borrow from a lender. (2) The right granted by a creditor to a customer to defer payment of a debt.

Credit line—The dollar limit for funds pre-approved for an individual or company by a financial institution.

Credit rating—The amount, type and terms of credit which a financial institution can extend to an individual or company. That extension of credit is based upon the lender's faith and confidence in the borrower's promise to repay the funds.

Credit risk—The uncertainty assumed by the lender for possible non-payment of the credit extended.

Cross-border leasing—This is a lease transaction where the lessee is in one country and the lessor is in another country.

Current asset—See under Asset, current.

Current ratio—The ratio of current assets to current liabilities is very important to short-term creditors because liquidation of current assets is a source of funds for current liabilities.

Debt service—The payments of principal and interest to lenders.

Default—Failure of lessee or lessor to meet or perform some obligation required under the lease contract. For example, the lessee wrongfully rejects acceptance of goods or fails to make a payment when due. The lessor fails to deliver conforming goods as specified under the lease contract.

Depreciation—Annual charges against income to write off the cost of an asset as a result of wear out during the useful life of that asset until original cost is recovered.

Direct financing lease—[Per FAS 13 ¶6(b) (ii)] Lease other than leveraged leases that do not give rise to manufacturer's or dealer's profit (or loss) to the lessor but that meets one or more of the four criteria of a capital lease plus the following two criteria listed in §8:

(1) Collectability of the minimum lease payments is reasonably predicted.
(2) No important uncertainties surround the amount of unreimbursable costs yet to be incurred by the lessor under the lease.

Direct investor—A lessor in a direct financing lease transaction.

Discounted cash flow—The present value of a future cash flow.

Direct lease—Same as a direct financing lease.

Disqualified leaseback or long-term agreement—[Per IRC Section 467(b)(4)] A disqualified leaseback or long-term agreement means any Section 467 rental agreement if:
(1) Such agreement is part of a leaseback transaction or such agreement is for a term in excess of 75% of the statutory recovery period, and
(2) a principal purpose for providing increasing rents under the agreement is the avoidance of tax.

Economic life of leased property—The estimated remaining period which the property is expected to be economically usable by one or more users, with normal repairs and maintenance, for the purpose for which it was intended at the inception of the lease, without limitation by the lease term.

Effective lease rate—The effective rate to the lessee of cash flows as a result of a lease transaction.

Equipment acceptance—See Certificate of acceptance.

Equipment schedule—A document which describes in detail the equipment being leased, location of the leased equipment, terms and inception date as well as the repayment schedule.

Equity—A right, claim, or interest existing in an asset or a company.

Equity participant—The owner participant, a trustor owner, or a grantor owner.

ERTA—Economic Recovery Tax Act of 1981.

Estimated residual value of leased property—The estimated fair value of the leased property at the end of the lease term.

Executory costs—Those costs such as insurance, maintenance, and taxes incurred for leased property, whether paid by lessor or lessee.

Factor—A multiplier which when applied to a known dollar amount will give the resultant desired future amount.

Fair market purchase option—The option a lessee has to purchase the leased property at the end of the lease term for its then fair market value.

Fair market value—The price for which the property could be sold in an arm's-length transaction. That is, the price a buyer is willing to pay and a seller is willing to accept for the property.

FASB—Financial Accounting Standards Board, the body which issues rules and regulations for the accounting profession.

FASB 13 (FAS 13)—Statement #13 of the Financial Accounting Standards Board that establishes standards of financial accounting and reporting for leases by lessees and lessors.

Finance lease—An equipment lease considered a 'true lease,' regardless of the fact that it may contain a purchase option more than 10% of the original cost of the leased equipment, was authorized under the Tax Equity and Fiscal Responsibility Act of 1982, to become effective January 1, 1984. This was postponed to January 1, 1988, by the Deficit Reduction Act of 1984. However, before it became effective, it was repealed by Public Law 99-514, second season (1986), except for certain property eligible under certain transition rules.

Financing agreement—An agreement under a leveraged lease between the owner trustee, the lenders, the equity participant and the lessee which specificize the rights and obligations of each.

Financing statement—The document which must be filed to perfect a security interest in property. (See UCC Sections 2A-309 and 9-302.)

Fixed asset—See Assets, fixed.

Fixed price purchase option—The lessee's option to purchase the equipment at a predetermined fixed price.

Floating interest payments—This is tied to some money benchmark, such as the prime rate, or Treasury bills or notes where the agreement allows for the interest payments to float up or down as changes occur.

Full-payout lease—The lessee's total payments returns to the lessor his original investment and costs plus interest over the lease term, and the lessee has the option to purchase the leased equipment at a nominal amount ($1.00).

Full service lease—Are true leases where the lessor owns the equipment at the end of the lease. The lessor provides repair and maintenance, insurance and pays the property taxes on the leased equipment.

Future value—The value of an investment at a specified time in the future increasing at a certain or floating rate of interest.

Goodwill—The intangible asset of an entity. The difference between the purchase price and the book value of assets.

Grandfather lease—A lease which qualifies for tax treatment under a prior law by a transitional rule for a limited time. The safe harbor leases created by the ERTA in 1981, was repealed by TEFRA of 1982, with a grandfather clause (P.L. 97-248, Section 209).

Gross lease—The opposite of a net lease. Maintenance, insurance and property tax are paid for by the lessor.

Guideline lease—Internal Revenue procedure 75-21 sets forth the guideline for "leveraged lease" transactions (Section 4).

Hedge—To protect oneself from losing by a counterbalancing transaction. To buy or sell futures as a protection against loss due to price fluctuation.

Hell-or-High-Water clause—A clause in a lease whereby the lessee is unconditionally obligated to pay rent over the entire term of the lease, regardless of what occurs to the equipment or any change in the circumstances of the lessee.

Inception of the lease—The date of the lease agreement or commitment. For purposes of this definition, a commitment shall be in writing, signed by the parties to the transaction, and shall specifically set forth the principal provisions of the transaction [FAS 23(6)].

Income statement—A document which presents the net results from its operations for a specified period of time.

Incremental borrowing rate—The interest rate a person would expect to pay to borrow an additional amount for a similar term.

Indemnity agreement—A provision in a lease agreement whereby the lessee indemnifies the lessor from loss of tax benefits.

Indenture trust—An agreement whereby the owner trustee mortgages the equipment and assigns the lease and rental payments under the lease as security for amounts due the lenders. Same as mortgage or security agreement.

Indenture trustee—In some leveraged leases there is a separate indenture trustee in addition to an owner trustee. The indenture trustee holds the security interest for the benefit of the lenders. The indenture trustee receives the rent or lease payments, paying the lenders the amount due and pays the balance to the owner trustee.

Independent lessor—A non-captive leasing company. Brokers without funds to invest in leases sometimes call themselves independent lessors rather than brokers.

Initial direct costs—Costs incurred by a lessor in negotiating and consummating a lease transaction. Included, but not limited, to commissions, legal fees, costs for credit checks, documents, salaries, etc.

Initial lease term—The initial period, exclusive of renewals, for which the equipment is leased.

Inspection—(1) The lessee's right to inspect the leased goods prior to acceptance. (2) The lessor's right to inspect leased equipment on the lessee's premises to determine its condition.

Installment lease contract—A lease contract that authorizes or requires the delivery of goods in separate lots, to be separately accepted.

Insured value—A schedule included in a lease contract which states the agreed value of the leased equipment at various times during the lease term thus establishing the lessee's liability to the lessor in event the equipment is lost or rendered unusable during the lease term. This is also known as casualty value.

Interest—The charge to use someone else's money.

International lease— See cross-border leasing.

IRC—Internal Revenue Code

IRR—Internal Rate of Return

IRS—Internal Revenue Service

ITC—Investment Tax Credit. Repealed effective December 31, 1985. Under transition rules, transition property must be place in service by specified dates, the last being December 31, 1990, for property with a useful life of 20 years.

Lease—An agreement whereby one party transfers the right to possession and use of property for a specified period of time for some consideration, usually a fee at a determined rate.

Lease intended as security—A lease whereby the lessee is considered the owner of the property for federal tax purposes. A conditional sale or installment purchase are examples of this.

Lease line—Similar to a bank line of credit which permits the lessee to add equipment, whenever needed, under the same basic terms and conditions without the need to negotiate a new lease contract.

Lease rate—The periodic rental charge to a lessee for the use of an asset. Usually refers to the monthly or quarterly or semiannual lease rental basis stated as a percentage of the original asset costs.

Lease term—(Per FAS 98, ¶22) A lease term is the fixed noncancellable term of the lease plus all fixed-rate renewal options reasonably assured to be exercised.

Lease with purchase option—A provision allowing the lessee at his option, to purchase the leased equipment at specific times during the lease term.

Lessee—The A person who acquires the right to possession and use of property under a lease.

Lessee's incremental borrowing rate—(Per FAS 13,¶5,1) The rate that, at the inception of the lease, the lessee would have incurred to borrow over a similar term the funds necessary to purchase the leased asset.

Lessor—A person who transfers the right to possession and use to property under a lease.

Level of payments—Equal payment over the term of the lease.

Leverage—The amount borrowed. The debt portion of the funds, used to purchase the asset, represents leverage of the equity holder.

Leveraged lease—A true lease or a finance lease where the lessor provides 20 to 40% of the equipment cost, and long-term lenders provide the balance on a nonrecourse debt basis. A leveraged lease is a true lease or a finance lease which meets the criteria of a direct financing lease plus all of these characteristics:

1. It involves at lease parties: a lessee; a lessor; and, a long-term lender.
2. The financing provided by the long-term lender is nonrecourse as to the general credit of the lessor.
3. The lessor's net investment declines during the early years and increases during the later years of the lease term.
4. Any investment credit retained by the lessor is accounted for as one of the cash flow components of the lessee.

Liability—An obligation according to law or equity, as an obligation to pay or perform a service.

Lien—[Per UCC Section 2A-103(r)] A charge against or interest in goods to secure payment of a debt or performance of an obligation, but the term does not include a security interest.

Limited-use property—Same as Special-purpose property.

Line of credit—A fixed limit of credit (the amount and conditions) that a financial institution or business will provide to a customer for a specified period of time.

Liquid asset—Those assets which can be quickly and easily converted to cash without significant loss in value.

Liquidation—The process of selling assets of an entity to pay off its creditors.

Loan participant—The lender(s) in a leveraged lease transaction.

Loan balance—The amount outstanding on a loan on equipment financed at any given time during the term of the loan.

MACRS (Modified Acceleration Cost Recovery System)—The new ACRS deductions for tax depreciation authorized by the Tax Reform Act of 1986 and is contained in the Internal Revenue Code of 1986 under Section 168. Also called Modified Accelerated Cost Recovery System.

Market value—The price at which property can be sold.

Master lease—A lease which permits a lessee to add equipment to a lease contract under the same terms and conditions without negotiating a new lease contract.

Merchant lessee—A lessee that is a merchant with respect to goods of the kind subject to the lease.

Middle market—That segment of the leasing market generally represented by financing under $2 million and dominated by singled investor leases.

Mortgage—[Per UCC Section 9-105(1)(j)] A consensual interest created by a real estate mortgage, a trust deed on real estate, or the like.

Modified Acceleration Cost Recovery System—See MACRS.

Net assets—Total assets less total liabilities.

Net delivered price or value—This includes the list price, transportation costs and taxes of the goods delivered.

Net lease—The rentals payable are net to the lessor. All costs in connection with the use of the equipment are paid for by the lessee and are not part of the payments to the lessor. These costs include maintenance, insurance and property taxes, and assumes risks of ownership.

Net-Net lease—Same as a net lease with the addition of requirement to returning the equipment having a pre-determined value, and is responsible for any variation between the actual resale value from the present value.

Net working capital—That amount remaining from the current assets over the current liabilities.

Net worth—Owner's equity. Same as net assets.

Nominal rate—The stated annual rate which when subdivided into compounding periods gives a higher effective rate.

Non-recourse loan—In a leveraged lease, the lenders cannot look to the lessor for repayment of the loan. They have recourse against the lessee.

Non-tax-oriented lease—A lease which does not meet the guidelines set by the IRS for a true lease.

Offering circular—This is a prospectus which contains a complete description of the terms of the lease being offered.

Open-end lease—A conditional sale lease in which the lessee guarantees that the lessor will realize a minimum value from the sale of the asset at the end of the lease term. The lease is called "open-end lease" because the lessee does not know his liability until a sale is consummated.

Operating lease—Also called a "true lease" or a "tax lease." It is generally used in short-term leasing where the lessee uses the asset for a fraction of that asset's useful life. In this type of lease, the lessor provides the maintenance, insurance, payment of property taxes, etc.

Optimum service life—The time during which maximum utilization of an asset can be obtained at the least cost.

Owner participant—Also known as the equity participant. This is a beneficial owner of the equipment, usually under an owner trust of the equipment of the lease with the legal title to the equipment held by an owner trustee.

Owner trustee—The owner trustee represents the owner participant (equity participant) and acts for them as the lessor of the lease transaction. The owner trustee is usually indemnified by the owner participant(s) against normal costs of the lease transaction.

Packager—This is the leasing company, investment banker, or broker, who arranges a leveraged lease.

Participation agreement—An agreement between the owner trustee, the equity participants, lenders, the supplier (manufacturer or dealer) and the lessee which spells out all the obligations of all parties entering a leveraged lease transaction.

Payback method—An analytical method of determining the amount of time that is required to recover the initial investment.

Payment stream—A series of payments as in a lease, the monthly rentals.

Payout lease—A lease transaction whereby the lessor expects to recover the investment, plus interest from rental payments cash flow from tax benefits and from residual disposition.

Performance bond—A bond (insurance) issued to protect one party against any loss due to default by another during the life of a contract.

Present value—The value today (present) of an amount of money to receive or pay in the future. The present value varies depending upon the discount rate applied.

Prime rate of interest—This is the simple interest rate that banks charge their "good" customers for short-term loans.

Principal—The actual sum upon which interest accrues. This is sometimes called capital. Any income, interest, or premium earned is NOT to be confused with principal.

Purchase option—A provision whereby the lessee can exercise his/her right to purchase the leased equipment at the end of the lease. The purchase price may be at a predetermined amount or at a fair market value.

Put option—In a lease agreement, the lessor negotiates an option to sell the leased equipment to the lessee or to a third part at a predetermined price at the end of the lease term.

Recovery property—Recovery property is property for which depreciation is allowed under the Internal Revenue Code Section 167. They can be tangible or intangible, real or personal, such as: buildings, machinery, vehicles, patents, copyrights, furniture and equipment.

Refinancing—Repaying an existing debt by entering a new loan agreement; the object being to lengthen the maturity date or obtaining a lower interest rate.

Related persons—[Per FAS 13 ¶5(a)] In leasing transactions, related persons include a parent company and its subsidiaries, an owner company and its joint ventures (corporate or otherwise) and partnerships, and an investor and investees, provided the parent company, owner or investor has the ability to exercise significant influence over operating and financial policies.

Renewal option—That provision in a lease agreement which provides for the lessee to have the option to renew the lease for a fair rental value.

Rent—The fee paid to lease (use and possess) another person's property. There is no legal difference between the terms "rent" or "lease."

Rental—The payment for the use, not ownership, of an asset.

Right of first refusal—When a lease contains a "right of first refusal," the lessor has the right to continue to own the equipment at the end of the lease and is not obligated to sell the equipment. However, if the lessor offers to sell the equipment at a stated price, the lessee has the first right to purchase the equipment or refuse the offer.

Required rate of return—The minimum future receipts that a company will accept when evaluating the acceptance of an investment proposal.

Residual risk—The "gamble" taken by the lessor or the lessee as to the loss or profit realized as to the value of the leased equipment at the end of the lease term.

Residual value—The value of the leased equipment when the lease term ends. For tax purposes, Internal Revenue Procedure 75-21, Section 4(1)(C) states the lessor must represent and demonstrate the 20% of the original cost of the property is a reasonable estimate of what the fair market value of the property at the end of the lease term.

Revenue procedures—The rulings and determination letters in regarding the interpretation or application of the Federal tax laws (other than those under the jurisdiction of the Alcohol, Tobacco and Firearms Division). Rev. Proc. 72-3 describes the procedure of the IRS in issuing rulings, determination, opinion, and information letters to taxpayers. Rev. Proc. 75-21, 75-28 and 76-30 concerns advance rulings on leveraged lease transactions.

Revenue ruling—This is a written statement issued to a taxpayer that interprets and applies the tax laws to a specific set of facts.

Risk—The uncertainty about the future.

Safe-harbor lease—Authorized by the Economic Recovery Tax Act of 1981, safe-harbor leases did not have to be a true lease, but the lessor could claim ITC and tax depreciation. Except for leases of mass-commuting vehicles, including transit buses, safe-harbor leases were repealed by the Tax Equity and Fiscal Responsibility Act of 1982, effective December 31, 1983.

Sale-and-leaseback—One transaction where the property of an owner is sold to another, and executing another transaction whereby that original owner leases the property for continuing use.

Sales type lease—Same as a direct financing lease except that the transaction gives rise to a manufacturer or dealer profits.

Section 38 property (per IRS)—Section 38 property means tangible personal property used as an integral part of manufacturing, production or of furnishing transportation (used in business or trade).

Security agreement—(Per UCC Section 9-105) Security agreement means an agreement which creates or provides for a security interest.

Security interest—Security interest means an interest in personal property or fixtures which secures payment or performance of an obligation. A lease does not create a security interest unless intended as security. For example, the consideration the lessee is to pay the lessor, for the right to possession and use of the property, is an obligation for the term of the lease not subject to termination by the lessee.

Selling price—The cost of property when acquired which may include freight, taxes, etc., but not interest or finance charges.

Sinking fund—A reserve fund established to repay a debt due at a future date.

Skip payment agreement—A financial scheduling where payments are set with seasonable business cycles.

Special purpose property—Also known as limited-use property. Unique property valuable to the lessee only and not valuable to anyone else except as scrap.

Sub-lease—A lease of property re-leased by the original lessee who becomes the lessor under an existing lease.

Straight-line depreciation—Depreciation of the depreciable amount of an asset divided by the estimated useful life. The amounts depreciated each year will be of equal amounts.

Tax benefit transfer lease—Authorized by the ERTA of 1981 and repealed by TEFRA of 1982 for all leveraged safe-harbor leases, but continued for mass-commuting transit vehicles such as buses.

Tax lease—Another name for a true lease or operating lease.

Tax title—The tax title held by either the lessor or lessee under the safe-harbor lease for tax purposes and the legal title held by the other party.

TEFRA—Tax Equity and Fiscal Responsibility Act of 1982.

Termination value—Leases can contain provisions which permit a lessee to terminate the lease during the lease term in event the equipment becomes obsolete and/or becomes surplus to the lessee's needs. The liability of the lessee is set forth in a "termination schedule" in the lease setting the value on the equipment at various times during the lease term. If the equipment is sold at a lower than termination value price, the lessee pays the difference. If sold at higher price, the lessor retains the excess.

TRA—Tax Reform Act of 1986

TRAC lease—A tax-oriented lease of motor vehicles or trailers which contains a "terminal rental adjustment clause."

True lease—[Per FAS 13 ¶6(a)] Leases that do not meet the criteria for capital leases are operating or true leases. Per IRS Ruling 55-540, under a true lease, the lessee deducts all rental payments and the lessor has the benefits of ownership.

Trustee—A bank or trust company that holds title to or a security interest in the leased property in trust lessee, lessor, and/or creditors of the lessor. Under a leveraged lease there can be one trustee performing all functions or there can be two trustees: the owner trustee and the indenture trustee, who divide the various functions.

Trustor owner—The lessor(s) under a leveraged lease transaction holding trust certificates as evidence of their interest as owners of the equipment. Also known as owner participants, grant owner, or equity participant.

UCC—The Uniform Commercial Code, prepared under the joint sponsorship of The American Law Institute and the National

Conference of Commissioners on Uniform State Laws, provides a comprehensive modernization of various statute relating to commercial transactions.

Useful life—The period of time during which an asset will be economically usable (profitable).

Vendor lease—A lease offered by a manufacturer or dealer to its customers as a means of financing their products.

Vendor leasing—A vendor lease offered through a captive leasing subsidiary or other third-party leasing company as a financing source to its customers. The leasing companies serve as an extension to the manufacturer's or dealer's leasing to their customers.

Yield—The interest rate earned by a lessor or lender in a lease that is measured by the rate at which the excess cash flows permit recovery of the investment.

APPENDIX

Factor Tables

The following tables are "multipliers" used to facilitate the calculations in the handling of money, whether to purchase or lease, borrow, or invest.

All factors have the basic bracket expression, $(1 + i)^n$, in all formulae, so the author calculated the compound-amount factor table to the 9th decimal. The other factor tables are only to the 6th decimal, which is sufficient for everyday calculation needs. If a more exacing determination is desired, the use of the 9th decimal of the compound-amount factors are recommended to obtain a more accurate factor number.

NOTE: The "n" column denotes the total number of interest compounding periods.

NOTE: The percentage columns denote the percentage rate of interest per compounding period. Thus, interest compounded quarterly for five years would be represented by 20 compounding periods (4 quarters per year × 5 years). If compounded monthly for five years would be indicated by 60 (12 × 5) under the "n" column.

NOTE: The annual interest percentage rate would be divided by the compounding periods per year to arrive at the interest rate per compounding period. Thus, 12% compounded quarterly would give 3% as the quarterly interest rate (12 * 4 = 3). For monthly compounding periods, the monthly rate would be 1% (12 * 12 = 1).

For more information concerning the factor tables see pages 55–57.

Table I Compound-Amount Factor (Compound-Interest Factor; Future Value Factor) $(1 + i)^n$

n	*0.0025 (¼%)*	*0.0050 (½%)*	*0.0075 (¾%)*	*0.01 (1%)*	*0.0125 (1¼%)*	*0.0150 (1½%)*
1	1.002500000	1.005000000	1.007500000	1.010000000	1.012500000	1.015000000
2	1.005006250	1.010025000	1.015056250	1.020100000	1.025156250	1.030225000
3	1.007518766	1.015075125	1.022669172	1.030301000	1.037970703	1.045678375
4	1.010037563	1.020150501	1.030339191	1.040604010	1.050945337	1.061363551
5	1.012562656	1.025251253	1.038066735	1.051010050	1.064082154	1.077284004
6	1.015094063	1.030377509	1.045852235	1.061520151	1.077383181	1.093443264
7	1.017631798	1.035529397	1.053696127	1.072135352	1.090850470	1.109844913
8	1.020175878	1.040707044	1.061598848	1.082856706	1.104486101	1.126492587
9	1.022726317	1.045910579	1.069560839	1.093685273	1.118292177	1.143389975
10	1.025283133	1.051140132	1.077582545	1.104622125	1.132270830	1.160540825
11	1.027846341	1.056395833	1.085664415	1.115668347	1.146424215	1.177948937
12	1.030415957	1.061677812	1.093806898	1.126825030	1.160754518	1.195618171
13	1.032991997	1.066986201	1.102010449	1.138093280	1.175263949	1.213552444
14	1.035574477	1.072321132	1.110275528	1.149474213	1.189954749	1.231755731
15	1.038163413	1.077682738	1.118602594	1.160968955	1.204829183	1.250232067
16	1.040758822	1.083071151	1.126992114	1.172578645	1.219889548	1.268985548
17	1.043360719	1.088486507	1.135444555	1.184304431	1.235138167	1.288020331
18	1.045969120	1.093928940	1.143960389	1.196147476	1.250577394	1.307340636
19	1.048584043	1.099398584	1.152540092	1.208108950	1.266209612	1.326950745
20	1.051205503	1.104895577	1.161184142	1.220190040	1.282037232	1.346855007
21	1.053833517	1.110420055	1.169893023	1.232391940	1.298062697	1.367057832
22	1.056468101	1.115972155	1.178667221	1.244715860	1.314288481	1.387563699
23	1.059109271	1.121552016	1.187507225	1.257163018	1.330717087	1.408377155
24	1.061757044	1.127159776	1.196413529	1.269734649	1.347351050	1.429502812
25	1.064411437	1.132795575	1.205386631	1.282431995	1.364192939	1.450945354
26	1.067072465	1.138459553	1.214427031	1.295256315	1.381245350	1.472709534
27	1.069740147	1.144151851	1.223535233	1.308208878	1.398510917	1.494800177
28	1.072414497	1.149872610	1.232711748	1.321290967	1.415992304	1.517222180
29	1.075095533	1.155621973	1.241957086	1.334503877	1.433692207	1.539980513
30	1.077783272	1.161400083	1.251271764	1.347848915	1.451613360	1.563080220
31	1.080477730	1.167207083	1.260656302	1.361327404	1.469758527	1.586526424
32	1.083178925	1.173043119	1.270111224	1.374940679	1.488130509	1.610324320
33	1.085886872	1.178908334	1.279637058	1.388690085	1.506732140	1.634479185
34	1.088601589	1.184802876	1.289234336	1.402576986	1.525566292	1.658996373
35	1.091323093	1.190726890	1.298903594	1.416602756	1.544635870	1.683881318
36	1.094051401	1.196680525	1.308645371	1.430768784	1.563943819	1.709139538
37	1.096786529	1.202663927	1.318460211	1.445076471	1.583493116	1.734776631
38	1.099528496	1.208677247	1.328348663	1.459527236	1.603286780	1.760798281
39	1.102277317	1.214720633	1.338311278	1.474122509	1.623327865	1.787210255
40	1.105033010	1.220794236	1.348348612	1.488863734	1.643619463	1.814018409
41	1.107795593	1.226898208	1.358461227	1.503752371	1.664164707	1.841228685
42	1.110565082	1.233032699	1.368649686	1.518789895	1.684966766	1.868847115
43	1.113341494	1.239197862	1.378914559	1.533977794	1.706028850	1.896879822
44	1.116124848	1.245393852	1.389256418	1.549317572	1.727354211	1.925333019
45	1.118915160	1.251620821	1.399675841	1.564810747	1.748946138	1.954213014
46	1.121712448	1.257878925	1.410173410	1.580458855	1.770807965	1.983526210
47	1.124516729	1.264168319	1.420749710	1.596263443	1.792943065	2.013279103
48	1.127328021	1.270489161	1.431405333	1.612226078	1.815354853	2.043478289
49	1.130146341	1.276841607	1.442140873	1.628348338	1.838046789	2.074130464
50	1.132971707	1.283225815	1.452956930	1.644631822	1.861022374	2.105242421
51	1.135804136	1.289641944	1.463854107	1.661078140	1.884285153	2.136821057
52	1.138643647	1.296090154	1.474833013	1.677688921	1.907838718	2.168873373
53	1.141490256	1.302570604	1.485894260	1.694465811	1.931686702	2.201406473
54	1.144343981	1.309083458	1.497038467	1.711410469	1.955832785	2.234427570
55	1.147204841	1.315628875	1.508266256	1.728524573	1.980280695	2.267943984
56	1.150072853	1.322207019	1.519578253	1.745809819	2.005034204	2.301963144
57	1.152948035	1.328818054	1.530975090	1.763267917	2.030097131	2.336492591
58	1.155830406	1.335462145	1.542457403	1.780900597	2.055473346	2.371539980
59	1.158719982	1.342139455	1.554025833	1.798709603	2.081166762	2.407113079
60	1.161616782	1.348850153	1.565681027	1.816696699	2.107181347	2.443219776

Table I Compound-Amount Factor (Compound-Interest Factor; Future Value Factor)(continued) $(1 + i)^n$

n	0.0025 (¼%)	0.0050 (½%)	0.0075 (¾%)	0.01 (1%)	0.0125 (1¼%)	0.0150 (1½%)
61	1.164520824	1.355594403	1.577423635	1.834863666	2.133521114	2.479868072
62	1.167432126	1.362372375	1.589254312	1.853212302	2.160190128	2.517066093
63	1.170350706	1.369184237	1.601173719	1.871744425	2.187192504	2.554822085
64	1.173276583	1.376030158	1.613182522	1.890461869	2.214532411	2.593144416
65	1.176209774	1.382910309	1.625281391	1.909366488	2.242214066	2.632041582
66	1.179150299	1.389824861	1.637471001	1.928460153	2.270241742	2.671522206
67	1.182098174	1.396773985	1.649752034	1.947744755	2.298619763	2.711595039
68	1.185053420	1.403757855	1.662125174	1.967222202	2.327352510	2.752268965
69	1.188016053	1.410776644	1.674591113	1.986894424	2.356444417	2.793552999
70	1.190986093	1.417830527	1.687150546	2.006763368	2.385899972	2.835456294
71	1.193963559	1.424919680	1.699804176	2.026831002	2.415723722	2.877988139
72	1.196948468	1.432044278	1.712552707	2.047099312	2.445920268	2.921157961
73	1.199940839	1.439204500	1.725396852	2.067570305	2.476494271	2.964975330
74	1.202940691	1.446400522	1.738337329	2.088246008	2.507450450	3.009449960
75	1.205948043	1.453632525	1.751374858	2.109128468	2.538793581	3.054591709
76	1.208962913	1.460900688	1.764510170	2.130219753	2.570528500	3.100410585
77	1.211985320	1.468205191	1.777743996	2.151521951	2.602660107	3.146916744
78	1.215015283	1.475546217	1.791077076	2.173037170	2.635193358	3.194120495
79	1.218052821	1.482923948	1.804510154	2.194767542	2.668133275	3.242032302
80	1.221097953	1.490338568	1.818043980	2.216715217	2.701484941	3.290662787
81	1.224150698	1.497790261	1.831679310	2.238882369	2.735253503	3.340022729
82	1.227211075	1.505279212	1.845416905	2.261271193	2.769444171	3.390123070
83	1.230279103	1.512805608	1.859257532	2.283883905	2.804062223	3.440974916
84	1.233354801	1.520369636	1.873201963	2.306722744	2.839113001	3.492589540
85	1.236438188	1.527971484	1.887250978	2.329789971	2.874601914	3.544978383
86	1.239529283	1.535611342	1.901405360	2.353087871	2.910534438	3.598153058
87	1.242628106	1.543289398	1.915665901	2.376618750	2.946916118	3.652125354
88	1.245734676	1.551005845	1.930033395	2.400384937	2.983752570	3.706907235
89	1.248849013	1.558760875	1.944508645	2.424388787	3.021049477	3.762510843
90	1.251971136	1.566554679	1.959092460	2.448632675	3.058812595	3.818948506
91	1.255101064	1.574387452	1.973785654	2.473119001	3.097047753	3.876232733
92	1.258238816	1.582259390	1.988589046	2.497850191	3.135760850	3.934376224
93	1.261384413	1.590170687	2.003503464	2.522828693	3.174957860	3.993391868
94	1.264537874	1.598121540	2.018529740	2.548056980	3.214644833	4.053292746
95	1.267699219	1.606112148	2.033668713	2.573537550	3.254827894	4.114092137
96	1.270868467	1.614142708	2.048921228	2.599272926	3.295513243	4.175803519
97	1.274045638	1.622213422	2.064288137	2.625265655	3.336707158	4.238440572
98	1.277230752	1.630324489	2.079770298	2.651518311	3.378415998	4.302017180
99	1.280423829	1.638476112	2.095368576	2.678033494	3.420646197	4.366547438
100	1.283624889	1.646668492	2.111083840	2.704813829	3.463404275	4.432045650
101	1.286833951	1.654901835	2.126916969	2.731861968	3.506696828	4.498526334
102	1.290051036	1.663176344	2.142868846	2.759180587	3.550530539	4.566004229
103	1.293276163	1.671492225	2.158940362	2.786772393	3.594912170	4.634494293
104	1.296509354	1.679849687	2.175132415	2.814640117	3.639848573	4.704011707
105	1.299750627	1.688248935	2.191445908	2.842786518	3.685346680	4.774571883
106	1.303000004	1.696690180	2.207881753	2.871214384	3.731413513	4.846190461
107	1.306257504	1.705173631	2.224440866	2.899926527	3.778056182	4.918883318
108	1.309523148	1.713699499	2.241124172	2.928925793	3.825281884	4.992666568
109	1.312796955	1.722267996	2.257932604	2.958215051	3.873097908	5.067556566
110	1.316078948	1.730879336	2.274867098	2.987797201	3.921511632	5.143569915
111	1.319369145	1.739533733	2.291928601	3.017675173	3.970530527	5.220723463
112	1.322667568	1.748231402	2.309118066	3.047851925	4.020162159	5.299034315
113	1.325974237	1.756972559	2.326436451	3.078330444	4.070414186	5.378519830
114	1.329289173	1.765757421	2.343884725	3.109113749	4.121294363	5.459197627
115	1.332612395	1.774586208	2.361463860	3.140204886	4.172810543	5.541085592
116	1.335943926	1.783459140	2.379174839	3.171606935	4.224970674	5.624201876
117	1.339283786	1.792376435	2.397018650	3.203323004	4.277782808	5.708564904
118	1.342631996	1.801338317	2.414996290	3.235356234	4.331255093	5.794193377
119	1.345988576	1.810345009	2.433108762	3.267709797	4.385395782	5.881106278
120	1.349353547	1.819396734	2.451357078	3.300386895	4.440213229	5.969322872

Table I Compound-Amount Factor (Compound-Interest Factor; Future Value Factor)(continued) $(1 + i)^n$

n	*0.0175 (1¾%)*	*0.02 (2%)*	*0.0225 (2¼%)*	*0.025 (2½%)*	*0.0275 (2¾%)*	*0.03 (3%)*
1	1.017500000	1.020000000	1.022500000	1.025000000	1.027500000	1.030000000
2	1.035306250	1.040400000	1.045506250	1.050625000	1.055756250	1.060900000
3	1.053424109	1.061208000	1.069030141	1.076890625	1.084789547	1.092727000
4	1.071859031	1.082432160	1.093083319	1.103812891	1.114621259	1.125508810
5	1.090616564	1.104080803	1.117677693	1.131408213	1.145273344	1.159274074
6	1.109702354	1.126162419	1.142825442	1.159693418	1.176768361	1.194052297
7	1.129122145	1.148685668	1.168539014	1.188685754	1.209129491	1.229873865
8	1.148881783	1.171659381	1.194831142	1.218402898	1.242380552	1.266770081
9	1.168987214	1.195092569	1.221714843	1.248862970	1.276546017	1.304773184
10	1.189444490	1.218994420	1.249203426	1.280084544	1.311651033	1.343916379
11	1.210259769	1.243374308	1.277310504	1.312086658	1.347721436	1.384233871
12	1.231439315	1.268241795	1.306049990	1.344888824	1.384783775	1.425760887
13	1.252989503	1.293606630	1.335436115	1.378511045	1.422865329	1.468533713
14	1.274916819	1.319478763	1.365483427	1.412973821	1.461994126	1.512589725
15	1.297227864	1.345868338	1.396206804	1.448298166	1.502198964	1.557967417
16	1.319929351	1.372785705	1.427621457	1.484505621	1.543509436	1.604706439
17	1.343028115	1.400241419	1.459742940	1.521618261	1.585955945	1.652847632
18	1.366531107	1.428246248	1.492587156	1.559658718	1.629569734	1.702433061
19	1.390445401	1.456811173	1.526170367	1.598650186	1.674382901	1.753506053
20	1.414778196	1.485947396	1.560509201	1.638616440	1.720428431	1.806111235
21	1.439536814	1.515666344	1.595620658	1.679581851	1.767740213	1.860294572
22	1.464728708	1.545979671	1.631522122	1.721571398	1.816353069	1.916103409
23	1.490361461	1.576899264	1.668231370	1.764610683	1.866302778	1.973586511
24	1.516442786	1.608437249	1.705766576	1.808725950	1.917626105	2.032794106
25	1.542980535	1.640605994	1.744146324	1.853944098	1.970360823	2.093777930
26	1.569982695	1.673418114	1.783389616	1.900292701	2.024545745	2.156591268
27	1.597457392	1.706886477	1.823515883	1.947800018	2.080220753	2.221289006
28	1.625412896	1.741024206	1.864544990	1.996495019	2.137426824	2.287927676
29	1.653857622	1.775844690	1.906497252	2.046407394	2.196206062	2.356565506
30	1.682800130	1.811361584	1.949393441	2.097567579	2.256601728	2.427262471
31	1.712249132	1.847588816	1.993254793	2.150006769	2.318658276	2.500080345
32	1.742213492	1.884540592	2.038103026	2.203756938	2.382421379	2.575082756
33	1.772702228	1.922231404	2.083960344	2.258850861	2.447937966	2.652335238
34	1.803724517	1.960676032	2.130849452	2.315322133	2.515256260	2.731905296
35	1.835289696	1.999889553	2.178793564	2.373205186	2.584425808	2.813862454
36	1.867407266	2.039887344	2.227816419	2.432535316	2.655497517	2.898278328
37	1.900086893	2.080685091	2.277942289	2.493348699	2.728523699	2.985226678
38	1.933338414	2.122298792	2.329195990	2.555682416	2.803558101	3.074783478
39	1.967171836	2.164744768	2.381602900	2.619574476	2.880655949	3.167026983
40	2.001597343	2.208039664	2.435188965	2.685063838	2.959873987	3.262037792
41	2.036625297	2.252200457	2.489980717	2.752190434	3.041270522	3.359898926
42	2.072266239	2.297244466	2.546005283	2.820995195	3.124905461	3.460695894
43	2.108530899	2.343189355	2.603290402	2.891520075	3.210840361	3.564516770
44	2.145430189	2.390053142	2.661864436	2.963808077	3.299138471	3.671452273
45	2.182975218	2.437854205	2.721756386	3.037903279	3.389864779	3.781595842
46	2.221177284	2.486611289	2.782995905	3.113850861	3.483086061	3.895043717
47	2.260047886	2.536343515	2.845613313	3.191697132	3.578870927	4.011895028
48	2.299598724	2.587070385	2.909639612	3.271489561	3.677289878	4.132251879
49	2.339841702	2.638811793	2.975106503	3.353276800	3.778415349	4.256219436
50	2.380788932	2.691588029	3.042046400	3.437108720	3.882321772	4.383906019
51	2.422452738	2.745419790	3.110492444	3.523036438	3.989085620	4.515423199
52	2.464845661	2.800328185	3.180478524	3.611112349	4.098785475	4.650885895
53	2.507980460	2.856334749	3.252039290	3.701390157	4.211502075	4.790412472
54	2.551870118	2.913461444	3.325210174	3.793924911	4.327318383	4.934124846
55	2.596527845	2.971730673	3.400027403	3.888773034	4.446319638	5.082148592
56	2.641967083	3.031165286	3.476528020	3.985992360	4.568593428	5.234613049
57	2.688201507	3.091788592	3.554749900	4.085642169	4.694229747	5.391651441
58	2.735245033	3.153624364	3.634731773	4.187783223	4.823321065	5.553400984
59	2.783111821	3.216696851	3.716513238	4.292477804	4.955962395	5.720003014
60	2.831816278	3.281030788	3.800134786	4.399789749	5.092251361	5.891603104

Table I **Compound-Amount Factor (Compound-Interest Factor; Future Value Factor)(continued)** $(1 + i)^n$

n	*0.0175 (1¾%)*	*0.02 (2%)*	*0.0225 (2¼%)*	*0.025 (2½%)*	*0.0275 (2¾%)*	*0.03 (3%)*
61	2.881373063	3.346651404	3.885637819	4.509784493	5.232288273	6.068351197
62	2.931797091	3.413584432	3.973064670	4.622529105	5.376176200	6.250401733
63	2.983103540	3.481856121	4.062458625	4.738092332	5.524021046	6.437913785
64	3.035307852	3.551493243	4.153863944	4.856544641	5.675931625	6.631051199
65	3.088425740	3.622523108	4.247325882	4.977958257	5.832019744	6.829982735
66	3.142473190	3.694973570	4.342890715	5.102407213	5.992400287	7.034882217
67	3.197466471	3.768873042	4.440605756	5.229967394	6.157191295	7.245928683
68	3.253422134	3.844250503	4.540519385	5.360716578	6.326514056	7.463306544
69	3.310357022	3.921135513	4.642681072	5.494734493	6.500493192	7.687205740
70	3.368288269	3.999558223	4.747141396	5.632102855	6.679256755	7.917821912
71	3.427233314	4.079549387	4.853952077	5.772905427	6.862936316	8.155356569
72	3.487209897	4.161140375	4.963165999	5.917228062	7.051667065	8.400017267
73	3.548236070	4.244363183	5.074837234	6.065158764	7.245587909	8.652017785
74	3.610330202	4.329250446	5.189021071	6.216787733	7.444841577	8.911578318
75	3.673510980	4.415835455	5.305774046	6.372207426	7.649574720	9.178925668
76	3.737797422	4.504152164	5.425153962	6.531512612	7.859938025	9.454293438
77	3.803208877	4.594235208	5.547219926	6.694800427	8.076086320	9.737922241
78	3.869765033	4.686119912	5.672032374	6.862170438	8.298178694	10.030059908
79	3.937485921	4.779842310	5.799653103	7.033724699	8.526378608	10.330961705
80	4.006391924	4.875439156	5.930145297	7.209567816	8.760854020	10.640890556
81	4.076503783	4.972947939	6.063573567	7.389807012	9.001777506	10.960117273
82	4.147842599	5.072406898	6.200003972	7.574552187	9.249326387	11.288920791
83	4.220429845	5.173855036	6.339504061	7.763915992	9.503682863	11.627588415
84	4.294287367	5.277332137	6.482142902	7.958013891	9.765034141	11.976416068
85	4.369437396	5.382878779	6.627991118	8.156964239	10.033572580	12.335708550
86	4.445902550	5.490536355	6.777120918	8.360888345	10.309495826	12.705779806
87	4.523705845	5.600347082	6.929606139	8.569910553	10.593006961	13.086953200
88	4.602870697	5.712354024	7.085522277	8.784158317	10.884314653	13.479561796
89	4.683420934	5.826601104	7.244946528	9.003762275	11.183633306	13.883948650
90	4.765380801	5.943133126	7.407957825	9.228856332	11.491183222	14.300467110
91	4.848774965	6.061995789	7.574636876	9.459577740	11.807190760	14.729481123
92	4.933628527	6.183235705	7.745066206	9.696067184	12.131888506	15.171365557
93	5.019967026	6.306900419	7.919330195	9.938468863	12.465515440	15.626506523
94	5.107816449	6.433038427	8.097515125	10.186930585	12.808317115	16.095301719
95	5.197203237	6.561699196	8.279709215	10.441603849	13.160545835	16.578160771
96	5.288154293	6.692933180	8.466002672	10.702643946	13.522460846	17.075505594
97	5.380696993	6.826791843	8.656487732	10.970210044	13.894328519	17.587770761
98	5.474859191	6.963327680	8.851258706	11.244465295	14.276422553	18.115403884
99	5.570669227	7.102594234	9.050412027	11.525576928	14.669024174	18.658866001
100	5.668155938	7.244646118	9.254046298	11.813716351	15.072422338	19.218631981
101	5.767348667	7.389539041	9.462262340	12.109059260	15.486913953	19.795190940
102	5.868277269	7.537329821	9.675163242	12.411785741	15.912804086	20.389046668
103	5.970972121	7.688076418	9.892854415	12.722080385	16.350406199	21.000718069
104	6.075464133	7.841837946	10.115443639	13.040132394	16.800042369	21.630739611
105	6.181784755	7.998674705	10.343041121	13.366135704	17.262043534	22.279661799
106	6.289965989	8.158648199	10.575759547	13.700289097	17.736749731	22.948051653
107	6.400040393	8.321821163	10.813714136	14.042796324	18.224510349	23.636493202
108	6.512041100	8.488257586	11.057022704	14.393866232	18.725684384	24.345587999
109	6.626001819	8.658022738	11.305805715	14.753712888	19.240640704	25.075955639
110	6.741956851	8.831183193	11.560186344	15.122555711	19.769758324	25.828234308
111	6.859941096	9.007806857	11.820290537	15.500619603	20.313426678	26.603081337
112	6.979990065	9.187962994	12.086247074	15.888135093	20.872045911	27.401173777
113	7.102139892	9.371722254	12.358187633	16.285338471	21.446027174	28.223208990
114	7.226427340	9.559156699	12.636246855	16.692471932	22.035792921	29.069905260
115	7.352889818	9.750339833	12.920562409	17.109783731	22.641777226	29.942002418
116	7.481565390	9.945346630	13.211275063	17.537528324	23.264426100	30.840262490
117	7.612492784	10.144253562	13.508528752	17.975966532	23.904197818	31.765470365
118	7.745711408	10.347138633	13.812470649	18.425365695	24.561563258	32.718434476
119	7.881261358	10.554081406	14.123251238	18.885999838	25.237006247	33.699987510
120	8.019183431	10.765163034	14.441024391	19.358149834	25.931023919	34.710987136

Table I Compound-Amount Factor (Compound-Interest Factor; Future Value Factor)(continued) $(1 + i)^n$

n	*0.035 (3½%)*	*0.04 (4%)*	*0.045 (4½%)*	*0.05 (5%)*	*0.055 (5½)*
1	1.035000000	1.040000000	1.045000000	1.050000000	1.055000000
2	1.071225000	1.081600000	1.092025000	1.102500000	1.113025000
3	1.108717875	1.124864000	1.141166125	1.157625000	1.174241375
4	1.147523001	1.169858560	1.192518601	1.215506250	1.238824651
5	1.187686306	1.216652902	1.246181938	1.276281563	1.306960006
6	1.229255326	1.265319018	1.302260125	1.340095641	1.378842807
7	1.272279263	1.315931779	1.360861830	1.407100423	1.454679161
8	1.316809037	1.368569050	1.422100613	1.477455444	1.534686515
9	1.362897353	1.423311812	1.486095140	1.551328216	1.619094273
10	1.410598761	1.480244285	1.552969422	1.628894627	1.708144458
11	1.459969717	1.539454056	1.622853046	1.710339358	1.802092404
12	1.511068657	1.601032219	1.695881433	1.795856326	1.901207486
13	1.563956060	1.665073507	1.772196097	1.885649142	2.005773897
14	1.618694522	1.731676448	1.851944922	1.979931599	2.116091462
15	1.675348831	1.800943506	1.935282443	2.078928179	2.232476492
16	1.733986040	1.872981246	2.022370153	2.182874588	2.355262699
17	1.794675551	1.947900496	2.113376810	2.292018318	2.484802148
18	1.857489196	2.025816515	2.208478766	2.406619234	2.621466266
19	1.922501317	2.106849176	2.307860311	2.526950195	2.765646911
20	1.989788863	2.191123143	2.411714025	2.653297705	2.917757491
21	2.059431474	2.278768069	2.520241156	2.785962590	3.078234153
22	2.131511575	2.369918792	2.633652008	2.925260720	3.247537031
23	2.206114480	2.464715543	2.752166348	3.071523756	3.426151568
24	2.283328487	2.563304165	2.876013834	3.225099944	3.614589904
25	2.363244984	2.665836331	3.005434457	3.386354941	3.813392349
26	2.445958559	2.772469785	3.140679007	3.555672688	4.023128928
27	2.531567108	2.883368576	3.282009562	3.733456322	4.244401019
28	2.620171957	2.998703319	3.429699993	3.920129138	4.477843075
29	2.711877976	3.118651452	3.584036492	4.116135595	4.724124444
30	2.806793705	3.243397510	3.745318135	4.321942375	4.983951288
31	2.905031484	3.373133410	3.913857451	4.538039494	5.258068609
32	3.006707586	3.508058747	4.089981036	4.764941469	5.547262383
33	3.111942352	3.648381097	4.274030182	5.003188542	5.852361814
34	3.220860334	3.794316341	4.466361541	5.253347969	6.174241714
35	3.333590446	3.946088994	4.667347810	5.516015368	6.513825008
36	3.450266111	4.103932554	4.877378461	5.791816136	6.872085383
37	3.571025425	4.268089856	5.096860492	6.081406943	7.250050079
38	3.696011315	4.438813450	5.326219214	6.385477290	7.648802834
39	3.825371711	4.616365988	5.565899079	6.704751154	8.069486990
40	3.959259721	4.801020628	5.816364538	7.039988712	8.513308774
41	4.097833811	4.993061453	6.078100942	7.391988148	8.981540757
42	4.241257995	5.192783911	6.351615484	7.761587555	9.475525498
43	4.389702025	5.400495268	6.637438181	8.149666933	9.996679401
44	4.543341595	5.616515078	6.936122899	8.557150280	10.546496768
45	4.702358551	5.841175681	7.248248430	8.985007793	11.126554090
46	4.866941101	6.074822709	7.574419609	9.434258183	11.738514565
47	5.037284039	6.317815617	7.915268491	9.905971092	12.384132866
48	5.213588981	6.570528242	8.271455573	10.401269647	13.065260173
49	5.396064595	6.833349371	8.643671074	10.921333129	13.783849483
50	5.584926856	7.106683346	9.032636273	11.467399786	14.541961205
51	5.780399296	7.390950680	9.439104905	12.040769775	15.341769071
52	5.982713271	7.686588707	9.863864626	12.642808264	16.185566370
53	6.192108235	7.994052256	10.307738534	13.274948677	17.075772520
54	6.408832024	8.313814346	10.771586768	13.938696111	18.014940009
55	6.633141145	8.646366920	11.256308172	14.635630916	19.005761709
56	6.865301085	8.992221596	11.762842040	15.367412462	20.051078603
57	7.105586623	9.351910460	12.292169932	16.135783085	21.153887926
58	7.354282154	9.725986879	12.845317579	16.942572240	22.317351762
59	7.611682030	10.115026354	13.423356870	17.789700852	23.54806109
60	7.878090901	10.519627408	14.027407929	18.679185894	24.839770445

Table I Compound-Amount Factor (Compound-Interest Factor; Future Value Factor)(continued) $(1 + i)^n$

n	*0.035 (3½%)*	*0.04 (4%)*	*0.045 (4½%)*	*0.05 (5%)*	*0.055 (5½)*
61	8.153824082	10.940412504	14.658641286	19.613145189	26.205957820
62	8.439207925	11.378029005	15.318280144	20.593802448	27.647285500
63	8.734580203	11.833150165	16.007602750	21.623492571	29.167886202
64	9.040290510	12.306476171	16.727944874	22.704667199	30.772119943
65	9.356700677	12.798735218	17.480702393	23.839900559	32.464586540
66	9.684185201	13.310684627	18.267334001	25.031895587	34.250138800
67	10.023131683	13.843112012	19.089364031	26.283490366	36.133896434
68	10.373941292	14.396836492	19.948385412	27.597664885	38.121260738
69	10.737029237	14.972709952	20.846062756	28.977548129	40.217930078
70	11.112825261	15.571618350	21.784135580	30.426425536	42.429916233
71	11.501774145	16.194483084	22.764421681	31.947746812	44.763561625
72	11.904336240	16.842262408	23.788820656	33.545134153	47.225557515
73	12.320988008	17.515952904	24.859317586	35.222390861	49.822963178
74	12.752222589	18.216591020	25.977986877	36.983510404	52.563226153
75	13.198550379	18.945254661	27.146996287	38.832685924	55.454203591
76	13.660499642	19.703064847	28.368611120	40.774320220	58.504184789
77	14.138617130	20.491187441	29.645198620	42.813036231	61.721914952
78	14.633468729	21.310834939	30.979232558	44.953688042	65.116620275
79	15.145640135	22.163268336	32.373298023	47.201372445	68.698034390
80	15.675737540	23.049799070	33.830096434	49.561441067	72.476426281
81	16.224388354	23.971791033	35.352450774	52.039513120	76.462629727
82	16.792241946	24.930662674	36.943311059	54.641488776	80.668074361
83	17.379970414	25.927889181	38.605760056	57.373563215	85.104818451
84	17.988269379	26.965004748	40.343019259	60.242241376	89.785583466
85	18.617858807	28.043604938	42.158455125	63.254353445	94.723790557
86	19.269483865	29.165349136	44.055585606	66.417071117	99.933599037
87	19.943915800	30.331963101	46.038086958	69.737924673	105.429946985
88	20.641952853	31.545241625	48.109800871	73.224820906	111.228594069
89	21.364421203	32.807051290	50.274741911	76.886061952	117.346166742
90	22.112175945	34.119333342	52.537105297	80.730365049	123.800205913
91	22.886102103	35.484106675	54.901275035	84.766883302	130.609217238
92	23.687115677	36.903470942	57.371832412	89.005227467	137.792724187
93	24.516164726	38.379609780	59.953564870	93.455488840	145.371324017
94	25.374230491	39.914794171	62.651475289	98.128263282	153.366746838
95	26.262328558	41.511385938	65.470791677	103.034676446	161.801917914
96	27.181510058	43.171841376	68.416977303	108.186410268	170.701023399
97	28.132862910	44.898715031	71.495741281	113.595730782	180.089579686
98	29.117513112	46.694663632	74.713049639	119.275517321	189.994506569
99	30.136626071	48.562450177	78.075136873	125.239293187	200.444204430
100	31.191407983	50.504948184	81.588518032	131.501257846	211.468635674
101	32.283107263	52.525146112	85.260001343	138.076320739	223.099410636
102	33.413016017	54.626151956	89.096701404	144.980136776	235.369878221
103	34.582471577	56.811198034	93.106052967	152.229143614	248.315221523
104	35.792858082	59.083645956	97.295825351	159.840600795	261.972558707
105	37.045608115	61.446991794	101.674137491	167.832630835	276.381049436
106	38.342204399	63.904871466	106.249473678	176.224262377	291.582007155
107	39.684181553	66.461066324	111.030699994	185.035475495	307.619017548
108	41.073127908	69.119508977	116.027081494	194.287249270	324.538063513
109	42.510687385	71.884289336	121.248300161	204.001611734	342.387657006
110	43.998561443	74.759660910	126.704473668	214.201692320	361.218978142
111	45.538511094	77.750047346	132.406174983	224.911776936	381.086021940
112	47.132358982	80.860049240	138.364452858	236.157365783	402.045753146
113	48.781991546	84.094451210	144.590853236	247.965234072	424.158269569
114	50.489361250	87.458229258	151.097441632	260.363495776	447.486974396
115	52.256488894	90.956558428	157.896826505	273.381670565	472.098757987
116	54.085466005	94.594820766	165.002183698	287.050754093	498.064189677
117	55.978457315	98.378613596	172.427281964	301.403291798	525.457720109
118	57.937703322	102.313758140	180.186509653	316.473456387	554.357894715
119	59.965522938	106.406308466	188.294902587	332.297129207	584.847578924
120	62.064316241	110.662560804	196.768173204	348.911985667	617.014195765

Table I Compound-Amount Factor (Compound-Interest Factor; Future Value Factor)(continued) $(1 + i)^n$

n	*0.06 (6%)*	*0.065 (6½%)*	*0.07 (7%)*	*0.075 (7½%)*	*0.08 (8%)*
1	1.060000000	1.065000000	1.070000000	1.075000000	1.080000000
2	1.123600000	1.134225000	1.144900000	1.155625000	1.166400000
3	1.191016000	1.207949625	1.225043000	1.242296875	1.259712000
4	1.262476960	1.286466351	1.310796010	1.335469141	1.360488960
5	1.338225578	1.370086663	1.402551731	1.435629326	1.469328077
6	1.418519112	1.459142297	1.500730352	1.543301526	1.586874323
7	1.503630259	1.553986546	1.605781476	1.659049140	1.713824269
8	1.593848075	1.654995671	1.718186180	1.783477826	1.850930210
9	1.689478959	1.762570390	1.838459212	1.917238662	1.999004627
10	1.790847697	1.877137465	1.967151357	2.061031562	2.158924997
11	1.898298558	1.999151401	2.104851952	2.215608929	2.331638997
12	2.012196472	2.129096242	2.252191589	2.381779599	2.518170117
13	2.132928260	2.267487497	2.409845000	2.560413069	2.719623726
14	2.260903956	2.414874185	2.578534150	2.752444049	2.937193624
15	2.396558193	2.571841007	2.759031541	2.958877353	3.172169114
16	2.540351685	2.739010672	2.952163749	3.180793154	3.425942643
17	2.692772786	2.917046366	3.158815211	3.419352641	3.700018055
18	2.854339153	3.106654379	3.379932276	3.675804089	3.996019499
19	3.025599502	3.308586914	3.616527535	3.951489396	4.315701059
20	3.207135472	3.523645064	3.869684462	4.247851100	4.660957144
21	3.399563601	3.752681993	4.140562375	4.566439933	5.033833715
22	3.603537417	3.996606322	4.430401741	4.908922928	5.436540413
23	3.819749662	4.256385733	4.740529863	5.277092147	5.871463646
24	4.048934641	4.533050806	5.072366953	5.672874058	6.341180737
25	4.291870720	4.827699108	5.427432640	6.098339613	6.848475196
26	4.549382963	5.141499550	5.807352925	6.555715084	7.396353212
27	4.822345941	5.475697021	6.213867630	7.047393715	7.988061469
28	5.111686697	5.831617327	6.648838364	7.575948244	8.627106386
29	5.418387899	6.210672454	7.114257049	8.144144362	9.317274897
30	5.743491173	6.614366163	7.612255043	8.754955189	10.062656889
31	6.088100643	7.044299964	8.145112896	9.411576828	10.867669440
32	6.453386682	7.502179461	8.715270798	10.117445090	11.737082995
33	6.840589883	7.989821126	9.325339754	10.876253472	12.676049635
34	7.251025276	8.509159499	9.978113537	11.691972482	13.690133606
35	7.686086792	9.062254867	10.676581485	12.568870419	14.785344294
36	8.147252000	9.651301433	11.423942189	13.511535700	15.968171838
37	8.636087120	10.278636026	12.223618142	14.524900877	17.245625585
38	9.154252347	10.946747368	13.079271412	15.614268443	18.625275632
39	9.703507488	11.658285947	13.994820410	16.785338577	20.115297682
40	10.285717937	12.416074534	14.974457839	18.044238970	21.724521497
41	10.902861013	13.223119378	16.022669888	19.397556893	23.462483217
42	11.557032674	14.082622138	17.144256780	20.852373659	25.339481874
43	12.250454635	14.997992577	18.344354755	22.416301684	27.366640424
44	12.985481913	15.972862094	19.628459588	24.097524310	29.555971658
45	13.764610827	17.011098131	21.002451759	25.904838634	31.920449390
46	14.590487477	18.116819509	22.472623382	27.847701531	34.474085342
47	15.465916726	19.294412777	24.045707019	29.936279146	37.232012169
48	16.393871729	20.548549608	25.728906510	32.181500082	40.210573142
49	17.377504033	21.884205332	27.529929965	34.595112588	43.427418994
50	18.420154275	23.306678679	29.457025063	37.189746032	46.901612513
51	19.525363531	24.821612793	31.519016817	39.978976984	50.653741514
52	20.696885343	26.435017624	33.725347995	42.977400258	54.706040835
53	21.938698464	28.153293770	36.086122354	46.200705278	59.082524102
54	23.255020372	29.983257865	38.612150919	49.665758173	63.809126030
55	24.650321594	31.932169626	41.315001483	53.390690036	68.913856113
56	26.129340890	34.007760652	44.207051587	57.394991789	74.426964602
57	27.697101343	36.218265094	47.301545198	61.699616173	80.381121770
58	29.358927424	38.572452325	50.612653362	66.327087386	86.811611512
59	31.120463069	41.079661727	54.155539098	71.301618940	93.756540433
60	32.987690853	43.749839739	57.946426835	76.649240361	101.257063667

Table I Compound-Amount Factor (Compound-Interest Factor; Future Value Factor)(continued) $(1 + i)^n$

n	0.06 (6%)	0.065 (6½%)	0.07 (7%)	0.075 (7½%)	0.08 (8%)
61	34.966952305	46.593579322	62.002676713	82.397933388	109.357628761
62	37.064969443	49.622161978	66.342864083	88.577778392	118.106239061
63	39.288867609	52.847602506	70.986864569	95.221111771	127.554738186
64	41.646199666	56.282696669	75.955945088	102.362695154	137.759117241
65	44.144971646	59.941071953	81.272861245	110.039897291	148.779846621
66	46.793669945	63.837241630	86.961961532	118.292889588	160.682234350
67	49.601290141	67.986662336	93.049298839	127.164856307	173.536813098
68	52.577367550	72.405795387	99.562749758	136.702220530	187.419758146
69	55.732009603	77.112172088	106.532142241	146.954887069	202.413338798
70	59.075930179	82.124463273	113.989392198	157.976503600	218.606405902
71	62.620485990	87.462553386	121.968649651	169.824741370	236.094918374
72	66.377715149	93.147619356	130.506455127	182.561596972	254.982511844
73	70.360378058	99.202214614	139.641906986	196.253716745	275.381112791
74	74.582000742	105.650358564	149.416840475	210.972745501	297.411601814
75	79.056920786	112.517631871	159.876019308	226.795701414	321.204529960
76	83.800336033	119.831277942	171.067340660	243.805379020	346.900892356
77	88.828356195	127.620311009	183.042054506	262.090782446	374.652963745
78	94.158057567	135.915631224	195.854998321	281.747591130	404.625200844
79	99.807541021	144.750147254	209.564848204	302.878660465	436.995216912
80	105.795993482	154.158906825	224.234387578	325.594559999	471.954834265
81	112.143753091	164.179235769	239.930794709	350.014151999	509.711221006
82	118.872378277	174.850886094	256.725950338	376.265213399	550.488118687
83	126.004720973	186.216193690	274.696766862	404.485104404	594.527168182
84	133.565004231	198.320246280	293.925540542	434.821487234	642.089341636
85	141.578904485	211.211062288	314.500328380	467.433098777	693.456488967
86	150.073638754	224.939781337	336.515351367	502.490581185	748.933008084
87	159.078057080	239.560867124	360.071425963	540.177374774	808.847648731
88	168.622740505	255.132323487	385.276425780	580.690677882	873.555460630
89	178.740104935	271.715924513	412.245775585	624.242478724	943.439897480
90	189.464511231	289.377459607	441.102979875	671.060664628	1018.915089278
91	200.832381905	308.186994481	471.980188467	721.390214475	1100.428296421
92	212.882324819	328.219149122	505.018801659	775.494480560	1188.462560134
93	225.655264308	349.553393815	540.370117776	833.656566603	1283.539564945
94	239.194580167	372.274364413	578.196026020	896.180809098	1386.222730141
95	253.546254977	396.472198100	618.669747841	963.394369780	1497.120548552
96	268.759030275	422.242890977	661.976630190	1035.648947514	1616.890192436
97	284.884572092	449.688678890	708.314994303	1113.322618577	1746.241407831
98	301.977646417	478.918443018	757.897043905	1196.821814970	1885.940720457
99	320.096305202	510.048141814	810.949836978	1286.583451093	2036.815978094
100	339.302083514	543.201271032	867.716325566	1383.077209925	2199.761256341
101	359.660208525	578.509353649	928.456468356	1486.808000669	2375.742156849
102	381.239821037	616.112461636	993.448421141	1598.318600720	2565.801529396
103	404.114210299	656.159771643	1062.989810621	1718.192495774	2771.065651748
104	428.361062917	698.810156800	1137.399097364	1847.056932957	2992.750903888
105	454.062726692	744.232816991	1217.017034180	1985.586202928	3232.170976199
106	481.306490294	792.607950096	1302.208226572	2134.505168148	3490.744654295
107	510.184879711	844.127466852	1393.362802432	2294.593055759	3770.004226639
108	540.795972494	898.995752198	1490.898198603	2466.687534941	4071.604564770
109	573.243730844	957.430476090	1595.261072505	2651.689100062	4397.332929951
110	607.638354694	1019.663457036	1706.929347580	2850.565782566	4749.119564347
111	644.096655976	1085.941581744	1826.414401911	3064.358216259	5129.049129495
112	682.742455334	1156.527784557	1954.263410045	3294.185082478	5539.373059855
113	723.707002654	1231.702090553	2091.061848748	3541.248963664	5982.522904643
114	767.129422814	1311.762726439	2237.436178160	3806.842635939	6461.124737015
115	813.157188182	1397.027303658	2394.056710631	4092.355833634	6978.014715976
116	861.946619473	1487.834078395	2561.640680376	4399.282521157	7536.255893254
117	913.663416642	1584.543293491	2740.955528002	4729.228710244	8139.156364714
118	968.483221640	1687.538607568	2932.822414962	5083.920863512	8790.288873891
119	1026.592214939	1797.228617060	3138.119984009	5465.214928275	9493.511983803
120	1088.187747835	1914.048477169	3357.788382890	5875.106047896	10252.992942507

Table I **Compound-Amount Factor (Compound-Interest Factor; Future Value Factor)(continued)** $(1 + i)^n$

n	*0.085 (8½%)*	*0.09 (9%)*	*0.095 (9½%)*
1	1.085000000	1.090000000	1.095000000
2	1.177225000	1.188100000	1.199025000
3	1.277289125	1.295029000	1.312932375
4	1.385858701	1.411581610	1.437660951
5	1.503656690	1.538623955	1.574238741
6	1.631467509	1.677100111	1.723791421
7	1.770142247	1.828039121	1.887551606
8	1.920604338	1.992562642	2.066869009
9	2.083855707	2.171893279	2.263221565
10	2.260983442	2.367363675	2.478227613
11	2.453167034	2.580426405	2.713659237
12	2.661686232	2.812664782	2.971456864
13	2.887929562	3.065804612	3.253745266
14	3.133403575	3.341727027	3.562851067
15	3.399742879	3.642482460	3.901321918
16	3.688721024	3.970305881	4.271947500
17	4.002262311	4.327633410	4.677782513
18	4.342454607	4.717120417	5.122171851
19	4.711563249	5.141661255	5.608778177
20	5.112046125	5.604410768	6.141612104
21	5.546570045	6.108807737	6.725065254
22	6.018028499	6.658600433	7.363946453
23	6.529560921	7.257874472	8.063521366
24	7.084573600	7.911083175	8.829555896
25	7.686762356	8.623080660	9.668363706
26	8.340137156	9.399157920	10.586858258
27	9.049048814	10.245082133	11.592609793
28	9.818217964	11.167139525	12.693907723
29	10.652766490	12.172182082	13.899828957
30	11.558251642	13.267678469	15.220312708
31	12.540703032	14.461769531	16.666242415
32	13.606662789	15.763328789	18.249535444
33	14.763229126	17.182028380	19.983241311
34	16.018103602	18.728410934	21.881649236
35	17.379642408	20.413967919	23.960405913
36	18.856912013	22.251225031	26.236644475
37	20.459749534	24.253835284	28.729125700
38	22.198828245	26.436680460	31.458392642
39	24.085728645	28.815981701	34.446939943
40	26.133015580	31.409420054	37.719399237
41	28.354321905	34.236267859	41.302742165
42	30.764439267	37.317531966	45.226502671
43	33.379416604	40.676109843	49.523020424
44	36.216667016	44.336959729	54.227707365
45	39.295083712	48.327286105	59.379339564
46	42.635165827	52.676741854	65.020376823
47	46.259154923	57.417648621	71.197312621
48	50.191183091	62.585236997	77.961057320
49	54.457433654	68.217908326	85.367357765
50	59.086315514	74.357520076	93.477256753
51	64.108652333	81.049696883	102.357596145
52	69.557887781	88.344169602	112.081567778
53	75.470308243	96.295144866	122.729316717
54	81.885284444	104.961707904	134.388601805
55	88.845533621	114.408261616	147.155518977
56	96.397403979	124.705005161	161.135293280
57	104.591183317	135.928455626	176.443146141
58	113.481433899	148.162016632	193.205245025
59	123.127355781	161.496598129	211.559743302
60	133.593181022	176.031291960	231.657918916

Table I Compound-Amount Factor (Compound-Interest Factor; Future Value Factor)(continued) $(1 + i)^n$

n	*0.085 (8½%)*	*0.09 (9%)*	*0.095 (9½%)*
61	144.948601409	191.874108237	
62	157.269232529	209.142777978	
63	170.637117294	227.965627996	
64	185.141272263	248.482534516	
65	200.878280406	270.845962622	
66	217.952934240	295.222099258	
67	236.478933651	321.792088191	
68	256.579643011	350.753376128	
69	278.388912667	382.321179980	
70	302.051970244	416.730086178	
71	327.726387715	454.235793934	
72	355.583130670	495.117015388	
73	385.807696777	539.677546773	
74	418.601351003	588.248525983	
75	454.182465839	641.190893321	
76	492.787975435	698.898073720	
77	534.674953347	761.798900355	
78	580.122324381	830.360801387	
79	629.432721954	905.093273512	
80	682.934503320	986.551668128	
81	740.983936102	1075.341318259	
82	803.967570671	1172.122036903	
83	872.304814178	1277.613020224	
84	946.450723383	1392.598192044	
85	1026.899034870	1517.932029328	
86	1114.185452834	1654.545911968	
87	1208.891216325	1803.455044045	
88	1311.646969713	1965.765998009	
89	1423.136962138	2142.684937830	
90	1544.103603920	2335.526582234	
91	1675.352410253	2545.723974635	
92	1817.757365125	2774.839132353	
93	1972.266741160	3024.574654264	
94	2139.909414159	3296.786373148	
95	2321.801714363	3593.497146732	
96	2519.154860083	3916.911889937	
97	2733.283023190	4269.433960032	
98	2965.612080162	4653.683016435	
99	3217.689106975	5072.514487914	
100	3491.192681068	5529.040791826	
101	3787.944058959	6026.654463090	
102	4109.919303971	6569.053364768	
103	4459.262444808	7160.268167598	
104	4838.299752617	7804.692302681	
105	5249.555231589	8507.114609923	
106	5695.767426274	9272.754924816	
107	6179.907657508	10107.302868049	
108	6705.199808396	11016.960126173	
109	7275.141792110	12008.486537529	
110	7893.528844439	13089.250325907	
111	8564.478796216	14267.282855238	
112	9292.459493894	15551.338312210	
113	10082.318550876	16950.958760309	
114	10939.315627700	18476.545048736	
115	11869.157456054	20139.434103123	
116	12878.035839819	21951.983172404	
117	13972.668886204	23927.661657920	
118	15160.345741531	26081.151207133	
119	16448.975129561	28428.454815775	
120	17847.138015574	30987.015749195	

Table I Compound-Amount Factor (Compound-Interest Factor; Future Value Factor)(continued) $(1 + i)^n$

n	*0.10 (10%)*	*0.105 (10½%)*	*0.11 (11%)*	*0.115 (11½%)*
1	1.100000000	1.105000000	1.110000000	1.115000000
2	1.210000000	1.221025000	1.232100000	1.243225000
3	1.331000000	1.349232625	1.367631000	1.386195875
4	1.464100000	1.490902051	1.518070410	1.545608401
5	1.610510000	1.647446766	1.685058155	1.723353367
6	1.771561000	1.820428676	1.870414552	1.921539004
7	1.948717100	2.011573687	2.076160153	2.142515989
8	2.143588810	2.222788925	2.304537770	2.388905328
9	2.357947691	2.456181762	2.558036924	2.663629441
10	2.593742460	2.714080847	2.839420986	2.969946827
11	2.853116706	2.999059336	3.151757295	3.311490712
12	3.138428377	3.313960566	3.498450597	3.692312143
13	3.452271214	3.661926425	3.883280163	4.116928040
14	3.797498336	4.046428700	4.310440980	4.590374764
15	4.177248169	4.471303713	4.784589488	5.118267862
16	4.594972986	4.940790603	5.310894332	5.706868667
17	5.054470285	5.459573616	5.895092709	6.363158563
18	5.559917313	6.032828846	6.543552907	7.094921798
19	6.115909045	6.666275875	7.263343726	7.910837805
20	6.727499949	7.366234842	8.062311536	8.820584152
21	7.400249944	8.139689500	8.949165805	9.834951330
22	8.140274939	8.994356898	9.933574044	10.965970733
23	8.954302433	9.938764372	11.026267188	12.227057367
24	9.849732676	10.982334631	12.239156579	13.633168964
25	10.834705943	12.135479767	13.585463803	15.200983395
26	11.918176538	13.409705143	15.079864821	16.949096485
27	13.109994191	14.817724183	16.738649952	18.898242581
28	14.420993611	16.373585222	18.579901446	21.071540478
29	15.863092972	18.092811671	20.623690605	23.494767633
30	17.449402269	19.992556896	22.892296572	26.196665911
31	19.194342496	22.091775370	25.410449195	29.209282491
32	21.113776745	24.411411784	28.205598606	32.568349977
33	23.225154420	26.974610021	31.308214453	36.313710225
34	25.547669862	29.806944074	34.752118043	40.489786900
35	28.102436848	32.936673201	38.574851027	45.146112394
36	30.912680533	36.395023887	42.818084640	50.337915319
37	34.003948586	40.216501396	47.528073951	56.126775581
38	37.404343445	44.439234042	52.756162086	62.581354773
39	41.144777789	49.105353617	58.559339915	69.778210572
40	45.259255568	54.261415746	65.000867306	77.802704787
41	49.785181125	59.958864400	72.150962709	86.750015838
42	54.763699237	66.254545162	80.087568607	96.726267659
43	60.240069161	73.211272404	88.897201154	107.849788440
44	66.264076077	80.898456006	98.675893281	120.252514111
45	72.890483685	89.392793887	109.530241542	134.081553233
46	80.179532054	98.779037245	121.578568111	149.500931855
47	88.197485259	109.150836156	134.952210604	166.693539018
48	97.017233785	120.611673952	149.796953770	185.863296006
49	106.718957163	133.275899717	166.274618685	207.237575046
50	117.390852880	147.269869187	184.564826740	231.069896177
51	129.129938168	162.733205452	204.866957682	257.642934237
52	142.042931984	179.820192024	227.402323027	287.271871674
53	156.247225183	198.701312187	252.416578560	320.308136917
54	171.871947701	219.564949966	280.182402201	357.143572662
55	189.059142471	242.619269713	311.002466443	398.215083518
56	207.965056718	268.094293033	345.212737752	444.009818123
57	228.761562390	296.244193801	383.186138905	495.070947207
58	251.637718629	327.349834150	425.336614184	552.004106136
59	276.801490492	361.721566736	472.123641744	615.484578341
60	304.481639541	399.702331243	524.057242336	686.265304850

Table I Compound-Amount Factor (Compound-Interest Factor; Future Value Factor)(continued) $(1 + i)^n$

n	*0.12 (12%)*	*0.125 (12½%)*	*0.13 (13%)*	*0.135 (13½%)*
1	1.120000000	1.125000000	1.130000000	1.135000000
2	1.254400000	1.265625000	1.276900000	1.288225000
3	1.404928000	1.423828125	1.442897000	1.462135375
4	1.573519360	1.601806641	1.630473610	1.659523651
5	1.762341683	1.802032471	1.842435179	1.883559343
6	1.973822685	2.027286530	2.081951753	2.137839855
7	2.210681407	2.280697346	2.352605480	2.426448235
8	2.475963176	2.565784514	2.658444193	2.754018747
9	2.773078757	2.886507578	3.004041938	3.125811278
10	3.105848208	3.247321025	3.394567390	3.547795800
11	3.478549993	3.653236154	3.835861151	4.026748233
12	3.895975993	4.109890673	4.334523100	4.570359245
13	4.363493112	4.623627007	4.898011103	5.187357743
14	4.887112285	5.201580383	5.534752547	5.887651038
15	5.473565759	5.851777931	6.254270378	6.682483928
16	6.130393650	6.583250172	7.067325527	7.584619259
17	6.866040888	7.406156444	7.986077845	8.608542859
18	7.689965795	8.331925999	9.024267965	9.770696145
19	8.612761690	9.373416749	10.197422801	11.089740124
20	9.646293093	10.545093842	11.523087765	12.586855041
21	10.803848264	11.863230573	13.021089174	14.286080471
22	12.100310056	13.346134394	14.713830767	16.214701335
23	13.552347263	15.014401194	16.626628766	18.403686015
24	15.178628935	16.891201343	18.788090506	20.888183627
25	17.000064407	19.002601511	21.230542272	23.708088417
26	19.040072135	21.377926700	23.990512767	26.908680353
27	21.324880792	24.050167537	27.109279427	30.541352201
28	23.883866487	27.056438479	30.633485752	34.664434748
29	26.749930465	30.438493289	34.615838900	39.344133439
30	29.959922121	34.243304950	39.115897957	44.655591453
31	33.555112775	38.523718069	44.200964692	50.684096300
32	37.581726308	43.339182827	49.947090102	57.526449300
33	42.091533465	48.756580681	56.440211815	65.292519956
34	47.142517481	54.851153266	63.777439351	74.107010150
35	52.799619579	61.707547424	72.068506467	84.111456520
36	59.135573929	69.420990852	81.437412307	95.466503150
37	66.231842800	78.098614709	92.024275907	108.354481075
38	74.179663936	87.860941548	103.987431775	122.982336020
39	83.081223608	98.843559241	117.505797906	139.584951383
40	93.050970441	111.199004146	132.781551634	158.428919820
41	104.217086894	125.098879664	150.043153346	179.816823995
42	116.723137322	140.736239622	169.548763281	204.092095235
43	130.729913800	158.328269575	191.590102507	231.644528091
44	146.417503456	178.119303272	216.496815833	262.916539384
45	163.987603871	200.384216181	244.641401892	298.410272200
46	183.666116336	225.432243204	276.444784138	338.695658948
47	205.706050296	253.611273604	312.382606075	384.419572905
48	230.390776331	285.312682805	352.992344865	436.316215248
49	258.037669491	320.976768155	398.881349698	495.218904306
50	289.002189830	361.098864175	450.735925158	562.073456387
51	323.682452610	406.236222196	509.331595429	637.953373000
52	362.524346923	457.015749971	575.544702835	724.077078355
53	406.027268553	514.142718717	650.365514203	821.827483933
54	454.750540780	578.410558557	734.913031050	932.774194264
55	509.320605673	650.711878377	830.451725086	1058.698710489
56	570.439078354	732.050863174	938.410449347	1201.623036405
57	638.891767757	823.557221071	1060.403807763	1363.842146320
58	715.558779888	926.501873704	1198.256302772	1547.960836073
59	801.425833474	1042.314607917	1354.029622132	1756.935548943
60	897.596933491	1172.603933907	1530.053473009	1994.121848050

Table I Compound-Amount Factor (Compound-Interest Factor; Future Value Factor)(continued) $(1 + i)^n$

n	*0.14 (14%)*	*0.145 (14½%)*	*0.15 (15%)*	*0.155 (15½%)*
1	1.140000000	1.145000000	1.150000000	1.155000000
2	1.299600000	1.311025000	1.322500000	1.334025000
3	1.481544000	1.501123625	1.520875000	1.540798875
4	1.688960160	1.718786551	1.749006250	1.779622701
5	1.925414582	1.968010600	2.011357187	2.055464219
6	2.194972624	2.253372138	2.313060766	2.374061173
7	2.502268791	2.580111097	2.660019880	2.742040655
8	2.852586422	2.954227207	3.059022863	3.167056957
9	3.251948521	3.382590152	3.517876292	3.657950785
10	3.707221314	3.873065724	4.045557736	4.224933157
11	4.226232298	4.434660253	4.652391396	4.879797796
12	4.817904820	5.077685990	5.350250105	5.636166454
13	5.492411495	5.813950459	6.152787621	6.509772254
14	6.261349104	6.656973275	7.075705764	7.518786954
15	7.137937978	7.622234400	8.137061629	8.684198932
16	8.137249295	8.727458388	9.357620874	10.030249766
17	9.276464197	9.992939855	10.761264005	11.584938480
18	10.575169184	11.441916133	12.375453605	13.380603944
19	12.055692870	13.100993973	14.231771646	15.454597556
20	13.743489872	15.000638099	16.366537393	17.850060177
21	15.667578454	17.175730623	18.821518002	20.616819504
22	17.861039437	19.666211564	21.644745702	23.812426527
23	20.361584959	22.517812240	24.891457557	27.503352639
24	23.212206853	25.782895015	28.625176191	31.766372298
25	26.461915812	29.521414792	32.918952620	36.690160005
26	30.166584026	33.802019937	37.856795513	42.377134805
27	34.389905790	38.703312828	43.535314840	48.945590700
28	39.204492600	44.315293188	50.065612066	56.532157259
29	44.693121564	50.741010701	57.575453875	65.294641634
30	50.950158583	58.098457252	66.211771957	75.415311087
31	58.083180785	66.522733554	76.143537750	87.104684305
32	66.214826095	76.168529919	87.565068413	100.605910373
33	75.484901748	87.212966757	100.699828675	116.199826481
34	86.052787993	99.858846937	115.804802976	134.210799585
35	98.100178312	114.338379743	133.175523422	155.013473521
36	111.834203276	130.917444806	153.151851936	179.040561916
37	127.490991734	149.900474302	176.124629726	206.791849013
38	145.339730577	171.636043076	202.543324185	238.844585611
39	165.687292858	196.523269322	232.924822813	275.865496380
40	188.883513858	225.019143374	267.863546235	318.624648319
41	215.327205798	257.646919163	308.043078170	368.011468809
42	245.473014610	295.005722442	354.249539895	425.053246474
43	279.839236655	337.781552196	407.386970880	490.936499677
44	319.016729787	386.759877265	468.495016512	567.031657127
45	363.679071957	442.840059468	538.769268988	654.921563982
46	414.594142031	507.051868091	619.584659337	756.434406399
47	472.637321915	580.574388964	712.522358237	873.681739391
48	538.806546983	664.757675364	819.400711973	1009.102408997
49	614.239463561	761.147538292	942.310818769	1165.513282391
50	700.232988459	871.513931344	1083.657441584	1346.167841162
51	798.265606843	997.883451389	1246.206057822	1554.823856542
52	910.022791802	1142.576551840	1433.136966495	1795.821554306
53	1037.425982654	1308.250151857	1648.107511469	2074.173895224
54	1182.665620225	1497.946423876	1895.323638189	2395.670848983
55	1348.238807057	1715.148655338	2179.622183918	2766.999830576
56	1536.992240045	1963.845210362	2506.565511505	3195.884804315
57	1752.171153651	2248.602765865	2882.550338231	3691.246948984
58	1997.475115162	2574.650166915	3314.932888966	4263.390226076
59	2277.121631285	2947.974441118	3812.172822311	4924.215711118
60	2595.918659665	3375.430735080	4383.998745657	5687.469146341

Table I Compound-Amount Factor (Compound-Interest Factor; Future Value Factor)(continued) $(1 + i)^n$

n	*0.16 (16%)*	*0.165 (16½%)*	*0.17 (17%)*	*0.175 (17½%)*
1	1.160000000	1.165000000	1.170000000	1.175000000
2	1.345600000	1.357225000	1.368900000	1.380625000
3	1.560896000	1.581167125	1.601613000	1.622234375
4	1.810639360	1.842059701	1.873887210	1.906125391
5	2.100341658	2.145999551	2.192448036	2.239697334
6	2.436396323	2.500089477	2.565164202	2.631644367
7	2.826219734	2.912604241	3.001242116	3.092182132
8	3.278414892	3.393183941	3.511453276	3.633314005
9	3.802961275	3.953059291	4.108400333	4.269143956
10	4.411435079	4.605314074	4.806828389	5.016244148
11	5.117264691	5.365190896	5.623989215	5.894086874
12	5.936027042	6.250447394	6.580067382	6.925552077
13	6.885791369	7.281771214	7.698678837	8.137523690
14	7.987517987	8.483263464	9.007454239	9.561590336
15	9.265520865	9.883001936	10.538721460	11.234868645
16	10.748004204	11.513697255	12.330304108	13.200970657
17	12.467684877	13.413457302	14.426455807	15.511140522
18	14.462514457	15.626677757	16.878953294	18.225590114
19	16.776516770	18.205079587	19.748375354	21.415068384
20	19.460759453	21.208917719	23.105599164	25.162705351

n	*0.18 (18%)*	*0.185 (18½%)*	*0.19 (19%)*	*0.195 (19½%)*
1	1.180000000	1.185000000	1.190000000	1.195000000
2	1.392400000	1.404225000	1.416100000	1.428025000
3	1.643032000	1.664006625	1.685159000	1.706489875
4	1.938777760	1.971847851	2.005339210	2.039255401
5	2.287757757	2.336639703	2.386353660	2.436910204
6	2.699554153	2.768918048	2.839760855	2.912107693
7	3.185473901	3.281167887	3.379315418	3.479968694
8	3.758859203	3.888183946	4.021385347	4.158562589
9	4.435453859	4.607497976	4.785448563	4.969482294
10	5.233835554	5.459885102	5.694683790	5.938531341
11	6.175925953	6.469963845	6.776673710	7.096544953
12	7.287592625	7.666907157	8.064241715	8.480371218
13	8.599359298	9.085284981	9.596447641	10.134043606
14	10.147243971	10.766062702	11.419772693	12.110182109
15	11.973747886	12.757784302	13.589529505	14.471667620
16	14.129022506	15.117974398	16.171540110	17.293642806
17	16.672246556	17.914799662	19.244132731	20.665903154
18	19.673250937	21.229037599	22.900517950	24.695754269
19	23.214436105	25.156409555	27.251616361	29.511426351
20	27.393034604	29.810345323	32.429423469	35.266154490

n	*0.20 (20%)*	*0.21 (21%)*	*0.22 (22%)*	*0.23 (23%)*
1	1.200000000	1.210000000	1.220000000	1.230000000
2	1.440000000	1.464100000	1.488400000	1.512900000
3	1.728000000	1.771561000	1.815848000	1.860867000
4	2.073600000	2.143588810	2.215334560	2.288866410
5	2.488320000	2.593742460	2.702708163	2.815305684
6	2.985984000	3.138428377	3.297303959	3.462825992
7	3.583180800	3.797498336	4.022710830	4.259275970
8	4.299816960	4.594972986	4.907707213	5.238909443
9	5.159780352	5.559917313	5.987402800	6.443858615
10	6.191736422	6.727499949	7.304631415	7.925946096
11	7.430083707	8.140274939	8.911650327	9.748913698
12	8.916100448	9.849732676	10.872213399	11.991163849
13	10.699320538	11.918176538	13.264100346	14.749131534
14	12.839184645	14.420993611	16.182202423	18.141431787
15	15.407021575	17.449402269	19.742286956	22.313961098
16	18.488425890	21.113776745	24.085590086	27.446172150
17	22.186111067	25.547669862	29.384419905	33.758791745
18	26.623333281	30.912680533	35.848992284	41.523313846
19	31.947999937	37.404343445	43.735770586	51.073676031
20	38.337599924	45.259255568	53.357640115	62.820621518

Table I Compound-Amount Factor (Compound-Interest Factor; Future Value Factor)(continued) $(1 + i)^n$

n	*0.24 (24%)*	*0.25 (25%)*	*0.30 (30%)*
1	1.240000000	1.250000000	1.300000000
2	1.537600000	1.562500000	1.690000000
3	1.906624000	1.953125000	2.197000000
4	2.364213760	2.441406250	2.856100000
5	2.931625062	3.051757812	3.712930000
6	3.635215077	3.814697266	4.826809000
7	4.507666696	4.768371582	6.274851700
8	5.589506703	5.960464478	8.157307210
9	6.930988312	7.450580597	10.604499373
10	8.594425506	9.313225746	13.785849185
11	10.657087628	11.641532183	17.921603940
12	13.214788659	14.551915228	23.298085122
13	16.386337937	18.189894035	30.287510659
14	20.319059042	22.737367544	39.373763857
15	25.195633212	28.421709430	51.185893014
16	31.242585183	35.527136788	66.541660918
17	38.740805626	44.408920985	86.504159194
18	48.038598977	55.511151231	112.455406952
19	59.567862731	69.388939039	146.192029038
20	73.864149787	86.736173799	190.049637749

n	*0.35 (35%)*	*0.40 (40%)*
1	1.350000000	1.400000000
2	1.822500000	1.960000000
3	2.460375000	2.744000000
4	3.321506250	3.841600000
5	4.484033438	5.378240000
6	6.053445141	7.529536000
7	8.172150940	10.541350400
8	11.032403769	14.757890560
9	14.893745088	20.661046784
10	20.106555869	28.925465498
11	27.143850423	40.495651697
12	36.644198071	56.693912375
13	49.469667395	79.371477325
14	66.784050984	111.120068256
15	90.158468828	155.568095558
16	121.713932918	217.795333781
17	164.313809439	304.913467293
18	221.823642742	426.878854211
19	299.461917702	597.630395895
20	404.273588898	836.682554253

Table II **Present Value Factor (Single Payment/Present Value Factor; Present Worth Factor)** $\frac{1}{(1+i)^n}$

n	*0.0025 (¼%)*	*0.0050 (½%)*	*0.0075 (¾%)*	*0.01 (1%)*	*0.0125 (1¼%)*	*0.0150 (1½%)*
1	0.997506	0.995025	0.992556	0.990099	0.987654	0.985222
2	0.995019	0.990075	0.985167	0.980296	0.975461	0.970662
3	0.992537	0.985149	0.977833	0.970590	0.963418	0.956317
4	0.990062	0.980248	0.970554	0.960980	0.951524	0.942184
5	0.987593	0.975371	0.963329	0.951466	0.939777	0.928260
6	0.985130	0.970518	0.956158	0.942045	0.928175	0.914542
7	0.982674	0.965690	0.949040	0.932718	0.916716	0.901027
8	0.980223	0.960885	0.941975	0.923483	0.905398	0.887711
9	0.977779	0.956105	0.934963	0.914340	0.894221	0.874592
10	0.975340	0.951348	0.928003	0.905287	0.883181	0.861667
11	0.972908	0.946615	0.921095	0.896324	0.872277	0.848933
12	0.970482	0.941905	0.914238	0.887449	0.861509	0.836387
13	0.968062	0.937219	0.907432	0.878663	0.850873	0.824027
14	0.965648	0.932556	0.900677	0.869963	0.840368	0.811849
15	0.963239	0.927917	0.893973	0.861349	0.829993	0.799852
16	0.960837	0.923300	0.887318	0.852821	0.819746	0.788031
17	0.958441	0.918707	0.880712	0.844377	0.809626	0.776385
18	0.956051	0.914136	0.874156	0.836017	0.799631	0.764912
19	0.953667	0.909588	0.867649	0.827740	0.789759	0.753607
20	0.951289	0.905063	0.861190	0.819544	0.780009	0.742470
21	0.948916	0.900560	0.854779	0.811430	0.770379	0.731498
22	0.946550	0.896080	0.848416	0.803396	0.760868	0.720688
23	0.944190	0.891622	0.842100	0.795442	0.751475	0.710037
24	0.941835	0.887186	0.835831	0.787566	0.742197	0.699544
25	0.939486	0.882772	0.829609	0.779768	0.733034	0.689206
26	0.937143	0.878380	0.823434	0.772048	0.723984	0.679021
27	0.934806	0.874010	0.817304	0.764404	0.715046	0.668986
28	0.932475	0.869662	0.811220	0.756836	0.706219	0.659099
29	0.930150	0.865335	0.805181	0.749342	0.697500	0.649359
30	0.927830	0.861030	0.799187	0.741923	0.688889	0.639762
31	0.925517	0.856746	0.793238	0.734577	0.680384	0.630308
32	0.923209	0.852484	0.787333	0.727304	0.671984	0.620993
33	0.920906	0.848242	0.781472	0.720103	0.663688	0.611816
34	0.918610	0.844022	0.775654	0.712973	0.655494	0.602774
35	0.916319	0.839823	0.769880	0.705914	0.647402	0.593866
36	0.914034	0.835645	0.764149	0.698925	0.639409	0.585090
37	0.911754	0.831487	0.758461	0.692005	0.631515	0.576443
38	0.909481	0.827351	0.752814	0.685153	0.623719	0.567924
39	0.907213	0.823235	0.747210	0.678370	0.616019	0.559531
40	0.904950	0.819139	0.741648	0.671653	0.608413	0.551262
41	0.902694	0.815064	0.736127	0.665003	0.600902	0.543116
42	0.900443	0.811009	0.730647	0.658419	0.593484	0.535089
43	0.898197	0.806974	0.725208	0.651900	0.586157	0.527182
44	0.895957	0.802959	0.719810	0.645445	0.578920	0.519391
45	0.893723	0.798964	0.714451	0.639055	0.571773	0.511715
46	0.891494	0.794989	0.709133	0.632728	0.564714	0.504153
47	0.889271	0.791034	0.703854	0.626463	0.557742	0.496702
48	0.887053	0.787098	0.698614	0.620260	0.550856	0.489362
49	0.884841	0.783182	0.693414	0.614119	0.544056	0.482130
50	0.882635	0.779286	0.688252	0.608039	0.537339	0.475005
51	0.880433	0.775409	0.683128	0.602019	0.530705	0.467985
52	0.878238	0.771551	0.678043	0.596058	0.524153	0.461069
53	0.876048	0.767713	0.672995	0.590156	0.517682	0.454255
54	0.873863	0.763893	0.667986	0.584313	0.511291	0.447542
55	0.871684	0.760093	0.663013	0.578528	0.504979	0.440928
56	0.869510	0.756311	0.658077	0.572800	0.498745	0.434412
57	0.867342	0.752548	0.653178	0.567129	0.492587	0.427992
58	0.865179	0.748804	0.648316	0.561514	0.486506	0.421667
59	0.863021	0.745079	0.643490	0.555954	0.480500	0.415435
60	0.860869	0.741372	0.638700	0.550450	0.474568	0.409296

Table II **Present Value Factor (Single Payment/Present Value Factor; Present Worth Factor)(continued)** $\frac{1}{(1+i)^n}$

n	*0.0025 (¼%)*	*0.0050 (½%)*	*0.0075 (¾%)*	*0.01 (1%)*	*0.0125 (1¼%)*	*0.0150 (1½%)*
61	0.858722	0.737684	0.633945	0.545000	0.468709	0.403247
62	0.856581	0.734014	0.629226	0.539604	0.462922	0.397288
63	0.854445	0.730362	0.624542	0.534261	0.457207	0.391417
64	0.852314	0.726728	0.619893	0.528971	0.451563	0.385632
65	0.850188	0.723113	0.615278	0.523734	0.445988	0.379933
66	0.848068	0.719515	0.610698	0.518548	0.440482	0.374318
67	0.845953	0.715935	0.606152	0.513414	0.435044	0.368787
68	0.843844	0.712374	0.601639	0.508331	0.429673	0.363337
69	0.841739	0.708829	0.597161	0.503298	0.424368	0.357967
70	0.839640	0.705303	0.592715	0.498315	0.419129	0.352677
71	0.837547	0.701794	0.588303	0.493381	0.413955	0.347465
72	0.835458	0.698302	0.583924	0.488496	0.408844	0.342330
73	0.833374	0.694828	0.579577	0.483659	0.403797	0.337271
74	0.831296	0.691371	0.575262	0.478871	0.398811	0.332287
75	0.829223	0.687932	0.570980	0.474129	0.393888	0.327376
76	0.827155	0.684509	0.566730	0.469435	0.389025	0.322538
77	0.825093	0.681104	0.562511	0.464787	0.384222	0.317771
78	0.823035	0.677715	0.558323	0.460185	0.379479	0.313075
79	0.820982	0.674343	0.554167	0.455629	0.374794	0.308448
80	0.818935	0.670988	0.550042	0.451118	0.370167	0.303890
81	0.816893	0.667650	0.545947	0.446651	0.365597	0.299399
82	0.814856	0.664329	0.541883	0.442229	0.361083	0.294975
83	0.812824	0.661023	0.537849	0.437851	0.356625	0.290615
84	0.810797	0.657735	0.533845	0.433515	0.352223	0.286321
85	0.808775	0.654462	0.529871	0.429223	0.347874	0.282089
86	0.806758	0.651206	0.525927	0.424974	0.343580	0.277920
87	0.804746	0.647967	0.522012	0.420766	0.339338	0.273813
88	0.802739	0.644743	0.518126	0.416600	0.335148	0.269767
89	0.800737	0.641535	0.514269	0.412475	0.331011	0.265780
90	0.798740	0.638344	0.510440	0.408391	0.326924	0.261852
91	0.796749	0.635168	0.506641	0.404348	0.322888	0.257982
92	0.794762	0.632008	0.502869	0.400344	0.318902	0.254170
93	0.792780	0.628863	0.499126	0.396380	0.314965	0.250414
94	0.790803	0.625735	0.495410	0.392456	0.311076	0.246713
95	0.788831	0.622622	0.491722	0.388570	0.307236	0.243067
96	0.786863	0.619524	0.488062	0.384723	0.303443	0.239475
97	0.784901	0.616442	0.484428	0.380914	0.299697	0.235936
98	0.782944	0.613375	0.480822	0.377142	0.295997	0.232449
99	0.780991	0.610323	0.477243	0.373408	0.292342	0.229014
100	0.779044	0.607287	0.473690	0.369711	0.288733	0.225629
101	0.777101	0.604265	0.470164	0.366051	0.285169	0.222295
102	0.775163	0.601259	0.466664	0.362426	0.281648	0.219010
103	0.773230	0.598268	0.463190	0.358838	0.278171	0.215773
104	0.771302	0.595291	0.459742	0.355285	0.274737	0.212585
105	0.769378	0.592330	0.456320	0.351768	0.271345	0.209443
106	0.767460	0.589383	0.452923	0.348285	0.267995	0.206348
107	0.765546	0.586451	0.449551	0.344836	0.264686	0.203298
108	0.763637	0.583533	0.446205	0.341422	0.261419	0.200294
109	0.761732	0.580630	0.442883	0.338042	0.258191	0.197334
110	0.759833	0.577741	0.439586	0.334695	0.255004	0.194417
111	0.757938	0.574867	0.436314	0.331381	0.251856	0.191544
112	0.756048	0.572007	0.433066	0.328100	0.248746	0.188714
113	0.754162	0.569161	0.429842	0.324851	0.245675	0.185925
114	0.752282	0.566329	0.426642	0.321635	0.242642	0.183177
115	0.750406	0.563512	0.423466	0.318451	0.239647	0.180470
116	0.748534	0.560708	0.420314	0.315298	0.236688	0.177803
117	0.746668	0.557919	0.417185	0.312176	0.233766	0.175175
118	0.744806	0.555143	0.414079	0.309085	0.230880	0.172587
119	0.742948	0.552381	0.410997	0.306025	0.228030	0.170036
120	0.741096	0.549633	0.407937	0.302995	0.225214	0.167523

Table II **Present Value Factor (Single Payment/Present Value Factor; Present Worth Factor)(continued)** $\frac{1}{(1+i)^n}$

n	*0.0175 (1¾%)*	*0.02 (2%)*	*0.0225 (2¼%)*	*0.025 (2½%)*	*0.0275 (2¾%)*	*0.03 (3%)*
1	0.982801	0.980392	0.977995	0.975610	0.973236	0.970874
2	0.965898	0.961169	0.956474	0.951814	0.947188	0.942596
3	0.949285	0.942322	0.935427	0.928599	0.921838	0.915142
4	0.932959	0.923845	0.914843	0.905951	0.897166	0.888487
5	0.916913	0.905731	0.894712	0.883854	0.873154	0.862609
6	0.901143	0.887971	0.875024	0.862297	0.849785	0.837484
7	0.885644	0.870560	0.855769	0.841265	0.827041	0.813092
8	0.870412	0.853490	0.836938	0.820747	0.804906	0.789409
9	0.855441	0.836755	0.818522	0.800728	0.783364	0.766417
10	0.840729	0.820348	0.800510	0.781198	0.762398	0.744094
11	0.826269	0.804263	0.782895	0.762145	0.741993	0.722421
12	0.812058	0.788493	0.765667	0.743556	0.722134	0.701380
13	0.798091	0.773033	0.748819	0.725420	0.702807	0.680951
14	0.784365	0.757875	0.732341	0.707727	0.683997	0.661118
15	0.770875	0.743015	0.716226	0.690466	0.665691	0.641862
16	0.757616	0.728446	0.700466	0.673625	0.647874	0.623167
17	0.744586	0.714163	0.685052	0.657195	0.630535	0.605016
18	0.731780	0.700159	0.669978	0.641166	0.613659	0.587395
19	0.719194	0.686431	0.655235	0.625528	0.597235	0.570286
20	0.706825	0.672971	0.640816	0.610271	0.581251	0.553676
21	0.694668	0.659776	0.626715	0.595386	0.565694	0.537549
22	0.682720	0.646839	0.612925	0.580865	0.550554	0.521893
23	0.670978	0.634156	0.599437	0.566697	0.535819	0.506692
24	0.659438	0.621721	0.586247	0.552875	0.521478	0.491934
25	0.648096	0.609531	0.573346	0.539391	0.507521	0.477606
26	0.636950	0.597579	0.560730	0.526235	0.493938	0.463695
27	0.625995	0.585862	0.548391	0.513400	0.480718	0.450189
28	0.615228	0.574375	0.536324	0.500878	0.467852	0.437077
29	0.604647	0.563112	0.524522	0.488661	0.455331	0.424346
30	0.594248	0.552071	0.512980	0.476743	0.443144	0.411987
31	0.584027	0.541246	0.501692	0.465115	0.431284	0.399987
32	0.573982	0.530633	0.490652	0.453771	0.419741	0.388337
33	0.564111	0.520229	0.479856	0.442703	0.408507	0.377026
34	0.554408	0.510028	0.469296	0.431905	0.397574	0.366045
35	0.544873	0.500028	0.458970	0.421371	0.386933	0.355383
36	0.535502	0.490223	0.448870	0.411094	0.376577	0.345032
37	0.526292	0.480611	0.438993	0.401067	0.366499	0.334983
38	0.517240	0.471187	0.429333	0.391285	0.356690	0.325226
39	0.508344	0.461948	0.419885	0.381741	0.347143	0.315754
40	0.499601	0.452890	0.410646	0.372431	0.337852	0.306557
41	0.491008	0.444010	0.401610	0.363347	0.328810	0.297628
42	0.482563	0.435304	0.392772	0.354485	0.320010	0.288959
43	0.474264	0.426769	0.384129	0.345839	0.311445	0.280543
44	0.466107	0.418401	0.375677	0.337404	0.303109	0.272372
45	0.458090	0.410197	0.367410	0.329174	0.294997	0.264439
46	0.450212	0.402154	0.359325	0.321146	0.287102	0.256737
47	0.442469	0.394268	0.351418	0.313313	0.279418	0.249259
48	0.434858	0.386538	0.343685	0.305671	0.271939	0.241999
49	0.427379	0.378958	0.336122	0.298216	0.264661	0.234950
50	0.420029	0.371528	0.328726	0.290942	0.257578	0.228107
51	0.412805	0.364243	0.321493	0.283846	0.250684	0.221463
52	0.405705	0.357101	0.314418	0.276923	0.243975	0.215013
53	0.398727	0.350099	0.307499	0.270169	0.237445	0.208750
54	0.391869	0.343234	0.300733	0.263579	0.231090	0.202670
55	0.385130	0.336504	0.294115	0.257151	0.224905	0.196767
56	0.378506	0.329906	0.287643	0.250879	0.218886	0.191036
57	0.371996	0.323437	0.281314	0.244760	0.213027	0.185472
58	0.365598	0.317095	0.275123	0.238790	0.207326	0.180070
59	0.359310	0.310878	0.269069	0.232966	0.201777	0.174825
60	0.353130	0.304782	0.263149	0.227284	0.196377	0.169733

Table II **Present Value Factor (Single Payment/Present Value Factor; Present Worth Factor)(continued)** $\frac{1}{(1+i)^n}$

n	*0.0175 (1¾%)*	*0.02 (2%)*	*0.0225 (2¼%)*	*0.025 (2½%)*	*0.0275 (2¾%)*	*0.03 (3%)*
61	0.347057	0.298806	0.257358	0.221740	0.191121	0.164789
62	0.341088	0.292947	0.251695	0.216332	0.186006	0.159990
63	0.335221	0.287203	0.246156	0.211055	0.181028	0.155330
64	0.329456	0.281572	0.240740	0.205908	0.176183	0.150806
65	0.323790	0.276051	0.235442	0.200886	0.171467	0.146413
66	0.318221	0.270638	0.230261	0.195986	0.166878	0.142149
67	0.312748	0.265331	0.225195	0.191206	0.162412	0.138009
68	0.307369	0.260129	0.220239	0.186542	0.158065	0.133989
69	0.302082	0.255028	0.215393	0.181992	0.153834	0.130086
70	0.296887	0.250028	0.210653	0.177554	0.149717	0.126297
71	0.291781	0.245125	0.206018	0.173223	0.145710	0.122619
72	0.286762	0.240319	0.201484	0.168998	0.141810	0.119047
73	0.281830	0.235607	0.197051	0.164876	0.138015	0.115580
74	0.276983	0.230987	0.192715	0.160855	0.134321	0.112214
75	0.272219	0.226458	0.188474	0.156931	0.130726	0.108945
76	0.267537	0.222017	0.184327	0.153104	0.127227	0.105772
77	0.262936	0.217664	0.180270	0.149370	0.123822	0.102691
78	0.258414	0.213396	0.176304	0.145726	0.120508	0.099700
79	0.253969	0.209212	0.172424	0.142172	0.117283	0.096796
80	0.249601	0.205110	0.168630	0.138705	0.114144	0.093977
81	0.245308	0.201088	0.164919	0.135322	0.111089	0.091240
82	0.241089	0.197145	0.161290	0.132021	0.108116	0.088582
83	0.236943	0.193279	0.157741	0.128801	0.105222	0.086002
84	0.232868	0.189490	0.154270	0.125659	0.102406	0.083497
85	0.228862	0.185774	0.150875	0.122595	0.099665	0.081065
86	0.224926	0.182132	0.147555	0.119605	0.096998	0.078704
87	0.221058	0.178560	0.144308	0.116687	0.094402	0.076412
88	0.217256	0.175059	0.141133	0.113841	0.091875	0.074186
89	0.213519	0.171627	0.138027	0.111065	0.089416	0.072026
90	0.209847	0.168261	0.134990	0.108356	0.087023	0.069928
91	0.206238	0.164962	0.132020	0.105713	0.084694	0.067891
92	0.202691	0.161728	0.129114	0.103135	0.082427	0.065914
93	0.199204	0.158556	0.126273	0.100619	0.080221	0.063994
94	0.195778	0.155448	0.123495	0.098165	0.078074	0.062130
95	0.192411	0.152400	0.120777	0.095771	0.075985	0.060320
96	0.189102	0.149411	0.118119	0.093435	0.073951	0.058563
97	0.185850	0.146482	0.115520	0.091156	0.071972	0.056858
98	0.182653	0.143609	0.112978	0.088933	0.070046	0.055202
99	0.179512	0.140794	0.110492	0.086764	0.068171	0.053594
100	0.176424	0.138033	0.108061	0.084647	0.066346	0.052033
101	0.173390	0.135326	0.105683	0.082583	0.064571	0.050517
102	0.170408	0.132673	0.103357	0.080569	0.062842	0.049046
103	0.167477	0.130072	0.101083	0.078603	0.061161	0.047617
104	0.164596	0.127521	0.098859	0.076686	0.059524	0.046231
105	0.161766	0.125021	0.096683	0.074816	0.057931	0.044884
106	0.158983	0.122569	0.094556	0.072991	0.056380	0.043577
107	0.156249	0.120166	0.092475	0.071211	0.054871	0.042307
108	0.153562	0.117810	0.090440	0.069474	0.053403	0.041075
109	0.150921	0.115500	0.088450	0.067780	0.051973	0.039879
110	0.148325	0.113235	0.086504	0.066126	0.050582	0.038717
111	0.145774	0.111015	0.084600	0.064514	0.049229	0.037590
112	0.143267	0.108838	0.082739	0.062940	0.047911	0.036495
113	0.140803	0.106704	0.080918	0.061405	0.046629	0.035432
114	0.138381	0.104612	0.079137	0.059907	0.045381	0.034400
115	0.136001	0.102561	0.077396	0.058446	0.044166	0.033398
116	0.133662	0.100550	0.075693	0.057021	0.042984	0.032425
117	0.131363	0.098578	0.074027	0.055630	0.041834	0.031481
118	0.129104	0.096645	0.072398	0.054273	0.040714	0.030564
119	0.126883	0.094750	0.070805	0.052949	0.039624	0.029674
120	0.124701	0.092892	0.069247	0.051658	0.038564	0.028809

Table II **Present Value Factor (Single Payment/Present Value Factor; Present Worth Factor)(continued)** $\frac{1}{(1+i)^n}$

n	0.035 (3½%)	0.04 (4%)	0.045 (4½%)	0.05 (5%)	0.055 (5½)	0.06 (6%)
1	0.966184	0.961538	0.956938	0.952381	0.947867	0.943396
2	0.933511	0.924556	0.915730	0.907029	0.898452	0.889996
3	0.901943	0.888996	0.876297	0.863838	0.851614	0.839619
4	0.871442	0.854804	0.838561	0.822702	0.807217	0.792094
5	0.841973	0.821927	0.802451	0.783526	0.765134	0.747258
6	0.813501	0.790315	0.767896	0.746215	0.725246	0.704961
7	0.785991	0.759918	0.734828	0.710681	0.687437	0.665057
8	0.759412	0.730690	0.703185	0.676839	0.651599	0.627412
9	0.733731	0.702587	0.672904	0.644609	0.617629	0.591898
10	0.708919	0.675564	0.643928	0.613913	0.585431	0.558395
11	0.684946	0.649581	0.616199	0.584679	0.554911	0.526788
12	0.661783	0.624597	0.589664	0.556837	0.525982	0.496969
13	0.639404	0.600574	0.564272	0.530321	0.498561	0.468839
14	0.617782	0.577475	0.539973	0.505068	0.472569	0.442301
15	0.596891	0.555265	0.516720	0.481017	0.447933	0.417265
16	0.576706	0.533908	0.494469	0.458112	0.424581	0.393646
17	0.557204	0.513373	0.473176	0.436297	0.402447	0.371364
18	0.538361	0.493628	0.452800	0.415521	0.381466	0.350344
19	0.520156	0.474642	0.433302	0.395734	0.361579	0.330513
20	0.502566	0.456387	0.414643	0.376889	0.342729	0.311805
21	0.485571	0.438834	0.396787	0.358942	0.324862	0.294155
22	0.469151	0.421955	0.379701	0.341850	0.307926	0.277505
23	0.453286	0.405726	0.363350	0.325571	0.291873	0.261797
24	0.437957	0.390121	0.347703	0.310068	0.276657	0.246979
25	0.423147	0.375117	0.332731	0.295303	0.262234	0.232999
26	0.408838	0.360689	0.318402	0.281241	0.248563	0.219810
27	0.395012	0.346817	0.304691	0.267848	0.235605	0.207368
28	0.381654	0.333477	0.291571	0.255094	0.223322	0.195630
29	0.368748	0.320651	0.279015	0.242946	0.211679	0.184557
30	0.356278	0.308319	0.267000	0.231377	0.200644	0.174110
31	0.344230	0.296460	0.255502	0.220359	0.190184	0.164255
32	0.332590	0.285058	0.244500	0.209866	0.180269	0.154957
33	0.321343	0.274094	0.233971	0.199873	0.170871	0.146186
34	0.310476	0.263552	0.223896	0.190355	0.161963	0.137912
35	0.299977	0.253415	0.214254	0.181290	0.153520	0.130105
36	0.289833	0.243669	0.205028	0.172657	0.145516	0.122741
37	0.280032	0.234297	0.196199	0.164436	0.137930	0.115793
38	0.270562	0.225285	0.187750	0.156605	0.130739	0.109239
39	0.261413	0.216621	0.179665	0.149148	0.123924	0.103056
40	0.252572	0.208289	0.171929	0.142046	0.117463	0.097222
41	0.244031	0.200278	0.164525	0.135282	0.111339	0.091719
42	0.235779	0.192575	0.157440	0.128840	0.105535	0.086527
43	0.227806	0.185168	0.150661	0.122704	0.100033	0.081630
44	0.220102	0.178046	0.144173	0.116861	0.094818	0.077009
45	0.212659	0.171198	0.137964	0.111297	0.089875	0.072650
46	0.205468	0.164614	0.132023	0.105997	0.085190	0.068538
47	0.198520	0.158283	0.126338	0.100949	0.080748	0.064658
48	0.191806	0.152195	0.120898	0.096142	0.076539	0.060998
49	0.185320	0.146341	0.115692	0.091564	0.072549	0.057546
50	0.179053	0.140713	0.110710	0.087204	0.068767	0.054288
51	0.172998	0.135301	0.105942	0.083051	0.065182	0.051215
52	0.167148	0.130097	0.101380	0.079096	0.061783	0.048316
53	0.161496	0.125093	0.097014	0.075330	0.058563	0.045582
54	0.156035	0.120282	0.092837	0.071743	0.055509	0.043001
55	0.150758	0.115656	0.088839	0.068326	0.052616	0.040567
56	0.145660	0.111207	0.085013	0.065073	0.049873	0.038271
57	0.140734	0.106930	0.081353	0.061974	0.047273	0.036105
58	0.135975	0.102817	0.077849	0.059023	0.044808	0.034061
59	0.131377	0.098863	0.074497	0.056212	0.042472	0.032133
60	0.126934	0.095060	0.071289	0.053536	0.040258	0.030314

Table II Present Value Factor (Single Payment/Present Value Factor; Present Worth Factor)(continued) $\frac{1}{(1+i)^n}$

n	0.035 (3½%)	0.04 (4%)	0.045 (4½%)	0.05 (5%)	0.055 (5½)	0.06 (6%)
61	0.122642	0.091404	0.068219	0.050986	0.038159	0.028598
62	0.118495	0.087889	0.065281	0.048558	0.036170	0.026980
63	0.114487	0.084508	0.062470	0.046246	0.034284	0.025453
64	0.110616	0.081258	0.059780	0.044044	0.032497	0.024012
65	0.106875	0.078133	0.057206	0.041946	0.030803	0.022653
66	0.103261	0.075128	0.054743	0.039949	0.029197	0.021370
67	0.099769	0.072238	0.052385	0.038047	0.027675	0.020161
68	0.096395	0.069460	0.050129	0.036235	0.026232	0.019020
69	0.093136	0.066788	0.047971	0.034509	0.024865	0.017943
70	0.089986	0.064219	0.045905	0.032866	0.023568	0.016927
71	0.086943	0.061749	0.043928	0.031301	0.022340	0.015969
72	0.084003	0.059374	0.042037	0.029811	0.021175	0.015065
73	0.081162	0.057091	0.040226	0.028391	0.020071	0.014213
74	0.078418	0.054895	0.038494	0.027039	0.019025	0.013408
75	0.075766	0.052784	0.036836	0.025752	0.018033	0.012649
76	0.073204	0.050754	0.035250	0.024525	0.017093	0.011933
77	0.070728	0.048801	0.033732	0.023357	0.016202	0.011258
78	0.068336	0.046924	0.032280	0.022245	0.015357	0.010620
79	0.066026	0.045120	0.030890	0.021186	0.014556	0.010019
80	0.063793	0.043384	0.029559	0.020177	0.013798	0.009452
81	0.061636	0.041716	0.028287	0.019216	0.013078	0.008917
82	0.059551	0.040111	0.027068	0.018301	0.012396	0.008412
83	0.057537	0.038569	0.025903	0.017430	0.011750	0.007936
84	0.055592	0.037085	0.024787	0.016600	0.011138	0.007487
85	0.053712	0.035659	0.023720	0.015809	0.010557	0.007063
86	0.051896	0.034287	0.022699	0.015056	0.010007	0.006663
87	0.050141	0.032969	0.021721	0.014339	0.009485	0.006286
88	0.048445	0.031701	0.020786	0.013657	0.008990	0.005930
89	0.046807	0.030481	0.019891	0.013006	0.008522	0.005595
90	0.045224	0.029309	0.019034	0.012387	0.008078	0.005278
91	0.043695	0.028182	0.018215	0.011797	0.007656	0.004979
92	0.042217	0.027098	0.017430	0.011235	0.007257	0.004697
93	0.040789	0.026056	0.016680	0.010700	0.006879	0.004432
94	0.039410	0.025053	0.015961	0.010191	0.006520	0.004181
95	0.038077	0.024090	0.015274	0.009705	0.006180	0.003944
96	0.036790	0.023163	0.014616	0.009243	0.005858	0.003721
97	0.035546	0.022272	0.013987	0.008803	0.005553	0.003510
98	0.034344	0.021416	0.013385	0.008384	0.005263	0.003312
99	0.033182	0.020592	0.012808	0.007985	0.004989	0.003124
100	0.032060	0.019800	0.012257	0.007604	0.004729	0.002947
101	0.030976	0.019039	0.011729	0.007242	0.004482	0.002780
102	0.029928	0.018306	0.011224	0.006897	0.004249	0.002623
103	0.028916	0.017602	0.010740	0.006569	0.004027	0.002475
104	0.027939	0.016925	0.010278	0.006256	0.003817	0.002334
105	0.026994	0.016274	0.009835	0.005958	0.003618	0.002202
106	0.026081	0.015648	0.009412	0.005675	0.003430	0.002078
107	0.025199	0.015046	0.009007	0.005404	0.003251	0.001960
108	0.024347	0.014468	0.008619	0.005147	0.003081	0.001849
109	0.023523	0.013911	0.008248	0.004902	0.002921	0.001744
110	0.022728	0.013376	0.007892	0.004668	0.002768	0.001646
111	0.021959	0.012862	0.007553	0.004446	0.002624	0.001553
112	0.021217	0.012367	0.007227	0.004234	0.002487	0.001465
113	0.020499	0.011891	0.006916	0.004033	0.002358	0.001382
114	0.019806	0.011434	0.006618	0.003841	0.002235	0.001304
115	0.019136	0.010994	0.006333	0.003658	0.002118	0.001230
116	0.018489	0.010571	0.006061	0.003484	0.002008	0.001160
117	0.017864	0.010165	0.005800	0.003318	0.001903	0.001094
118	0.017260	0.009774	0.005550	0.003160	0.001804	0.001033
119	0.016676	0.009398	0.005311	0.003009	0.001710	0.000974
120	0.016112	0.009036	0.005082	0.002866	0.001621	0.000919

Table II **Present Value Factor (Single Payment/Present Value Factor; Present Worth Factor)(continued)** $\frac{1}{(1+i)^n}$

n	0.065 (6½%)	0.07 (7%)	0.075 (7½%)	0.08 (8%)	0.085 (8½%)	0.09 (9%)
1	0.938967	0.934579	0.930233	0.925926	0.921659	0.917431
2	0.881659	0.873439	0.865333	0.857339	0.849455	0.841680
3	0.827849	0.816298	0.804961	0.793832	0.782908	0.772183
4	0.777323	0.762895	0.748801	0.735030	0.721574	0.708425
5	0.729881	0.712986	0.696559	0.680583	0.665045	0.649931
6	0.685334	0.666342	0.647962	0.630170	0.612945	0.596267
7	0.643506	0.622750	0.602755	0.583490	0.564926	0.547034
8	0.604231	0.582009	0.560702	0.540269	0.520669	0.501866
9	0.567353	0.543934	0.521583	0.500249	0.479880	0.460428
10	0.532726	0.508349	0.485194	0.463193	0.442285	0.422411
11	0.500212	0.475093	0.451343	0.428883	0.407636	0.387533
12	0.469683	0.444012	0.419854	0.397114	0.375702	0.355535
13	0.441017	0.414964	0.390562	0.367698	0.346269	0.326179
14	0.414100	0.387817	0.363313	0.340461	0.319142	0.299246
15	0.388827	0.362446	0.337966	0.315242	0.294140	0.274538
16	0.365095	0.338735	0.314387	0.291890	0.271097	0.251870
17	0.342813	0.316574	0.292453	0.270269	0.249859	0.231073
18	0.321890	0.295864	0.272049	0.250249	0.230285	0.211994
19	0.302244	0.276508	0.253069	0.231712	0.212244	0.194490
20	0.283797	0.258419	0.235413	0.214548	0.195616	0.178431
21	0.266476	0.241513	0.218989	0.198656	0.180292	0.163698
22	0.250212	0.225713	0.203711	0.183941	0.166167	0.150182
23	0.234941	0.210947	0.189498	0.170315	0.153150	0.137781
24	0.220602	0.197147	0.176277	0.157699	0.141152	0.126405
25	0.207138	0.184249	0.163979	0.146018	0.130094	0.115968
26	0.194496	0.172195	0.152539	0.135202	0.119902	0.106393
27	0.182625	0.160930	0.141896	0.125187	0.110509	0.097608
28	0.171479	0.150402	0.131997	0.115914	0.101851	0.089548
29	0.161013	0.140563	0.122788	0.107328	0.093872	0.082155
30	0.151186	0.131367	0.114221	0.099377	0.086518	0.075371
31	0.141959	0.122773	0.106252	0.092016	0.079740	0.069148
32	0.133295	0.114741	0.098839	0.085200	0.073493	0.063438
33	0.125159	0.107235	0.091943	0.078889	0.067736	0.058200
34	0.117520	0.100219	0.085529	0.073045	0.062429	0.053395
35	0.110348	0.093663	0.079562	0.067635	0.057539	0.048986
36	0.103613	0.087535	0.074011	0.062625	0.053031	0.044941
37	0.097289	0.081809	0.068847	0.057986	0.048876	0.041231
38	0.091351	0.076457	0.064044	0.053690	0.045047	0.037826
39	0.085776	0.071455	0.059576	0.049713	0.041518	0.034703
40	0.080541	0.066780	0.055419	0.046031	0.038266	0.031838
41	0.075625	0.062412	0.051553	0.042621	0.035268	0.029209
42	0.071010	0.058329	0.047956	0.039464	0.032505	0.026797
43	0.066676	0.054513	0.044610	0.036541	0.029959	0.024584
44	0.062606	0.050946	0.041498	0.033834	0.027612	0.022555
45	0.058785	0.047613	0.038603	0.031328	0.025448	0.020692
46	0.055197	0.044499	0.035910	0.029007	0.023455	0.018984
47	0.051828	0.041587	0.033404	0.026859	0.021617	0.017416
48	0.048665	0.038867	0.031074	0.024869	0.019924	0.015978
49	0.045695	0.036324	0.028906	0.023027	0.018363	0.014659
50	0.042906	0.033948	0.026889	0.021321	0.016924	0.013449
51	0.040287	0.031727	0.025013	0.019742	0.015599	0.012338
52	0.037829	0.029651	0.023268	0.018280	0.014377	0.011319
53	0.035520	0.027711	0.021645	0.016925	0.013250	0.010385
54	0.033352	0.025899	0.020135	0.015672	0.012212	0.009527
55	0.031316	0.024204	0.018730	0.014511	0.011255	0.008741
56	0.029405	0.022621	0.017423	0.013436	0.010374	0.008019
57	0.027610	0.021141	0.016208	0.012441	0.009561	0.007357
58	0.025925	0.019758	0.015077	0.011519	0.008812	0.006749
59	0.024343	0.018465	0.014025	0.010666	0.008122	0.006192
60	0.022857	0.017257	0.013046	0.009876	0.007485	0.005681

Table II Present Value Factor (Single Payment/Present Value Factor; Present Worth Factor)(continued) $\frac{1}{(1+i)^n}$

n	*0.065 (6½%)*	*0.07 (7%)*	*0.075 (7½%)*	*0.08 (8%)*	*0.085 (8½%)*	*0.09 (9%)*
61	0.021462	0.016128	0.012136	0.009144	0.006899	0.005212
62	0.020152	0.015073	0.011290	0.008467	0.006359	0.004781
63	0.018922	0.014087	0.010502	0.007840	0.005860	0.004387
64	0.017767	0.013166	0.009769	0.007259	0.005401	0.004024
65	0.016683	0.012304	0.009088	0.006721	0.004978	0.003692
66	0.015665	0.011499	0.008454	0.006223	0.004588	0.003387
67	0.014709	0.010747	0.007864	0.005762	0.004229	0.003108
68	0.013811	0.010044	0.007315	0.005336	0.003897	0.002851
69	0.012968	0.009387	0.006805	0.004940	0.003592	0.002616
70	0.012177	0.008773	0.006330	0.004574	0.003311	0.002400
71	0.011433	0.008199	0.005888	0.004236	0.003051	0.002201
72	0.010736	0.007662	0.005478	0.003922	0.002812	0.002020
73	0.010080	0.007161	0.005095	0.003631	0.002592	0.001853
74	0.009465	0.006693	0.004740	0.003362	0.002389	0.001700
75	0.008887	0.006255	0.004409	0.003113	0.002202	0.001560
76	0.008345	0.005846	0.004102	0.002883	0.002029	0.001431
77	0.007836	0.005463	0.003815	0.002669	0.001870	0.001313
78	0.007358	0.005106	0.003549	0.002471	0.001724	0.001204
79	0.006908	0.004772	0.003302	0.002288	0.001589	0.001105
80	0.006487	0.004460	0.003071	0.002119	0.001464	0.001014
81	0.006091	0.004168	0.002857	0.001962	0.001350	0.000930
82	0.005719	0.003895	0.002658	0.001817	0.001244	0.000853
83	0.005370	0.003640	0.002472	0.001682	0.001146	0.000783
84	0.005042	0.003402	0.002300	0.001557	0.001057	0.000718
85	0.004735	0.003180	0.002139	0.001442	0.000974	0.000659
86	0.004446	0.002972	0.001990	0.001335	0.000898	0.000604
87	0.004174	0.002777	0.001851	0.001236	0.000827	0.000554
88	0.003920	0.002596	0.001722	0.001145	0.000762	0.000509
89	0.003680	0.002426	0.001602	0.001060	0.000703	0.000467
90	0.003456	0.002267	0.001490	0.000981	0.000648	0.000428
91	0.003245	0.002119	0.001386	0.000909	0.000597	0.000393
92	0.003047	0.001980	0.001289	0.000841	0.000550	0.000360
93	0.002861	0.001851	0.001200	0.000779	0.000507	0.000331
94	0.002686	0.001730	0.001116	0.000721	0.000467	0.000303
95	0.002522	0.001616	0.001038	0.000668	0.000431	0.000278
96	0.002368	0.001511	0.000966	0.000618	0.000397	0.000255
97	0.002224	0.001412	0.000898	0.000573	0.000366	0.000234
98	0.002088	0.001319	0.000836	0.000530	0.000337	0.000215
99	0.001961	0.001233	0.000777	0.000491	0.000311	0.000197
100	0.001841	0.001152	0.000723	0.000455	0.000286	0.000181
101	0.001729	0.001077	0.000673	0.000421	0.000264	0.000166
102	0.001623	0.001007	0.000626	0.000390	0.000243	0.000152
103	0.001524	0.000941	0.000582	0.000361	0.000224	0.000140
104	0.001431	0.000879	0.000541	0.000334	0.000207	0.000128
105	0.001344	0.000822	0.000504	0.000309	0.000190	0.000118
106	0.001262	0.000768	0.000468	0.000286	0.000176	0.000108
107	0.001185	0.000718	0.000436	0.000265	0.000162	0.000099
108	0.001112	0.000671	0.000405	0.000246	0.000149	0.000091
109	0.001044	0.000627	0.000377	0.000227	0.000137	0.000083
110	0.000981	0.000586	0.000351	0.000211	0.000127	0.000076
111	0.000921	0.000548	0.000326	0.000195	0.000117	0.000070
112	0.000865	0.000512	0.000304	0.000181	0.000108	0.000064
113	0.000812	0.000478	0.000282	0.000167	0.000099	0.000059
114	0.000762	0.000447	0.000263	0.000155	0.000091	0.000054
115	0.000716	0.000418	0.000244	0.000143	0.000084	0.000050
116	0.000672	0.000390	0.000227	0.000133	0.000078	0.000046
117	0.000631	0.000365	0.000211	0.000123	0.000072	0.000042
118	0.000593	0.000341	0.000197	0.000114	0.000066	0.000038
119	0.000556	0.000319	0.000183	0.000105	0.000061	0.000035
120	0.000522	0.000298	0.000170	0.000098	0.000056	0.000032

Table II **Present Value Factor (Single Payment/Present Value Factor; Present Worth Factor)(continued)** $\frac{1}{(1+i)^n}$

n	0.095 (9½%)	0.10 (10%)	0.105 (10½%)	0.11 (11%)	0.115 (11½%)	0.12 (12%)
1	0.913242	0.909091	0.904977	0.900901	0.896861	0.892857
2	0.834011	0.826446	0.818984	0.811622	0.804360	0.797194
3	0.761654	0.751315	0.741162	0.731191	0.721399	0.711780
4	0.695574	0.683013	0.670735	0.658731	0.646994	0.635518
5	0.635228	0.620921	0.607000	0.593451	0.580264	0.567427
6	0.580117	0.564474	0.549321	0.534641	0.520416	0.506631
7	0.529787	0.513158	0.497123	0.481658	0.466741	0.452349
8	0.483824	0.466507	0.449885	0.433926	0.418602	0.403883
9	0.441848	0.424098	0.407136	0.390925	0.375428	0.360610
10	0.403514	0.385543	0.368449	0.352184	0.336706	0.321973
11	0.368506	0.350494	0.333438	0.317283	0.301979	0.287476
12	0.336535	0.318631	0.301754	0.285841	0.270833	0.256675
13	0.307338	0.289664	0.273080	0.257514	0.242900	0.229174
14	0.280674	0.263331	0.247132	0.231995	0.217847	0.204620
15	0.256323	0.239392	0.223648	0.209004	0.195379	0.182696
16	0.234085	0.217629	0.202397	0.188292	0.175227	0.163122
17	0.213777	0.197845	0.183164	0.169633	0.157155	0.145644
18	0.195230	0.179859	0.165760	0.152822	0.140946	0.130040
19	0.178292	0.163508	0.150009	0.137678	0.126409	0.116107
20	0.162824	0.148644	0.135755	0.124034	0.113371	0.103667
21	0.148697	0.135131	0.122855	0.111742	0.101678	0.092560
22	0.135797	0.122846	0.111181	0.100669	0.091191	0.082643
23	0.124015	0.111678	0.100616	0.090693	0.081786	0.073788
24	0.113256	0.101526	0.091055	0.081705	0.073351	0.065882
25	0.103430	0.092296	0.082403	0.073608	0.065785	0.058823
26	0.094457	0.083905	0.074573	0.066314	0.059000	0.052521
27	0.086262	0.076278	0.067487	0.059742	0.052915	0.046894
28	0.078778	0.069343	0.061074	0.053822	0.047457	0.041869
29	0.071943	0.063039	0.055271	0.048488	0.042563	0.037383
30	0.065702	0.057309	0.050019	0.043683	0.038173	0.033378
31	0.060002	0.052099	0.045266	0.039354	0.034236	0.029802
32	0.054796	0.047362	0.040964	0.035454	0.030705	0.026609
33	0.050042	0.043057	0.037072	0.031940	0.027538	0.023758
34	0.045700	0.039143	0.033549	0.028775	0.024698	0.021212
35	0.041736	0.035584	0.030361	0.025924	0.022150	0.018940
36	0.038115	0.032349	0.027476	0.023355	0.019866	0.016910
37	0.034808	0.029408	0.024865	0.021040	0.017817	0.015098
38	0.031788	0.026735	0.022503	0.018955	0.015979	0.013481
39	0.029030	0.024304	0.020364	0.017077	0.014331	0.012036
40	0.026512	0.022095	0.018429	0.015384	0.012853	0.010747
41	0.024211	0.020086	0.016678	0.013860	0.011527	0.009595
42	0.022111	0.018260	0.015093	0.012486	0.010338	0.008567
43	0.020193	0.016600	0.013659	0.011249	0.009272	0.007649
44	0.018441	0.015091	0.012361	0.010134	0.008316	0.006830
45	0.016841	0.013719	0.011187	0.009130	0.007458	0.006098
46	0.015380	0.012472	0.010124	0.008225	0.006689	0.005445
47	0.014045	0.011338	0.009162	0.007410	0.005999	0.004861
48	0.012827	0.010307	0.008291	0.006676	0.005380	0.004340
49	0.011714	0.009370	0.007503	0.006014	0.004825	0.003875
50	0.010698	0.008519	0.006790	0.005418	0.004328	0.003460
51	0.009770	0.007744	0.006145	0.004881	0.003881	0.003089
52	0.008922	0.007040	0.005561	0.004397	0.003481	0.002758
53	0.008148	0.006400	0.005033	0.003962	0.003122	0.002463
54	0.007441	0.005818	0.004554	0.003569	0.002800	0.002199
55	0.006796	0.005289	0.004122	0.003215	0.002511	0.001963
56	0.006206	0.004809	0.003730	0.002897	0.002252	0.001753
57	0.005668	0.004371	0.003376	0.002610	0.002020	0.001565
58	0.005176	0.003974	0.003055	0.002351	0.001812	0.001398
59	0.004727	0.003613	0.002765	0.002118	0.001625	0.001248
60	0.004317	0.003284	0.002502	0.001908	0.001457	0.001114

Table II Present Value Factor (Single Payment/Present Value Factor; Present Worth Factor)(continued) $\frac{1}{(1+i)^n}$

n	*0.125 (12½%)*	*0.13 (13%)*	*0.135 (13½%)*	*0.14 (14%)*	*0.145 (14½%)*	*0.15 (15%)*
1	0.888889	0.884956	0.881057	0.877193	0.873362	0.869565
2	0.790123	0.783147	0.776262	0.769468	0.762762	0.756144
3	0.702332	0.693050	0.683931	0.674972	0.666168	0.657516
4	0.624295	0.613319	0.602583	0.592080	0.581806	0.571753
5	0.554929	0.542760	0.530910	0.519369	0.508127	0.497177
6	0.493270	0.480319	0.467762	0.455587	0.443779	0.432328
7	0.438462	0.425061	0.412125	0.399637	0.387580	0.375937
8	0.389744	0.376160	0.363106	0.350559	0.338498	0.326902
9	0.346439	0.332885	0.319917	0.307508	0.295631	0.284262
10	0.307946	0.294588	0.281865	0.269744	0.258193	0.247185
11	0.273730	0.260698	0.248339	0.236617	0.225496	0.214943
12	0.243315	0.230706	0.218801	0.207559	0.196940	0.186907
13	0.216280	0.204165	0.192776	0.182069	0.172000	0.162528
14	0.192249	0.180677	0.169847	0.159710	0.150218	0.141329
15	0.170888	0.159891	0.149645	0.140096	0.131195	0.122894
16	0.151901	0.141496	0.131846	0.122892	0.114581	0.106865
17	0.135023	0.125218	0.116164	0.107800	0.100071	0.092926
18	0.120020	0.110812	0.102347	0.094561	0.087398	0.080805
19	0.106685	0.098064	0.090173	0.082948	0.076330	0.070265
20	0.094831	0.086782	0.079448	0.072762	0.066664	0.061100
21	0.084294	0.076798	0.069998	0.063826	0.058222	0.053131
22	0.074928	0.067963	0.061672	0.055988	0.050849	0.046201
23	0.066603	0.060144	0.054337	0.049112	0.044409	0.040174
24	0.059202	0.053225	0.047874	0.043081	0.038785	0.034934
25	0.052624	0.047102	0.042180	0.037790	0.033874	0.030378
26	0.046777	0.041683	0.037163	0.033149	0.029584	0.026415
27	0.041580	0.036888	0.032742	0.029078	0.025838	0.022970
28	0.036960	0.032644	0.028848	0.025507	0.022566	0.019974
29	0.032853	0.028889	0.025417	0.022375	0.019708	0.017369
30	0.029203	0.025565	0.022394	0.019627	0.017212	0.015103
31	0.025958	0.022624	0.019730	0.017217	0.015032	0.013133
32	0.023074	0.020021	0.017383	0.015102	0.013129	0.011420
33	0.020510	0.017718	0.015316	0.013248	0.011466	0.009931
34	0.018231	0.015680	0.013494	0.011621	0.010014	0.008635
35	0.016205	0.013876	0.011889	0.010194	0.008746	0.007509
36	0.014405	0.012279	0.010475	0.008942	0.007638	0.006529
37	0.012804	0.010867	0.009229	0.007844	0.006671	0.005678
38	0.011382	0.009617	0.008131	0.006880	0.005826	0.004937
39	0.010117	0.008510	0.007164	0.006035	0.005088	0.004293
40	0.008993	0.007531	0.006312	0.005294	0.004444	0.003733
41	0.007994	0.006665	0.005561	0.004644	0.003881	0.003246
42	0.007105	0.005898	0.004900	0.004074	0.003390	0.002823
43	0.006316	0.005219	0.004317	0.003573	0.002960	0.002455
44	0.005614	0.004619	0.003803	0.003135	0.002586	0.002134
45	0.004990	0.004088	0.003351	0.002750	0.002258	0.001856
46	0.004436	0.003617	0.002953	0.002412	0.001972	0.001614
47	0.003943	0.003201	0.002601	0.002116	0.001722	0.001403
48	0.003505	0.002833	0.002292	0.001856	0.001504	0.001220
49	0.003115	0.002507	0.002019	0.001628	0.001314	0.001061
50	0.002769	0.002219	0.001779	0.001428	0.001147	0.000923
51	0.002462	0.001963	0.001568	0.001253	0.001002	0.000802
52	0.002188	0.001737	0.001381	0.001099	0.000875	0.000698
53	0.001945	0.001538	0.001217	0.000964	0.000764	0.000607
54	0.001729	0.001361	0.001072	0.000846	0.000668	0.000528
55	0.001537	0.001204	0.000945	0.000742	0.000583	0.000459
56	0.001366	0.001066	0.000832	0.000651	0.000509	0.000399
57	0.001214	0.000943	0.000733	0.000571	0.000445	0.000347
58	0.001079	0.000835	0.000646	0.000501	0.000388	0.000302
59	0.000959	0.000739	0.000569	0.000439	0.000339	0.000262
60	0.000853	0.000654	0.000501	0.000385	0.000296	0.000228

Table II **Present Value Factor (Single Payment/Present Value Factor; Present Worth Factor)(continued)** $\frac{1}{(1+i)^n}$

n	0.155 (15½%)	0.16 (16%)	0.165 (16½%)	0.17 (17%)	0.175 (17½%)	0.18 (18%)
1	0.865801	0.862069	0.858369	0.854701	0.851064	0.847458
2	0.749611	0.743163	0.736798	0.730514	0.724310	0.718184
3	0.649014	0.640658	0.632444	0.624371	0.616434	0.608631
4	0.561917	0.552291	0.542871	0.533650	0.524624	0.515789
5	0.486508	0.476113	0.465983	0.456111	0.446489	0.437109
6	0.421219	0.410442	0.399986	0.389839	0.379991	0.370432
7	0.364692	0.353830	0.343335	0.333195	0.323396	0.313925
8	0.315751	0.305025	0.294708	0.284782	0.275231	0.266038
9	0.273377	0.262953	0.252969	0.243404	0.234239	0.225456
10	0.236690	0.226684	0.217140	0.208037	0.199352	0.191064
11	0.204927	0.195417	0.186387	0.177810	0.169662	0.161919
12	0.177426	0.168463	0.159989	0.151974	0.144393	0.137220
13	0.153615	0.145227	0.137329	0.129892	0.122888	0.116288
14	0.133000	0.125195	0.117879	0.111019	0.104585	0.098549
15	0.115152	0.107927	0.101184	0.094888	0.089009	0.083516
16	0.099698	0.093041	0.086853	0.081101	0.075752	0.070776
17	0.086319	0.080207	0.074552	0.069317	0.064470	0.059980
18	0.074735	0.069144	0.063993	0.059245	0.054868	0.050830
19	0.064706	0.059607	0.054930	0.050637	0.046696	0.043077
20	0.056022	0.051385	0.047150	0.043280	0.039741	0.036506
21	0.048504					
22	0.041995					
23	0.036359					
24	0.031480					
25	0.027255					
26	0.023598					
27	0.020431					
28	0.017689					
29	0.015315					
30	0.013260					
31	0.011480					
32	0.009940					
33	0.008606					
34	0.007451					
35	0.006451					
36	0.005585					
37	0.004836					
38	0.004187					
39	0.003625					
40	0.003138					
41	0.002717					
42	0.002353					
43	0.002037					
44	0.001764					
45	0.001527					
46	0.001322					
47	0.001145					
48	0.000991					
49	0.000858					
50	0.000743					
51	0.000643					
52	0.000557					
53	0.000482					
54	0.000417					
55	0.000361					
56	0.000313					
57	0.000271					
58	0.000235					
59	0.000203					
60	0.000176					

Table II **Present Value Factor (Single Payment/Present Value Factor; Present Worth Factor)(continued)** $\frac{1}{(1+i)^n}$

n	0.185 (18½%)	0.19 (19%)	0.195 (19½%)	0.20 (20%)	0.21 (21%)	0.22 (22%)
1	0.843882	0.840336	0.836820	0.833333	0.826446	0.819672
2	0.712137	0.706165	0.700268	0.694444	0.683013	0.671862
3	0.600959	0.593416	0.585998	0.578704	0.564474	0.550707
4	0.507139	0.498669	0.490375	0.482253	0.466507	0.451399
5	0.427965	0.419049	0.410356	0.401878	0.385543	0.369999
6	0.361152	0.352142	0.343394	0.334898	0.318631	0.303278
7	0.304770	0.295918	0.287359	0.279082	0.263331	0.248589
8	0.257189	0.248671	0.240468	0.232568	0.217629	0.203761
9	0.217038	0.208967	0.201228	0.193807	0.179859	0.167017
10	0.183154	0.175602	0.168392	0.161506	0.148644	0.136899
11	0.154560	0.147565	0.140914	0.134588	0.122846	0.112213
12	0.130431	0.124004	0.117919	0.112157	0.101526	0.091978
13	0.110068	0.104205	0.098677	0.093464	0.083905	0.075391
14	0.092884	0.087567	0.082575	0.077887	0.069343	0.061796
15	0.078384	0.073586	0.069101	0.064905	0.057309	0.050653
16	0.066146	0.061837	0.057825	0.054088	0.047362	0.041519
17	0.055820	0.051964	0.048389	0.045073	0.039143	0.034032
18	0.047105	0.043667	0.040493	0.037561	0.032349	0.027895
19	0.039751	0.036695	0.033885	0.031301	0.026735	0.022865
20	0.033545	0.030836	0.028356	0.026084	0.022095	0.018741

n	0.23 (23%)	0.24 (24%)	0.25 (25%)	0.30 (30%)	0.35 (35%)	0.40 (40%)
1	0.813008	0.806452	0.800000	0.769231	0.740741	0.714286
2	0.660982	0.650364	0.640000	0.591716	0.548697	0.510204
3	0.537384	0.524487	0.512000	0.455166	0.406442	0.364431
4	0.436897	0.422974	0.409600	0.350128	0.301068	0.260308
5	0.355201	0.341108	0.327680	0.269329	0.223014	0.185934
6	0.288781	0.275087	0.262144	0.207176	0.165195	0.132810
7	0.234782	0.221844	0.209715	0.159366	0.122367	0.094865
8	0.190879	0.178907	0.167772	0.122589	0.090642	0.067760
9	0.155187	0.144280	0.134218	0.094300	0.067142	0.048400
10	0.126168	0.116354	0.107374	0.072538	0.049735	0.034572
11	0.102576	0.093834	0.085899	0.055799	0.036841	0.024694
12	0.083395	0.075673	0.068719	0.042922	0.027289	0.017639
13	0.067801	0.061026	0.054976	0.033017	0.020214	0.012599
14	0.055122	0.049215	0.043980	0.025398	0.014974	0.008999
15	0.044815	0.039689	0.035184	0.019537	0.011092	0.006428
16	0.036435	0.032008	0.028147	0.015028	0.008216	0.004591
17	0.029622	0.025813	0.022518	0.011560	0.006086	0.003280
18	0.024083	0.020817	0.018014	0.008892	0.004508	0.002343
19	0.019580	0.016788	0.014412	0.006840	0.003339	0.001673
20	0.015918	0.013538	0.011529	0.005262	0.002474	0.001195

Table III Uniform Series/Compound-Amount Factor (Future Value of Annuity)

$$\frac{(1 + i)^n - 1}{i}$$

n	0.0025 (1/4%)	0.0050 (1/2%)	0.0075 (3/4%)	0.01 (1%)	0.0125 (1 1/4%)	0.0150 (1 1/2%)
1	1.000000	1.000000	1.000000	1.000000	1.000000	1.000000
2	2.002500	2.005000	2.007500	2.010000	2.012500	2.015000
3	3.007506	3.015025	3.022556	3.030100	3.037656	3.045225
4	4.015025	4.030100	4.045225	4.060401	4.075627	4.090903
5	5.025063	5.050251	5.075565	5.101005	5.126572	5.152267
6	6.037625	6.075502	6.113631	6.152015	6.190654	6.229551
7	7.052719	7.105879	7.159484	7.213535	7.268038	7.322994
8	8.070351	8.141409	8.213180	8.285671	8.358888	8.432839
9	9.090527	9.182116	9.274779	9.368527	9.463374	9.559332
10	10.113253	10.228026	10.344339	10.462213	10.581666	10.702722
11	11.138536	11.279167	11.421922	11.566835	11.713937	11.863262
12	12.166383	12.335562	12.507586	12.682503	12.860361	13.041211
13	13.196799	13.397240	13.601393	13.809328	14.021116	14.236830
14	14.229791	14.464226	14.703404	14.947421	15.196380	15.450382
15	15.265365	15.536548	15.813679	16.096896	16.386335	16.682138
16	16.303529	16.614230	16.932282	17.257864	17.591164	17.932370
17	17.344287	17.697301	18.059274	18.430443	18.811053	19.201355
18	18.387648	18.785788	19.194718	19.614748	20.046192	20.489376
19	19.433617	19.879717	20.338679	20.810895	21.296769	21.796716
20	20.482201	20.979115	21.491219	22.019004	22.562979	23.123667
21	21.533407	22.084011	22.652403	23.239194	23.845016	24.470522
22	22.587240	23.194431	23.822296	24.471586	25.143078	25.837580
23	23.643708	24.310403	25.000963	25.716302	26.457367	27.225144
24	24.702818	25.431955	26.188471	26.973465	27.788084	28.633521
25	25.764575	26.559115	27.384884	28.243200	29.135435	30.063024
26	26.828986	27.691911	28.590271	29.525631	30.499628	31.513969
27	27.896059	28.830370	29.804698	30.820888	31.880873	32.986678
28	28.965799	29.974522	31.028233	32.129097	33.279384	34.481479
29	30.038213	31.124395	32.260945	33.450388	34.695377	35.998701
30	31.113309	32.280017	33.502902	34.784892	36.129069	37.538681
31	32.191092	33.441417	34.754174	36.132740	37.580682	39.101762
32	33.271570	34.608624	36.014830	37.494068	39.050441	40.688288
33	34.354749	35.781667	37.284941	38.869009	40.538571	42.298612
34	35.440636	36.960575	38.564578	40.257699	42.045303	43.933092
35	36.529237	38.145378	39.853813	41.660276	43.570870	45.592088
36	37.620560	39.336105	41.152716	43.076878	45.115505	47.275969
37	38.714612	40.532785	42.461361	44.507647	46.679449	48.985109
38	39.811398	41.735449	43.779822	45.952724	48.262942	50.719885
39	40.910927	42.944127	45.108170	47.412251	49.866229	52.480684
40	42.013204	44.158847	46.446482	48.886373	51.489557	54.267894
41	43.118237	45.379642	47.794830	50.375237	53.133177	56.081912
42	44.226033	46.606540	49.153291	51.878989	54.797341	57.923141
43	45.336598	47.839572	50.521941	53.397779	56.482308	59.791988
44	46.449939	49.078770	51.900856	54.931757	58.188337	61.688868
45	47.566064	50.324164	53.290112	56.481075	59.915691	63.614201
46	48.684979	51.575785	54.689788	58.045885	61.664637	65.568414
47	49.806692	52.833664	56.099961	59.626344	63.435445	67.551940
48	50.931208	54.097832	57.520711	61.222608	65.228388	69.565219
49	52.058536	55.368321	58.952116	62.834834	67.043743	71.608698
50	53.188683	56.645163	60.394257	64.463182	68.881790	73.682828
51	54.321654	57.928389	61.847214	66.107814	70.742812	75.788070
52	55.457459	59.218031	63.311068	67.768892	72.627097	77.924892
53	56.596102	60.514121	64.785901	69.446581	74.534936	80.093765
54	57.737593	61.816692	66.271796	71.141047	76.466623	82.295171
55	58.881937	63.125775	67.768834	72.852457	78.422456	84.529599
56	60.029141	64.441404	69.277100	74.580982	80.402736	86.797543
57	61.179214	65.763611	70.796679	76.326792	82.407771	89.099506
58	62.332162	67.092429	72.327654	78.090060	84.437868	91.435999
59	63.487993	68.427891	73.870111	79.870960	86.493341	93.807539
60	64.646713	69.770031	75.424137	81.669670	88.574508	96.214652

Table III Uniform Series/Compound-Amount Factor (Future Value of Annuity) (continued)

$$\frac{(1 + i)^n - 1}{i}$$

n	0.0025 (1/4%)	0.0050 (1/2%)	0.0075 (3/4%)	0.01 (1%)	0.0125 (1 1/4%)	0.0150 (1 1/2%)
61	65.808329	71.118881	76.989818	83.486367	90.681689	98.657871
62	66.972850	72.474475	78.567242	85.321230	92.815210	101.137740
63	68.140282	73.836847	80.156496	87.174443	94.975400	103.654806
64	69.310633	75.206032	81.757670	89.046187	97.162593	106.209628
65	70.483910	76.582062	83.370852	90.936649	99.377125	108.802772
66	71.660119	77.964972	84.996134	92.846015	101.619339	111.434814
67	72.839270	79.354797	86.633605	94.774475	103.889581	114.106336
68	74.021368	80.751571	88.283357	96.722220	106.188201	116.817931
69	75.206421	82.155329	89.945482	98.689442	108.515553	119.570200
70	76.394437	83.566105	91.620073	100.676337	110.871998	122.363753
71	77.585423	84.983936	93.307223	102.683100	113.257898	125.199209
72	78.779387	86.408856	95.007028	104.709931	115.673621	128.077197
73	79.976335	87.840900	96.719580	106.757031	118.119542	130.998355
74	81.176276	89.280104	98.444977	108.824601	120.596036	133.963331
75	82.379217	90.726505	100.183314	110.912847	123.103486	136.972781
76	83.585165	92.180138	101.934689	113.021975	125.642280	140.027372
77	84.794128	93.641038	103.699199	115.152195	128.212809	143.127783
78	86.006113	95.109243	105.476943	117.303717	130.815469	146.274700
79	87.221129	96.584790	107.268021	119.476754	133.450662	149.468820
80	88.439181	98.067714	109.072531	121.671522	136.118795	152.710852
81	89.660279	99.558052	110.890575	123.888237	138.820280	156.001515
82	90.884430	101.055842	112.722254	126.127119	141.555534	159.341538
83	92.111641	102.561122	114.567671	128.388390	144.324978	162.731661
84	93.341920	104.073927	116.426928	130.672274	147.129040	166.172636
85	94.575275	105.594297	118.300130	132.978997	149.968153	169.665226
86	95.811713	107.122268	120.187381	135.308787	152.842755	173.210204
87	97.051242	108.657880	122.088787	137.661875	155.753289	176.808357
88	98.293871	110.201169	124.004453	140.038494	158.700206	180.460482
89	99.539605	111.752175	125.934486	142.438879	161.683958	184.167390
90	100.788454	113.310936	127.878995	144.863267	164.705008	187.929900
91	102.040425	114.877490	129.838087	147.311900	167.763820	191.748849
92	103.295526	116.451878	131.811873	149.785019	170.860868	195.625082
93	104.553765	118.034137	133.800462	152.282869	173.996629	199.559458
94	105.815150	119.624308	135.803965	154.805698	177.171587	203.552850
95	107.079688	121.222430	137.822495	157.353755	180.386232	207.606142
96	108.347387	122.828542	139.856164	159.927293	183.641059	211.720235
97	109.618255	124.442684	141.905085	162.526565	186.936573	215.896038
98	110.892301	126.064898	143.969373	165.151831	190.273280	220.134479
99	112.169532	127.695222	146.049143	167.803349	193.651696	224.436496
100	113.449955	129.333698	148.144512	170.481383	197.072342	228.803043
101	114.733580	130.980367	150.255596	173.186197	200.535746	233.235089
102	116.020414	132.635269	152.382513	175.918059	204.042443	237.733615
103	117.310465	134.298445	154.525382	178.677239	207.592974	242.299620
104	118.603742	135.969937	156.684322	181.464012	211.187886	246.934114
105	119.900251	137.649787	158.859454	184.278652	214.827734	251.638126
106	121.200002	139.338036	161.050900	187.121438	218.513081	256.412697
107	122.503002	141.034726	163.258782	189.992653	222.244495	261.258888
108	123.809259	142.739900	165.483223	192.892579	226.022551	266.177771
109	125.118782	144.453599	167.724347	195.821505	229.847833	271.170438
110	126.431579	146.175867	169.982280	198.779720	233.720931	276.237994
111	127.747658	147.906747	172.257147	201.767517	237.642442	281.381564
112	129.067027	149.646280	174.549075	204.785192	241.612973	286.602288
113	130.389695	151.394512	176.858194	207.833044	245.633135	291.901322
114	131.715669	153.151484	179.184630	210.911375	249.703549	297.279842
115	133.044958	154.917242	181.528515	214.020489	253.824843	302.739039
116	134.377571	156.691828	183.889979	217.160693	257.997654	308.280125
117	135.713515	158.475287	186.269153	220.332300	262.222625	313.904327
118	137.052798	160.267663	188.666172	223.535623	266.500407	319.612892
119	138.395430	162.069002	191.081168	226.770980	270.831663	325.407085
120	139.741419	163.879347	193.514277	230.038689	275.217058	331.288191

Table III Uniform Series/Compound-Amount Factor (Future Value of Annuity) (continued)

$$\frac{(1 + i)^n - 1}{i}$$

n	0.0175 (1¾%)	0.02 (2%)	0.0225 (2¼%)	0.025 (2½%)	0.0275 (2¾%)	0.03 (3%)
1	1.000000	1.000000	1.000000	1.000000	1.000000	1.000000
2	2.017500	2.020000	2.022500	2.025000	2.027500	2.030000
3	3.052806	3.060400	3.068006	3.075625	3.083256	3.090900
4	4.106230	4.121608	4.137036	4.152516	4.168046	4.183627
5	5.178089	5.204040	5.230120	5.256329	5.282667	5.309136
6	6.268706	6.308121	6.347797	6.387737	6.427940	6.468410
7	7.378408	7.434283	7.490623	7.547430	7.604709	7.662462
8	8.507530	8.582969	8.659162	8.736116	8.813838	8.892336
9	9.656412	9.754628	9.853993	9.954519	10.056219	10.159106
10	10.825399	10.949721	11.075708	11.203382	11.332765	11.463879
11	12.014844	12.168715	12.324911	12.483466	12.644416	12.807796
12	13.225104	13.412090	13.602222	13.795553	13.992137	14.192030
13	14.456543	14.680332	14.908272	15.140442	15.376921	15.617790
14	15.709533	15.973938	16.243708	16.518953	16.799786	17.086324
15	16.984449	17.293417	17.609191	17.931927	18.261781	18.598914
16	18.281677	18.639285	19.005398	19.380225	19.763979	20.156881
17	19.601607	20.012071	20.433020	20.864730	21.307489	21.761588
18	20.944635	21.412312	21.892763	22.386349	22.893445	23.414435
19	22.311166	22.840559	23.385350	23.946007	24.523015	25.116868
20	23.701611	24.297370	24.911520	25.544658	26.197398	26.870374
21	25.116389	25.783317	26.472029	27.183274	27.917826	28.676486
22	26.555926	27.298984	28.067650	28.862856	29.685566	30.536780
23	28.020655	28.844963	29.699172	30.584427	31.501919	32.452884
24	29.511016	30.421862	31.367403	32.349038	33.368222	34.426470
25	31.027459	32.030300	33.073170	34.157764	35.285848	36.459264
26	32.570440	33.670906	34.817316	36.011708	37.256209	38.553042
27	34.140422	35.344324	36.600706	37.912001	39.280755	40.709634
28	35.737880	37.051210	38.424222	39.859801	41.360975	42.930923
29	37.363293	38.792235	40.288767	41.856296	43.498402	45.218850
30	39.017150	40.568079	42.195264	43.902703	45.694608	47.575416
31	40.699950	42.379441	44.144657	46.000271	47.951210	50.002678
32	42.412200	44.227030	46.137912	48.150278	50.269868	52.502759
33	44.154413	46.111570	48.176015	50.354034	52.652290	55.077841
34	45.927115	48.033802	50.259976	52.612885	55.100228	57.730177
35	47.730840	49.994478	52.390825	54.928207	57.615484	60.462082
36	49.566129	51.994367	54.569619	57.301413	60.199910	63.275944
37	51.433537	54.034255	56.797435	59.733948	62.855407	66.174223
38	53.333624	56.114940	59.075377	62.227297	65.583931	69.159449
39	55.266962	58.237238	61.404573	64.782979	68.387489	72.234233
40	57.234134	60.401983	63.786176	67.402554	71.268145	75.401260
41	59.235731	62.610023	66.221365	70.087617	74.228019	78.663298
42	61.272357	64.862223	68.711346	72.839808	77.269289	82.023196
43	63.344623	67.159468	71.257351	75.660803	80.394195	85.483892
44	65.453154	69.502657	73.860642	78.552323	83.605035	89.048409
45	67.598584	71.892710	76.522506	81.516131	86.904174	92.719861
46	69.781559	74.330564	79.244262	84.554034	90.294039	96.501457
47	72.002736	76.817176	82.027258	87.667885	93.777125	100.396501
48	74.262784	79.353519	84.872872	90.859582	97.355996	104.408396
49	76.562383	81.940590	87.782511	94.131072	101.033285	108.540648
50	78.902225	84.579401	90.757618	97.484349	104.811701	112.796867
51	81.283014	87.270989	93.799664	100.921458	108.694023	117.180773
52	83.705466	90.016409	96.910157	104.444494	112.683108	121.696197
53	86.170312	92.816737	100.090635	108.055606	116.781894	126.347082
54	88.678292	95.673072	103.342674	111.756996	120.993396	131.137495
55	91.230163	98.586534	106.667885	115.550921	125.320714	136.071620
56	93.826690	101.558264	110.067912	119.439694	129.767034	141.153768
57	96.468658	104.589430	113.544440	123.425687	134.335627	146.388381
58	99.156859	107.681218	117.099190	127.511329	139.029857	151.780033
59	101.892104	110.834843	120.733922	131.699112	143.853178	157.333434
60	104.675216	114.051539	124.450435	135.991590	148.809140	163.053437

Table III **Uniform Series/Compound-Amount Factor (Future Value of Annuity) (continued)**

$$\frac{(1+i)^n - 1}{i}$$

n	*0.0175 (1¾%)*	*0.02 (2%)*	*0.0225 (2¼%)*	*0.025 (2½%)*	*0.0275 (2¾%)*	*0.03 (3%)*
61	107.507032	117.332570	128.250570	140.391380	153.901392	168.945040
62	110.388405	120.679222	132.136208	144.901164	159.133680	175.013391
63	113.320202	124.092806	136.109272	149.523693	164.509856	181.263793
64	116.303306	127.574662	140.171731	154.261786	170.033877	187.701707
65	119.338614	131.126155	144.325595	159.118330	175.709809	194.332758
66	122.427039	134.748679	148.572921	164.096289	181.541829	201.162741
67	125.569513	138.443652	152.915811	169.198696	187.534229	208.197623
68	128.766979	142.212525	157.356417	174.428663	193.691420	215.443551
69	132.020401	146.056776	161.896937	179.789380	200.017934	222.906858
70	135.330758	149.977911	166.539618	185.284114	206.518427	230.594064
71	138.699047	153.977469	171.286759	190.916217	213.197684	238.511886
72	142.126280	158.057019	176.140711	196.689122	220.060621	246.667242
73	145.613490	162.218159	181.103877	202.606351	227.112288	255.067259
74	149.161726	166.462522	186.178714	208.671509	234.357876	263.719277
75	152.772056	170.791773	191.367735	214.888297	241.802717	272.630856
76	156.445567	175.207608	196.673509	221.260504	249.452292	281.809781
77	160.183364	179.711760	202.098663	227.792017	257.312230	291.264075
78	163.986573	184.305996	207.645883	234.486818	265.388316	301.001997
79	167.856338	188.992115	213.317916	241.348988	273.686495	311.032057
80	171.793824	193.771958	219.117569	248.382713	282.212873	321.363019
81	175.800216	198.647397	225.047714	255.592280	290.973727	332.003909
82	179.876720	203.620345	231.111288	262.982087	299.975505	342.964026
83	184.024563	208.692752	237.311292	270.556640	309.224831	354.252947
84	188.244992	213.866607	243.650796	278.320556	318.728514	365.880536
85	192.539280	219.143939	250.132939	286.278570	328.493548	377.856952
86	196.908717	224.526818	256.760930	294.435534	338.527121	390.192660
87	201.354620	230.017354	263.538051	302.796422	348.836617	402.898440
88	205.878326	235.617701	270.467657	311.366333	359.429624	415.985393
89	210.481196	241.330055	277.553179	320.150491	370.313938	429.464955
90	215.164617	247.156656	284.798126	329.154253	381.497572	443.348904
91	219.929998	253.099789	292.206083	338.383110	392.988755	457.649371
92	224.778773	259.161785	299.780720	347.842687	404.795946	472.378852
93	229.712401	265.345021	307.525786	357.538755	416.927834	487.550217
94	234.732369	271.651921	315.445117	367.477223	429.393350	503.176724
95	239.840185	278.084960	323.542632	377.664154	442.201667	519.272026
96	245.037388	284.646659	331.822341	388.105758	455.362213	535.850186
97	250.325542	291.339592	340.288344	398.808402	468.884673	552.925692
98	255.706239	298.166384	348.944831	409.778612	482.779002	570.513463
99	261.181099	305.129712	357.796090	421.023077	497.055424	588.628867
100	266.751768	312.232306	366.846502	432.548654	511.724449	607.287733
101	272.419924	319.476952	376.100548	444.362370	526.796871	626.506365
102	278.187272	326.866491	385.562811	456.471430	542.283785	646.301556
103	284.055550	334.403821	395.237974	468.883215	558.196589	666.690602
104	290.026522	342.091897	405.130828	481.605296	574.546995	687.691320
105	296.101986	349.933735	415.246272	494.645428	591.347038	709.322060
106	302.283771	357.932410	425.589313	508.011564	608.609081	731.601722
107	308.573737	366.091058	436.165073	521.711853	626.345831	754.549773
108	314.973777	374.412879	446.978787	535.754649	644.570341	778.186267
109	321.485818	382.901137	458.035810	550.148516	663.296026	802.531855
110	328.111820	391.559160	469.341615	564.902228	682.536666	827.607810
111	334.853777	400.390343	480.901802	580.024784	702.306425	853.436045
112	341.713718	409.398150	492.722092	595.525404	722.619851	880.039126
113	348.693708	418.586113	504.808339	611.413539	743.491897	907.440300
114	355.795848	427.957835	517.166527	627.698877	764.937924	935.663509
115	363.022275	437.516992	529.802774	644.391349	786.973717	964.733414
116	370.375165	447.267331	542.723336	661.501133	809.615495	994.675416
117	377.856731	457.212678	555.934611	679.038661	832.879921	1025.515679
118	385.469223	467.356932	569.443140	697.014628	856.784118	1057.281149
119	393.214935	477.704070	583.255611	715.439994	881.345682	1089.999584
120	401.096196	488.258152	597.378862	734.325993	906.582688	1123.699571

Table III Uniform Series/Compound-Amount Factor (Future Value of Annuity) (continued)

$$\frac{(1+i)^n - 1}{i}$$

n	0.035 (3½%)	0.04 (4%)	0.045 (4½%)	0.05 (5%)	0.055 (5½)	0.06 (6%)
1	1.000000	1.000000	1.000000	1.000000	1.000000	1.000000
2	2.035000	2.040000	2.045000	2.050000	2.055000	2.060000
3	3.106225	3.121600	3.137025	3.152500	3.168025	3.183600
4	4.214943	4.246464	4.278191	4.310125	4.342266	4.374616
5	5.362466	5.416323	5.470710	5.525631	5.581091	5.637093
6	6.550152	6.632975	6.716892	6.801913	6.888051	6.975319
7	7.779408	7.898294	8.019152	8.142008	8.266894	8.393838
8	9.051687	9.214226	9.380014	9.549109	9.721573	9.897468
9	10.368496	10.582795	10.802114	11.026564	11.256260	11.491316
10	11.731393	12.006107	12.288209	12.577893	12.875354	13.180795
11	13.141992	13.486351	13.841179	14.206787	14.583498	14.971643
12	14.601962	15.025805	15.464032	15.917127	16.385591	16.869941
13	16.113030	16.626838	17.159913	17.712983	18.286798	18.882138
14	17.676986	18.291911	18.932109	19.598632	20.292572	21.015066
15	19.295681	20.023588	20.784054	21.578564	22.408663	23.275970
16	20.971030	21.824531	22.719337	23.657492	24.641140	25.672528
17	22.705016	23.697512	24.741707	25.840366	26.996403	28.212880
18	24.499691	25.645413	26.855084	28.132385	29.481205	30.905653
19	26.357180	27.671229	29.063562	30.539004	32.102671	33.759992
20	28.279682	29.778079	31.371423	33.065954	34.868318	36.785591
21	30.269471	31.969202	33.783137	35.719252	37.786076	39.992727
22	32.328902	34.247970	36.303378	38.505214	40.864310	43.392290
23	34.460414	36.617889	38.937030	41.430475	44.111847	46.995828
24	36.666528	39.082604	41.689196	44.501999	47.537998	50.815577
25	38.949857	41.645908	44.565210	47.727099	51.152588	54.864512
26	41.313102	44.311745	47.570645	51.113454	54.965981	59.156383
27	43.759060	47.084214	50.711324	54.669126	58.989109	63.705766
28	46.290627	49.967583	53.993333	58.402583	63.233510	68.528112
29	48.910799	52.966286	57.423033	62.322712	67.711354	73.639798
30	51.622677	56.084938	61.007070	66.438848	72.435478	79.058186
31	54.429471	59.328335	64.752388	70.760790	77.419429	84.801677
32	57.334502	62.701469	68.666245	75.298829	82.677498	90.889778
33	60.341210	66.209527	72.756226	80.063771	88.224760	97.343165
34	63.453152	69.857909	77.030256	85.066959	94.077122	104.183755
35	66.674013	73.652225	81.496618	90.320307	100.251364	111.434780
36	70.007603	77.598314	86.163966	95.836323	106.765189	119.120867
37	73.457869	81.702246	91.041344	101.628139	113.637274	127.268119
38	77.028895	85.970336	96.138205	107.709546	120.887324	135.904206
39	80.724906	90.409150	101.464424	114.095023	128.536127	145.058458
40	84.550278	95.025516	107.030323	120.799774	136.605614	154.761966
41	88.509537	99.826536	112.846688	127.839763	145.118923	165.047684
42	92.607371	104.819598	118.924789	135.231751	154.100464	175.950545
43	96.848629	110.012382	125.276404	142.993339	163.575989	187.507577
44	101.238331	115.412877	131.913842	151.143006	173.572669	199.758032
45	105.781673	121.029392	138.849965	159.700156	184.119165	212.743514
46	110.484031	126.870568	146.098214	168.685164	195.245719	226.508125
47	115.350973	132.945390	153.672633	178.119422	206.984234	241.098612
48	120.388257	139.263206	161.587902	188.025393	219.368367	256.564529
49	125.601846	145.833734	169.859357	198.426663	232.433627	272.958401
50	130.997910	152.667084	178.503028	209.347996	246.217476	290.335905
51	136.582837	159.773767	187.535665	220.815396	260.759438	308.756059
52	142.363236	167.164718	196.974769	232.856165	276.101207	328.281422
53	148.345950	174.851306	206.838634	245.498974	292.286773	348.978308
54	154.538058	182.845359	217.146373	258.773922	309.362546	370.917006
55	160.946890	191.159173	227.917959	272.712618	327.377486	394.172027
56	167.580031	199.805540	239.174268	287.348249	346.383247	418.822348
57	174.445332	208.797762	250.937110	302.715662	366.434326	444.951689
58	181.550919	218.149672	263.229280	318.851445	387.588214	472.648790
59	188.905201	227.875659	276.074597	335.794017	409.905566	502.007718
60	196.516883	237.990685	289.497954	353.583718	433.450372	533.128181

Table III Uniform Series/Compound-Amount Factor (Future Value of Annuity) (continued)

$$\frac{(1 + i)^n - 1}{i}$$

n	0.035 (3½%)	0.04 (4%)	0.045 (4½%)	0.05 (5%)	0.055 (5½)	0.06 (6%)
61	204.394974	248.510313	303.525362	372.262904	458.290142	566.115872
62	212.548798	259.450725	318.184003	391.876049	484.496100	601.082824
63	220.988006	270.828754	333.502283	412.469851	512.143385	638.147793
64	229.722586	282.661904	349.509886	434.093344	541.311272	677.436661
65	238.762876	294.968380	366.237831	456.798011	572.083392	719.082861
66	248.119577	307.767116	383.718533	480.637912	604.547978	763.227832
67	257.803762	321.077800	401.985867	505.669807	638.798117	810.021502
68	267.826894	334.920912	421.075231	531.953298	674.932013	859.622792
69	278.200835	349.317749	441.023617	559.550963	713.053274	912.200160
70	288.937865	364.290459	461.869680	588.528511	753.271204	967.932170
71	300.050690	379.862077	483.653815	618.954936	795.701120	1027.008100
72	311.552464	396.056560	506.418237	650.902683	840.464682	1089.628586
73	323.456800	412.898823	530.207057	684.447817	887.690240	1156.006301
74	335.777788	430.414776	555.066375	719.670208	937.513203	1226.366679
75	348.530011	448.631367	581.044362	756.653718	990.076429	1300.948680
76	361.728561	467.576621	608.191358	795.486404	1045.530633	1380.005601
77	375.389061	487.279686	636.559969	836.260725	1104.034817	1463.805937
78	389.527678	507.770873	666.205168	879.073761	1165.756732	1552.634293
79	404.161147	529.081708	697.184401	924.027449	1230.873353	1646.792350
80	419.306787	551.244977	729.557699	971.228821	1299.571387	1746.599891
81	434.982524	574.294776	763.387795	1020.790262	1372.047813	1852.395885
82	451.206913	598.266567	798.740246	1072.829776	1448.510443	1964.539638
83	467.999155	623.197230	835.683557	1127.471264	1529.178517	2083.412016
84	485.379125	649.125119	874.289317	1184.844828	1614.283336	2209.416737
85	503.367394	676.090123	914.632336	1245.087069	1704.068919	2342.981741
86	521.985253	704.133728	956.790791	1308.341422	1798.792710	2484.560646
87	541.254737	733.299078	1000.846377	1374.758493	1898.726309	2634.634285
88	561.198653	763.631041	1046.884464	1444.496418	2004.156256	2793.712342
89	581.840606	795.176282	1094.994265	1517.721239	2115.384850	2962.335082
90	603.205027	827.983334	1145.269007	1594.607301	2232.731017	3141.075187
91	625.317203	862.102667	1197.806112	1675.337666	2356.531223	3330.539698
92	648.203305	897.586774	1252.707387	1760.104549	2487.140440	3531.372080
93	671.890421	934.490245	1310.079219	1849.109777	2624.933164	3744.254405
94	696.406585	972.869854	1370.032784	1942.565266	2770.304488	3969.909669
95	721.780816	1012.784648	1432.684259	2040.693529	2923.671235	4209.104250
96	748.043145	1054.296034	1498.155051	2143.728205	3085.473153	4462.650505
97	775.224655	1097.467876	1566.572028	2251.914616	3256.174176	4731.409535
98	803.357517	1142.366591	1638.067770	2365.510346	3436.263756	5016.294107
99	832.475031	1189.061254	1712.780819	2484.785864	3626.258262	5318.271753
100	862.611657	1237.623705	1790.855956	2610.025157	3826.702467	5638.368059
101	893.803065	1288.128653	1872.444474	2741.526415	4038.171102	5977.670142
102	926.086172	1340.653799	1957.704476	2879.602736	4261.270513	6337.330351
103	959.499188	1395.279951	2046.801177	3024.582872	4496.640391	6718.570172
104	994.081659	1452.091149	2139.907230	3176.812016	4744.955613	7122.684382
105	1029.874518	1511.174795	2237.203055	3336.652617	5006.928172	7551.045445
106	1066.920126	1572.621787	2338.877193	3504.485248	5283.309221	8005.108172
107	1105.262330	1636.526658	2445.126667	3680.709510	5574.891228	8486.414662
108	1144.946512	1702.987724	2556.157367	3865.744985	5882.510246	8996.599542
109	1186.019640	1772.107233	2672.184448	4060.032235	6207.048309	9537.395514
110	1228.530327	1843.991523	2793.432748	4264.033846	6549.435966	10110.639245
111	1272.528888	1918.751184	2920.137222	4478.235539	6910.654944	10718.277600
112	1318.067399	1996.501231	3052.543397	4703.147316	7291.740966	11362.374256
113	1365.199758	2077.361280	3190.907850	4939.304681	7693.786719	12045.116711
114	1413.981750	2161.455731	3335.498703	5187.269916	8117.944989	12768.823714
115	1464.471111	2248.913961	3486.596145	5447.633411	8565.431963	13535.953136
116	1516.727600	2339.870519	3644.492971	5721.015082	9037.530721	14349.110325
117	1570.813066	2434.465340	3809.495155	6008.065836	9535.594911	15211.056944
118	1626.791523	2532.843954	3981.922437	6309.469128	10061.052631	16124.720361
119	1684.729227	2635.157712	4162.108946	6625.942584	10615.410526	17093.203582
120	1744.694750	2741.564020	4350.403849	6958.239713	11200.258105	18119.795797

Table III **Uniform Series/Compound-Amount Factor (Future Value of Annuity) (continued)**

$$\frac{(1+i)^n - 1}{i}$$

n	0.065 (6½%)	0.07 (7%)	0.075 (7½%)	0.08 (8%)	0.085 (8½%)	0.09 (9%)
1	1.000000	1.000000	1.000000	1.000000	1.000000	1.000000
2	2.065000	2.070000	2.075000	2.080000	2.085000	2.090000
3	3.199225	3.214900	3.230625	3.246400	3.262225	3.278100
4	4.407175	4.439943	4.472922	4.506112	4.539514	4.573129
5	5.693641	5.750739	5.808391	5.866601	5.925373	5.984711
6	7.063728	7.153291	7.244020	7.335929	7.429030	7.523335
7	8.522870	8.654021	8.787322	8.922803	9.060497	9.200435
8	10.076856	10.259803	10.446371	10.636628	10.830639	11.028474
9	11.731852	11.977989	12.229849	12.487558	12.751244	13.021036
10	13.494423	13.816448	14.147087	14.486562	14.835099	15.192930
11	15.371560	15.783599	16.208119	16.645487	17.096083	17.560293
12	17.370711	17.888451	18.423728	18.977126	19.549250	20.140720
13	19.499808	20.140643	20.805508	21.495297	22.210936	22.953385
14	21.767295	22.550488	23.365921	24.214920	25.098866	26.019189
15	24.182169	25.129022	26.118365	27.152114	28.232269	29.360916
16	26.754010	27.888054	29.077242	30.324283	31.632012	33.003399
17	29.493021	30.840217	32.258035	33.750226	35.320733	36.973705
18	32.410067	33.999033	35.677388	37.450244	39.322995	41.301338
19	35.516722	37.378965	39.353192	41.446263	43.665450	46.018458
20	38.825309	40.995492	43.304681	45.761964	48.377013	51.160120
21	42.348954	44.865177	47.552532	50.422921	53.489059	56.764530
22	46.101636	49.005739	52.118972	55.456755	59.035629	62.873338
23	50.098242	53.436141	57.027895	60.893296	65.053658	69.531939
24	54.354628	58.176671	62.304987	66.764759	71.583219	76.789813
25	58.887679	63.249038	67.977862	73.105940	78.667792	84.700896
26	63.715378	68.676470	74.076201	79.954415	86.354555	93.323977
27	68.856877	74.483823	80.631916	87.350768	94.694692	102.723135
28	74.332574	80.697691	87.679310	95.338830	103.743741	112.968217
29	80.164192	87.346529	95.255258	103.965936	113.561959	124.135356
30	86.374864	94.460786	103.399403	113.283211	124.214725	136.307539
31	92.989230	102.073041	112.154358	123.345868	135.772977	149.575217
32	100.033530	110.218154	121.565935	134.213537	148.313680	164.036987
33	107.535710	118.933425	131.683380	145.950620	161.920343	179.800315
34	115.525531	128.258765	142.559633	158.626670	176.683572	196.982344
35	124.034690	138.236878	154.251606	172.316804	192.701675	215.710755
36	133.096945	148.913460	166.820476	187.102148	210.081318	236.124723
37	142.748247	160.337402	180.332012	203.070320	228.938230	258.375948
38	153.026883	172.561020	194.856913	220.315945	249.397979	282.629783
39	163.973630	185.640292	210.471181	238.941221	271.596808	309.066463
40	175.631916	199.635112	227.256520	259.056519	295.682536	337.882445
41	188.047990	214.609570	245.300759	280.781040	321.815552	369.291865
42	201.271110	230.632240	264.698315	304.243523	350.169874	403.528133
43	215.353732	247.776496	285.550689	329.583005	380.934313	440.845665
44	230.351725	266.120851	307.966991	356.949646	414.313730	481.521775
45	246.324587	285.749311	332.064515	386.505617	450.530397	525.858734
46	263.335685	306.751763	357.969354	418.426067	489.825480	574.186021
47	281.452504	329.224386	385.817055	452.900152	532.460646	626.862762
48	300.746917	353.270093	415.753334	490.132164	578.719801	684.280411
49	321.295467	378.999000	447.934835	530.342737	628.910984	746.865648
50	343.179672	406.528929	482.529947	573.770156	683.368418	815.083556
51	366.486351	435.985955	519.719693	620.671769	742.454733	889.441076
52	391.307963	467.504971	559.698670	671.325510	806.563386	970.490773
53	417.742981	501.230319	602.676070	726.031551	876.121273	1058.834943
54	445.896275	537.316442	648.876776	785.114075	951.591582	1155.130088
55	475.879533	575.928593	698.542534	848.923201	1033.476866	1260.091796
56	507.811702	617.243594	751.933224	917.837058	1122.322400	1374.500057
57	541.819463	661.450646	809.328216	992.264022	1218.719804	1499.205063
58	578.037728	708.752191	871.027832	1072.645144	1323.310987	1635.133518
59	616.610180	759.364844	937.354919	1159.456755	1436.792421	1783.295535
60	657.689842	813.520383	1008.656538	1253.213296	1559.919777	1944.792133

Table III Uniform Series/Compound-Amount Factor (Future Value of Annuity) (continued)

$$\frac{(1+i)^n - 1}{i}$$

n	0.065 (6½%)	0.07 (7%)	0.075 (7½%)	0.08 (8%)	0.085 (8½%)	0.09 (9%)
61	701.439682	871.466810	1085.305779	1354.470360	1693.512958	2120.823425
62	748.033261	933.469487	1167.703712	1463.827988	1838.461559	2312.697533
63	797.655423	999.812351	1256.281490	1581.934227	1995.730792	2521.840311
64	850.503026	1070.799216	1351.502602	1709.488966	2166.367909	2749.805939
65	906.785722	1146.755161	1453.865297	1847.248083	2351.509181	2998.288474
66	966.726794	1228.028022	1563.905195	1996.027929	2552.387462	3269.134436
67	1030.564036	1314.989983	1682.198084	2156.710164	2770.340396	3564.356535
68	1098.550698	1408.039282	1809.362940	2330.246977	3006.819330	3886.148624
69	1170.956494	1507.602032	1946.065161	2517.666735	3263.398973	4236.902000
70	1248.068666	1614.134174	2093.020048	2720.080074	3541.787885	4619.223180
71	1330.193129	1728.123566	2250.996552	2938.686480	3843.839855	5035.953266
72	1417.655682	1850.092216	2420.821293	3174.781398	4171.566243	5490.189060
73	1510.803302	1980.598671	2603.382890	3429.763910	4527.149374	5985.306075
74	1610.005516	2120.240578	2799.636607	3705.145023	4912.957071	6524.983622
75	1715.655875	2269.657419	3010.609352	4002.556624	5331.558422	7113.232148
76	1828.173507	2429.533438	3237.405054	4323.761154	5785.740887	7754.423041
77	1948.004785	2600.600779	3481.210433	4670.662047	6278.528863	8453.321115
78	2075.625096	2783.642833	3743.301215	5045.315011	6813.203816	9215.120015
79	2211.540727	2979.497831	4025.048806	5449.940211	7393.326141	10045.480817
80	2356.290874	3189.062680	4327.927467	5886.935428	8022.758863	10950.574090
81	2510.449781	3413.297067	4653.522027	6358.890263	8705.693366	11937.125758
82	2674.629017	3653.227862	5003.536179	6868.601484	9446.677302	13012.467077
83	2849.479903	3909.953812	5379.801392	7419.089602	10250.644873	14184.589114
84	3035.696097	4184.650579	5784.286496	8013.616770	11122.949687	15462.202134
85	3234.016343	4478.576120	6219.107984	8655.706112	12069.400410	16854.800326
86	3445.227405	4793.076448	6686.541082	9349.162601	13096.299445	18372.732355
87	3670.167187	5129.591799	7189.031664	10098.095609	14210.484898	20027.278267
88	3909.728054	5489.663225	7729.209038	10906.943258	15419.376114	21830.733311
89	4164.860377	5874.939651	8309.899716	11780.498718	16731.023084	23796.499309
90	4436.576302	6287.185427	8934.142195	12723.938616	18154.160046	25939.184247
91	4725.953761	6728.288407	9605.202860	13742.853705	19698.263650	28274.710829
92	5034.140756	7200.268595	10326.593074	14843.282002	21373.616060	30820.434804
93	5362.359905	7705.287397	11102.087555	16031.744562	23191.373425	33595.273936
94	5711.913299	8245.657515	11935.744121	17315.284127	25163.640167	36619.848591
95	6084.187663	8823.853541	12831.924930	18701.506857	27303.549581	39916.634964
96	6480.659861	9442.523288	13795.319300	20198.627405	29625.351295	43510.132110
97	6902.902752	10104.499919	14830.968248	21815.517598	32144.506155	47427.044000
98	7352.591431	10812.814913	15944.290866	23561.759006	34877.789178	51696.477960
99	7831.509874	11570.711957	17141.112681	25447.699726	37843.401259	56350.160977
100	8341.558016	12381.661794	18427.696132	27484.515704	41061.090366	61422.675465
101	8884.759287	13249.378119	19810.773342	29684.276961	44552.283047	66951.716257
102	9463.268641	14177.834588	21297.581343	32060.019117	48340.227106	72978.370720
103	10079.381102	15171.283009	22895.899944	34625.820647	52450.146410	79547.424084
104	10735.540874	16234.272819	24614.092439	37396.886299	56909.408854	86707.692252
105	11434.351031	17371.671917	26461.149372	40389.637202	61747.708607	94512.384555
106	12178.583848	18588.688951	28446.735575	43621.808179	66997.263839	103019.499165
107	12971.191798	19890.897178	30581.240743	47112.552833	72693.031265	112292.154089
108	13815.319265	21284.259980	32875.833799	50882.557060	78872.938922	122399.356957
109	14714.315017	22775.158179	35342.521334	54954.161624	85578.138731	133416.517084
110	15671.745493	24370.419251	37994.210434	59351.494554	92853.280523	145415.003621
111	16691.408950	26077.348599	40844.776217	64100.614119	100746.809367	158514.253947
112	17777.350532	27903.763001	43909.134433	69229.663248	109311.288163	172781.536802
113	18933.878316	29858.026411	47203.319516	74769.036308	118603.641775	188332.875115
114	20165.580407	31949.088259	50744.568479	80751.559213	128686.066280	205283.833875
115	21477.343133	34186.524438	54551.411115	87212.683950	139623.391836	223760.378924
116	22874.370437	36580.581148	58643.766949	94190.698666	151494.539293	243899.813027
117	24362.204515	39142.221829	63043.049470	101726.954559	164384.292779	265851.796199
118	25946.747809	41883.177357	67772.278180	109866.110924	178345.244018	289779.457857
119	27634.286416	44815.999772	72856.199044	118656.399798	193505.589760	315860.609064
120	29431.515033	47954.119756	78321.413972	128149.811781	209954.564889	344289.063880

Table III **Uniform Series/Compound-Amount Factor (Future Value of Annuity) (continued)**

$$\frac{(1+i)^n - 1}{i}$$

n	0.095 (9½%)	0.10 (10%)	0.105 (10½%)	0.11 (11%)	0.115 (11½%)	0.12 (12%)
1	1.000000	1.000000	1.000000	1.000000	1.000000	1.000000
2	2.095000	2.100000	2.105000	2.110000	2.115000	2.120000
3	3.294025	3.310000	3.326025	3.342100	3.358225	3.374400
4	4.606957	4.641000	4.675258	4.709731	4.744421	4.779328
5	6.044618	6.105100	6.166160	6.227801	6.290029	6.352847
6	7.618857	7.715610	7.813606	7.912860	8.013383	8.115189
7	9.342648	9.487171	9.634035	9.783274	9.934922	10.089012
8	11.230200	11.435888	11.645609	11.859434	12.077438	12.299693
9	13.297069	13.579477	13.868398	14.163972	14.466343	14.775656
10	15.560291	15.937425	16.324579	16.722009	17.129972	17.548735
11	18.038518	18.531167	19.038660	19.561430	20.099919	20.654583
12	20.752178	21.384284	22.037720	22.713187	23.411410	24.133133
13	23.723634	24.522712	25.351680	26.211638	27.103722	28.029109
14	26.977380	27.974983	29.013607	30.094918	31.220650	32.392602
15	30.540231	31.772482	33.060035	34.405359	35.811025	37.279715
16	34.441553	35.949730	37.531339	39.189948	40.929293	42.753280
17	38.713500	40.544703	42.472130	44.500843	46.636161	48.883674
18	43.391283	45.599173	47.931703	50.395936	52.999320	55.749715
19	48.513454	51.159090	53.964532	56.939488	60.094242	63.439681
20	54.122233	57.274999	60.630808	64.202832	68.005080	72.052442
21	60.263845	64.002499	67.997043	72.265144	76.825664	81.698736
22	66.988910	71.402749	76.136732	81.214309	86.660615	92.502584
23	74.352856	79.543024	85.131089	91.147884	97.626586	104.602894
24	82.416378	88.497327	95.069854	102.174151	109.853643	118.155241
25	91.245934	98.347059	106.052188	114.413307	123.486812	133.333870
26	100.914297	109.181765	118.187668	127.998771	138.687796	150.333934
27	111.501156	121.099942	131.597373	143.078636	155.636892	169.374007
28	123.093766	134.209936	146.415097	159.817286	174.535135	190.698887
29	135.787673	148.630930	162.788683	178.397187	195.606675	214.582754
30	149.687502	164.494023	180.881494	199.020878	219.101443	241.332684
31	164.907815	181.943425	200.874051	221.913174	245.298109	271.292606
32	181.574057	201.137767	222.965827	247.323624	274.507391	304.847719
33	199.823593	222.251544	247.377238	275.529222	307.075741	342.429446
34	219.806834	245.476699	274.351848	306.837437	343.389451	384.520979
35	241.688483	271.024368	304.158792	341.589555	383.879238	431.663496
36	265.648889	299.126805	337.095466	380.164406	429.025351	484.463116
37	291.885534	330.039486	373.490489	422.982490	479.363266	543.598690
38	320.614659	364.043434	413.706991	470.510564	535.490042	609.830533
39	352.073052	401.447778	458.146225	523.266726	598.071396	684.010197
40	386.519992	442.592556	507.251579	581.826066	667.849607	767.091420
41	424.239391	487.851811	561.512994	646.826934	745.652312	860.142391
42	465.542133	537.636992	621.471859	718.977896	832.402327	964.359478
43	510.768636	592.400692	687.726404	799.065465	929.128595	1081.082615
44	560.291656	652.640761	760.937676	887.962666	1036.978384	1211.812529
45	614.519364	718.904837	841.836132	986.638559	1157.230898	1358.230032
46	673.898703	791.795321	931.228926	1096.168801	1291.312451	1522.217636
47	738.919080	871.974853	1030.007963	1217.747369	1440.813383	1705.883752
48	810.116393	960.172338	1139.158800	1352.699580	1607.506922	1911.589803
49	888.077450	1057.189572	1259.770473	1502.496533	1793.370218	2141.980579
50	973.444808	1163.908529	1393.046373	1668.771152	2000.607793	2400.018249
51	1066.922065	1281.299382	1540.316242	1853.335979	2231.677689	2689.020438
52	1169.279661	1410.429320	1703.049448	2058.202937	2489.320623	3012.702891
53	1281.361229	1552.472252	1882.869640	2285.605260	2776.592495	3375.227238
54	1404.090545	1708.719477	2081.570952	2538.021838	3096.900632	3781.254506
55	1538.479147	1880.591425	2301.135902	2818.204240	3454.044205	4236.005047
56	1685.634666	2069.650567	2543.755172	3129.206707	3852.259288	4745.325653
57	1846.769959	2277.615624	2811.849465	3474.419445	4296.269106	5315.764731
58	2023.213106	2506.377186	3108.093659	3857.605583	4791.340053	5954.656499
59	2216.418351	2758.014905	3435.443493	4282.942198	5343.344159	6670.215279
60	2427.978094	3034.816395	3797.165059	4755.065839	5958.828738	7471.641112

Table III Uniform Series/Compound-Amount Factor (Future Value of Annuity) (continued)

$$\frac{(1+i)^n - 1}{i}$$

n	*0.125 (12½%)*	*0.13 (13%)*	*0.135 (13½%)*	*0.14 (14%)*	*0.145 (14½%)*	*0.15 (15%)*
1	1.000000	1.000000	1.000000	1.000000	1.000000	1.000000
2	2.125000	2.130000	2.135000	2.140000	2.145000	2.150000
3	3.390625	3.406900	3.423225	3.439600	3.456025	3.472500
4	4.814453	4.849797	4.885360	4.921144	4.957149	4.993375
5	6.416260	6.480271	6.544884	6.610104	6.675935	6.742381
6	8.218292	8.322706	8.428443	8.535519	8.643946	8.753738
7	10.245579	10.404658	10.566283	10.730491	10.897318	11.066799
8	12.526276	12.757263	12.992731	13.232760	13.477429	13.726819
9	15.092061	15.415707	15.746750	16.085347	16.431656	16.785842
10	17.978568	18.419749	18.872561	19.337295	19.814246	20.303718
11	21.225889	21.814317	22.420357	23.044516	23.687312	24.349276
12	24.879125	25.650178	26.447106	27.270749	28.121972	29.001667
13	28.989016	29.984701	31.017465	32.088654	33.199658	34.351917
14	33.612643	34.882712	36.204823	37.581065	39.013609	40.504705
15	38.814223	40.417464	42.092474	43.842414	45.670582	47.580411
16	44.666001	46.671735	48.774957	50.980352	53.292816	55.717472
17	51.249252	53.739060	56.359577	59.117601	62.020275	65.075093
18	58.655408	61.725138	64.968120	68.394066	72.013215	75.836357
19	66.987334	70.749406	74.738816	78.969235	83.455131	88.211811
20	76.360751	80.946829	85.828556	91.024928	96.556125	102.443583
21	86.905845	92.469917	98.415411	104.768418	111.556763	118.810120
22	98.769075	105.491006	112.701491	120.435996	128.732494	137.631638
23	112.115210	120.204837	128.916193	138.297035	148.398705	159.276384
24	127.129611	136.831465	147.319879	158.658620	170.916517	184.167841
25	144.020812	155.619556	168.208062	181.870827	196.699412	212.793017
26	163.023414	176.850098	191.916151	208.332743	226.220827	245.711970
27	184.401340	200.840611	218.824831	238.499327	260.022847	283.568766
28	208.451508	227.949890	249.366183	272.889233	298.726160	327.104080
29	235.507946	258.583376	284.030618	312.093725	343.041453	377.169693
30	265.946440	293.199215	323.374752	356.786847	393.782464	434.745146
31	300.189745	332.315113	368.030343	407.737006	451.880921	500.956918
32	338.713463	376.516078	418.714439	465.820186	518.403655	577.100456
33	382.052645	426.463168	476.240889	532.035012	594.572185	664.665524
34	430.809226	482.903380	541.533409	607.519914	681.785151	765.365353
35	485.660379	546.680819	615.640419	693.572702	781.643998	881.170156
36	547.367927	618.749325	699.751875	791.672881	895.982378	1014.345680
37	616.788918	700.186738	795.218378	903.507084	1026.899823	1167.497532
38	694.887532	792.211014	903.572859	1030.998076	1176.800297	1343.622161
39	782.748474	896.198445	1026.555195	1176.337806	1348.436340	1546.165485
40	881.592033	1013.704243	1166.140147	1342.025099	1544.959609	1779.090308
41	992.791037	1146.485795	1324.569067	1530.908613	1769.978753	2046.953854
42	1117.889917	1296.528948	1504.385891	1746.235819	2027.625672	2354.996933
43	1258.626157	1466.077712	1708.477986	1991.708833	2322.631394	2709.246473
44	1416.954426	1657.667814	1940.122514	2271.548070	2660.412947	3116.633443
45	1595.073729	1874.164630	2203.039053	2590.564800	3047.172824	3585.128460
46	1795.457946	2118.806032	2501.449326	2954.243872	3490.012883	4123.897729
47	2020.890189	2395.250816	2840.144984	3368.838014	3997.064751	4743.482388
48	2274.501462	2707.633422	3224.564557	3841.475336	4577.639140	5456.004746
49	2559.814145	3060.625767	3660.880773	4380.281883	5242.396816	6275.405458
50	2880.790913	3459.507117	4156.099677	4994.521346	6003.544354	7217.716277
51	3241.889778	3910.243042	4718.173133	5694.754335	6875.058285	8301.373719
52	3648.126000	4419.574637	5356.126506	6493.019941	7872.941737	9547.579777
53	4105.141750	4995.119340	6080.203585	7403.042733	9015.518289	10980.716743
54	4619.284468	5645.484854	6902.031069	8440.468716	10323.768441	12628.824255
55	5197.695027	6380.397885	7834.805263	9623.134336	11821.714864	14524.147893
56	5848.406905	7210.849610	8893.503973	10971.373143	13536.863520	16703.770077
57	6580.457769	8149.260060	10095.127010	12508.365383	15500.708730	19210.335588
58	7404.014990	9209.663867	11458.969156	14260.536537	17749.311496	22092.885926
59	8330.516863	10407.920170	13006.929992	16258.011652	20323.961663	25407.818815
60	9372.831471	11761.949792	14763.865541	18535.133283	23271.936104	29219.991638

Table III **Uniform Series/Compound-Amount Factor (Future Value of Annuity) (continued)**

$$\frac{(1+i)^n - 1}{i}$$

n	*0.155 (15½%)*	*0.16 (16%)*	*0.165 (16½%)*	*0.17 (17%)*	*0.175 (17½%)*	*0.18 (18%)*
1	1.000000	1.000000	1.000000	1.000000	1.000000	1.000000
2	2.155000	2.160000	2.165000	2.170000	2.175000	2.180000
3	3.489025	3.505600	3.522225	3.538900	3.555625	3.572400
4	5.029824	5.066496	5.103392	5.140513	5.177859	5.215432
5	6.809447	6.877135	6.945452	7.014400	7.083985	7.154210
6	8.864911	8.977477	9.091451	9.206848	9.323682	9.441968
7	11.238972	11.413873	11.591541	11.772012	11.955326	12.141522
8	13.981013	14.240093	14.504145	14.773255	15.047509	15.326996
9	17.148070	17.518508	17.897329	18.284708	18.680823	19.085855
10	20.806020	21.321469	21.850388	22.393108	22.949967	23.521309
11	25.030954	25.732904	26.455702	27.199937	27.966211	28.755144
12	29.910751	30.850169	31.820893	32.823926	33.860298	34.931070
13	35.546918	36.786196	38.071341	39.403993	40.785850	42.218663
14	42.056690	43.671987	45.353112	47.102672	48.923373	50.818022
15	49.575477	51.659505	53.836375	56.110126	58.484964	60.965266
16	58.259676	60.925026	63.719377	66.648848	69.719832	72.939014
17	68.289926	71.673030	75.233075	78.979152	82.920803	87.068036
18	79.874864	84.140715	88.646532	93.405608	98.431944	103.740283
19	93.255468	98.603230	104.273210	110.284561	116.657534	123.413534
20	108.710066	115.379747	122.478289	130.032936	138.072602	146.627970
21	126.560126					
22	147.176945					
23	170.989372					
24	198.492725					
25	230.259097					
26	266.949257					
27	309.326392					
28	358.271982					
29	414.804140					
30	480.098781					
31	555.514092					
32	642.618777					
33	743.224687					
34	859.424513					
35	993.635313					
36	1148.648787					
37	1327.689348					
38	1534.481197					
39	1773.325783					
40	2049.191279					
41	2367.815928					
42	2735.827397					
43	3160.880643					
44	3651.817143					
45	4218.848800					
46	4873.770364					
47	5630.204770					
48	6503.886510					
49	7512.988919					
50	8678.502201					
51	10024.670042					
52	11579.493899					
53	13375.315453					
54	15449.489348					
55	17845.160197					
56	20612.160028					
57	23808.044832					
58	27499.291781					
59	31762.682007					
60	36686.897718					

Table III Uniform Series/Compound-Amount Factor (Future Value of Annuity) (continued)

$$\frac{(1+i)^n - 1}{i}$$

n	0.185 (18½%)	0.19 (19%)	0.195 (19½%)	0.20 (20%)	0.21 (21%)	0.22 (22%)
1	1.000000	1.000000	1.000000	1.000000	1.000000	1.000000
2	2.185000	2.190000	2.195000	2.200000	2.210000	2.220000
3	3.589225	3.606100	3.623025	3.640000	3.674100	3.708400
4	5.253232	5.291259	5.329515	5.368000	5.445661	5.524248
5	7.225079	7.296598	7.368770	7.441600	7.589250	7.739583
6	9.561719	9.682952	9.805680	9.929920	10.182992	10.442291
7	12.330637	12.522713	12.717788	12.915904	13.321421	13.739595
8	15.611805	15.902028	16.197757	16.499085	17.118919	17.762306
9	19.499989	19.923413	20.356319	20.798902	21.713892	22.670013
10	24.107487	24.708862	25.325802	25.958682	27.273809	28.657416
11	29.567372	30.403546	31.264333	32.150419	34.001309	35.962047
12	36.037336	37.180220	38.360878	39.580502	42.141584	44.873697
13	43.704243	45.244461	46.841249	48.496603	51.991317	55.745911
14	52.789528	54.840909	56.975293	59.195923	63.909493	69.010011
15	63.555591	66.260682	69.085475	72.035108	78.330487	85.192213
16	76.313375	79.850211	83.557143	87.442129	95.779889	104.934500
17	91.431350	96.021751	100.850785	105.930555	116.893666	129.020090
18	109.346149	115.265884	121.516689	128.116666	142.441336	158.404510
19	130.575187	138.166402	146.212443	154.740000	173.354016	194.253503
20	155.731596	165.418018	175.723869	186.688000	210.758360	237.989273

n	0.23 (23%)	0.24 (24%)	0.25 (25%)
1	1.000000	1.000000	1.000000
2	2.230000	2.240000	2.250000
3	3.742900	3.777600	3.812500
4	5.603767	5.684224	5.765625
5	7.892633	8.048438	8.207031
6	10.707939	10.980063	11.258789
7	14.170765	14.615278	15.073486
8	18.430041	19.122945	19.841858
9	23.668950	24.712451	25.802322
10	30.112809	31.643440	33.252903
11	38.038755	40.237865	42.566129
12	47.787669	50.894953	54.207661
13	59.778833	64.109741	68.759576
14	74.527964	80.496079	86.949470
15	92.669396	100.815138	109.686838
16	114.983357	126.010772	138.108547
17	142.429529	157.253357	173.635684
18	176.188321	195.994162	218.044605
19	217.711635	244.032761	273.555756
20	268.785311	303.600624	342.944695

n	0.30 (30%)	0.35 (35%)	0.40 (40%)
1	1.000000	1.000000	1.000000
2	2.300000	2.350000	2.400000
3	3.990000	4.172500	4.360000
4	6.187000	6.632875	7.104000
5	9.043100	9.954381	10.945600
6	12.756030	14.438415	16.323840
7	17.582839	20.491860	23.853376
8	23.857691	28.664011	34.394726
9	32.014998	39.696415	49.152617
10	42.619497	54.590160	69.813644
11	56.405346	74.696715	98.739129
12	74.326950	101.840566	139.234871
13	97.625036	138.484764	195.928693
14	127.912546	187.954431	275.300171
15	167.286310	254.738482	386.420239
16	218.472203	344.896951	541.099334
17	285.013864	466.610884	759.783667
18	371.518023	630.924694	1064.697134
19	483.973430	852.748336	1491.575987
20	630.165459	1152.210254	2089.206382

Table IV Uniform Series/Present Value Factor (Present Value of Annuity Factor; Uniform Series/Present Worth Factor)

$$\frac{(1 + i)^n - 1}{i\,(1 + i)^n}$$

n	0.0025 (¼%)	0.0050 (½%)	0.0075 (¾%)	0.01 (1%)	0.0125 (1¼%)	0.0150 (1½%)
1	0.997506	0.995025	0.992556	0.990099	0.987654	0.985222
2	1.992525	1.985099	1.977723	1.970395	1.963115	1.955883
3	2.985062	2.970248	2.955556	2.940985	2.926534	2.912200
4	3.975124	3.950496	3.926110	3.901966	3.878058	3.854385
5	4.962718	4.925866	4.889440	4.853431	4.817835	4.782645
6	5.947848	5.896384	5.845598	5.795476	5.746010	5.697187
7	6.930522	6.862074	6.794638	6.728195	6.662726	6.598214
8	7.910745	7.822959	7.736613	7.651678	7.568124	7.485925
9	8.888524	8.779064	8.671576	8.566018	8.462345	8.360517
10	9.863864	9.730412	9.599580	9.471305	9.345526	9.222185
11	10.836772	10.677027	10.520675	10.367628	10.217803	10.071118
12	11.807254	11.618932	11.434913	11.255077	11.079312	10.907505
13	12.775316	12.556151	12.342345	12.133740	11.930185	11.731532
14	13.740963	13.488708	13.243022	13.003703	12.770553	12.543382
15	14.704203	14.416625	14.136995	13.865053	13.600546	13.343233
16	15.665040	15.339925	15.024313	14.717874	14.420292	14.131264
17	16.623481	16.258632	15.905025	15.562251	15.229918	14.907649
18	17.579533	17.172768	16.779181	16.398269	16.029549	15.672561
19	18.533200	18.082356	17.646830	17.226008	16.819308	16.426168
20	19.484488	18.987419	18.508020	18.045553	17.599316	17.168639
21	20.433405	19.887979	19.362799	18.856983	18.369695	17.900137
22	21.379955	20.784059	20.211215	19.660379	19.130563	18.620824
23	22.324145	21.675681	21.053315	20.455821	19.882037	19.330861
24	23.265980	22.562866	21.889146	21.243387	20.624235	20.030405
25	24.205466	23.445638	22.718755	22.023156	21.357269	20.719611
26	25.142609	24.324018	23.542189	22.795204	22.081253	21.398632
27	26.077416	25.198028	24.359493	23.559608	22.796299	22.067617
28	27.009891	26.067689	25.170713	24.316443	23.502518	22.726717
29	27.940041	26.933024	25.975893	25.065785	24.200018	23.376076
30	28.867871	27.794054	26.775080	25.807708	24.888906	24.015838
31	29.793388	28.650800	27.568318	26.542285	25.569290	24.646146
32	30.716596	29.503284	28.355650	27.269589	26.241274	25.267139
33	31.637503	30.351526	29.137122	27.989693	26.904962	25.878954
34	32.556112	31.195548	29.912776	28.702666	27.560456	26.481728
35	33.472431	32.035371	30.682656	29.408580	28.207858	27.075595
36	34.386465	32.871016	31.446805	30.107505	28.847267	27.660684
37	35.298220	33.702504	32.205266	30.799510	29.478783	28.237127
38	36.207700	34.529854	32.958080	31.484663	30.102501	28.805052
39	37.114913	35.353089	33.705290	32.163033	30.718520	29.364583
40	38.019863	36.172228	34.446938	32.834686	31.326933	29.915845
41	38.922557	36.987291	35.183065	33.499689	31.927835	30.458961
42	39.822999	37.798300	35.913713	34.158108	32.521319	30.994050
43	40.721196	38.605274	36.638921	34.810008	33.107475	31.521232
44	41.617154	39.408232	37.358730	35.455454	33.686395	32.040622
45	42.510876	40.207196	38.073181	36.094508	34.258168	32.552337
46	43.402370	41.002185	38.782314	36.727236	34.822882	33.056490
47	44.291641	41.793219	39.486168	37.353699	35.380624	33.553192
48	45.178695	42.580318	40.184782	37.973959	35.931481	34.042554
49	46.063536	43.363500	40.878195	38.588079	36.475537	34.524683
50	46.946170	44.142786	41.566447	39.196118	37.012876	34.999688
51	47.826604	44.918195	42.249575	39.798136	37.543581	35.467673
52	48.704842	45.689747	42.927618	40.394194	38.067734	35.928742
53	49.580890	46.457459	43.600614	40.984351	38.585417	36.382997
54	50.454753	47.221353	44.268599	41.568664	39.096708	36.830539
55	51.326437	47.981445	44.931612	42.147192	39.601687	37.271467
56	52.195947	48.737757	45.589689	42.719992	40.100431	37.705879
57	53.063288	49.490305	46.242868	43.287121	40.593019	38.133871
58	53.928467	50.239109	46.891184	43.848635	41.079524	38.555538
59	54.791489	50.984189	47.534674	44.404589	41.560024	38.970973
60	55.652358	51.725561	48.173374	44.955038	42.034592	39.380269

Table IV Uniform Series/Present Value Factor (Present Value of Annuity Factor; Uniform Series/Present Worth Factor)(continued)

$$\frac{(1+i)^n - 1}{i(1+i)^n}$$

n	0.0025 (¼%)	0.0050 (½%)	0.0075 (¾%)	0.01 (1%)	0.0125 (1¼%)	0.0150 (1½%)
61	56.511080	52.463245	48.807319	45.500038	42.503301	39.783516
62	57.367661	53.197258	49.436545	46.039642	42.966223	40.180804
63	58.222106	53.927620	50.061086	46.573903	43.423430	40.572221
64	59.074420	54.654348	50.680979	47.102874	43.874992	40.957853
65	59.924608	55.377461	51.296257	47.626608	44.320980	41.337786
66	60.772676	56.096976	51.906955	48.145156	44.761462	41.712105
67	61.618630	56.812912	52.513107	48.658571	45.196506	42.080891
68	62.462474	57.525285	53.114746	49.166901	45.626178	42.444228
69	63.304213	58.234115	53.711907	49.670199	46.050547	42.802195
70	64.143853	58.939418	54.304622	50.168514	46.469676	43.154872
71	64.981400	59.641212	54.892925	50.661895	46.883630	43.502337
72	65.816858	60.339514	55.476849	51.150391	47.292474	43.844667
73	66.650232	61.034342	56.056426	51.634051	47.696271	44.181938
74	67.481528	61.725714	56.631688	52.112922	48.095082	44.514224
75	68.310751	62.413645	57.202668	52.587051	48.488970	44.841600
76	69.137907	63.098155	57.769397	53.056486	48.877995	45.164138
77	69.962999	63.779258	58.331908	53.521274	49.262218	45.481910
78	70.786034	64.456973	58.890231	53.981459	49.641696	45.794985
79	71.607017	65.131317	59.444398	54.437088	50.016490	46.103433
80	72.425952	65.802305	59.994440	54.888206	50.386657	46.407323
81	73.242845	66.469956	60.540387	55.334858	50.752254	46.706723
82	74.057700	67.134284	61.082270	55.777087	51.113337	47.001697
83	74.870524	67.795308	61.620119	56.214937	51.469963	47.292313
84	75.681321	68.453042	62.153965	56.648453	51.822185	47.578633
85	76.490095	69.107505	62.683836	57.077676	52.170060	47.860722
86	77.296853	69.758711	63.209763	57.502650	52.513639	48.138643
87	78.101599	70.406678	63.731774	57.923415	52.852977	48.412456
88	78.904339	71.051421	64.249900	58.340015	53.188125	48.682222
89	79.705076	71.692956	64.764169	58.752490	53.519136	48.948002
90	80.503816	72.331300	65.274609	59.160881	53.846060	49.209855
91	81.300565	72.966467	65.781250	59.565229	54.168948	49.467837
92	82.095327	73.598475	66.284119	59.965573	54.487850	49.722007
93	82.888106	74.227338	66.783245	60.361954	54.802815	49.972421
94	83.678909	74.853073	67.278655	60.754410	55.113892	50.219134
95	84.467740	75.475694	67.770377	61.142980	55.421127	50.462201
96	85.254603	76.095218	68.258439	61.527703	55.724570	50.701675
97	86.039504	76.711660	68.742867	61.908617	56.024267	50.937611
98	86.822448	77.325035	69.223689	62.285759	56.320264	51.170060
99	87.603440	77.935358	69.700932	62.659168	56.612606	51.399074
100	88.382483	78.542645	70.174623	63.028879	56.901339	51.624704
101	89.159584	79.146910	70.644787	63.394929	57.186508	51.846999
102	89.934748	79.748169	71.111451	63.757356	57.468156	52.066009
103	90.707978	80.346437	71.574641	64.116194	57.746327	52.281782
104	91.479279	80.941729	72.034383	64.471479	58.021064	52.494366
105	92.248658	81.534058	72.490703	64.823247	58.292409	52.703809
106	93.016118	82.123441	72.943626	65.171531	58.560404	52.910157
107	93.781663	82.709892	73.393177	65.516368	58.825090	53.113455
108	94.545300	83.293424	73.839382	65.857790	59.086509	53.313749
109	95.307033	83.874054	74.282265	66.195832	59.344700	53.511083
110	96.066865	84.451795	74.721851	66.530526	59.599704	53.705500
111	96.824803	85.026662	75.158165	66.861907	59.851559	53.897044
112	97.580851	85.598669	75.591230	67.190007	60.100305	54.085758
113	98.335014	86.167829	76.021072	67.514859	60.345980	54.271683
114	99.087295	86.734159	76.447714	67.836494	60.588623	54.454860
115	99.837701	87.297670	76.871181	68.154944	60.828269	54.635330
116	100.586236	87.858378	77.291494	68.470242	61.064957	54.813133
117	101.332903	88.416297	77.708679	68.782418	61.298723	54.988308
118	102.077709	88.971440	78.122759	69.091503	61.529603	55.160895
119	102.820657	89.523821	78.533755	69.397527	61.757633	55.330931
120	103.561753	90.073453	78.941693	69.700522	61.982847	55.498454

Table IV **Uniform Series/Present Value Factor (Present Value of Annuity Factor; Uniform Series/Present Worth Factor)(continued)**

$$\frac{(1+i)^n - 1}{i(1+i)^n}$$

n	0.0175 (1¾%)	0.02 (2%)	0.0225 (2¼%)	0.025 (2½%)	0.0275 (2¾%)	0.03 (3%)
1	0.982801	0.980392	0.977995	0.975610	0.973236	0.970874
2	1.948699	1.941561	1.934470	1.927424	1.920424	1.913470
3	2.897984	2.883883	2.869897	2.856024	2.842262	2.828611
4	3.830943	3.807729	3.784740	3.761974	3.739428	3.717098
5	4.747855	4.713460	4.679453	4.645828	4.612582	4.579707
6	5.648998	5.601431	5.554477	5.508125	5.462367	5.417191
7	6.534641	6.471991	6.410246	6.349391	6.289408	6.230283
8	7.405053	7.325481	7.247185	7.170137	7.094314	7.019692
9	8.260494	8.162237	8.065706	7.970866	7.877678	7.786109
10	9.101223	8.982585	8.866216	8.752064	8.640076	8.530203
11	9.927492	9.786848	9.649111	9.514209	9.382069	9.252624
12	10.739550	10.575341	10.414779	10.257765	10.104204	9.954004
13	11.537641	11.348374	11.163598	10.983185	10.807011	10.634955
14	12.322006	12.106249	11.895939	11.690912	11.491008	11.296073
15	13.092880	12.849264	12.612166	12.381378	12.156699	11.937935
16	13.850497	13.577709	13.312631	13.055003	12.804573	12.561102
17	14.595083	14.291872	13.997683	13.712198	13.435108	13.166118
18	15.326863	14.992031	14.667661	14.353364	14.048767	13.753513
19	16.046057	15.678462	15.322896	14.978891	14.646002	14.323799
20	16.752881	16.351433	15.963712	15.589162	15.227252	14.877475
21	17.447549	17.011209	16.590428	16.184549	15.792946	15.415024
22	18.130269	17.658048	17.203352	16.765413	16.343500	15.936917
23	18.801248	18.292204	17.802790	17.332110	16.879319	16.443608
24	19.460686	18.913926	18.389036	17.884986	17.400797	16.935542
25	20.108782	19.523456	18.962383	18.424376	17.908318	17.413148
26	20.745732	20.121036	19.523113	18.950611	18.402256	17.876842
27	21.371726	20.706898	20.071504	19.464011	18.882974	18.327031
28	21.986955	21.281272	20.607828	19.964889	19.350826	18.764108
29	22.591602	21.844385	21.132350	20.453550	19.806157	19.188455
30	23.185849	22.396456	21.645330	20.930293	20.249301	19.600441
31	23.769877	22.937702	22.147022	21.395407	20.680585	20.000428
32	24.343859	23.468335	22.637674	21.849178	21.100326	20.388766
33	24.907970	23.988564	23.117530	22.291881	21.508833	20.765792
34	25.462378	24.498592	23.586826	22.723786	21.906407	21.131837
35	26.007251	24.998619	24.045796	23.145157	22.293340	21.487220
36	26.542753	25.488842	24.494666	23.556251	22.669918	21.832252
37	27.069045	25.969453	24.933658	23.957318	23.036416	22.167235
38	27.586285	26.440641	25.362991	24.348603	23.393106	22.492462
39	28.094629	26.902589	25.782876	24.730344	23.740249	22.808215
40	28.594230	27.355479	26.193522	25.102775	24.078101	23.114772
41	29.085238	27.799489	26.595132	25.466122	24.406911	23.412400
42	29.567801	28.234794	26.987904	25.820607	24.726921	23.701359
43	30.042065	28.661562	27.372033	26.166446	25.038366	23.981902
44	30.508172	29.079963	27.747710	26.503849	25.341475	24.254274
45	30.966263	29.490160	28.115120	26.833024	25.636472	24.518713
46	31.416474	29.892314	28.474444	27.154170	25.923574	24.775449
47	31.858943	30.286582	28.825863	27.467483	26.202992	25.024708
48	32.293801	30.673120	29.169548	27.773154	26.474931	25.266707
49	32.721181	31.052078	29.505670	28.071369	26.739592	25.501657
50	33.141209	31.423606	29.834396	28.362312	26.997170	25.729764
51	33.554014	31.787849	30.155889	28.646158	27.247854	25.951227
52	33.959719	32.144950	30.470307	28.923081	27.491829	26.166240
53	34.358446	32.495049	30.777806	29.193249	27.729274	26.374990
54	34.750316	32.838283	31.078539	29.456829	27.960364	26.577660
55	35.135445	33.174788	31.372654	29.713979	28.185269	26.774428
56	35.513951	33.504694	31.660298	29.964858	28.404155	26.965464
57	35.885947	33.828131	31.941611	30.209617	28.617182	27.150936
58	36.251545	34.145226	32.216735	30.448407	28.824508	27.331005
59	36.610855	34.456104	32.485804	30.681373	29.026285	27.505831
60	36.963986	34.760887	32.748953	30.908656	29.222662	27.675564

Table IV **Uniform Series/Present Value Factor (Present Value of Annuity Factor; Uniform Series/Present Worth Factor)(continued)**

$$\frac{(1 + i)^n - 1}{i(1 + i)^n}$$

n	0.0175 (1¾%)	0.02 (2%)	0.0225 (2¼%)	0.025 (2½%)	0.0275 (2¾%)	0.03 (3%)
61	37.311042	35.059693	33.006311	31.130397	29.413783	27.840353
62	37.652130	35.352640	33.258006	31.346728	29.599789	28.000343
63	37.987351	35.639843	33.504162	31.557784	29.780816	28.155673
64	38.316807	35.921415	33.744902	31.763691	29.956999	28.306478
65	38.640597	36.197466	33.980344	31.964577	30.128466	28.452892
66	38.958817	36.468103	34.210605	32.160563	30.295344	28.595040
67	39.271565	36.733435	34.435800	32.351769	30.457756	28.733049
68	39.578934	36.993564	34.656039	32.538311	30.615821	28.867038
69	39.881016	37.248592	34.871432	32.720303	30.769655	28.997124
70	40.177903	37.498619	35.082085	32.897857	30.919372	29.123421
71	40.469683	37.743744	35.288103	33.071080	31.065083	29.246040
72	40.756445	37.984063	35.489587	33.240078	31.206893	29.365088
73	41.038276	38.219670	35.686638	33.404954	31.344908	29.480667
74	41.315259	38.450657	35.879352	33.565809	31.479229	29.592881
75	41.587478	38.677114	36.067826	33.722740	31.609956	29.701826
76	41.855015	38.899132	36.252153	33.875844	31.737183	29.807598
77	42.117951	39.116796	36.432423	34.025214	31.861005	29.910290
78	42.376364	39.330192	36.608727	34.170940	31.981514	30.009990
79	42.630334	39.539404	36.781151	34.313113	32.098797	30.106786
80	42.879935	39.744514	36.949781	34.451817	32.212941	30.200763
81	43.125243	39.945602	37.114700	34.587139	32.324030	30.292003
82	43.366332	40.142747	37.275990	34.719160	32.432146	30.380586
83	43.603275	40.336026	37.433731	34.847961	32.537368	30.466588
84	43.836142	40.525516	37.588001	34.973620	32.639775	30.550086
85	44.065005	40.711290	37.738877	35.096215	32.739440	30.631151
86	44.289931	40.893422	37.886432	35.215819	32.836438	30.709855
87	44.510989	41.071982	38.030740	35.332507	32.930840	30.786267
88	44.728244	41.247041	38.171873	35.446348	33.022715	30.860454
89	44.941764	41.418668	38.309900	35.557413	33.112132	30.932479
90	45.151610	41.586929	38.444890	35.665768	33.199155	31.002407
91	45.357848	41.751891	38.576910	35.771481	33.283849	31.070298
92	45.560539	41.913619	38.706024	35.874616	33.366276	31.136212
93	45.759743	42.072175	38.832298	35.975235	33.446498	31.200206
94	45.955521	42.227623	38.955792	36.073400	33.524572	31.262336
95	46.147933	42.380023	39.076569	36.169171	33.600557	31.322656
96	46.337035	42.529434	39.194689	36.262606	33.674508	31.381219
97	46.522884	42.675916	39.310209	36.353762	33.746480	31.438077
98	46.705537	42.819525	39.423187	36.442694	33.816525	31.493279
99	46.885049	42.960319	39.533680	36.529458	33.884696	31.546872
100	47.061473	43.098352	39.641741	36.614105	33.951042	31.598905
101	47.234863	43.233678	39.747423	36.696688	34.015613	31.649423
102	47.405271	43.366351	39.850781	36.777257	34.078455	31.698469
103	47.572748	43.496423	39.951864	36.855860	34.139616	31.746086
104	47.737344	43.623944	40.050723	36.932546	34.199140	31.792317
105	47.899110	43.748964	40.147406	37.007362	34.257070	31.837201
106	48.058093	43.871534	40.241962	37.080354	34.313450	31.880777
107	48.214342	43.991700	40.334437	37.151564	34.368322	31.923085
108	48.367904	44.109510	40.424877	37.221039	34.421724	31.964160
109	48.518824	44.225009	40.513327	37.288818	34.473697	32.004039
110	48.667149	44.338245	40.599831	37.354944	34.524280	32.042756
111	48.812923	44.449259	40.684432	37.419458	34.573508	32.080346
112	48.956190	44.558097	40.767170	37.482398	34.621419	32.116840
113	49.096992	44.664801	40.848088	37.543803	34.668048	32.152272
114	49.235373	44.769413	40.927226	37.603710	34.713429	32.186672
115	49.371374	44.871974	41.004622	37.662156	34.757595	32.220070
116	49.505036	44.972523	41.080315	37.719177	34.800579	32.252495
117	49.636399	45.071101	41.154342	37.774807	34.842412	32.283976
118	49.765503	45.167746	41.226740	37.829080	34.883127	32.314540
119	49.892386	45.262496	41.297545	37.882029	34.922751	32.344213
120	50.017087	45.355389	41.366793	37.933687	34.961315	32.373023

Table IV **Uniform Series/Present Value Factor (Present Value of Annuity Factor; Uniform Series/Present Worth Factor)(continued)**

$$\frac{(1+i)^n - 1}{i(1+i)^n}$$

n	0.035 (3½%)	0.04 (4%)	0.045 (4½%)	0.05 (5%)	0.055 (5½)	0.06 (6%)
1	0.966184	0.961538	0.956938	0.952381	0.947867	0.943396
2	1.899694	1.886095	1.872668	1.859410	1.846320	1.833393
3	2.801637	2.775091	2.748964	2.723248	2.697933	2.673012
4	3.673079	3.629895	3.587526	3.545951	3.505150	3.465106
5	4.515052	4.451822	4.389977	4.329477	4.270284	4.212364
6	5.328553	5.242137	5.157872	5.075692	4.995530	4.917324
7	6.114544	6.002055	5.892701	5.786373	5.682967	5.582381
8	6.873956	6.732745	6.595886	6.463213	6.334566	6.209794
9	7.607687	7.435332	7.268790	7.107822	6.952195	6.801692
10	8.316605	8.110896	7.912718	7.721735	7.537626	7.360087
11	9.001551	8.760477	8.528917	8.306414	8.092536	7.886875
12	9.663334	9.385074	9.118581	8.863252	8.618518	8.383844
13	10.302738	9.985648	9.682852	9.393573	9.117079	8.852683
14	10.920520	10.563123	10.222825	9.898641	9.589648	9.294984
15	11.517411	11.118387	10.739546	10.379658	10.037581	9.712249
16	12.094117	11.652296	11.234015	10.837770	10.462162	10.105895
17	12.651321	12.165669	11.707191	11.274066	10.864609	10.477260
18	13.189682	12.659297	12.159992	11.689587	11.246074	10.827603
19	13.709837	13.133939	12.593294	12.085321	11.607654	11.158116
20	14.212403	13.590326	13.007936	12.462210	11.950382	11.469921
21	14.697974	14.029160	13.404724	12.821153	12.275244	11.764077
22	15.167125	14.451115	13.784425	13.163003	12.583170	12.041582
23	15.620410	14.856842	14.147775	13.488574	12.875042	12.303379
24	16.058368	15.246963	14.495478	13.798642	13.151699	12.550358
25	16.481515	15.622080	14.828209	14.093945	13.413933	12.783356
26	16.890352	15.982769	15.146611	14.375185	13.662495	13.003166
27	17.285365	16.329586	15.451303	14.643034	13.898100	13.210534
28	17.667019	16.663063	15.742874	14.898127	14.121422	13.406164
29	18.035767	16.983715	16.021889	15.141074	14.333101	13.590721
30	18.392045	17.292033	16.288889	15.372451	14.533745	13.764831
31	18.736276	17.588494	16.544391	15.592811	14.723929	13.929086
32	19.068865	17.873551	16.788891	15.802677	14.904198	14.084043
33	19.390208	18.147646	17.022862	16.002549	15.075069	14.230230
34	19.700684	18.411198	17.246758	16.192904	15.237033	14.368141
35	20.000661	18.664613	17.461012	16.374194	15.390552	14.498246
36	20.290494	18.908282	17.666041	16.546852	15.536068	14.620987
37	20.570525	19.142579	17.862240	16.711287	15.673999	14.736780
38	20.841087	19.367864	18.049990	16.867893	15.804738	14.846019
39	21.102500	19.584485	18.229656	17.017041	15.928662	14.949075
40	21.355072	19.792774	18.401584	17.159086	16.046125	15.046297
41	21.599104	19.993052	18.566109	17.294368	16.157464	15.138016
42	21.834883	20.185627	18.723550	17.423208	16.262999	15.224543
43	22.062689	20.370795	18.874210	17.545912	16.363032	15.306173
44	22.282791	20.548841	19.018383	17.662773	16.457851	15.383182
45	22.495450	20.720040	19.156347	17.774070	16.547726	15.455832
46	22.700918	20.884654	19.288371	17.880066	16.632915	15.524370
47	22.899438	21.042936	19.414709	17.981016	16.713664	15.589028
48	23.091244	21.195131	19.535607	18.077158	16.790203	15.650027
49	23.276564	21.341472	19.651298	18.168722	16.862751	15.707572
50	23.455618	21.482185	19.762008	18.255925	16.931518	15.761861
51	23.628616	21.617485	19.867950	18.338977	16.996699	15.813076
52	23.795765	21.747582	19.969330	18.418073	17.058483	15.861393
53	23.957260	21.872675	20.066345	18.493403	17.117045	15.906974
54	24.113295	21.992957	20.159181	18.565146	17.172555	15.949976
55	24.264053	22.108612	20.248021	18.633472	17.225170	15.990543
56	24.409713	22.219819	20.333034	18.698545	17.275043	16.028814
57	24.550448	22.326749	20.414387	18.760519	17.322316	16.064919
58	24.686423	22.429567	20.492236	18.819542	17.367124	16.098980
59	24.817800	22.528430	20.566733	18.875754	17.409596	16.131113
60	24.944734	22.623490	20.638022	18.929290	17.449854	16.161428

Table IV Uniform Series/Present Value Factor (Present Value of Annuity Factor; Uniform Series/Present Worth Factor)(continued)

$$\frac{(1+i)^n - 1}{i(1+i)^n}$$

n	0.035 (3½%)	0.04 (4%)	0.045 (4½%)	0.05 (5%)	0.055 (5½)	0.06 (6%)
61	25.067376	22.714894	20.706241	18.980276	17.488013	16.190026
62	25.185870	22.802783	20.771523	19.028834	17.524183	16.217006
63	25.300358	22.887291	20.833993	19.075080	17.558468	16.242458
64	25.410974	22.968549	20.893773	19.119124	17.590965	16.266470
65	25.517849	23.046682	20.950979	19.161070	17.621767	16.289123
66	25.621110	23.121810	21.005722	19.201019	17.650964	16.310493
67	25.720880	23.194048	21.058107	19.239066	17.678639	16.330654
68	25.817275	23.263507	21.108236	19.275301	17.704871	16.349673
69	25.910411	23.330296	21.156207	19.309810	17.729736	16.367617
70	26.000397	23.394515	21.202112	19.342677	17.753304	16.384544
71	26.087340	23.456264	21.246040	19.373978	17.775644	16.400513
72	26.171343	23.515639	21.288077	19.403788	17.796819	16.415578
73	26.252505	23.572730	21.328303	19.432179	17.816890	16.429791
74	26.330923	23.627625	21.366797	19.459218	17.835914	16.443199
75	26.406689	23.680408	21.403634	19.484970	17.853947	16.455848
76	26.479892	23.731162	21.438884	19.509495	17.871040	16.467781
77	26.550621	23.779963	21.472616	19.532853	17.887242	16.479039
78	26.618957	23.826888	21.504896	19.555098	17.902599	16.489659
79	26.684983	23.872008	21.535785	19.576284	17.917155	16.499679
80	26.748776	23.915392	21.565345	19.596460	17.930953	16.509131
81	26.810411	23.957108	21.593632	19.615677	17.944031	16.518048
82	26.869963	23.997219	21.620700	19.633978	17.956428	16.526460
83	26.927500	24.035787	21.646603	19.651407	17.968178	16.534396
84	26.983092	24.072872	21.671390	19.668007	17.979316	16.541883
85	27.036804	24.108531	21.695110	19.683816	17.989873	16.548947
86	27.088699	24.142818	21.717809	19.698873	17.999879	16.555610
87	27.138840	24.175787	21.739530	19.713212	18.009364	16.561896
88	27.187285	24.207487	21.760316	19.726869	18.018355	16.567827
89	27.234092	24.237969	21.780207	19.739875	18.026876	16.573421
90	27.279316	24.267278	21.799241	19.752262	18.034954	16.578699
91	27.323010	24.295459	21.817455	19.764059	18.042610	16.583679
92	27.365227	24.322557	21.834885	19.775294	18.049868	16.588376
93	27.406017	24.348612	21.851565	19.785994	18.056747	16.592808
94	27.445427	24.373666	21.867526	19.796185	18.063267	16.596988
95	27.483504	24.397756	21.882800	19.805891	18.069447	16.600932
96	27.520294	24.420919	21.897417	19.815134	18.075306	16.604653
97	27.555839	24.443191	21.911403	19.823937	18.080858	16.608163
98	27.590183	24.464607	21.924788	19.832321	18.086122	16.611475
99	27.623365	24.485199	21.937596	19.840306	18.091111	16.614599
100	27.655425	24.504999	21.949853	19.847910	18.095839	16.617546
101	27.686401	24.524037	21.961582	19.855153	18.100322	16.620327
102	27.716330	24.542344	21.972805	19.862050	18.104570	16.622950
103	27.745246	24.559946	21.983546	19.868619	18.108597	16.625424
104	27.773185	24.576871	21.993824	19.874875	18.112415	16.627759
105	27.800178	24.593145	22.003659	19.880834	18.116033	16.629961
106	27.826259	24.608794	22.013071	19.886508	18.119462	16.632039
107	27.851458	24.623840	22.022077	19.891913	18.122713	16.633999
108	27.875805	24.638308	22.030696	19.897060	18.125794	16.635848
109	27.899329	24.652219	22.038944	19.901962	18.128715	16.637592
110	27.922057	24.665595	22.046836	19.906630	18.131484	16.639238
111	27.944016	24.678457	22.054388	19.911076	18.134108	16.640791
112	27.965233	24.690824	22.061616	19.915311	18.136595	16.642255
113	27.985732	24.702715	22.068532	19.919344	18.138953	16.643637
114	28.005538	24.714149	22.075150	19.923184	18.141187	16.644941
115	28.024675	24.725144	22.081483	19.926842	18.143305	16.646170
116	28.043164	24.735715	22.087544	19.930326	18.145313	16.647331
117	28.061028	24.745880	22.093343	19.933644	18.147216	16.648425
118	28.078288	24.755654	22.098893	19.936804	18.149020	16.649458
119	28.094964	24.765052	22.104204	19.939813	18.150730	16.650432
120	28.111077	24.774088	22.109286	19.942679	18.152351	16.651351

Table IV **Uniform Series/Present Value Factor (Present Value of Annuity Factor; Uniform Series/Present Worth Factor)(continued)**

$$\frac{(1+i)^n - 1}{i(1+i)^n}$$

n	*0.065 (6½%)*	*0.07 (7%)*	*0.075 (7½%)*	*0.08 (8%)*	*0.085 (8½%)*	*0.09 (9%)*
1	0.938967	0.934579	0.930233	0.925926	0.921659	0.917431
2	1.820626	1.808018	1.795565	1.783265	1.771114	1.759111
3	2.648476	2.624316	2.600526	2.577097	2.554022	2.531295
4	3.425799	3.387211	3.349326	3.312127	3.275597	3.239720
5	4.155679	4.100197	4.045885	3.992710	3.940642	3.889651
6	4.841014	4.766540	4.693846	4.622880	4.553587	4.485919
7	5.484520	5.389289	5.296601	5.206370	5.118514	5.032953
8	6.088751	5.971299	5.857304	5.746639	5.639183	5.534819
9	6.656104	6.515232	6.378887	6.246888	6.119063	5.995247
10	7.188830	7.023582	6.864081	6.710081	6.561348	6.417658
11	7.689042	7.498674	7.315424	7.138964	6.968984	6.805191
12	8.158725	7.942686	7.735278	7.536078	7.344686	7.160725
13	8.599742	8.357651	8.125840	7.903776	7.690955	7.486904
14	9.013842	8.745468	8.489154	8.244237	8.010097	7.786150
15	9.402669	9.107914	8.827120	8.559479	8.304237	8.060688
16	9.767764	9.446649	9.141507	8.851369	8.575333	8.312558
17	10.110577	9.763223	9.433960	9.121638	8.825192	8.543631
18	10.432466	10.059087	9.706009	9.371887	9.055476	8.755625
19	10.734710	10.335595	9.959078	9.603599	9.267720	8.950115
20	11.018507	10.594014	10.194491	9.818147	9.463337	9.128546
21	11.284983	10.835527	10.413480	10.016803	9.643628	9.292244
22	11.535196	11.061240	10.617191	10.200744	9.809796	9.442425
23	11.770137	11.272187	10.806689	10.371059	9.962945	9.580207
24	11.990739	11.469334	10.982967	10.528758	10.104097	9.706612
25	12.197877	11.653583	11.146946	10.674776	10.234191	9.822580
26	12.392373	11.825779	11.299485	10.809978	10.354093	9.928972
27	12.574998	11.986709	11.441381	10.935165	10.464602	10.026580
28	12.746477	12.137111	11.573378	11.051078	10.566453	10.116128
29	12.907490	12.277674	11.696165	11.158406	10.660326	10.198283
30	13.058676	12.409041	11.810386	11.257783	10.746844	10.273654
31	13.200635	12.531814	11.916638	11.349799	10.826584	10.342802
32	13.333929	12.646555	12.015478	11.434999	10.900078	10.406240
33	13.459088	12.753790	12.107421	11.513888	10.967813	10.464441
34	13.576609	12.854009	12.192950	11.586934	11.030243	10.517835
35	13.686957	12.947672	12.272511	11.654568	11.087781	10.566821
36	13.790570	13.035208	12.346522	11.717193	11.140812	10.611763
37	13.887859	13.117017	12.415370	11.775179	11.189689	10.652993
38	13.979210	13.193473	12.479414	11.828869	11.234736	10.690820
39	14.064986	13.264928	12.538989	11.878582	11.276255	10.725523
40	14.145527	13.331709	12.594409	11.924613	11.314520	10.757360
41	14.221152	13.394120	12.645962	11.967235	11.349788	10.786569
42	14.292161	13.452449	12.693918	12.006699	11.382293	10.813366
43	14.358837	13.506962	12.738528	12.043240	11.412252	10.837950
44	14.421443	13.557908	12.780026	12.077074	11.439864	10.860505
45	14.480228	13.605522	12.818629	12.108402	11.465312	10.881197
46	14.535426	13.650020	12.854539	12.137409	11.488767	10.900181
47	14.587254	13.691608	12.887943	12.164267	11.510384	10.917597
48	14.635919	13.730474	12.919017	12.189136	11.530308	10.933575
49	14.681615	13.766799	12.947922	12.212163	11.548671	10.948234
50	14.724521	13.800746	12.974812	12.233485	11.565595	10.961683
51	14.764808	13.832473	12.999825	12.253227	11.581194	10.974021
52	14.802637	13.862124	13.023093	12.271506	11.595570	10.985340
53	14.838157	13.889836	13.044737	12.288432	11.608821	10.995725
54	14.871509	13.915735	13.064872	12.304103	11.621033	11.005252
55	14.902825	13.939939	13.083602	12.318614	11.632288	11.013993
56	14.932230	13.962560	13.101025	12.332050	11.642662	11.022012
57	14.959840	13.983701	13.117233	12.344491	11.652223	11.029369
58	14.985766	14.003458	13.132309	12.356010	11.661035	11.036118
59	15.010109	14.021924	13.146334	12.366676	11.669157	11.042310
60	15.032966	14.039181	13.159381	12.376552	11.676642	11.047991

Table IV **Uniform Series/Present Value Factor (Present Value of Annuity Factor; Uniform Series/Present Worth Factor)(continued)**

$$\frac{(1+i)^n - 1}{i(1+i)^n}$$

n	*0.065 (6½%)*	*0.07 (7%)*	*0.075 (7½%)*	*0.08 (8%)*	*0.085 (8½%)*	*0.09 (9%)*
61	15.054428	14.055309	13.171517	12.385696	11.683541	11.053203
62	15.074580	14.070383	13.182806	12.394163	11.689900	11.057984
63	15.093503	14.084470	13.193308	12.402003	11.695760	11.062371
64	15.111270	14.097635	13.203078	12.409262	11.701161	11.066395
65	15.127953	14.109940	13.212165	12.415983	11.706140	11.070087
66	15.143618	14.121439	13.220619	12.422207	11.710728	11.073475
67	15.158327	14.132186	13.228483	12.427969	11.714956	11.076582
68	15.172138	14.142230	13.235798	12.433305	11.718854	11.079433
69	15.185106	14.151617	13.242603	12.438245	11.722446	11.082049
70	15.197282	14.160389	13.248933	12.442820	11.725757	11.084449
71	15.208716	14.168588	13.254821	12.447055	11.728808	11.086650
72	15.219452	14.176251	13.260299	12.450977	11.731620	11.088670
73	15.229532	14.183412	13.265394	12.454608	11.734212	11.090523
74	15.238997	14.190104	13.270134	12.457971	11.736601	11.092223
75	15.247885	14.196359	13.274543	12.461084	11.738803	11.093782
76	15.256230	14.202205	13.278645	12.463967	11.740832	11.095213
77	15.264065	14.207668	13.282460	12.466636	11.742702	11.096526
78	15.271423	14.212774	13.286010	12.469107	11.744426	11.097730
79	15.278331	14.217546	13.289311	12.471396	11.746015	11.098835
80	15.284818	14.222005	13.292383	12.473514	11.747479	11.099849
81	15.290909	14.226173	13.295240	12.475476	11.748829	11.100778
82	15.296628	14.230069	13.297897	12.477293	11.750073	11.101632
83	15.301998	14.233709	13.300370	12.478975	11.751219	11.102414
84	15.307041	14.237111	13.302669	12.480532	11.752276	11.103132
85	15.311775	14.240291	13.304809	12.481974	11.753249	11.103791
86	15.316221	14.243262	13.306799	12.483310	11.754147	11.104396
87	15.320395	14.246040	13.308650	12.484546	11.754974	11.104950
88	15.324315	14.248635	13.310372	12.485691	11.755736	11.105459
89	15.327995	14.251061	13.311974	12.486751	11.756439	11.105926
90	15.331451	14.253328	13.313464	12.487732	11.757087	11.106354
91	15.334696	14.255447	13.314851	12.488641	11.757684	11.106746
92	15.337742	14.257427	13.316140	12.489482	11.758234	11.107107
93	15.340603	14.259277	13.317340	12.490261	11.758741	11.107437
94	15.343289	14.261007	13.318455	12.490983	11.759208	11.107741
95	15.345812	14.262623	13.319493	12.491651	11.759639	11.108019
96	15.348180	14.264134	13.320459	12.492269	11.760036	11.108274
97	15.350404	14.265546	13.321357	12.492842	11.760402	11.108509
98	15.352492	14.266865	13.322193	12.493372	11.760739	11.108724
99	15.354452	14.268098	13.322970	12.493863	11.761050	11.108921
100	15.356293	14.269251	13.323693	12.494318	11.761336	11.109102
101	15.358022	14.270328	13.324366	12.494738	11.761600	11.109267
102	15.359645	14.271334	13.324991	12.495128	11.761843	11.109420
103	15.361169	14.272275	13.325573	12.495489	11.762068	11.109559
104	15.362600	14.273154	13.326115	12.495823	11.762274	11.109687
105	15.363944	14.273976	13.326618	12.496133	11.762465	11.109805
106	15.365205	14.274744	13.327087	12.496419	11.762640	11.109913
107	15.366390	14.275462	13.327523	12.496684	11.762802	11.110012
108	15.367502	14.276132	13.327928	12.496930	11.762951	11.110103
109	15.368547	14.276759	13.328305	12.497157	11.763089	11.110186
110	15.369527	14.277345	13.328656	12.497368	11.763215	11.110262
111	15.370448	14.277893	13.328982	12.497563	11.763332	11.110332
112	15.371313	14.278404	13.329286	12.497743	11.763440	11.110397
113	15.372125	14.278882	13.329568	12.497911	11.763539	11.110456
114	15.372887	14.279329	13.329831	12.498065	11.763630	11.110510
115	15.373603	14.279747	13.330075	12.498209	11.763715	11.110559
116	15.374275	14.280138	13.330303	12.498341	11.763792	11.110605
117	15.374906	14.280502	13.330514	12.498464	11.763864	11.110647
118	15.375499	14.280843	13.330711	12.498578	11.763930	11.110685
119	15.376055	14.281162	13.330894	12.498683	11.763991	11.110720
120	15.376578	14.281460	13.331064	12.498781	11.764047	11.110753

Table IV **Uniform Series/Present Value Factor (Present Value of Annuity Factor; Uniform Series/Present Worth Factor)(continued)**

$$\frac{(1+i)^n - 1}{i(1+i)^n}$$

n	*0.095 (9½%)*	*0.10 (10%)*	*0.105 (10½%)*	*0.11 (11%)*	*0.115 (11½%)*	*0.12 (12%)*
1	0.913242	0.909091	0.904977	0.900901	0.896861	0.892857
2	1.747253	1.735537	1.723961	1.712523	1.701221	1.690051
3	2.508907	2.486852	2.465123	2.443715	2.422619	2.401831
4	3.204481	3.169865	3.135858	3.102446	3.069614	3.037349
5	3.839709	3.790787	3.742858	3.695897	3.649878	3.604776
6	4.419825	4.355261	4.292179	4.230538	4.170294	4.111407
7	4.949612	4.868419	4.789303	4.712196	4.637035	4.563757
8	5.433436	5.334926	5.239188	5.146123	5.055637	4.967640
9	5.875284	5.759024	5.646324	5.537048	5.431064	5.328250
10	6.278798	6.144567	6.014773	5.889232	5.767771	5.650223
11	6.647304	6.495061	6.348211	6.206515	6.069750	5.937699
12	6.983839	6.813692	6.649964	6.492356	6.340583	6.194374
13	7.291178	7.103356	6.923045	6.749870	6.583482	6.423548
14	7.571852	7.366687	7.170176	6.981865	6.801329	6.628168
15	7.828175	7.606080	7.393825	7.190870	6.996708	6.810864
16	8.062260	7.823709	7.596221	7.379162	7.171935	6.973986
17	8.276037	8.021553	7.779386	7.548794	7.329090	7.119630
18	8.471266	8.201412	7.945146	7.701617	7.470036	7.249670
19	8.649558	8.364920	8.095154	7.839294	7.596445	7.365777
20	8.812382	8.513564	8.230909	7.963328	7.709816	7.469444
21	8.961080	8.648694	8.353764	8.075070	7.811494	7.562003
22	9.096876	8.771540	8.464945	8.175739	7.902685	7.644646
23	9.220892	8.883218	8.565561	8.266432	7.984471	7.718434
24	9.334148	8.984744	8.656616	8.348137	8.057822	7.784316
25	9.437578	9.077040	8.739019	8.421745	8.123607	7.843139
26	9.532034	9.160945	8.813592	8.488058	8.182607	7.895660
27	9.618296	9.237223	8.881079	8.547800	8.235522	7.942554
28	9.697074	9.306567	8.942153	8.601622	8.282979	7.984423
29	9.769018	9.369606	8.997423	8.650110	8.325542	8.021806
30	9.834719	9.426914	9.047442	8.693793	8.363715	8.055184
31	9.894721	9.479013	9.092707	8.733146	8.397951	8.084986
32	9.949517	9.526376	9.133672	8.768600	8.428655	8.111594
33	9.999559	9.569432	9.170744	8.800541	8.456193	8.135352
34	10.045259	9.608575	9.204293	8.829316	8.480891	8.156564
35	10.086995	9.644159	9.234654	8.855240	8.503041	8.175504
36	10.125109	9.676508	9.262131	8.878594	8.522907	8.192414
37	10.159917	9.705917	9.286996	8.899635	8.540723	8.207513
38	10.191705	9.732651	9.309499	8.918590	8.556703	8.220993
39	10.220735	9.756956	9.329863	8.935666	8.571034	8.233030
40	10.247247	9.779051	9.348292	8.951051	8.583887	8.243777
41	10.271458	9.799137	9.364970	8.964911	8.595414	8.253372
42	10.293569	9.817397	9.380064	8.977397	8.605753	8.261939
43	10.313762	9.833998	9.393723	8.988646	8.615025	8.269589
44	10.332203	9.849089	9.406084	8.998780	8.623341	8.276418
45	10.349043	9.862808	9.417271	9.007910	8.630799	8.282516
46	10.364423	9.875280	9.427394	9.016135	8.637488	8.287961
47	10.378469	9.886618	9.436556	9.023545	8.643487	8.292822
48	10.391296	9.896926	9.444847	9.030221	8.648867	8.297163
49	10.403010	9.906296	9.452350	9.036235	8.653692	8.301038
50	10.413707	9.914814	9.459140	9.041653	8.658020	8.304498
51	10.423477	9.922559	9.465285	9.046534	8.661901	8.307588
52	10.432399	9.929599	9.470847	9.050932	8.665382	8.310346
53	10.440547	9.935999	9.475879	9.054894	8.668504	8.312809
54	10.447988	9.941817	9.480434	9.058463	8.671304	8.315008
55	10.454784	9.947106	9.484555	9.061678	8.673816	8.316972
56	10.460990	9.951915	9.488285	9.064575	8.676068	8.318725
57	10.466657	9.956286	9.491661	9.067185	8.678088	8.320290
58	10.471833	9.960260	9.494716	9.069536	8.679899	8.321687
59	10.476560	9.963873	9.497480	9.071654	8.681524	8.322935
60	10.480877	9.967157	9.499982	9.073562	8.682981	8.324049

Table IV Uniform Series/Present Value Factor (Present Value of Annuity Factor; Uniform Series/Present Worth Factor)(continued)

$$\frac{(1+i)^n - 1}{i(1+i)^n}$$

n	*0.125 (12½%)*	*0.13 (13%)*	*0.135 (13½%)*	*0.14 (14%)*	*0.145 (14½%)*	*0.15 (15%)*
1	0.888889	0.884956	0.881057	0.877193	0.873362	0.869565
2	1.679012	1.668102	1.657319	1.646661	1.636124	1.625709
3	2.381344	2.361153	2.341250	2.321632	2.302292	2.283225
4	3.005639	2.974471	2.943833	2.913712	2.884098	2.854978
5	3.560568	3.517231	3.474743	3.433081	3.392225	3.352155
6	4.053839	3.997550	3.942505	3.888668	3.836005	3.784483
7	4.492301	4.422610	4.354630	4.288305	4.223585	4.160420
8	4.882045	4.798770	4.717735	4.638864	4.562083	4.487322
9	5.228485	5.131655	5.037652	4.946372	4.857714	4.771584
10	5.536431	5.426243	5.319517	5.216116	5.115908	5.018769
11	5.810161	5.686941	5.567857	5.452733	5.341404	5.233712
12	6.053476	5.917647	5.786658	5.660292	5.538344	5.420619
13	6.269757	6.121812	5.979434	5.842362	5.710344	5.583147
14	6.462006	6.302488	6.149281	6.002072	5.860563	5.724476
15	6.632894	6.462379	6.298926	6.142168	5.991758	5.847370
16	6.784795	6.603875	6.430772	6.265060	6.106339	5.954235
17	6.919818	6.729093	6.546936	6.372859	6.206409	6.047161
18	7.039838	6.839905	6.649283	6.467420	6.293807	6.127966
19	7.146523	6.937969	6.739456	6.550369	6.370137	6.198231
20	7.241353	7.024752	6.818904	6.623131	6.436801	6.259331
21	7.325647	7.101550	6.888902	6.686957	6.495023	6.312462
22	7.400575	7.169513	6.950575	6.742944	6.545871	6.358663
23	7.467178	7.229658	7.004912	6.792056	6.590281	6.398837
24	7.526381	7.282883	7.052786	6.835137	6.629066	6.433771
25	7.579005	7.329985	7.094965	6.872927	6.662940	6.464149
26	7.625782	7.371668	7.132128	6.906077	6.692524	6.490564
27	7.667362	7.408556	7.164870	6.935155	6.718362	6.513534
28	7.704322	7.441200	7.193718	6.960662	6.740927	6.533508
29	7.737175	7.470088	7.219135	6.983037	6.760635	6.550877
30	7.766378	7.495653	7.241529	7.002664	6.777847	6.565980
31	7.792336	7.518277	7.261259	7.019881	6.792880	6.579113
32	7.815410	7.538299	7.278642	7.034983	6.806008	6.590533
33	7.835920	7.556016	7.293958	7.048231	6.817475	6.600463
34	7.854151	7.571696	7.307452	7.059852	6.827489	6.609099
35	7.870356	7.585572	7.319341	7.070045	6.836235	6.616607
36	7.884761	7.597851	7.329816	7.078987	6.843873	6.623137
37	7.897565	7.608718	7.339045	7.086831	6.850544	6.628815
38	7.908947	7.618334	7.347176	7.093711	6.856370	6.633752
39	7.919064	7.626844	7.354340	7.099747	6.861459	6.638045
40	7.928057	7.634376	7.360652	7.105041	6.865903	6.641778
41	7.936051	7.641040	7.366213	7.109685	6.869784	6.645025
42	7.943156	7.646938	7.371113	7.113759	6.873174	6.647848
43	7.949472	7.652158	7.375430	7.117332	6.876135	6.650302
44	7.955086	7.656777	7.379233	7.120467	6.878720	6.652437
45	7.960077	7.660864	7.382585	7.123217	6.880978	6.654293
46	7.964513	7.664482	7.385537	7.125629	6.882950	6.655907
47	7.968456	7.667683	7.388138	7.127744	6.884673	6.657310
48	7.971961	7.670516	7.390430	7.129600	6.886177	6.658531
49	7.975076	7.673023	7.392450	7.131228	6.887491	6.659592
50	7.977845	7.675242	7.394229	7.132656	6.888638	6.660515
51	7.980307	7.677205	7.395796	7.133909	6.889641	6.661317
52	7.982495	7.678942	7.397177	7.135008	6.890516	6.662015
53	7.984440	7.680480	7.398394	7.135972	6.891280	6.662622
54	7.986169	7.681841	7.399466	7.136818	6.891948	6.663149
55	7.987706	7.683045	7.400411	7.137559	6.892531	6.663608
56	7.989072	7.684111	7.401243	7.138210	6.893040	6.664007
57	7.990286	7.685054	7.401976	7.138781	6.893485	6.664354
58	7.991365	7.685888	7.402622	7.139281	6.893873	6.664656
59	7.992325	7.686627	7.403191	7.139720	6.894212	6.664918
60	7.993178	7.687280	7.403693	7.140106	6.894509	6.665146

Table IV **Uniform Series/Present Value Factor (Present Value of Annuity Factor; Uniform Series/Present Worth Factor)(continued)**

$$\frac{(1+i)^n - 1}{i(1+i)^n}$$

n	0.155 (15½%)	0.16 (16%)	0.165 (16½%)	0.17 (17%)	0.175 (17½%)	0.18 (18%)
1	0.865801	0.862069	0.858369	0.854701	0.851064	0.847458
2	1.615412	1.605232	1.595167	1.585214	1.575373	1.565642
3	2.264426	2.245890	2.227611	2.209585	2.191807	2.174273
4	2.826343	2.798181	2.770481	2.743235	2.716432	2.690062
5	3.312851	3.274294	3.236465	3.199346	3.162921	3.127171
6	3.734070	3.684736	3.636450	3.589185	3.542911	3.497603
7	4.098762	4.038565	3.979786	3.922380	3.866307	3.811528
8	4.414513	4.343591	4.274494	4.207163	4.141538	4.077566
9	4.687890	4.606544	4.527463	4.450566	4.375777	4.303022
10	4.924580	4.833227	4.744603	4.658604	4.575129	4.494086
11	5.129506	5.028644	4.930990	4.836413	4.744791	4.656005
12	5.306932	5.197107	5.090978	4.988387	4.889184	4.793225
13	5.460547	5.342334	5.228308	5.118280	5.012071	4.909513
14	5.593547	5.467529	5.346187	5.229299	5.116657	5.008062
15	5.708699	5.575456	5.447371	5.324187	5.205665	5.091578
16	5.808397	5.668497	5.534224	5.405288	5.281417	5.162354
17	5.894716	5.748704	5.608776	5.474605	5.345887	5.222334
18	5.969451	5.817848	5.672769	5.533851	5.400755	5.273164
19	6.034157	5.877455	5.727699	5.584488	5.447451	5.316241
20	6.090179	5.928841	5.774849	5.627767	5.487192	5.352746
21	6.138683					
22	6.180678					
23	6.217037					
24	6.248517					
25	6.275772					
26	6.299370					
27	6.319801					
28	6.337490					
29	6.352805					
30	6.366065					
31	6.377546					
32	6.387485					
33	6.396091					
34	6.403542					
35	6.409993					
36	6.415579					
37	6.420414					
38	6.424601					
39	6.428226					
40	6.431365					
41	6.434082					
42	6.436435					
43	6.438471					
44	6.440235					
45	6.441762					
46	6.443084					
47	6.444229					
48	6.445219					
49	6.446077					
50	6.446820					
51	6.447463					
52	6.448020					
53	6.448502					
54	6.448920					
55	6.449281					
56	6.449594					
57	6.449865					
58	6.450100					
59	6.450303					
60	6.450479					

Table IV Uniform Series/Present Value Factor (Present Value of Annuity Factor; Uniform Series/Present Worth Factor)(continued)

$$\frac{(1 + i)^n - 1}{i\,(1 + i)^n}$$

n	*0.185 (18½%)*	*0.19 (19%)*	*0.195 (19½%)*	*0.20 (20%)*	*0.21 (21%)*	*0.22 (22%)*
1	0.843882	0.840336	0.836820	0.833333	0.826446	0.819672
2	1.556018	1.546501	1.537088	1.527778	1.509460	1.491535
3	2.156978	2.139917	2.123086	2.106481	2.073934	2.042241
4	2.664116	2.638586	2.613461	2.588735	2.540441	2.493641
5	3.092081	3.057635	3.023817	2.990612	2.925984	2.863640
6	3.453233	3.409777	3.367211	3.325510	3.244615	3.166918
7	3.758003	3.705695	3.654570	3.604592	3.507946	3.415506
8	4.015192	3.954366	3.895037	3.837160	3.725576	3.619268
9	4.232230	4.163332	4.096266	4.030967	3.905434	3.786285
10	4.415384	4.338935	4.264657	4.192472	4.054078	3.923184
11	4.569944	4.486500	4.405571	4.327060	4.176924	4.035397
12	4.700375	4.610504	4.523490	4.439217	4.278450	4.127375
13	4.810443	4.714709	4.622168	4.532681	4.362355	4.202766
14	4.903327	4.802277	4.704743	4.610567	4.431698	4.264562
15	4.981711	4.875863	4.773843	4.675473	4.489007	4.315215
16	5.047857	4.937700	4.831668	4.729561	4.536369	4.356734
17	5.103677	4.989664	4.880057	4.774634	4.575512	4.390765
18	5.150782	5.033331	4.920550	4.812195	4.607861	4.418660
19	5.190534	5.070026	4.954435	4.843496	4.634596	4.441525
20	5.224079	5.100862	4.982791	4.869580	4.656691	4.460266

n	*0.23 (23%)*	*0.24 (24%)*	*0.25 (25%)*	*0.30 (30%)*	*0.35 (35%)*	*0.40 (40%)*
1	0.813008	0.806452	0.800000	0.769231	0.740741	0.714286
2	1.473990	1.456816	1.440000	1.360947	1.289438	1.224490
3	2.011374	1.981303	1.952000	1.816113	1.695880	1.588921
4	2.448272	2.404277	2.361600	2.166241	1.996948	1.849229
5	2.803473	2.745384	2.689280	2.435570	2.219961	2.035164
6	3.092254	3.020471	2.951424	2.642746	2.385157	2.167974
7	3.327036	3.242316	3.161139	2.802112	2.507523	2.262839
8	3.517916	3.421222	3.328911	2.924702	2.598165	2.330599
9	3.673102	3.565502	3.463129	3.019001	2.665308	2.378999
10	3.799270	3.681856	3.570503	3.091539	2.715043	2.413571
11	3.901846	3.775691	3.656403	3.147338	2.751884	2.438265
12	3.985240	3.851363	3.725122	3.190260	2.779173	2.455904
13	4.053041	3.912390	3.780098	3.223277	2.799387	2.468503
14	4.108163	3.961605	3.824078	3.248675	2.814361	2.477502
15	4.152978	4.001294	3.859263	3.268211	2.825453	2.483930
16	4.189413	4.033302	3.887410	3.283239	2.833669	2.488521
17	4.219035	4.059114	3.909928	3.294800	2.839755	2.491801
18	4.243118	4.079931	3.927942	3.303692	2.844263	2.494144
19	4.262698	4.096718	3.942354	3.310532	2.847602	2.495817
20	4.278616	4.110257	3.953883	3.315794	2.850076	2.497012

Table V Capital Recovery Factor (Amortization Factor)

$$\frac{i(1+i)^n}{(1+i)^n - 1}$$

n	0.0025 (1/4%)	0.0050 (1/2%)	0.0075 (3/4%)	0.01 (1%)	0.0125 (1 1/4%)	0.0150 (1 1/2%)
1	1.002500	1.005000	1.007500	1.010000	1.012500	1.015000
2	0.501876	0.503753	0.505632	0.507512	0.509394	0.511278
3	0.335001	0.336672	0.338346	0.340022	0.341701	0.343383
4	0.251564	0.253133	0.254705	0.256281	0.257861	0.259445
5	0.201502	0.203010	0.204522	0.206040	0.207562	0.209089
6	0.168128	0.169595	0.171069	0.172548	0.174034	0.175525
7	0.144289	0.145729	0.147175	0.148628	0.150089	0.151556
8	0.126410	0.127829	0.129256	0.130690	0.132133	0.133584
9	0.112505	0.113907	0.115319	0.116740	0.118171	0.119610
10	0.101380	0.102771	0.104171	0.105582	0.107003	0.108434
11	0.092278	0.093659	0.095051	0.096454	0.097868	0.099294
12	0.084694	0.086066	0.087451	0.088849	0.090258	0.091680
13	0.078276	0.079642	0.081022	0.082415	0.083821	0.085240
14	0.072775	0.074136	0.075511	0.076901	0.078305	0.079723
15	0.068008	0.069364	0.070736	0.072124	0.073526	0.074944
16	0.063836	0.065189	0.066559	0.067945	0.069347	0.070765
17	0.060156	0.061506	0.062873	0.064258	0.065660	0.067080
18	0.056884	0.058232	0.059598	0.060982	0.062385	0.063806
19	0.053957	0.055303	0.056667	0.058052	0.059455	0.060878
20	0.051323	0.052666	0.054031	0.055415	0.056820	0.058246
21	0.048939	0.050282	0.051645	0.053031	0.054437	0.055865
22	0.046773	0.048114	0.049477	0.050864	0.052272	0.053703
23	0.044795	0.046135	0.047498	0.048886	0.050297	0.051731
24	0.042981	0.044321	0.045685	0.047073	0.048487	0.049924
25	0.041313	0.042652	0.044016	0.045407	0.046822	0.048263
26	0.039773	0.041112	0.042477	0.043869	0.045287	0.046732
27	0.038347	0.039686	0.041052	0.042446	0.043867	0.045315
28	0.037023	0.038362	0.039729	0.041124	0.042549	0.044001
29	0.035791	0.037129	0.038497	0.039895	0.041322	0.042779
30	0.034641	0.035979	0.037348	0.038748	0.040179	0.041639
31	0.033564	0.034903	0.036274	0.037676	0.039109	0.040574
32	0.032556	0.033895	0.035266	0.036671	0.038108	0.039577
33	0.031608	0.032947	0.034320	0.035727	0.037168	0.038641
34	0.030716	0.032056	0.033431	0.034840	0.036284	0.037762
35	0.029875	0.031215	0.032592	0.034004	0.035451	0.036934
36	0.029081	0.030422	0.031800	0.033214	0.034665	0.036152
37	0.028330	0.029671	0.031051	0.032468	0.033923	0.035414
38	0.027618	0.028960	0.030342	0.031761	0.033220	0.034716
39	0.026943	0.028286	0.029669	0.031092	0.032554	0.034055
40	0.026302	0.027646	0.029030	0.030456	0.031921	0.033427
41	0.025692	0.027036	0.028423	0.029851	0.031321	0.032831
42	0.025111	0.026456	0.027845	0.029276	0.030749	0.032264
43	0.024557	0.025903	0.027293	0.028727	0.030205	0.031725
44	0.024029	0.025375	0.026768	0.028204	0.029686	0.031210
45	0.023523	0.024871	0.026265	0.027705	0.029190	0.030720
46	0.023040	0.024389	0.025785	0.027228	0.028717	0.030251
47	0.022578	0.023927	0.025325	0.026771	0.028264	0.029803
48	0.022134	0.023485	0.024885	0.026334	0.027831	0.029375
49	0.021709	0.023061	0.024463	0.025915	0.027416	0.028965
50	0.021301	0.022654	0.024058	0.025513	0.027018	0.028572
51	0.020909	0.022263	0.023669	0.025127	0.026636	0.028195
52	0.020532	0.021887	0.023295	0.024756	0.026269	0.027833
53	0.020169	0.021525	0.022935	0.024400	0.025917	0.027485
54	0.019820	0.021177	0.022589	0.024057	0.025578	0.027151
55	0.019483	0.020841	0.022256	0.023726	0.025251	0.026830
56	0.019159	0.020518	0.021935	0.023408	0.024937	0.026521
57	0.018845	0.020206	0.021625	0.023102	0.024635	0.026223
58	0.018543	0.019905	0.021326	0.022806	0.024343	0.025937
59	0.018251	0.019614	0.021037	0.022520	0.024062	0.025660
60	0.017969	0.019333	0.020758	0.022244	0.023790	0.025393

Table V Capital Recovery Factor (Amortization Factor) (continued)

$$\frac{i(1+i)^n}{(1+i)^n - 1}$$

n	0.0025 (1/4%)	0.0050 (1/2%)	0.0075 (3/4%)	0.01 (1%)	0.0125 (1 1/4%)	0.0150 (1 1/2%)
61	0.017696	0.019061	0.020489	0.021978	0.023528	0.025136
62	0.017431	0.018798	0.020228	0.021720	0.023274	0.024888
63	0.017176	0.018543	0.019976	0.021471	0.023029	0.024647
64	0.016928	0.018297	0.019731	0.021230	0.022792	0.024415
65	0.016688	0.018058	0.019495	0.020997	0.022563	0.024191
66	0.016455	0.017826	0.019265	0.020771	0.022341	0.023974
67	0.016229	0.017602	0.019043	0.020551	0.022126	0.023764
68	0.016010	0.017384	0.018827	0.020339	0.021917	0.023560
69	0.015797	0.017172	0.018618	0.020133	0.021715	0.023363
70	0.015590	0.016967	0.018415	0.019933	0.021519	0.023172
71	0.015389	0.016767	0.018217	0.019739	0.021329	0.022987
72	0.015194	0.016573	0.018026	0.019550	0.021145	0.022808
73	0.015004	0.016384	0.017839	0.019367	0.020966	0.022634
74	0.014819	0.016201	0.017658	0.019189	0.020792	0.022465
75	0.014639	0.016022	0.017482	0.019016	0.020623	0.022301
76	0.014464	0.015848	0.017310	0.018848	0.020459	0.022141
77	0.014293	0.015679	0.017143	0.018684	0.020300	0.021987
78	0.014127	0.015514	0.016981	0.018525	0.020144	0.021836
79	0.013965	0.015354	0.016822	0.018370	0.019993	0.021690
80	0.013807	0.015197	0.016668	0.018219	0.019847	0.021548
81	0.013653	0.015044	0.016518	0.018072	0.019704	0.021410
82	0.013503	0.014896	0.016371	0.017929	0.019564	0.021276
83	0.013356	0.014750	0.016228	0.017789	0.019429	0.021145
84	0.013213	0.014609	0.016089	0.017653	0.019297	0.021018
85	0.013074	0.014470	0.015953	0.017520	0.019168	0.020894
86	0.012937	0.014335	0.015820	0.017391	0.019043	0.020773
87	0.012804	0.014203	0.015691	0.017264	0.018920	0.020656
88	0.012674	0.014074	0.015564	0.017141	0.018801	0.020541
89	0.012546	0.013948	0.015441	0.017021	0.018685	0.020430
90	0.012422	0.013825	0.015320	0.016903	0.018571	0.020321
91	0.012300	0.013705	0.015202	0.016788	0.018461	0.020215
92	0.012181	0.013587	0.015087	0.016676	0.018353	0.020112
93	0.012064	0.013472	0.014974	0.016567	0.018247	0.020011
94	0.011950	0.013360	0.014864	0.016460	0.018144	0.019913
95	0.011839	0.013249	0.014756	0.016355	0.018044	0.019817
96	0.011730	0.013141	0.014650	0.016253	0.017945	0.019723
97	0.011623	0.013036	0.014547	0.016153	0.017849	0.019632
98	0.011518	0.012932	0.014446	0.016055	0.017756	0.019543
99	0.011415	0.012831	0.014347	0.015959	0.017664	0.019456
100	0.011314	0.012732	0.014250	0.015866	0.017574	0.019371
101	0.011216	0.012635	0.014155	0.015774	0.017487	0.019288
102	0.011119	0.012539	0.014062	0.015684	0.017401	0.019206
103	0.011024	0.012446	0.013971	0.015597	0.017317	0.019127
104	0.010931	0.012355	0.013882	0.015511	0.017235	0.019050
105	0.010840	0.012265	0.013795	0.015427	0.017155	0.018974
106	0.010751	0.012177	0.013709	0.015344	0.017076	0.018900
107	0.010663	0.012090	0.013625	0.015263	0.017000	0.018828
108	0.010577	0.012006	0.013543	0.015184	0.016924	0.018757
109	0.010492	0.011923	0.013462	0.015107	0.016851	0.018688
110	0.010409	0.011841	0.013383	0.015031	0.016779	0.018620
111	0.010328	0.011761	0.013305	0.014956	0.016708	0.018554
112	0.010248	0.011682	0.013229	0.014883	0.016639	0.018489
113	0.010169	0.011605	0.013154	0.014812	0.016571	0.018426
114	0.010092	0.011529	0.013081	0.014741	0.016505	0.018364
115	0.010016	0.011455	0.013009	0.014672	0.016440	0.018303
116	0.009942	0.011382	0.012938	0.014605	0.016376	0.018244
117	0.009868	0.011310	0.012869	0.014539	0.016314	0.018186
118	0.009796	0.011240	0.012800	0.014474	0.016252	0.018129
119	0.009726	0.011170	0.012733	0.014410	0.016192	0.018073
120	0.009656	0.011102	0.012668	0.014347	0.016133	0.018019

Table V **Capital Recovery Factor (Amortization Factor) (continued)**

$$\frac{i(1+i)^n}{(1+i)^n - 1}$$

n	0.0175 (1¾%)	0.02 (2%)	0.0225 (2¼%)	0.025 (2½%)	0.0275 (2¾%)	0.03 (3%)
1	1.017500	1.020000	1.022500	1.025000	1.027500	1.030000
2	0.513163	0.515050	0.516938	0.518827	0.520718	0.522611
3	0.345067	0.346755	0.348445	0.350137	0.351832	0.353530
4	0.261032	0.262624	0.264219	0.265818	0.267421	0.269027
5	0.210621	0.212158	0.213700	0.215247	0.216798	0.218355
6	0.177023	0.178526	0.180035	0.181550	0.183071	0.184598
7	0.153031	0.154512	0.156000	0.157495	0.158997	0.160506
8	0.135043	0.136510	0.137985	0.139467	0.140958	0.142456
9	0.121058	0.122515	0.123982	0.125457	0.126941	0.128434
10	0.109875	0.111327	0.112788	0.114259	0.115740	0.117231
11	0.100730	0.102178	0.103636	0.105106	0.106586	0.108077
12	0.093114	0.094560	0.096017	0.097487	0.098969	0.100462
13	0.086673	0.088118	0.089577	0.091048	0.092533	0.094030
14	0.081156	0.082602	0.084062	0.085537	0.087025	0.088526
15	0.076377	0.077825	0.079289	0.080766	0.082259	0.083767
16	0.072200	0.073650	0.075117	0.076599	0.078097	0.079611
17	0.068516	0.069970	0.071440	0.072928	0.074432	0.075953
18	0.065245	0.066702	0.068177	0.069670	0.071181	0.072709
19	0.062321	0.063782	0.065262	0.066761	0.068278	0.069814
20	0.059691	0.061157	0.062642	0.064147	0.065672	0.067216
21	0.057315	0.058785	0.060276	0.061787	0.063319	0.064872
22	0.055156	0.056631	0.058128	0.059647	0.061186	0.062747
23	0.053188	0.054668	0.056171	0.057696	0.059244	0.060814
24	0.051386	0.052871	0.054380	0.055913	0.057469	0.059047
25	0.049730	0.051220	0.052736	0.054276	0.055840	0.057428
26	0.048203	0.049699	0.051221	0.052769	0.054341	0.055938
27	0.046791	0.048293	0.049822	0.051377	0.052958	0.054564
28	0.045482	0.046990	0.048525	0.050088	0.051677	0.053293
29	0.044264	0.045778	0.047321	0.048891	0.050489	0.052115
30	0.043130	0.044650	0.046199	0.047778	0.049384	0.051019
31	0.042070	0.043596	0.045153	0.046739	0.048355	0.049999
32	0.041078	0.042611	0.044174	0.045768	0.047393	0.049047
33	0.040148	0.041687	0.043257	0.044859	0.046493	0.048156
34	0.039274	0.040819	0.042397	0.044007	0.045649	0.047322
35	0.038451	0.040002	0.041587	0.043206	0.044856	0.046539
36	0.037675	0.039233	0.040825	0.042452	0.044111	0.045804
37	0.036943	0.038507	0.040106	0.041741	0.043410	0.045112
38	0.036250	0.037821	0.039428	0.041070	0.042748	0.044459
39	0.035594	0.037171	0.038785	0.040436	0.042123	0.043844
40	0.034972	0.036556	0.038177	0.039836	0.041532	0.043262
41	0.034382	0.035972	0.037601	0.039268	0.040972	0.042712
42	0.033821	0.035417	0.037054	0.038729	0.040442	0.042192
43	0.033287	0.034890	0.036534	0.038217	0.039939	0.041698
44	0.032778	0.034388	0.036039	0.037730	0.039461	0.041230
45	0.032293	0.033910	0.035568	0.037268	0.039007	0.040785
46	0.031830	0.033453	0.035119	0.036827	0.038575	0.040363
47	0.031388	0.033018	0.034691	0.036407	0.038164	0.039961
48	0.030966	0.032602	0.034282	0.036006	0.037772	0.039578
49	0.030561	0.032204	0.033892	0.035623	0.037398	0.039213
50	0.030174	0.031823	0.033518	0.035258	0.037041	0.038865
51	0.029803	0.031459	0.033161	0.034909	0.036700	0.038534
52	0.029447	0.031109	0.032819	0.034574	0.036374	0.038217
53	0.029105	0.030774	0.032491	0.034254	0.036063	0.037915
54	0.028777	0.030452	0.032177	0.033948	0.035765	0.037626
55	0.028461	0.030143	0.031875	0.033654	0.035480	0.037349
56	0.028158	0.029847	0.031585	0.033372	0.035206	0.037084
57	0.027866	0.029561	0.031307	0.033102	0.034944	0.036831
58	0.027585	0.029287	0.031040	0.032842	0.034693	0.036588
59	0.027314	0.029022	0.030783	0.032593	0.034452	0.036356
60	0.027053	0.028768	0.030535	0.032353	0.034220	0.036133

Table V Capital Recovery Factor (Amortization Factor) (continued)

$$\frac{i(1+i)^n}{(1+i)^n - 1}$$

n	0.0175 (1¾%)	0.02 (2%)	0.0225 (2¼%)	0.025 (2½%)	0.0275 (2¾%)	0.03 (3%)
61	0.026802	0.028523	0.030297	0.032123	0.033998	0.035919
62	0.026559	0.028286	0.030068	0.031901	0.033784	0.035714
63	0.026325	0.028058	0.029847	0.031688	0.033579	0.035517
64	0.026098	0.027839	0.029634	0.031482	0.033381	0.035328
65	0.025880	0.027626	0.029429	0.031285	0.033191	0.035146
66	0.025668	0.027421	0.029231	0.031094	0.033008	0.034971
67	0.025464	0.027223	0.029040	0.030910	0.032832	0.034803
68	0.025266	0.027032	0.028855	0.030733	0.032663	0.034642
69	0.025075	0.026847	0.028677	0.030562	0.032500	0.034486
70	0.024889	0.026668	0.028505	0.030397	0.032342	0.034337
71	0.024710	0.026494	0.028338	0.030238	0.032190	0.034193
72	0.024536	0.026327	0.028177	0.030084	0.032044	0.034054
73	0.024367	0.026165	0.028022	0.029936	0.031903	0.033921
74	0.024204	0.026007	0.027871	0.029792	0.031767	0.033792
75	0.024046	0.025855	0.027726	0.029654	0.031636	0.033668
76	0.023892	0.025708	0.027585	0.029520	0.031509	0.033548
77	0.023743	0.025564	0.027448	0.029390	0.031386	0.033433
78	0.023598	0.025426	0.027316	0.029265	0.031268	0.033322
79	0.023457	0.025291	0.027188	0.029143	0.031154	0.033215
80	0.023321	0.025161	0.027064	0.029026	0.031043	0.033112
81	0.023188	0.025034	0.026944	0.028912	0.030937	0.033012
82	0.023059	0.024911	0.026827	0.028803	0.030834	0.032916
83	0.022934	0.024792	0.026714	0.028696	0.030734	0.032823
84	0.022812	0.024676	0.026604	0.028593	0.030637	0.032733
85	0.022694	0.024563	0.026498	0.028493	0.030544	0.032647
86	0.022578	0.024454	0.026395	0.028396	0.030454	0.032563
87	0.022466	0.024347	0.026295	0.028303	0.030367	0.032482
88	0.022357	0.024244	0.026197	0.028212	0.030282	0.032404
89	0.022251	0.024144	0.026103	0.028124	0.030200	0.032328
90	0.022148	0.024046	0.026011	0.028038	0.030121	0.032256
91	0.022047	0.023951	0.025922	0.027955	0.030045	0.032185
92	0.021949	0.023859	0.025836	0.027875	0.029970	0.032117
93	0.021853	0.023769	0.025752	0.027797	0.029898	0.032051
94	0.021760	0.023681	0.025670	0.027721	0.029829	0.031987
95	0.021669	0.023596	0.025591	0.027648	0.029761	0.031926
96	0.021581	0.023513	0.025514	0.027577	0.029696	0.031866
97	0.021495	0.023432	0.025439	0.027507	0.029633	0.031809
98	0.021411	0.023354	0.025366	0.027440	0.029571	0.031753
99	0.021329	0.023277	0.025295	0.027375	0.029512	0.031699
100	0.021249	0.023203	0.025226	0.027312	0.029454	0.031647
101	0.021171	0.023130	0.025159	0.027250	0.029398	0.031596
102	0.021095	0.023059	0.025094	0.027191	0.029344	0.031547
103	0.021020	0.022990	0.025030	0.027133	0.029291	0.031500
104	0.020948	0.022923	0.024968	0.027076	0.029241	0.031454
105	0.020877	0.022858	0.024908	0.027022	0.029191	0.031410
106	0.020808	0.022794	0.024850	0.026968	0.029143	0.031367
107	0.020741	0.022732	0.024793	0.026917	0.029097	0.031325
108	0.020675	0.022671	0.024737	0.026867	0.029051	0.031285
109	0.020611	0.022612	0.024683	0.026818	0.029008	0.031246
110	0.020548	0.022554	0.024631	0.026770	0.028965	0.031208
111	0.020486	0.022498	0.024579	0.026724	0.028924	0.031172
112	0.020426	0.022443	0.024530	0.026679	0.028884	0.031136
113	0.020368	0.022389	0.024481	0.026636	0.028845	0.031102
114	0.020311	0.022337	0.024434	0.026593	0.028807	0.031069
115	0.020255	0.022286	0.024387	0.026552	0.028771	0.031037
116	0.020200	0.022236	0.024343	0.026512	0.028735	0.031005
117	0.020147	0.022187	0.024299	0.026473	0.028701	0.030975
118	0.020094	0.022140	0.024256	0.026435	0.028667	0.030946
119	0.020043	0.022093	0.024215	0.026398	0.028635	0.030917
120	0.019993	0.022048	0.024174	0.026362	0.028603	0.030890

Table V Capital Recovery Factor (Amortization Factor) (continued)

$$\frac{i(1+i)^n}{(1+i)^n - 1}$$

n	0.035 (3½%)	0.04 (4%)	0.045 (4½%)	0.05 (5%)	0.055 (5½)	0.06 (6%)
1	1.035000	1.040000	1.045000	1.050000	1.055000	1.060000
2	0.526400	0.530196	0.533998	0.537805	0.541618	0.545437
3	0.356934	0.360349	0.363773	0.367209	0.370654	0.374110
4	0.272251	0.275490	0.278744	0.282012	0.285294	0.288591
5	0.221481	0.224627	0.227792	0.230975	0.234176	0.237396
6	0.187668	0.190762	0.193878	0.197017	0.200179	0.203363
7	0.163544	0.166610	0.169701	0.172820	0.175964	0.179135
8	0.145477	0.148528	0.151610	0.154722	0.157864	0.161036
9	0.131446	0.134493	0.137574	0.140690	0.143839	0.147022
10	0.120241	0.123291	0.126379	0.129505	0.132668	0.135868
11	0.111092	0.114149	0.117248	0.120389	0.123571	0.126793
12	0.103484	0.106552	0.109666	0.112825	0.116029	0.119277
13	0.097062	0.100144	0.103275	0.106456	0.109684	0.112960
14	0.091571	0.094669	0.097820	0.101024	0.104279	0.107585
15	0.086825	0.089941	0.093114	0.096342	0.099626	0.102963
16	0.082685	0.085820	0.089015	0.092270	0.095583	0.098952
17	0.079043	0.082199	0.085418	0.088699	0.092042	0.095445
18	0.075817	0.078993	0.082237	0.085546	0.088920	0.092357
19	0.072940	0.076139	0.079407	0.082745	0.086150	0.089621
20	0.070361	0.073582	0.076876	0.080243	0.083679	0.087185
21	0.068037	0.071280	0.074601	0.077996	0.081465	0.085005
22	0.065932	0.069199	0.072546	0.075971	0.079471	0.083046
23	0.064019	0.067309	0.070682	0.074137	0.077670	0.081278
24	0.062273	0.065587	0.068987	0.072471	0.076036	0.079679
25	0.060674	0.064012	0.067439	0.070952	0.074549	0.078227
26	0.059205	0.062567	0.066021	0.069564	0.073193	0.076904
27	0.057852	0.061239	0.064719	0.068292	0.071952	0.075697
28	0.056603	0.060013	0.063521	0.067123	0.070814	0.074593
29	0.055445	0.058880	0.062415	0.066046	0.069769	0.073580
30	0.054371	0.057830	0.061392	0.065051	0.068805	0.072649
31	0.053372	0.056855	0.060443	0.064132	0.067917	0.071792
32	0.052442	0.055949	0.059563	0.063280	0.067095	0.071002
33	0.051572	0.055104	0.058745	0.062490	0.066335	0.070273
34	0.050760	0.054315	0.057982	0.061755	0.065630	0.069598
35	0.049998	0.053577	0.057270	0.061072	0.064975	0.068974
36	0.049284	0.052887	0.056606	0.060434	0.064366	0.068395
37	0.048613	0.052240	0.055984	0.059840	0.063800	0.067857
38	0.047982	0.051632	0.055402	0.059284	0.063272	0.067358
39	0.047388	0.051061	0.054856	0.058765	0.062780	0.066894
40	0.046827	0.050523	0.054343	0.058278	0.062320	0.066462
41	0.046298	0.050017	0.053862	0.057822	0.061891	0.066059
42	0.045798	0.049540	0.053409	0.057395	0.061489	0.065683
43	0.045325	0.049090	0.052982	0.056993	0.061113	0.065333
44	0.044878	0.048665	0.052581	0.056616	0.060761	0.065006
45	0.044453	0.048262	0.052202	0.056262	0.060431	0.064700
46	0.044051	0.047882	0.051845	0.055928	0.060122	0.064415
47	0.043669	0.047522	0.051507	0.055614	0.059831	0.064148
48	0.043306	0.047181	0.051189	0.055318	0.059559	0.063898
49	0.042962	0.046857	0.050887	0.055040	0.059302	0.063664
50	0.042634	0.046550	0.050602	0.054777	0.059061	0.063444
51	0.042322	0.046259	0.050332	0.054529	0.058835	0.063239
52	0.042024	0.045982	0.050077	0.054294	0.058622	0.063046
53	0.041741	0.045719	0.049835	0.054073	0.058421	0.062866
54	0.041471	0.045469	0.049605	0.053864	0.058232	0.062696
55	0.041213	0.045231	0.049388	0.053667	0.058055	0.062537
56	0.040967	0.045005	0.049181	0.053480	0.057887	0.062388
57	0.040732	0.044789	0.048985	0.053303	0.057729	0.062247
58	0.040508	0.044584	0.048799	0.053136	0.057580	0.062116
59	0.040294	0.044388	0.048622	0.052978	0.057440	0.061992
60	0.040089	0.044202	0.048454	0.052828	0.057307	0.061876

Table V Capital Recovery Factor (Amortization Factor) (continued)

$$\frac{i(1+i)^n}{(1+i)^n - 1}$$

n	0.035 (3½%)	0.04 (4%)	0.045 (4½%)	0.05 (5%)	0.055 (5½)	0.06 (6%)
61	0.039892	0.044024	0.048295	0.052686	0.057182	0.061766
62	0.039705	0.043854	0.048143	0.052552	0.057064	0.061664
63	0.039525	0.043692	0.047998	0.052424	0.056953	0.061567
64	0.039353	0.043538	0.047861	0.052304	0.056847	0.061476
65	0.039188	0.043390	0.047730	0.052189	0.056748	0.061391
66	0.039030	0.043249	0.047606	0.052081	0.056654	0.061310
67	0.038879	0.043115	0.047488	0.051978	0.056565	0.061235
68	0.038734	0.042986	0.047375	0.051880	0.056482	0.061163
69	0.038595	0.042863	0.047267	0.051787	0.056402	0.061096
70	0.038461	0.042745	0.047165	0.051699	0.056328	0.061033
71	0.038333	0.042633	0.047068	0.051616	0.056257	0.060974
72	0.038210	0.042525	0.046975	0.051536	0.056190	0.060918
73	0.038092	0.042422	0.046886	0.051461	0.056127	0.060865
74	0.037978	0.042323	0.046802	0.051390	0.056067	0.060815
75	0.037869	0.042229	0.046721	0.051322	0.056010	0.060769
76	0.037765	0.042139	0.046644	0.051257	0.055956	0.060725
77	0.037664	0.042052	0.046571	0.051196	0.055906	0.060683
78	0.037567	0.041969	0.046501	0.051138	0.055858	0.060644
79	0.037474	0.041890	0.046434	0.051082	0.055812	0.060607
80	0.037385	0.041814	0.046371	0.051030	0.055769	0.060573
81	0.037299	0.041741	0.046310	0.050980	0.055729	0.060540
82	0.037216	0.041671	0.046252	0.050932	0.055690	0.060509
83	0.037137	0.041605	0.046197	0.050887	0.055654	0.060480
84	0.037060	0.041541	0.046144	0.050844	0.055619	0.060453
85	0.036987	0.041479	0.046093	0.050803	0.055587	0.060427
86	0.036916	0.041420	0.046045	0.050764	0.055556	0.060402
87	0.036848	0.041364	0.045999	0.050727	0.055527	0.060380
88	0.036782	0.041310	0.045955	0.050692	0.055499	0.060358
89	0.036719	0.041258	0.045913	0.050659	0.055473	0.060338
90	0.036658	0.041208	0.045873	0.050627	0.055448	0.060318
91	0.036599	0.041160	0.045835	0.050597	0.055424	0.060300
92	0.036543	0.041114	0.045798	0.050568	0.055402	0.060283
93	0.036488	0.041070	0.045763	0.050541	0.055381	0.060267
94	0.036436	0.041028	0.045730	0.050515	0.055361	0.060252
95	0.036385	0.040987	0.045698	0.050490	0.055342	0.060238
96	0.036337	0.040949	0.045667	0.050466	0.055324	0.060224
97	0.036290	0.040911	0.045638	0.050444	0.055307	0.060211
98	0.036245	0.040875	0.045610	0.050423	0.055291	0.060199
99	0.036201	0.040841	0.045584	0.050402	0.055276	0.060188
100	0.036159	0.040808	0.045558	0.050383	0.055261	0.060177
101	0.036119	0.040776	0.045534	0.050365	0.055248	0.060167
102	0.036080	0.040746	0.045511	0.050347	0.055235	0.060158
103	0.036042	0.040717	0.045489	0.050331	0.055222	0.060149
104	0.036006	0.040689	0.045467	0.050315	0.055211	0.060140
105	0.035971	0.040662	0.045447	0.050300	0.055200	0.060132
106	0.035937	0.040636	0.045428	0.050285	0.055189	0.060125
107	0.035905	0.040611	0.045409	0.050272	0.055179	0.060118
108	0.035873	0.040587	0.045391	0.050259	0.055170	0.060111
109	0.035843	0.040564	0.045374	0.050246	0.055161	0.060105
110	0.035814	0.040542	0.045358	0.050235	0.055153	0.060099
111	0.035786	0.040521	0.045342	0.050223	0.055145	0.060093
112	0.035759	0.040501	0.045328	0.050213	0.055137	0.060088
113	0.035732	0.040481	0.045313	0.050202	0.055130	0.060083
114	0.035707	0.040463	0.045300	0.050193	0.055123	0.060078
115	0.035683	0.040445	0.045287	0.050184	0.055117	0.060074
116	0.035659	0.040427	0.045274	0.050175	0.055111	0.060070
117	0.035637	0.040411	0.045263	0.050166	0.055105	0.060066
118	0.035615	0.040395	0.045251	0.050158	0.055099	0.060062
119	0.035594	0.040379	0.045240	0.050151	0.055094	0.060059
120	0.035573	0.040365	0.045230	0.050144	0.055089	0.060055

Table V **Capital Recovery Factor (Amortization Factor) (continued)**

$$\frac{i(1+i)^n}{(1+i)^n - 1}$$

n	0.065 (6½%)	0.07 (7%)	0.075 (7½%)	0.08 (8%)	0.085 (8½%)	0.09 (9%)
1	1.065000	1.070000	1.075000	1.080000	1.085000	1.090000
2	0.549262	0.553092	0.556928	0.560769	0.564616	0.568469
3	0.377576	0.381052	0.384538	0.388034	0.391539	0.395055
4	0.291903	0.295228	0.298568	0.301921	0.305288	0.308669
5	0.240635	0.243891	0.247165	0.250456	0.253766	0.257092
6	0.206568	0.209796	0.213045	0.216315	0.219607	0.222920
7	0.182331	0.185553	0.188800	0.192072	0.195369	0.198691
8	0.164237	0.167468	0.170727	0.174015	0.177331	0.180674
9	0.150238	0.153486	0.156767	0.160080	0.163424	0.166799
10	0.139105	0.142378	0.145686	0.149029	0.152408	0.155820
11	0.130055	0.133357	0.136697	0.140076	0.143493	0.146947
12	0.122568	0.125902	0.129278	0.132695	0.136153	0.139651
13	0.116283	0.119651	0.123064	0.126522	0.130023	0.133567
14	0.110940	0.114345	0.117797	0.121297	0.124842	0.128433
15	0.106353	0.109795	0.113287	0.116830	0.120420	0.124059
16	0.102378	0.105858	0.109391	0.112977	0.116614	0.120300
17	0.098906	0.102425	0.106000	0.109629	0.113312	0.117046
18	0.095855	0.099413	0.103029	0.106702	0.110430	0.114212
19	0.093156	0.096753	0.100411	0.104128	0.107901	0.111730
20	0.090756	0.094393	0.098092	0.101852	0.105671	0.109546
21	0.088613	0.092289	0.096029	0.099832	0.103695	0.107617
22	0.086691	0.090406	0.094187	0.098032	0.101939	0.105905
23	0.084961	0.088714	0.092535	0.096422	0.100372	0.104382
24	0.083398	0.087189	0.091050	0.094978	0.098970	0.103023
25	0.081981	0.085811	0.089711	0.093679	0.097712	0.101806
26	0.080695	0.084561	0.088500	0.092507	0.096580	0.100715
27	0.079523	0.083426	0.087402	0.091448	0.095560	0.099735
28	0.078453	0.082392	0.086405	0.090489	0.094639	0.098852
29	0.077474	0.081449	0.085498	0.089619	0.093806	0.098056
30	0.076577	0.080586	0.084671	0.088827	0.093051	0.097336
31	0.075754	0.079797	0.083916	0.088107	0.092365	0.096686
32	0.074997	0.079073	0.083226	0.087451	0.091742	0.096096
33	0.074299	0.078408	0.082594	0.086852	0.091176	0.095562
34	0.073656	0.077797	0.082015	0.086304	0.090660	0.095077
35	0.073062	0.077234	0.081483	0.085803	0.090189	0.094636
36	0.072513	0.076715	0.080994	0.085345	0.089760	0.094235
37	0.072005	0.076237	0.080545	0.084924	0.089368	0.093870
38	0.071535	0.075795	0.080132	0.084539	0.089010	0.093538
39	0.071099	0.075387	0.079751	0.084185	0.088682	0.093236
40	0.070694	0.075009	0.079400	0.083860	0.088382	0.092960
41	0.070318	0.074660	0.079077	0.083561	0.088107	0.092708
42	0.069968	0.074336	0.078778	0.083287	0.087856	0.092478
43	0.069644	0.074036	0.078502	0.083034	0.087625	0.092268
44	0.069341	0.073758	0.078247	0.082802	0.087414	0.092077
45	0.069060	0.073500	0.078011	0.082587	0.087220	0.091902
46	0.068797	0.073260	0.077794	0.082390	0.087042	0.091742
47	0.068553	0.073037	0.077592	0.082208	0.086878	0.091595
48	0.068325	0.072831	0.077405	0.082040	0.086728	0.091461
49	0.068112	0.072639	0.077232	0.081886	0.086590	0.091339
50	0.067914	0.072460	0.077072	0.081743	0.086463	0.091227
51	0.067729	0.072294	0.076924	0.081611	0.086347	0.091124
52	0.067556	0.072139	0.076787	0.081490	0.086240	0.091030
53	0.067394	0.071995	0.076659	0.081377	0.086141	0.090944
54	0.067243	0.071861	0.076541	0.081274	0.086051	0.090866
55	0.067101	0.071736	0.076432	0.081178	0.085968	0.090794
56	0.066969	0.071620	0.076330	0.081090	0.085891	0.090728
57	0.066846	0.071512	0.076236	0.081008	0.085821	0.090667
58	0.066730	0.071411	0.076148	0.080932	0.085756	0.090612
59	0.066622	0.071317	0.076067	0.080862	0.085696	0.090561
60	0.066520	0.071229	0.075991	0.080798	0.085641	0.090514

Table V **Capital Recovery Factor (Amortization Factor) (continued)**

$$\frac{i(1+i)^n}{(1+i)^n - 1}$$

n	0.065 (6½%)	0.07 (7%)	0.075 (7½%)	0.08 (8%)	0.085 (8½%)	0.09 (9%)
61	0.066426	0.071147	0.075921	0.080738	0.085590	0.090472
62	0.066337	0.071071	0.075856	0.080683	0.085544	0.090432
63	0.066254	0.071000	0.075796	0.080632	0.085501	0.090397
64	0.066176	0.070934	0.075740	0.080585	0.085462	0.090364
65	0.066103	0.070872	0.075688	0.080541	0.085425	0.090334
66	0.066034	0.070814	0.075639	0.080501	0.085392	0.090306
67	0.065970	0.070760	0.075594	0.080464	0.085361	0.090281
68	0.065910	0.070710	0.075553	0.080429	0.085333	0.090257
69	0.065854	0.070663	0.075514	0.080397	0.085306	0.090236
70	0.065801	0.070620	0.075478	0.080368	0.085282	0.090216
71	0.065752	0.070579	0.075444	0.080340	0.085260	0.090199
72	0.065705	0.070541	0.075413	0.080315	0.085240	0.090182
73	0.065662	0.070505	0.075384	0.080292	0.085221	0.090167
74	0.065621	0.070472	0.075357	0.080270	0.085204	0.090153
75	0.065583	0.070441	0.075332	0.080250	0.085188	0.090141
76	0.065547	0.070412	0.075309	0.080231	0.085173	0.090129
77	0.065513	0.070385	0.075287	0.080214	0.085159	0.090118
78	0.065482	0.070359	0.075267	0.080198	0.085147	0.090109
79	0.065452	0.070336	0.075248	0.080183	0.085135	0.090100
80	0.065424	0.070314	0.075231	0.080170	0.085125	0.090091
81	0.065398	0.070293	0.075215	0.080157	0.085115	0.090084
82	0.065374	0.070274	0.075200	0.080146	0.085106	0.090077
83	0.065351	0.070256	0.075186	0.080135	0.085098	0.090070
84	0.065329	0.070239	0.075173	0.080125	0.085090	0.090065
85	0.065309	0.070223	0.075161	0.080116	0.085083	0.090059
86	0.065290	0.070209	0.075150	0.080107	0.085076	0.090054
87	0.065272	0.070195	0.075139	0.080099	0.085070	0.090050
88	0.065256	0.070182	0.075129	0.080092	0.085065	0.090046
89	0.065240	0.070170	0.075120	0.080085	0.085060	0.090042
90	0.065225	0.070159	0.075112	0.080079	0.085055	0.090039
91	0.065212	0.070149	0.075104	0.080073	0.085051	0.090035
92	0.065199	0.070139	0.075097	0.080067	0.085047	0.090032
93	0.065186	0.070130	0.075090	0.080062	0.085043	0.090030
94	0.065175	0.070121	0.075084	0.080058	0.085040	0.090027
95	0.065164	0.070113	0.075078	0.080053	0.085037	0.090025
96	0.065154	0.070106	0.075072	0.080050	0.085034	0.090023
97	0.065145	0.070099	0.075067	0.080046	0.085031	0.090021
98	0.065136	0.070092	0.075063	0.080042	0.085029	0.090019
99	0.065128	0.070086	0.075058	0.080039	0.085026	0.090018
100	0.065120	0.070081	0.075054	0.080036	0.085024	0.090016
101	0.065113	0.070075	0.075050	0.080034	0.085022	0.090015
102	0.065106	0.070071	0.075047	0.080031	0.085021	0.090014
103	0.065099	0.070066	0.075044	0.080029	0.085019	0.090013
104	0.065093	0.070062	0.075041	0.080027	0.085018	0.090012
105	0.065087	0.070058	0.075038	0.080025	0.085016	0.090011
106	0.065082	0.070054	0.075035	0.080023	0.085015	0.090010
107	0.065077	0.070050	0.075033	0.080021	0.085014	0.090009
108	0.065072	0.070047	0.075030	0.080020	0.085013	0.090008
109	0.065068	0.070044	0.075028	0.080018	0.085012	0.090007
110	0.065064	0.070041	0.075026	0.080017	0.085011	0.090007
111	0.065060	0.070038	0.075024	0.080016	0.085010	0.090006
112	0.065056	0.070036	0.075023	0.080014	0.085009	0.090006
113	0.065053	0.070033	0.075021	0.080013	0.085008	0.090005
114	0.065050	0.070031	0.075020	0.080012	0.085008	0.090005
115	0.065047	0.070029	0.075018	0.080011	0.085007	0.090004
116	0.065044	0.070027	0.075017	0.080011	0.085007	0.090004
117	0.065041	0.070026	0.075016	0.080010	0.085006	0.090004
118	0.065039	0.070024	0.075015	0.080009	0.085006	0.090003
119	0.065036	0.070022	0.075014	0.080008	0.085005	0.090003
120	0.065034	0.070021	0.075013	0.080008	0.085005	0.090003

Table V Capital Recovery Factor (Amortization Factor) (continued)

$$\frac{i(1+i)^n}{(1+i)^n-1}$$

n	0.095 (9½%)	0.10 (10%)	0.105 (10½%)	0.11 (11%)	0.115 (11½%)	0.12 (12%)
1	1.095000	1.100000	1.105000	1.110000	1.115000	1.120000
2	0.572327	0.576190	0.580059	0.583934	0.587813	0.591698
3	0.398580	0.402115	0.405659	0.409213	0.412776	0.416349
4	0.312063	0.315471	0.318892	0.322326	0.325774	0.329234
5	0.260436	0.263797	0.267175	0.270570	0.273982	0.277410
6	0.226253	0.229607	0.232982	0.236377	0.239791	0.243226
7	0.202036	0.205405	0.208799	0.212215	0.215655	0.219118
8	0.184046	0.187444	0.190869	0.194321	0.197799	0.201303
9	0.170205	0.173641	0.177106	0.180602	0.184126	0.187679
10	0.159266	0.162745	0.166257	0.169801	0.173377	0.176984
11	0.150437	0.153963	0.157525	0.161121	0.164751	0.168415
12	0.143188	0.146763	0.150377	0.154027	0.157714	0.161437
13	0.137152	0.140779	0.144445	0.148151	0.151895	0.155677
14	0.132068	0.135746	0.139467	0.143228	0.147030	0.150871
15	0.127744	0.131474	0.135248	0.139065	0.142924	0.146824
16	0.124035	0.127817	0.131644	0.135517	0.139432	0.143390
17	0.120831	0.124664	0.128545	0.132471	0.136443	0.140457
18	0.118046	0.121930	0.125863	0.129843	0.133868	0.137937
19	0.115613	0.119547	0.123531	0.127563	0.131641	0.135763
20	0.113477	0.117460	0.121493	0.125576	0.129705	0.133879
21	0.111594	0.115624	0.119707	0.123838	0.128016	0.132240
22	0.109928	0.114005	0.118134	0.122313	0.126539	0.130811
23	0.108449	0.112572	0.116747	0.120971	0.125243	0.129560
24	0.107134	0.111300	0.115519	0.119787	0.124103	0.128463
25	0.105959	0.110168	0.114429	0.118740	0.123098	0.127500
26	0.104909	0.109159	0.113461	0.117813	0.122210	0.126652
27	0.103969	0.108258	0.112599	0.116989	0.121425	0.125904
28	0.103124	0.107451	0.111830	0.116257	0.120730	0.125244
29	0.102364	0.106728	0.111143	0.115605	0.120112	0.124660
30	0.101681	0.106079	0.110528	0.115025	0.119564	0.124144
31	0.101064	0.105496	0.109978	0.114506	0.119077	0.123686
32	0.100507	0.104972	0.109485	0.114043	0.118643	0.123280
33	0.100004	0.104499	0.109042	0.113629	0.118257	0.122920
34	0.099549	0.104074	0.108645	0.113259	0.117912	0.122601
35	0.099138	0.103690	0.108288	0.112927	0.117605	0.122317
36	0.098764	0.103343	0.107967	0.112630	0.117331	0.122064
37	0.098426	0.103030	0.107677	0.112364	0.117086	0.121840
38	0.098119	0.102747	0.107417	0.112125	0.116867	0.121640
39	0.097840	0.102491	0.107183	0.111911	0.116672	0.121462
40	0.097587	0.102259	0.106971	0.111719	0.116497	0.121304
41	0.097357	0.102050	0.106781	0.111546	0.116341	0.121163
42	0.097148	0.101860	0.106609	0.111391	0.116201	0.121037
43	0.096958	0.101688	0.106454	0.111251	0.116076	0.120925
44	0.096785	0.101532	0.106314	0.111126	0.115964	0.120825
45	0.096627	0.101391	0.106188	0.111014	0.115864	0.120736
46	0.096484	0.101263	0.106074	0.110912	0.115774	0.120657
47	0.096353	0.101147	0.105971	0.110821	0.115694	0.120586
48	0.096234	0.101041	0.105878	0.110739	0.115622	0.120523
49	0.096126	0.100946	0.105794	0.110666	0.115558	0.120467
50	0.096027	0.100859	0.105718	0.110599	0.115500	0.120417
51	0.095937	0.100780	0.105649	0.110540	0.115448	0.120372
52	0.095855	0.100709	0.105587	0.110486	0.115402	0.120332
53	0.095780	0.100644	0.105531	0.110438	0.115360	0.120296
54	0.095712	0.100585	0.105480	0.110394	0.115323	0.120264
55	0.095650	0.100532	0.105435	0.110355	0.115290	0.120236
56	0.095593	0.100483	0.105393	0.110320	0.115260	0.120211
57	0.095541	0.100439	0.105356	0.110288	0.115233	0.120188
58	0.095494	0.100399	0.105322	0.110259	0.115209	0.120168
59	0.095451	0.100363	0.105291	0.110233	0.115187	0.120150
60	0.095412	0.100330	0.105263	0.110210	0.115168	0.120134

Table V Capital Recovery Factor (Amortization Factor) (continued)

$$\frac{i(1+i)^n}{(1+i)^n - 1}$$

n	0.125 (12½%)	0.13 (13%)	0.135 (13½%)	0.14 (14%)	0.145 (14½%)	0.15 (15%)
1	1.125000	1.130000	1.135000	1.140000	1.145000	1.150000
2	0.595588	0.599484	0.603384	0.607290	0.611200	0.615116
3	0.419931	0.423522	0.427122	0.430731	0.434350	0.437977
4	0.332708	0.336194	0.339693	0.343205	0.346729	0.350265
5	0.280854	0.284315	0.287791	0.291284	0.294792	0.298316
6	0.246680	0.250153	0.253646	0.257157	0.260688	0.264237
7	0.222603	0.226111	0.229641	0.233192	0.236766	0.240360
8	0.204832	0.208387	0.211966	0.215570	0.219198	0.222850
9	0.191260	0.194869	0.198505	0.202168	0.205858	0.209574
10	0.180622	0.184290	0.187987	0.191714	0.195469	0.199252
11	0.172112	0.175841	0.179602	0.183394	0.187217	0.191069
12	0.165194	0.168986	0.172811	0.176669	0.180559	0.184481
13	0.159496	0.163350	0.167240	0.171164	0.175121	0.179110
14	0.154751	0.158667	0.162621	0.166609	0.170632	0.174688
15	0.150764	0.154742	0.158757	0.162809	0.166896	0.171017
16	0.147388	0.151426	0.155502	0.159615	0.163764	0.167948
17	0.144512	0.148608	0.152743	0.156915	0.161124	0.165367
18	0.142049	0.146201	0.150392	0.154621	0.158886	0.163186
19	0.139928	0.144134	0.148380	0.152663	0.156982	0.161336
20	0.138096	0.142354	0.146651	0.150986	0.155357	0.159761
21	0.136507	0.140814	0.145161	0.149545	0.153964	0.158417
22	0.135125	0.139479	0.143873	0.148303	0.152768	0.157266
23	0.133919	0.138319	0.142757	0.147231	0.151739	0.156278
24	0.132866	0.137308	0.141788	0.146303	0.150851	0.155430
25	0.131943	0.136426	0.140945	0.145498	0.150084	0.154699
26	0.131134	0.135655	0.140211	0.144800	0.149420	0.154070
27	0.130423	0.134979	0.139570	0.144193	0.148846	0.153526
28	0.129797	0.134387	0.139010	0.143664	0.148348	0.153057
29	0.129246	0.133867	0.138521	0.143204	0.147915	0.152651
30	0.128760	0.133411	0.138092	0.142803	0.147539	0.152300
31	0.128331	0.133009	0.137717	0.142453	0.147213	0.151996
32	0.127952	0.132656	0.137388	0.142147	0.146929	0.151733
33	0.127617	0.132345	0.137100	0.141880	0.146682	0.151505
34	0.127321	0.132071	0.136847	0.141646	0.146467	0.151307
35	0.127059	0.131829	0.136624	0.141442	0.146279	0.151135
36	0.126827	0.131616	0.136429	0.141263	0.146116	0.150986
37	0.126621	0.131428	0.136258	0.141107	0.145974	0.150857
38	0.126439	0.131262	0.136107	0.140970	0.145850	0.150744
39	0.126278	0.131116	0.135974	0.140850	0.145742	0.150647
40	0.126134	0.130986	0.135858	0.140745	0.145647	0.150562
41	0.126007	0.130872	0.135755	0.140653	0.145565	0.150489
42	0.125895	0.130771	0.135665	0.140573	0.145493	0.150425
43	0.125795	0.130682	0.135585	0.140502	0.145431	0.150369
44	0.125706	0.130603	0.135515	0.140440	0.145376	0.150321
45	0.125627	0.130534	0.135454	0.140386	0.145328	0.150279
46	0.125557	0.130472	0.135400	0.140338	0.145287	0.150242
47	0.125495	0.130417	0.135352	0.140297	0.145250	0.150211
48	0.125440	0.130369	0.135310	0.140260	0.145218	0.150183
49	0.125391	0.130327	0.135273	0.140228	0.145191	0.150159
50	0.125347	0.130289	0.135241	0.140200	0.145167	0.150139
51	0.125308	0.130256	0.135212	0.140176	0.145145	0.150120
52	0.125274	0.130226	0.135187	0.140154	0.145127	0.150105
53	0.125244	0.130200	0.135164	0.140135	0.145111	0.150091
54	0.125216	0.130177	0.135145	0.140118	0.145097	0.150079
55	0.125192	0.130157	0.135128	0.140104	0.145085	0.150069
56	0.125171	0.130139	0.135112	0.140091	0.145074	0.150060
57	0.125152	0.130123	0.135099	0.140080	0.145065	0.150052
58	0.125135	0.130109	0.135087	0.140070	0.145056	0.150045
59	0.125120	0.130096	0.135077	0.140062	0.145049	0.150039
60	0.125107	0.130085	0.135068	0.140054	0.145043	0.150034

Table V **Capital Recovery Factor (Amortization Factor) (continued)**

$$\frac{i(1+i)^n}{(1+i)^n-1}$$

n	*0.155 (15½%)*	*0.16 (16%)*	*0.165 (16½%)*	*0.17 (17%)*	*0.175 (17½%)*	*0.18 (18%)*
1	1.155000	1.160000	1.165000	1.170000	1.175000	1.180000
2	0.619037	0.622963	0.626894	0.630829	0.634770	0.638716
3	0.441613	0.445258	0.448911	0.452574	0.456245	0.459924
4	0.353814	0.357375	0.360948	0.364533	0.368130	0.371739
5	0.301855	0.305409	0.308979	0.312564	0.316163	0.319778
6	0.267804	0.271390	0.274993	0.278615	0.282254	0.285910
7	0.243976	0.247613	0.251270	0.254947	0.258645	0.262362
8	0.226526	0.230224	0.233946	0.237690	0.241456	0.245244
9	0.213316	0.217082	0.220874	0.224691	0.228531	0.232395
10	0.203063	0.206901	0.210766	0.214657	0.218573	0.222515
11	0.194951	0.198861	0.202799	0.206765	0.210757	0.214776
12	0.188433	0.192415	0.196426	0.200466	0.204533	0.208628
13	0.183132	0.187184	0.191266	0.195378	0.199518	0.203686
14	0.178777	0.182898	0.187049	0.191230	0.195440	0.199678
15	0.175171	0.179358	0.183575	0.187822	0.192098	0.196403
16	0.172165	0.176414	0.180694	0.185004	0.189343	0.193710
17	0.169643	0.173952	0.178292	0.182662	0.187060	0.191485
18	0.167520	0.171885	0.176281	0.180706	0.185159	0.189639
19	0.165723	0.170142	0.174590	0.179067	0.183572	0.188103
20	0.164199	0.168667	0.173165	0.177690	0.182243	0.186820
21	0.162901					
22	0.161795					
23	0.160848					
24	0.160038					
25	0.159343					
26	0.158746					
27	0.158233					
28	0.157791					
29	0.157411					
30	0.157083					
31	0.156800					
32	0.156556					
33	0.156345					
34	0.156164					
35	0.156006					
36	0.155871					
37	0.155753					
38	0.155652					
39	0.155564					
40	0.155488					
41	0.155422					
42	0.155366					
43	0.155316					
44	0.155274					
45	0.155237					
46	0.155205					
47	0.155178					
48	0.155154					
49	0.155133					
50	0.155115					
51	0.155100					
52	0.155086					
53	0.155075					
54	0.155065					
55	0.155056					
56	0.155049					
57	0.155042					
58	0.155036					
59	0.155031					
60	0.155027					

Table V Capital Recovery Factor (Amortization Factor) (continued)

$$\frac{i(1+i)^n}{(1+i)^n - 1}$$

n	*0.185 (18½%)*	*0.19 (19%)*	*0.195 (19½%)*	*0.20 (20%)*	*0.21 (21%)*	*0.22 (22%)*
1	1.185000	1.190000	1.195000	1.200000	1.210000	1.220000
2	0.642666	0.646621	0.650581	0.654545	0.662489	0.670450
3	0.463612	0.467308	0.471012	0.474725	0.482175	0.489658
4	0.375359	0.378991	0.382634	0.386289	0.393632	0.401020
5	0.323407	0.327050	0.330708	0.334380	0.341765	0.349206
6	0.289584	0.293274	0.296982	0.300706	0.308203	0.315764
7	0.266099	0.269855	0.273630	0.277424	0.285067	0.292782
8	0.249054	0.252885	0.256737	0.260609	0.268415	0.276299
9	0.236282	0.240192	0.244125	0.248079	0.256053	0.264111
10	0.226481	0.230471	0.234485	0.238523	0.246665	0.254895
11	0.218821	0.222891	0.226985	0.231104	0.239411	0.247807
12	0.212749	0.216896	0.221068	0.225265	0.233730	0.242285
13	0.207881	0.212102	0.216349	0.220620	0.229234	0.237939
14	0.203943	0.208235	0.212551	0.216893	0.225647	0.234491
15	0.200734	0.205092	0.209475	0.213882	0.222766	0.231738
16	0.198104	0.202523	0.206968	0.211436	0.220441	0.229530
17	0.195937	0.200414	0.204916	0.209440	0.218555	0.227751
18	0.194145	0.198676	0.203229	0.207805	0.217020	0.226313
19	0.192658	0.197238	0.201839	0.206462	0.215769	0.225148
20	0.191421	0.196045	0.200691	0.205357	0.214745	0.224202

n	*0.23 (23%)*	*0.24 (24%)*	*0.25 (25%)*	*0.30 (30%)*	*0.35 (35%)*	*0.40 (40%)*
1	1.230000	1.240000	1.250000	1.300000	1.350000	1.400000
2	0.678430	0.686429	0.694444	0.734783	0.775532	0.816667
3	0.497173	0.504718	0.512295	0.550627	0.589664	0.629358
4	0.408451	0.415926	0.423442	0.461629	0.500764	0.540766
5	0.356700	0.364248	0.371847	0.410582	0.450458	0.491361
6	0.323389	0.331074	0.338819	0.378394	0.419260	0.461260
7	0.300568	0.308422	0.316342	0.356874	0.398800	0.441923
8	0.284259	0.292293	0.300399	0.341915	0.384887	0.429074
9	0.272249	0.280465	0.288756	0.331235	0.375191	0.420345
10	0.263208	0.271602	0.280073	0.323463	0.368318	0.414324
11	0.256289	0.264852	0.273493	0.317729	0.363387	0.410128
12	0.250926	0.259648	0.268448	0.313454	0.359819	0.407182
13	0.246728	0.255598	0.264543	0.310243	0.357221	0.405104
14	0.243418	0.252423	0.261501	0.307818	0.355320	0.403632
15	0.240791	0.249919	0.259117	0.305978	0.353926	0.402588
16	0.238697	0.247936	0.257241	0.304577	0.352899	0.401845
17	0.237021	0.246359	0.255759	0.303509	0.352143	0.401316
18	0.235676	0.245102	0.254586	0.302692	0.351585	0.400939
19	0.234593	0.244098	0.253656	0.302066	0.351173	0.400670
20	0.233720	0.243294	0.252916	0.301587	0.350868	0.400479

Table VI Sinking Fund Factor $\frac{1}{(1+i)^n - 1}$

n	0.0025 (¼%)	0.0050 (½%)	0.0075 (¾%)	0.01 (1%)	0.0125 (1¼%)	0.0150 (1½%)
1	1.000000	1.000000	1.000000	1.000000	1.000000	1.000000
2	0.499376	0.498753	0.498132	0.497512	0.496894	0.496278
3	0.332501	0.331672	0.330846	0.330022	0.329201	0.328383
4	0.249064	0.248133	0.247205	0.246281	0.245361	0.244445
5	0.199002	0.198010	0.197022	0.196040	0.195062	0.194089
6	0.165628	0.164595	0.163569	0.162548	0.161534	0.160525
7	0.141789	0.140729	0.139675	0.138628	0.137589	0.136556
8	0.123910	0.122829	0.121756	0.120690	0.119633	0.118584
9	0.110005	0.108907	0.107819	0.106740	0.105671	0.104610
10	0.098880	0.097771	0.096671	0.095582	0.094503	0.093434
11	0.089778	0.088659	0.087551	0.086454	0.085368	0.084294
12	0.082194	0.081066	0.079951	0.078849	0.077758	0.076680
13	0.075776	0.074642	0.073522	0.072415	0.071321	0.070240
14	0.070275	0.069136	0.068011	0.066901	0.065805	0.064723
15	0.065508	0.064364	0.063236	0.062124	0.061026	0.059944
16	0.061336	0.060189	0.059059	0.057945	0.056847	0.055765
17	0.057656	0.056506	0.055373	0.054258	0.053160	0.052080
18	0.054384	0.053232	0.052098	0.050982	0.049885	0.048806
19	0.051457	0.050303	0.049167	0.048052	0.046955	0.045878
20	0.048823	0.047666	0.046531	0.045415	0.044320	0.043246
21	0.046439	0.045282	0.044145	0.043031	0.041937	0.040865
22	0.044273	0.043114	0.041977	0.040864	0.039772	0.038703
23	0.042295	0.041135	0.039998	0.038886	0.037797	0.036731
24	0.040481	0.039321	0.038185	0.037073	0.035987	0.034924
25	0.038813	0.037652	0.036516	0.035407	0.034322	0.033263
26	0.037273	0.036112	0.034977	0.033869	0.032787	0.031732
27	0.035847	0.034686	0.033552	0.032446	0.031367	0.030315
28	0.034523	0.033362	0.032229	0.031124	0.030049	0.029001
29	0.033291	0.032129	0.030997	0.029895	0.028822	0.027779
30	0.032141	0.030979	0.029848	0.028748	0.027679	0.026639
31	0.031064	0.029903	0.028774	0.027676	0.026609	0.025574
32	0.030056	0.028895	0.027766	0.026671	0.025608	0.024577
33	0.029108	0.027947	0.026820	0.025727	0.024668	0.023641
34	0.028216	0.027056	0.025931	0.024840	0.023784	0.022762
35	0.027375	0.026215	0.025092	0.024004	0.022951	0.021934
36	0.026581	0.025422	0.024300	0.023214	0.022165	0.021152
37	0.025830	0.024671	0.023551	0.022468	0.021423	0.020414
38	0.025118	0.023960	0.022842	0.021761	0.020720	0.019716
39	0.024443	0.023286	0.022169	0.021092	0.020054	0.019055
40	0.023802	0.022646	0.021530	0.020456	0.019421	0.018427
41	0.023192	0.022036	0.020923	0.019851	0.018821	0.017831
42	0.022611	0.021456	0.020345	0.019276	0.018249	0.017264
43	0.022057	0.020903	0.019793	0.018727	0.017705	0.016725
44	0.021529	0.020375	0.019268	0.018204	0.017186	0.016210
45	0.021023	0.019871	0.018765	0.017705	0.016690	0.015720
46	0.020540	0.019389	0.018285	0.017228	0.016217	0.015251
47	0.020078	0.018927	0.017825	0.016771	0.015764	0.014803
48	0.019634	0.018485	0.017385	0.016334	0.015331	0.014375
49	0.019209	0.018061	0.016963	0.015915	0.014916	0.013965
50	0.018801	0.017654	0.016558	0.015513	0.014518	0.013572
51	0.018409	0.017263	0.016169	0.015127	0.014136	0.013195
52	0.018032	0.016887	0.015795	0.014756	0.013769	0.012833
53	0.017669	0.016525	0.015435	0.014400	0.013417	0.012485
54	0.017320	0.016177	0.015089	0.014057	0.013078	0.012151
55	0.016983	0.015841	0.014756	0.013726	0.012751	0.011830
56	0.016659	0.015518	0.014435	0.013408	0.012437	0.011521
57	0.016345	0.015206	0.014125	0.013102	0.012135	0.011223
58	0.016043	0.014905	0.013826	0.012806	0.011843	0.010937
59	0.015751	0.014614	0.013537	0.012520	0.011562	0.010660
60	0.015469	0.014333	0.013258	0.012244	0.011290	0.010393

Table VI Sinking Fund Factor (continued) $\frac{1}{(1+i)^n - 1}$

n	0.0025 (1/4%)	0.0050 (1/2%)	0.0075 (3/4%)	0.01 (1%)	0.0125 (1 1/4%)	0.0150 (1 1/2%)
61	0.015196	0.014061	0.012989	0.011978	0.011028	0.010136
62	0.014931	0.013798	0.012728	0.011720	0.010774	0.009888
63	0.014676	0.013543	0.012476	0.011471	0.010529	0.009647
64	0.014428	0.013297	0.012231	0.011230	0.010292	0.009415
65	0.014188	0.013058	0.011995	0.010997	0.010063	0.009191
66	0.013955	0.012826	0.011765	0.010771	0.009841	0.008974
67	0.013729	0.012602	0.011543	0.010551	0.009626	0.008764
68	0.013510	0.012384	0.011327	0.010339	0.009417	0.008560
69	0.013297	0.012172	0.011118	0.010133	0.009215	0.008363
70	0.013090	0.011967	0.010915	0.009933	0.009019	0.008172
71	0.012889	0.011767	0.010717	0.009739	0.008829	0.007987
72	0.012694	0.011573	0.010526	0.009550	0.008645	0.007808
73	0.012504	0.011384	0.010339	0.009367	0.008466	0.007634
74	0.012319	0.011201	0.010158	0.009189	0.008292	0.007465
75	0.012139	0.011022	0.009982	0.009016	0.008123	0.007301
76	0.011964	0.010848	0.009810	0.008848	0.007959	0.007141
77	0.011793	0.010679	0.009643	0.008684	0.007800	0.006987
78	0.011627	0.010514	0.009481	0.008525	0.007644	0.006836
79	0.011465	0.010354	0.009322	0.008370	0.007493	0.006690
80	0.011307	0.010197	0.009168	0.008219	0.007347	0.006548
81	0.011153	0.010044	0.009018	0.008072	0.007204	0.006410
82	0.011003	0.009896	0.008871	0.007929	0.007064	0.006276
83	0.010856	0.009750	0.008728	0.007789	0.006929	0.006145
84	0.010713	0.009609	0.008589	0.007653	0.006797	0.006018
85	0.010574	0.009470	0.008453	0.007520	0.006668	0.005894
86	0.010437	0.009335	0.008320	0.007391	0.006543	0.005773
87	0.010304	0.009203	0.008191	0.007264	0.006420	0.005656
88	0.010174	0.009074	0.008064	0.007141	0.006301	0.005541
89	0.010046	0.008948	0.007941	0.007021	0.006185	0.005430
90	0.009922	0.008825	0.007820	0.006903	0.006071	0.005321
91	0.009800	0.008705	0.007702	0.006788	0.005961	0.005215
92	0.009681	0.008587	0.007587	0.006676	0.005853	0.005112
93	0.009564	0.008472	0.007474	0.006567	0.005747	0.005011
94	0.009450	0.008360	0.007364	0.006460	0.005644	0.004913
95	0.009339	0.008249	0.007256	0.006355	0.005544	0.004817
96	0.009230	0.008141	0.007150	0.006253	0.005445	0.004723
97	0.009123	0.008036	0.007047	0.006153	0.005349	0.004632
98	0.009018	0.007932	0.006946	0.006055	0.005256	0.004543
99	0.008915	0.007831	0.006847	0.005959	0.005164	0.004456
100	0.008814	0.007732	0.006750	0.005866	0.005074	0.004371
101	0.008716	0.007635	0.006655	0.005774	0.004987	0.004288
102	0.008619	0.007539	0.006562	0.005684	0.004901	0.004206
103	0.008524	0.007446	0.006471	0.005597	0.004817	0.004127
104	0.008431	0.007355	0.006382	0.005511	0.004735	0.004050
105	0.008340	0.007265	0.006295	0.005427	0.004655	0.003974
106	0.008251	0.007177	0.006209	0.005344	0.004576	0.003900
107	0.008163	0.007090	0.006125	0.005263	0.004500	0.003828
108	0.008077	0.007006	0.006043	0.005184	0.004424	0.003757
109	0.007992	0.006923	0.005962	0.005107	0.004351	0.003688
110	0.007909	0.006841	0.005883	0.005031	0.004279	0.003620
111	0.007828	0.006761	0.005805	0.004956	0.004208	0.003554
112	0.007748	0.006682	0.005729	0.004883	0.004139	0.003489
113	0.007669	0.006605	0.005654	0.004812	0.004071	0.003426
114	0.007592	0.006529	0.005581	0.004741	0.004005	0.003364
115	0.007516	0.006455	0.005509	0.004672	0.003940	0.003303
116	0.007442	0.006382	0.005438	0.004605	0.003876	0.003244
117	0.007368	0.006310	0.005369	0.004539	0.003814	0.003186
118	0.007296	0.006240	0.005300	0.004474	0.003752	0.003129
119	0.007226	0.006170	0.005233	0.004410	0.003692	0.003073
120	0.007156	0.006102	0.005168	0.004347	0.003633	0.003019

Table VI Sinking Fund Factor (continued) $\frac{1}{(1+i)^n - 1}$

n	0.0175 (1¾%)	0.02 (2%)	0.0225 (2¼%)	0.025 (2½%)	0.0275 (2¾%)	0.03 (3%)
1	1.000000	1.000000	1.000000	1.000000	1.000000	1.000000
2	0.495663	0.495050	0.494438	0.493827	0.493218	0.492611
3	0.327567	0.326755	0.325945	0.325137	0.324332	0.323530
4	0.243532	0.242624	0.241719	0.240818	0.239921	0.239027
5	0.193121	0.192158	0.191200	0.190247	0.189298	0.188355
6	0.159523	0.158526	0.157535	0.156550	0.155571	0.154598
7	0.135531	0.134512	0.133500	0.132495	0.131497	0.130506
8	0.117543	0.116510	0.115485	0.114467	0.113458	0.112456
9	0.103558	0.102515	0.101482	0.100457	0.099441	0.098434
10	0.092375	0.091327	0.090288	0.089259	0.088240	0.087231
11	0.083230	0.082178	0.081136	0.080106	0.079086	0.078077
12	0.075614	0.074560	0.073517	0.072487	0.071469	0.070462
13	0.069173	0.068118	0.067077	0.066048	0.065033	0.064030
14	0.063656	0.062602	0.061562	0.060537	0.059525	0.058526
15	0.058877	0.057825	0.056789	0.055766	0.054759	0.053767
16	0.054700	0.053650	0.052617	0.051599	0.050597	0.049611
17	0.051016	0.049970	0.048940	0.047928	0.046932	0.045953
18	0.047745	0.046702	0.045677	0.044670	0.043681	0.042709
19	0.044821	0.043782	0.042762	0.041761	0.040778	0.039814
20	0.042191	0.041157	0.040142	0.039147	0.038172	0.037216
21	0.039815	0.038785	0.037776	0.036787	0.035819	0.034872
22	0.037656	0.036631	0.035628	0.034647	0.033686	0.032747
23	0.035688	0.034668	0.033671	0.032696	0.031744	0.030814
24	0.033886	0.032871	0.031880	0.030913	0.029969	0.029047
25	0.032230	0.031220	0.030236	0.029276	0.028340	0.027428
26	0.030703	0.029699	0.028721	0.027769	0.026841	0.025938
27	0.029291	0.028293	0.027322	0.026377	0.025458	0.024564
28	0.027982	0.026990	0.026025	0.025088	0.024177	0.023293
29	0.026764	0.025778	0.024821	0.023891	0.022989	0.022115
30	0.025630	0.024650	0.023699	0.022778	0.021884	0.021019
31	0.024570	0.023596	0.022653	0.021739	0.020855	0.019999
32	0.023578	0.022611	0.021674	0.020768	0.019893	0.019047
33	0.022648	0.021687	0.020757	0.019859	0.018993	0.018156
34	0.021774	0.020819	0.019897	0.019007	0.018149	0.017322
35	0.020951	0.020002	0.019087	0.018206	0.017356	0.016539
36	0.020175	0.019233	0.018325	0.017452	0.016611	0.015804
37	0.019443	0.018507	0.017606	0.016741	0.015910	0.015112
38	0.018750	0.017821	0.016928	0.016070	0.015248	0.014459
39	0.018094	0.017171	0.016285	0.015436	0.014623	0.013844
40	0.017472	0.016556	0.015677	0.014836	0.014032	0.013262
41	0.016882	0.015972	0.015101	0.014268	0.013472	0.012712
42	0.016321	0.015417	0.014554	0.013729	0.012942	0.012192
43	0.015787	0.014890	0.014034	0.013217	0.012439	0.011698
44	0.015278	0.014388	0.013539	0.012730	0.011961	0.011230
45	0.014793	0.013910	0.013068	0.012268	0.011507	0.010785
46	0.014330	0.013453	0.012619	0.011827	0.011075	0.010363
47	0.013888	0.013018	0.012191	0.011407	0.010664	0.009961
48	0.013466	0.012602	0.011782	0.011006	0.010272	0.009578
49	0.013061	0.012204	0.011392	0.010623	0.009898	0.009213
50	0.012674	0.011823	0.011018	0.010258	0.009541	0.008865
51	0.012303	0.011459	0.010661	0.009909	0.009200	0.008534
52	0.011947	0.011109	0.010319	0.009574	0.008874	0.008217
53	0.011605	0.010774	0.009991	0.009254	0.008563	0.007915
54	0.011277	0.010452	0.009677	0.008948	0.008265	0.007626
55	0.010961	0.010143	0.009375	0.008654	0.007980	0.007349
56	0.010658	0.009847	0.009085	0.008372	0.007706	0.007084
57	0.010366	0.009561	0.008807	0.008102	0.007444	0.006831
58	0.010085	0.009287	0.008540	0.007842	0.007193	0.006588
59	0.009814	0.009022	0.008283	0.007593	0.006952	0.006356
60	0.009553	0.008768	0.008035	0.007353	0.006720	0.006133

Table VI Sinking Fund Factor (continued) $\frac{1}{(1+i)^n - 1}$

n	0.0175 (1¾%)	0.02 (2%)	0.0225 (2¼%)	0.025 (2½%)	0.0275 (2¾%)	0.03 (3%)
61	0.009302	0.008523	0.007797	0.007123	0.006498	0.005919
62	0.009059	0.008286	0.007568	0.006901	0.006284	0.005714
63	0.008825	0.008058	0.007347	0.006688	0.006079	0.005517
64	0.008598	0.007839	0.007134	0.006482	0.005881	0.005328
65	0.008380	0.007626	0.006929	0.006285	0.005691	0.005146
66	0.008168	0.007421	0.006731	0.006094	0.005508	0.004971
67	0.007964	0.007223	0.006540	0.005910	0.005332	0.004803
68	0.007766	0.007032	0.006355	0.005733	0.005163	0.004642
69	0.007575	0.006847	0.006177	0.005562	0.005000	0.004486
70	0.007389	0.006668	0.006005	0.005397	0.004842	0.004337
71	0.007210	0.006494	0.005838	0.005238	0.004690	0.004193
72	0.007036	0.006327	0.005677	0.005084	0.004544	0.004054
73	0.006867	0.006165	0.005522	0.004936	0.004403	0.003921
74	0.006704	0.006007	0.005371	0.004792	0.004267	0.003792
75	0.006546	0.005855	0.005226	0.004654	0.004136	0.003668
76	0.006392	0.005708	0.005085	0.004520	0.004009	0.003548
77	0.006243	0.005564	0.004948	0.004390	0.003886	0.003433
78	0.006098	0.005426	0.004816	0.004265	0.003768	0.003322
79	0.005957	0.005291	0.004688	0.004143	0.003654	0.003215
80	0.005821	0.005161	0.004564	0.004026	0.003543	0.003112
81	0.005688	0.005034	0.004444	0.003912	0.003437	0.003012
82	0.005559	0.004911	0.004327	0.003803	0.003334	0.002916
83	0.005434	0.004792	0.004214	0.003696	0.003234	0.002823
84	0.005312	0.004676	0.004104	0.003593	0.003137	0.002733
85	0.005194	0.004563	0.003998	0.003493	0.003044	0.002647
86	0.005078	0.004454	0.003895	0.003396	0.002954	0.002563
87	0.004966	0.004347	0.003795	0.003303	0.002867	0.002482
88	0.004857	0.004244	0.003697	0.003212	0.002782	0.002404
89	0.004751	0.004144	0.003603	0.003124	0.002700	0.002328
90	0.004648	0.004046	0.003511	0.003038	0.002621	0.002256
91	0.004547	0.003951	0.003422	0.002955	0.002545	0.002185
92	0.004449	0.003859	0.003336	0.002875	0.002470	0.002117
93	0.004353	0.003769	0.003252	0.002797	0.002398	0.002051
94	0.004260	0.003681	0.003170	0.002721	0.002329	0.001987
95	0.004169	0.003596	0.003091	0.002648	0.002261	0.001926
96	0.004081	0.003513	0.003014	0.002577	0.002196	0.001866
97	0.003995	0.003432	0.002939	0.002507	0.002133	0.001809
98	0.003911	0.003354	0.002866	0.002440	0.002071	0.001753
99	0.003829	0.003277	0.002795	0.002375	0.002012	0.001699
100	0.003749	0.003203	0.002726	0.002312	0.001954	0.001647
101	0.003671	0.003130	0.002659	0.002250	0.001898	0.001596
102	0.003595	0.003059	0.002594	0.002191	0.001844	0.001547
103	0.003520	0.002990	0.002530	0.002133	0.001791	0.001500
104	0.003448	0.002923	0.002468	0.002076	0.001741	0.001454
105	0.003377	0.002858	0.002408	0.002022	0.001691	0.001410
106	0.003308	0.002794	0.002350	0.001968	0.001643	0.001367
107	0.003241	0.002732	0.002293	0.001917	0.001597	0.001325
108	0.003175	0.002671	0.002237	0.001867	0.001551	0.001285
109	0.003111	0.002612	0.002183	0.001818	0.001508	0.001246
110	0.003048	0.002554	0.002131	0.001770	0.001465	0.001208
111	0.002986	0.002498	0.002079	0.001724	0.001424	0.001172
112	0.002926	0.002443	0.002030	0.001679	0.001384	0.001136
113	0.002868	0.002389	0.001981	0.001636	0.001345	0.001102
114	0.002811	0.002337	0.001934	0.001593	0.001307	0.001069
115	0.002755	0.002286	0.001887	0.001552	0.001271	0.001037
116	0.002700	0.002236	0.001843	0.001512	0.001235	0.001005
117	0.002647	0.002187	0.001799	0.001473	0.001201	0.000975
118	0.002594	0.002140	0.001756	0.001435	0.001167	0.000946
119	0.002543	0.002093	0.001715	0.001398	0.001135	0.000917
120	0.002493	0.002048	0.001674	0.001362	0.001103	0.000890

Table VI Sinking Fund Factor (continued)

$$\frac{1}{(1+i)^n - 1}$$

n	0.035 (3½%)	0.04 (4%)	0.045 (4½%)	0.05 (5%)	0.055 (5½)	0.06 (6%)
1	1.000000	1.000000	1.000000	1.000000	1.000000	1.000000
2	0.491400	0.490196	0.488998	0.487805	0.486618	0.485437
3	0.321934	0.320349	0.318773	0.317209	0.315654	0.314110
4	0.237251	0.235490	0.233744	0.232012	0.230294	0.228591
5	0.186481	0.184627	0.182792	0.180975	0.179176	0.177396
6	0.152668	0.150762	0.148878	0.147017	0.145179	0.143363
7	0.128544	0.126610	0.124701	0.122820	0.120964	0.119135
8	0.110477	0.108528	0.106610	0.104722	0.102864	0.101036
9	0.096446	0.094493	0.092574	0.090690	0.088839	0.087022
10	0.085241	0.083291	0.081379	0.079505	0.077668	0.075868
11	0.076092	0.074149	0.072248	0.070389	0.068571	0.066793
12	0.068484	0.066552	0.064666	0.062825	0.061029	0.059277
13	0.062062	0.060144	0.058275	0.056456	0.054684	0.052960
14	0.056571	0.054669	0.052820	0.051024	0.049279	0.047585
15	0.051825	0.049941	0.048114	0.046342	0.044626	0.042963
16	0.047685	0.045820	0.044015	0.042270	0.040583	0.038952
17	0.044043	0.042199	0.040418	0.038699	0.037042	0.035445
18	0.040817	0.038993	0.037237	0.035546	0.033920	0.032357
19	0.037940	0.036139	0.034407	0.032745	0.031150	0.029621
20	0.035361	0.033582	0.031876	0.030243	0.028679	0.027185
21	0.033037	0.031280	0.029601	0.027996	0.026465	0.025005
22	0.030932	0.029199	0.027546	0.025971	0.024471	0.023046
23	0.029019	0.027309	0.025682	0.024137	0.022670	0.021278
24	0.027273	0.025587	0.023987	0.022471	0.021036	0.019679
25	0.025674	0.024012	0.022439	0.020952	0.019549	0.018227
26	0.024205	0.022567	0.021021	0.019564	0.018193	0.016904
27	0.022852	0.021239	0.019719	0.018292	0.016952	0.015697
28	0.021603	0.020013	0.018521	0.017123	0.015814	0.014593
29	0.020445	0.018880	0.017415	0.016046	0.014769	0.013580
30	0.019371	0.017830	0.016392	0.015051	0.013805	0.012649
31	0.018372	0.016855	0.015443	0.014132	0.012917	0.011792
32	0.017442	0.015949	0.014563	0.013280	0.012095	0.011002
33	0.016572	0.015104	0.013745	0.012490	0.011335	0.010273
34	0.015760	0.014315	0.012982	0.011755	0.010630	0.009598
35	0.014998	0.013577	0.012270	0.011072	0.009975	0.008974
36	0.014284	0.012887	0.011606	0.010434	0.009366	0.008395
37	0.013613	0.012240	0.010984	0.009840	0.008800	0.007857
38	0.012982	0.011632	0.010402	0.009284	0.008272	0.007358
39	0.012388	0.011061	0.009856	0.008765	0.007780	0.006894
40	0.011827	0.010523	0.009343	0.008278	0.007320	0.006462
41	0.011298	0.010017	0.008862	0.007822	0.006891	0.006059
42	0.010798	0.009540	0.008409	0.007395	0.006489	0.005683
43	0.010325	0.009090	0.007982	0.006993	0.006113	0.005333
44	0.009878	0.008665	0.007581	0.006616	0.005761	0.005006
45	0.009453	0.008262	0.007202	0.006262	0.005431	0.004700
46	0.009051	0.007882	0.006845	0.005928	0.005122	0.004415
47	0.008669	0.007522	0.006507	0.005614	0.004831	0.004148
48	0.008306	0.007181	0.006189	0.005318	0.004559	0.003898
49	0.007962	0.006857	0.005887	0.005040	0.004302	0.003664
50	0.007634	0.006550	0.005602	0.004777	0.004061	0.003444
51	0.007322	0.006259	0.005332	0.004529	0.003835	0.003239
52	0.007024	0.005982	0.005077	0.004294	0.003622	0.003046
53	0.006741	0.005719	0.004835	0.004073	0.003421	0.002866
54	0.006471	0.005469	0.004605	0.003864	0.003232	0.002696
55	0.006213	0.005231	0.004388	0.003667	0.003055	0.002537
56	0.005967	0.005005	0.004181	0.003480	0.002887	0.002388
57	0.005732	0.004789	0.003985	0.003303	0.002729	0.002247
58	0.005508	0.004584	0.003799	0.003136	0.002580	0.002116
59	0.005294	0.004388	0.003622	0.002978	0.002440	0.001992
60	0.005089	0.004202	0.003454	0.002828	0.002307	0.001876

Table VI Sinking Fund Factor (continued)

$$\frac{1}{(1+i)^n - 1}$$

n	0.035 (3½%)	0.04 (4%)	0.045 (4½%)	0.05 (5%)	0.055 (5½)	0.06 (6%)
61	0.004892	0.004024	0.003295	0.002686	0.002182	0.001766
62	0.004705	0.003854	0.003143	0.002552	0.002064	0.001664
63	0.004525	0.003692	0.002998	0.002424	0.001953	0.001567
64	0.004353	0.003538	0.002861	0.002304	0.001847	0.001476
65	0.004188	0.003390	0.002730	0.002189	0.001748	0.001391
66	0.004030	0.003249	0.002606	0.002081	0.001654	0.001310
67	0.003879	0.003115	0.002488	0.001978	0.001565	0.001235
68	0.003734	0.002986	0.002375	0.001880	0.001482	0.001163
69	0.003595	0.002863	0.002267	0.001787	0.001402	0.001096
70	0.003461	0.002745	0.002165	0.001699	0.001328	0.001033
71	0.003333	0.002633	0.002068	0.001616	0.001257	0.000974
72	0.003210	0.002525	0.001975	0.001536	0.001190	0.000918
73	0.003092	0.002422	0.001886	0.001461	0.001127	0.000865
74	0.002978	0.002323	0.001802	0.001390	0.001067	0.000815
75	0.002869	0.002229	0.001721	0.001322	0.001010	0.000769
76	0.002765	0.002139	0.001644	0.001257	0.000956	0.000725
77	0.002664	0.002052	0.001571	0.001196	0.000906	0.000683
78	0.002567	0.001969	0.001501	0.001138	0.000858	0.000644
79	0.002474	0.001890	0.001434	0.001082	0.000812	0.000607
80	0.002385	0.001814	0.001371	0.001030	0.000769	0.000573
81	0.002299	0.001741	0.001310	0.000980	0.000729	0.000540
82	0.002216	0.001671	0.001252	0.000932	0.000690	0.000509
83	0.002137	0.001605	0.001197	0.000887	0.000654	0.000480
84	0.002060	0.001541	0.001144	0.000844	0.000619	0.000453
85	0.001987	0.001479	0.001093	0.000803	0.000587	0.000427
86	0.001916	0.001420	0.001045	0.000764	0.000556	0.000402
87	0.001848	0.001364	0.000999	0.000727	0.000527	0.000380
88	0.001782	0.001310	0.000955	0.000692	0.000499	0.000358
89	0.001719	0.001258	0.000913	0.000659	0.000473	0.000338
90	0.001658	0.001208	0.000873	0.000627	0.000448	0.000318
91	0.001599	0.001160	0.000835	0.000597	0.000424	0.000300
92	0.001543	0.001114	0.000798	0.000568	0.000402	0.000283
93	0.001488	0.001070	0.000763	0.000541	0.000381	0.000267
94	0.001436	0.001028	0.000730	0.000515	0.000361	0.000252
95	0.001385	0.000987	0.000698	0.000490	0.000342	0.000238
96	0.001337	0.000949	0.000667	0.000466	0.000324	0.000224
97	0.001290	0.000911	0.000638	0.000444	0.000307	0.000211
98	0.001245	0.000875	0.000610	0.000423	0.000291	0.000199
99	0.001201	0.000841	0.000584	0.000402	0.000276	0.000188
100	0.001159	0.000808	0.000558	0.000383	0.000261	0.000177
101	0.001119	0.000776	0.000534	0.000365	0.000248	0.000167
102	0.001080	0.000746	0.000511	0.000347	0.000235	0.000158
103	0.001042	0.000717	0.000489	0.000331	0.000222	0.000149
104	0.001006	0.000689	0.000467	0.000315	0.000211	0.000140
105	0.000971	0.000662	0.000447	0.000300	0.000200	0.000132
106	0.000937	0.000636	0.000428	0.000285	0.000189	0.000125
107	0.000905	0.000611	0.000409	0.000272	0.000179	0.000118
108	0.000873	0.000587	0.000391	0.000259	0.000170	0.000111
109	0.000843	0.000564	0.000374	0.000246	0.000161	0.000105
110	0.000814	0.000542	0.000358	0.000235	0.000153	0.000099
111	0.000786	0.000521	0.000342	0.000223	0.000145	0.000093
112	0.000759	0.000501	0.000328	0.000213	0.000137	0.000088
113	0.000732	0.000481	0.000313	0.000202	0.000130	0.000083
114	0.000707	0.000463	0.000300	0.000193	0.000123	0.000078
115	0.000683	0.000445	0.000287	0.000184	0.000117	0.000074
116	0.000659	0.000427	0.000274	0.000175	0.000111	0.000070
117	0.000637	0.000411	0.000263	0.000166	0.000105	0.000066
118	0.000615	0.000395	0.000251	0.000158	0.000099	0.000062
119	0.000594	0.000379	0.000240	0.000151	0.000094	0.000059
120	0.000573	0.000365	0.000230	0.000144	0.000089	0.000055

Table VI Sinking Fund Factor (continued)

$$\frac{1}{(1+i)^n - 1}$$

n	0.065 (6½%)	0.07 (7%)	0.075 (7½%)	0.08 (8%)	0.085 (8½%)	0.09 (9%)
1	1.000000	1.000000	1.000000	1.000000	1.000000	1.000000
2	0.484262	0.483092	0.481928	0.480769	0.479616	0.478469
3	0.312576	0.311052	0.309538	0.308034	0.306539	0.305055
4	0.226903	0.225228	0.223568	0.221921	0.220288	0.218669
5	0.175635	0.173891	0.172165	0.170456	0.168766	0.167092
6	0.141568	0.139796	0.138045	0.136315	0.134607	0.132920
7	0.117331	0.115553	0.113800	0.112072	0.110369	0.108691
8	0.099237	0.097468	0.095727	0.094015	0.092331	0.090674
9	0.085238	0.083486	0.081767	0.080080	0.078424	0.076799
10	0.074105	0.072378	0.070686	0.069029	0.067408	0.065820
11	0.065055	0.063357	0.061697	0.060076	0.058493	0.056947
12	0.057568	0.055902	0.054278	0.052695	0.051153	0.049651
13	0.051283	0.049651	0.048064	0.046522	0.045023	0.043567
14	0.045940	0.044345	0.042797	0.041297	0.039842	0.038433
15	0.041353	0.039795	0.038287	0.036830	0.035420	0.034059
16	0.037378	0.035858	0.034391	0.032977	0.031614	0.030300
17	0.033906	0.032425	0.031000	0.029629	0.028312	0.027046
18	0.030855	0.029413	0.028029	0.026702	0.025430	0.024212
19	0.028156	0.026753	0.025411	0.024128	0.022901	0.021730
20	0.025756	0.024393	0.023092	0.021852	0.020671	0.019546
21	0.023613	0.022289	0.021029	0.019832	0.018695	0.017617
22	0.021691	0.020406	0.019187	0.018032	0.016939	0.015905
23	0.019961	0.018714	0.017535	0.016422	0.015372	0.014382
24	0.018398	0.017189	0.016050	0.014978	0.013970	0.013023
25	0.016981	0.015811	0.014711	0.013679	0.012712	0.011806
26	0.015695	0.014561	0.013500	0.012507	0.011580	0.010715
27	0.014523	0.013426	0.012402	0.011448	0.010560	0.009735
28	0.013453	0.012392	0.011405	0.010489	0.009639	0.008852
29	0.012474	0.011449	0.010498	0.009619	0.008806	0.008056
30	0.011577	0.010586	0.009671	0.008827	0.008051	0.007336
31	0.010754	0.009797	0.008916	0.008107	0.007365	0.006686
32	0.009997	0.009073	0.008226	0.007451	0.006742	0.006096
33	0.009299	0.008408	0.007594	0.006852	0.006176	0.005562
34	0.008656	0.007797	0.007015	0.006304	0.005660	0.005077
35	0.008062	0.007234	0.006483	0.005803	0.005189	0.004636
36	0.007513	0.006715	0.005994	0.005345	0.004760	0.004235
37	0.007005	0.006237	0.005545	0.004924	0.004368	0.003870
38	0.006535	0.005795	0.005132	0.004539	0.004010	0.003538
39	0.006099	0.005387	0.004751	0.004185	0.003682	0.003236
40	0.005694	0.005009	0.004400	0.003860	0.003382	0.002960
41	0.005318	0.004660	0.004077	0.003561	0.003107	0.002708
42	0.004968	0.004336	0.003778	0.003287	0.002856	0.002478
43	0.004644	0.004036	0.003502	0.003034	0.002625	0.002268
44	0.004341	0.003758	0.003247	0.002802	0.002414	0.002077
45	0.004060	0.003500	0.003011	0.002587	0.002220	0.001902
46	0.003797	0.003260	0.002794	0.002390	0.002042	0.001742
47	0.003553	0.003037	0.002592	0.002208	0.001878	0.001595
48	0.003325	0.002831	0.002405	0.002040	0.001728	0.001461
49	0.003112	0.002639	0.002232	0.001886	0.001590	0.001339
50	0.002914	0.002460	0.002072	0.001743	0.001463	0.001227
51	0.002729	0.002294	0.001924	0.001611	0.001347	0.001124
52	0.002556	0.002139	0.001787	0.001490	0.001240	0.001030
53	0.002394	0.001995	0.001659	0.001377	0.001141	0.000944
54	0.002243	0.001861	0.001541	0.001274	0.001051	0.000866
55	0.002101	0.001736	0.001432	0.001178	0.000968	0.000794
56	0.001969	0.001620	0.001330	0.001090	0.000891	0.000728
57	0.001846	0.001512	0.001236	0.001008	0.000821	0.000667
58	0.001730	0.001411	0.001148	0.000932	0.000756	0.000612
59	0.001622	0.001317	0.001067	0.000862	0.000696	0.000561
60	0.001520	0.001229	0.000991	0.000798	0.000641	0.000514

Table VI Sinking Fund Factor (continued) $\frac{1}{(1+i)^n - 1}$

n	0.065 (6½%)	0.07 (7%)	0.075 (7½%)	0.08 (8%)	0.085 (8½%)	0.09 (9%)
61	0.001426	0.001147	0.000921	0.000738	0.000590	0.000472
62	0.001337	0.001071	0.000856	0.000683	0.000544	0.000432
63	0.001254	0.001000	0.000796	0.000632	0.000501	0.000397
64	0.001176	0.000934	0.000740	0.000585	0.000462	0.000364
65	0.001103	0.000872	0.000688	0.000541	0.000425	0.000334
66	0.001034	0.000814	0.000639	0.000501	0.000392	0.000306
67	0.000970	0.000760	0.000594	0.000464	0.000361	0.000281
68	0.000910	0.000710	0.000553	0.000429	0.000333	0.000257
69	0.000854	0.000663	0.000514	0.000397	0.000306	0.000236
70	0.000801	0.000620	0.000478	0.000368	0.000282	0.000216
71	0.000752	0.000579	0.000444	0.000340	0.000260	0.000199
72	0.000705	0.000541	0.000413	0.000315	0.000240	0.000182
73	0.000662	0.000505	0.000384	0.000292	0.000221	0.000167
74	0.000621	0.000472	0.000357	0.000270	0.000204	0.000153
75	0.000583	0.000441	0.000332	0.000250	0.000188	0.000141
76	0.000547	0.000412	0.000309	0.000231	0.000173	0.000129
77	0.000513	0.000385	0.000287	0.000214	0.000159	0.000118
78	0.000482	0.000359	0.000267	0.000198	0.000147	0.000109
79	0.000452	0.000336	0.000248	0.000183	0.000135	0.000100
80	0.000424	0.000314	0.000231	0.000170	0.000125	0.000091
81	0.000398	0.000293	0.000215	0.000157	0.000115	0.000084
82	0.000374	0.000274	0.000200	0.000146	0.000106	0.000077
83	0.000351	0.000256	0.000186	0.000135	0.000098	0.000070
84	0.000329	0.000239	0.000173	0.000125	0.000090	0.000065
85	0.000309	0.000223	0.000161	0.000116	0.000083	0.000059
86	0.000290	0.000209	0.000150	0.000107	0.000076	0.000054
87	0.000272	0.000195	0.000139	0.000099	0.000070	0.000050
88	0.000256	0.000182	0.000129	0.000092	0.000065	0.000046
89	0.000240	0.000170	0.000120	0.000085	0.000060	0.000042
90	0.000225	0.000159	0.000112	0.000079	0.000055	0.000039
91	0.000212	0.000149	0.000104	0.000073	0.000051	0.000035
92	0.000199	0.000139	0.000097	0.000067	0.000047	0.000032
93	0.000186	0.000130	0.000090	0.000062	0.000043	0.000030
94	0.000175	0.000121	0.000084	0.000058	0.000040	0.000027
95	0.000164	0.000113	0.000078	0.000053	0.000037	0.000025
96	0.000154	0.000106	0.000072	0.000050	0.000034	0.000023
97	0.000145	0.000099	0.000067	0.000046	0.000031	0.000021
98	0.000136	0.000092	0.000063	0.000042	0.000029	0.000019
99	0.000128	0.000086	0.000058	0.000039	0.000026	0.000018
100	0.000120	0.000081	0.000054	0.000036	0.000024	0.000016
101	0.000113	0.000075	0.000050	0.000034	0.000022	0.000015
102	0.000106	0.000071	0.000047	0.000031	0.000021	0.000014
103	0.000099	0.000066	0.000044	0.000029	0.000019	0.000013
104	0.000093	0.000062	0.000041	0.000027	0.000018	0.000012
105	0.000087	0.000058	0.000038	0.000025	0.000016	0.000011
106	0.000082	0.000054	0.000035	0.000023	0.000015	0.000010
107	0.000077	0.000050	0.000033	0.000021	0.000014	0.000009
108	0.000072	0.000047	0.000030	0.000020	0.000013	0.000008
109	0.000068	0.000044	0.000028	0.000018	0.000012	0.000007
110	0.000064	0.000041	0.000026	0.000017	0.000011	0.000007
111	0.000060	0.000038	0.000024	0.000016	0.000010	0.000006
112	0.000056	0.000036	0.000023	0.000014	0.000009	0.000006
113	0.000053	0.000033	0.000021	0.000013	0.000008	0.000005
114	0.000050	0.000031	0.000020	0.000012	0.000008	0.000005
115	0.000047	0.000029	0.000018	0.000011	0.000007	0.000004
116	0.000044	0.000027	0.000017	0.000011	0.000007	0.000004
117	0.000041	0.000026	0.000016	0.000010	0.000006	0.000004
118	0.000039	0.000024	0.000015	0.000009	0.000006	0.000003
119	0.000036	0.000022	0.000014	0.000008	0.000005	0.000003
120	0.000034	0.000021	0.000013	0.000008	0.000005	0.000003

Table VI Sinking Fund Factor (continued) $\frac{1}{(1+i)^n - 1}$

n	0.095 (9½%)	0.10 (10%)	0.105 (10½%)	0.11 (11%)	0.115 (11½%)	0.12 (12%)
1	1.000000	1.000000	1.000000	1.000000	1.000000	1.000000
2	0.477327	0.476190	0.475059	0.473934	0.472813	0.471698
3	0.303580	0.302115	0.300659	0.299213	0.297776	0.296349
4	0.217063	0.215471	0.213892	0.212326	0.210774	0.209234
5	0.165436	0.163797	0.162175	0.160570	0.158982	0.157410
6	0.131253	0.129607	0.127982	0.126377	0.124791	0.123226
7	0.107036	0.105405	0.103799	0.102215	0.100655	0.099118
8	0.089046	0.087444	0.085869	0.084321	0.082799	0.081303
9	0.075205	0.073641	0.072106	0.070602	0.069126	0.067679
10	0.064266	0.062745	0.061257	0.059801	0.058377	0.056984
11	0.055437	0.053963	0.052525	0.051121	0.049751	0.048415
12	0.048188	0.046763	0.045377	0.044027	0.042714	0.041437
13	0.042152	0.040779	0.039445	0.038151	0.036895	0.035677
14	0.037068	0.035746	0.034467	0.033228	0.032030	0.030871
15	0.032744	0.031474	0.030248	0.029065	0.027924	0.026824
16	0.029035	0.027817	0.026644	0.025517	0.024432	0.023390
17	0.025831	0.024664	0.023545	0.022471	0.021443	0.020457
18	0.023046	0.021930	0.020863	0.019843	0.018868	0.017937
19	0.020613	0.019547	0.018531	0.017563	0.016641	0.015763
20	0.018477	0.017460	0.016493	0.015576	0.014705	0.013879
21	0.016594	0.015624	0.014707	0.013838	0.013016	0.012240
22	0.014928	0.014005	0.013134	0.012313	0.011539	0.010811
23	0.013449	0.012572	0.011747	0.010971	0.010243	0.009560
24	0.012134	0.011300	0.010519	0.009787	0.009103	0.008463
25	0.010959	0.010168	0.009429	0.008740	0.008098	0.007500
26	0.009909	0.009159	0.008461	0.007813	0.007210	0.006652
27	0.008969	0.008258	0.007599	0.006989	0.006425	0.005904
28	0.008124	0.007451	0.006830	0.006257	0.005730	0.005244
29	0.007364	0.006728	0.006143	0.005605	0.005112	0.004660
30	0.006681	0.006079	0.005528	0.005025	0.004564	0.004144
31	0.006064	0.005496	0.004978	0.004506	0.004077	0.003686
32	0.005507	0.004972	0.004485	0.004043	0.003643	0.003280
33	0.005004	0.004499	0.004042	0.003629	0.003257	0.002920
34	0.004549	0.004074	0.003645	0.003259	0.002912	0.002601
35	0.004138	0.003690	0.003288	0.002927	0.002605	0.002317
36	0.003764	0.003343	0.002967	0.002630	0.002331	0.002064
37	0.003426	0.003030	0.002677	0.002364	0.002086	0.001840
38	0.003119	0.002747	0.002417	0.002125	0.001867	0.001640
39	0.002840	0.002491	0.002183	0.001911	0.001672	0.001462
40	0.002587	0.002259	0.001971	0.001719	0.001497	0.001304
41	0.002357	0.002050	0.001781	0.001546	0.001341	0.001163
42	0.002148	0.001860	0.001609	0.001391	0.001201	0.001037
43	0.001958	0.001688	0.001454	0.001251	0.001076	0.000925
44	0.001785	0.001532	0.001314	0.001126	0.000964	0.000825
45	0.001627	0.001391	0.001188	0.001014	0.000864	0.000736
46	0.001484	0.001263	0.001074	0.000912	0.000774	0.000657
47	0.001353	0.001147	0.000971	0.000821	0.000694	0.000586
48	0.001234	0.001041	0.000878	0.000739	0.000622	0.000523
49	0.001126	0.000946	0.000794	0.000666	0.000558	0.000467
50	0.001027	0.000859	0.000718	0.000599	0.000500	0.000417
51	0.000937	0.000780	0.000649	0.000540	0.000448	0.000372
52	0.000855	0.000709	0.000587	0.000486	0.000402	0.000332
53	0.000780	0.000644	0.000531	0.000438	0.000360	0.000296
54	0.000712	0.000585	0.000480	0.000394	0.000323	0.000264
55	0.000650	0.000532	0.000435	0.000355	0.000290	0.000236
56	0.000593	0.000483	0.000393	0.000320	0.000260	0.000211
57	0.000541	0.000439	0.000356	0.000288	0.000233	0.000188
58	0.000494	0.000399	0.000322	0.000259	0.000209	0.000168
59	0.000451	0.000363	0.000291	0.000233	0.000187	0.000150
60	0.000412	0.000330	0.000263	0.000210	0.000168	0.000134

Table VI Sinking Fund Factor (continued)

$$\frac{1}{(1+i)^n - 1}$$

n	0.125 (12½%)	0.13 (13%)	0.135 (13½%)	0.14 (14%)	0.145 (14½%)	0.15 (15%)
1	1.000000	1.000000	1.000000	1.000000	1.000000	1.000000
2	0.470588	0.469484	0.468384	0.467290	0.466200	0.465116
3	0.294931	0.293522	0.292122	0.290731	0.289350	0.287977
4	0.207708	0.206194	0.204693	0.203205	0.201729	0.200265
5	0.155854	0.154315	0.152791	0.151284	0.149792	0.148316
6	0.121680	0.120153	0.118646	0.117157	0.115688	0.114237
7	0.097603	0.096111	0.094641	0.093192	0.091766	0.090360
8	0.079832	0.078387	0.076966	0.075570	0.074198	0.072850
9	0.066260	0.064869	0.063505	0.062168	0.060858	0.059574
10	0.055622	0.054290	0.052987	0.051714	0.050469	0.049252
11	0.047112	0.045841	0.044602	0.043394	0.042217	0.041069
12	0.040194	0.038986	0.037811	0.036669	0.035559	0.034481
13	0.034496	0.033350	0.032240	0.031164	0.030121	0.029110
14	0.029751	0.028667	0.027621	0.026609	0.025632	0.024688
15	0.025764	0.024742	0.023757	0.022809	0.021896	0.021017
16	0.022388	0.021426	0.020502	0.019615	0.018764	0.017948
17	0.019512	0.018608	0.017743	0.016915	0.016124	0.015367
18	0.017049	0.016201	0.015392	0.014621	0.013886	0.013186
19	0.014928	0.014134	0.013380	0.012663	0.011982	0.011336
20	0.013096	0.012354	0.011651	0.010986	0.010357	0.009761
21	0.011507	0.010814	0.010161	0.009545	0.008964	0.008417
22	0.010125	0.009479	0.008873	0.008303	0.007768	0.007266
23	0.008919	0.008319	0.007757	0.007231	0.006739	0.006278
24	0.007866	0.007308	0.006788	0.006303	0.005851	0.005430
25	0.006943	0.006426	0.005945	0.005498	0.005084	0.004699
26	0.006134	0.005655	0.005211	0.004800	0.004420	0.004070
27	0.005423	0.004979	0.004570	0.004193	0.003846	0.003526
28	0.004797	0.004387	0.004010	0.003664	0.003348	0.003057
29	0.004246	0.003867	0.003521	0.003204	0.002915	0.002651
30	0.003760	0.003411	0.003092	0.002803	0.002539	0.002300
31	0.003331	0.003009	0.002717	0.002453	0.002213	0.001996
32	0.002952	0.002656	0.002388	0.002147	0.001929	0.001733
33	0.002617	0.002345	0.002100	0.001880	0.001682	0.001505
34	0.002321	0.002071	0.001847	0.001646	0.001467	0.001307
35	0.002059	0.001829	0.001624	0.001442	0.001279	0.001135
36	0.001827	0.001616	0.001429	0.001263	0.001116	0.000986
37	0.001621	0.001428	0.001258	0.001107	0.000974	0.000857
38	0.001439	0.001262	0.001107	0.000970	0.000850	0.000744
39	0.001278	0.001116	0.000974	0.000850	0.000742	0.000647
40	0.001134	0.000986	0.000858	0.000745	0.000647	0.000562
41	0.001007	0.000872	0.000755	0.000653	0.000565	0.000489
42	0.000895	0.000771	0.000665	0.000573	0.000493	0.000425
43	0.000795	0.000682	0.000585	0.000502	0.000431	0.000369
44	0.000706	0.000603	0.000515	0.000440	0.000376	0.000321
45	0.000627	0.000534	0.000454	0.000386	0.000328	0.000279
46	0.000557	0.000472	0.000400	0.000338	0.000287	0.000242
47	0.000495	0.000417	0.000352	0.000297	0.000250	0.000211
48	0.000440	0.000369	0.000310	0.000260	0.000218	0.000183
49	0.000391	0.000327	0.000273	0.000228	0.000191	0.000159
50	0.000347	0.000289	0.000241	0.000200	0.000167	0.000139
51	0.000308	0.000256	0.000212	0.000176	0.000145	0.000120
52	0.000274	0.000226	0.000187	0.000154	0.000127	0.000105
53	0.000244	0.000200	0.000164	0.000135	0.000111	0.000091
54	0.000216	0.000177	0.000145	0.000118	0.000097	0.000079
55	0.000192	0.000157	0.000128	0.000104	0.000085	0.000069
56	0.000171	0.000139	0.000112	0.000091	0.000074	0.000060
57	0.000152	0.000123	0.000099	0.000080	0.000065	0.000052
58	0.000135	0.000109	0.000087	0.000070	0.000056	0.000045
59	0.000120	0.000096	0.000077	0.000062	0.000049	0.000039
60	0.000107	0.000085	0.000068	0.000054	0.000043	0.000034

Table VI Sinking Fund Factor (continued) $\frac{1}{(1+i)^n - 1}$

n	*0.155 (15½%)*	*0.16 (16%)*	*0.165 (16½%)*	*0.17 (17%)*	*0.175 (17½%)*	*0.18 (18%)*
1	1.000000	1.000000	1.000000	1.000000	1.000000	1.000000
2	0.464037	0.462963	0.461894	0.460829	0.459770	0.458716
3	0.286613	0.285258	0.283911	0.282574	0.281245	0.279924
4	0.198814	0.197375	0.195948	0.194533	0.193130	0.191739
5	0.146855	0.145409	0.143979	0.142564	0.141163	0.139778
6	0.112804	0.111390	0.109993	0.108615	0.107254	0.105910
7	0.088976	0.087613	0.086270	0.084947	0.083645	0.082362
8	0.071526	0.070224	0.068946	0.067690	0.066456	0.065244
9	0.058316	0.057082	0.055874	0.054691	0.053531	0.052395
10	0.048063	0.046901	0.045766	0.044657	0.043573	0.042515
11	0.039951	0.038861	0.037799	0.036765	0.035757	0.034776
12	0.033433	0.032415	0.031426	0.030466	0.029533	0.028628
13	0.028132	0.027184	0.026266	0.025378	0.024518	0.023686
14	0.023777	0.022898	0.022049	0.021230	0.020440	0.019678
15	0.020171	0.019358	0.018575	0.017822	0.017098	0.016403
16	0.017165	0.016414	0.015694	0.015004	0.014343	0.013710
17	0.014643	0.013952	0.013292	0.012662	0.012060	0.011485
18	0.012520	0.011885	0.011281	0.010706	0.010159	0.009639
19	0.010723	0.010142	0.009590	0.009067	0.008572	0.008103
20	0.009199	0.008667	0.008165	0.007690	0.007243	0.006820
21	0.007901					
22	0.006795					
23	0.005848					
24	0.005038					
25	0.004343					
26	0.003746					
27	0.003233					
28	0.002791					
29	0.002411					
30	0.002083					
31	0.001800					
32	0.001556					
33	0.001345					
34	0.001164					
35	0.001006					
36	0.000871					
37	0.000753					
38	0.000652					
39	0.000564					
40	0.000488					
41	0.000422					
42	0.000366					
43	0.000316					
44	0.000274					
45	0.000237					
46	0.000205					
47	0.000178					
48	0.000154					
49	0.000133					
50	0.000115					
51	0.000100					
52	0.000086					
53	0.000075					
54	0.000065					
55	0.000056					
56	0.000049					
57	0.000042					
58	0.000036					
59	0.000031					
60	0.000027					

Table VI Sinking Fund Factor (continued) $\frac{1}{(1+i)^n - 1}$

n	0.185 (18½%)	0.19 (19%)	0.195 (19½%)	0.20 (20%)	0.21 (21%)	0.22 (22%)
1	1.000000	1.000000	1.000000	1.000000	1.000000	1.000000
2	0.457666	0.456621	0.455581	0.454545	0.452489	0.450450
3	0.278612	0.277308	0.276012	0.274725	0.272175	0.269658
4	0.190359	0.188991	0.187634	0.186289	0.183632	0.181020
5	0.138407	0.137050	0.135708	0.134380	0.131765	0.129206
6	0.104584	0.103274	0.101982	0.100706	0.098203	0.095764
7	0.081099	0.079855	0.078630	0.077424	0.075067	0.072782
8	0.064054	0.062885	0.061737	0.060609	0.058415	0.056299
9	0.051282	0.050192	0.049125	0.048079	0.046053	0.044111
10	0.041481	0.040471	0.039485	0.038523	0.036665	0.034895
11	0.033821	0.032891	0.031985	0.031104	0.029411	0.027807
12	0.027749	0.026896	0.026068	0.025265	0.023730	0.022285
13	0.022881	0.022102	0.021349	0.020620	0.019234	0.017939
14	0.018943	0.018235	0.017551	0.016893	0.015647	0.014491
15	0.015734	0.015092	0.014475	0.013882	0.012766	0.011738
16	0.013104	0.012523	0.011968	0.011436	0.010441	0.009530
17	0.010937	0.010414	0.009916	0.009440	0.008555	0.007751
18	0.009145	0.008676	0.008229	0.007805	0.007020	0.006313
19	0.007658	0.007238	0.006839	0.006462	0.005769	0.005148
20	0.006421	0.006045	0.005691	0.005357	0.004745	0.004202

n	0.23 (23%)	0.24 (24%)	0.25 (25%)	0.30 (30%)	0.35 (35%)	0.40 (40%)
1	1.000000	1.000000	1.000000	1.000000	1.000000	1.000000
2	0.448430	0.446429	0.444444	0.434783	0.425532	0.416667
3	0.267173	0.264718	0.262295	0.250627	0.239664	0.229358
4	0.178451	0.175926	0.173442	0.161629	0.150764	0.140766
5	0.126700	0.124248	0.121847	0.110582	0.100458	0.091361
6	0.093389	0.091074	0.088819	0.078394	0.069260	0.061260
7	0.070568	0.068422	0.066342	0.056874	0.048800	0.041923
8	0.054259	0.052293	0.050399	0.041915	0.034887	0.029074
9	0.042249	0.040465	0.038756	0.031235	0.025191	0.020345
10	0.033208	0.031602	0.030073	0.023463	0.018318	0.014324
11	0.026289	0.024852	0.023493	0.017729	0.013387	0.010128
12	0.020926	0.019648	0.018448	0.013454	0.009819	0.007182
13	0.016728	0.015598	0.014543	0.010243	0.007221	0.005104
14	0.013418	0.012423	0.011501	0.007818	0.005320	0.003632
15	0.010791	0.009919	0.009117	0.005978	0.003926	0.002588
16	0.008697	0.007936	0.007241	0.004577	0.002899	0.001845
17	0.007021	0.006359	0.005759	0.003509	0.002143	0.001316
18	0.005676	0.005102	0.004586	0.002692	0.001585	0.000939
19	0.004593	0.004098	0.003656	0.002066	0.001173	0.000670
20	0.003720	0.003294	0.002916	0.001587	0.000868	0.000479

Index